Strategic Thinking

A Learning-Focused Approach to Strategic Management

Scott Kuban, PhD & Ryan Cooper, PhD

Published by ConvergX Publishing, Knoxville, TN

ISBN: 979-8-9972327-0-2

First Edition

Printed in the United States of America

10 9 8 7 6 5 4 3 2 1

Contents

Preface

0.1 The Strategy of Teaching Strategy

Strategic Management textbooks rarely present concepts in an order optimized for undergraduate learning. Instead, concepts and frameworks are organized into over-arching frameworks that provide a structure appealing to strategy professors. For instance, most texts ask students to consider how changes to the global socio-political environment impact industries and firms before they understand what differentiation is or how firms create value. Further, because so many aspects of strategic management are interrelated, the framework-first approach often draws on ideas from future chapters to explain the current one. Some of this is unavoidable, but excessive anticipatory previews often confuse rather than clarify.

Our approach optimizes for learning. We move from foundational concepts to frameworks, from smaller to larger scope (firm → industry → external environment), and from the entrepreneur's perspective to the corporate executive's. Each concept builds logically on previous material with as little redundancy or anticipatory preview as possible. This concept-first, building-out approach represents a deliberate departure from traditional structures and proved more effective in the classroom throughout development.

Finally, the text is organized into compact chapter sections to increase instructor flexibility. A typical semester course can cover two sections per class meeting while leaving sufficient days for exams and group presentations. The modular structure also supports flexibility within a class meeting: instructors can cover a single section and use the remaining time for experiential learning activities or case discussions, or move through several sections when a lecture-focused session fits the day's goals.

0.2 About the Authors

Dr. Scott Kuban has over a decade of experience teaching Strategic Management at the Mays Business School at Texas A&M University, the Freeman School of Business at Tulane University, and the Walton College of Business at the University of Arkansas. He received his PhD from Texas A&M University.

Dr. Ryan Cooper joined the Walton College of Business at the University of Arkansas in 2022 after previously teaching at the Robert H. Smith School of Business at the University of Maryland. He received his PhD in 2016 from the Olin Business School at Washington University in St. Louis.

Chapter 1

Foundations of Strategy

1.1 The Theory of the Firm — *Why do firms exist?*

Before we can study how firms compete, we need to answer a more fundamental question: why do firms exist in the first place? This may seem obvious at first glance. Firms exist to make products and provide services, to employ people, to generate profits. But if you think more carefully, the question becomes surprisingly difficult. After all, every activity a firm performs could theoretically be performed by independent individuals coordinating through the open market. A person could design a product, hire a freelance engineer to build it, contract with a logistics company to ship it, and pay a commissioned salesperson to sell it, all without ever forming a company. So why do people organize into firms at all?

This question is not just an academic exercise. Understanding why firms exist is the starting point for understanding how firms grow, how they decide what activities to perform internally versus outsource, and ultimately how they compete. The theory of the firm provides the economic logic that underpins many of the strategic decisions we will study throughout this book.

1.1.1 The Puzzle of Firm Existence

In a perfectly functioning free market, all economic activity could be coordinated through individual transactions. A buyer and a seller would find each other, agree on a price, exchange goods or services, and move on. There would be no need for employment contracts, organizational hierarchies, or corporate structures. Every person would operate as an independent agent, buying and selling their labor and output in a vast open marketplace.

Yet this is obviously not how the real world works. Instead, economic activity is overwhelmingly organized within firms, entities where individuals work together under common ownership and management, coordinating their activities through internal direction rather than market exchange. The question of why this happens puzzled economists for a long time, because classical economic theory assumed that markets were the most efficient way to allocate resources. If markets are so efficient, why would anyone choose the seemingly more rigid and bureaucratic structure of a firm?

1.1.2 The Market Alternative

To appreciate why firms form, consider what it would look like if they did not. Imagine you want to start selling custom bicycles. Without forming a firm, you would need to operate entirely through market transactions. You would search for and negotiate separate contracts with a frame supplier, a component manufacturer, a wheel builder, a painter, an assembler, a retail partner, a sales person, a shipping provider, and a warranty service provider. Each of these relationships would require its own agreement, its own price negotiation, its own quality standards, and its own enforcement mechanisms.

On paper, this approach has real appeal. You could shop around for the best price on every input. You would have no employees to manage, no office space to maintain, no payroll taxes to pay. You could swap out any contractor who underperformed and replace them with a better one. The market, in theory, would discipline every participant to deliver quality at a fair price through the forces of competition.

But anyone who has tried to coordinate even a moderately complex project through independent contractors knows that reality is far messier than theory. Contracts are incomplete; you cannot anticipate every possible contingency and write it into an agreement. Suppliers may deliver late or cut corners on quality in ways that are difficult to detect. Negotiating, monitoring, and enforcing each of these agreements takes time, money, and attention. The more complex the product and the more parties involved, the more these costs multiply.

1.1.3 Coase's Insight: Transaction Costs

In 1937, economist Ronald Coase published a groundbreaking paper, "The Nature of the Firm," that provided an elegant answer to the puzzle of firm existence. Coase observed that using the market to coordinate economic activity is not free. Every market exchange carries costs beyond the price of the good or service itself. Coase called these *transaction costs*, the expenses incurred when making an economic exchange beyond the price of the item being exchanged (Coase, 1937).

Coase's central insight was that firms exist because, in many situations, organizing activities internally under a single management structure is cheaper than coordinating those same activities through market transactions. When the transaction costs of using the market become high enough, it becomes more efficient to bring activities inside the firm and coordinate them through managerial authority rather than through contracts and price signals (Coase, 1937).

This idea was revolutionary because it shifted the focus from what firms produce to why firms produce it internally rather than buying it from the market. The boundary of the firm — what it does in-house versus what it contracts out — is determined by the relative cost of internal organization versus market exchange. When market transaction costs are low, firms stay small and outsource. When market transaction costs are high, firms grow larger and bring more activities in-house.

1.1.4 Types of Transaction Costs

Transaction costs come in three primary categories, each of which contributes to the friction inherent in market exchanges.

Search and information costs are the expenses associated with finding a suitable trading partner and gathering the information needed to make a good decision. Before you can buy a component or hire a contractor, you need to identify who is available, evaluate their quality and reliability, compare prices, and assess whether they can meet your specifications. In some markets this is relatively easy; buying office supplies, for example, involves minimal search costs. In others it is enormously expensive and time-consuming, such as finding a specialized manufacturer capable of producing a custom part to tight tolerances.

Bargaining and decision costs arise from negotiating the terms of an exchange. Once you have identified a potential trading partner, you must agree on price, delivery schedule, quality standards, payment terms, liability, and numerous other provisions. The more complex the transaction, the more costly and time-consuming these negotiations become. Each party has an incentive to secure favorable terms, and the process of reaching mutually acceptable conditions requires time, legal expertise, and often significant back-and-forth.

Enforcement and monitoring costs are the expenses involved in ensuring that both parties uphold their end of the agreement after a deal is struck. Contracts are only as good as the ability to enforce them. If a supplier delivers substandard materials, you need to detect the deficiency, document it, and either negotiate a remedy or pursue legal enforcement. Monitoring quality, tracking compliance with delivery schedules, and resolving disputes all consume resources. The more transactions you manage through the market, the more of these monitoring and enforcement costs you incur.

Together, these three categories of transaction costs can make market-based coordination far more expensive than it appears on the surface. The price quoted by a supplier may be attractive, but once you add the cost of finding that supplier, negotiating terms, and ensuring they perform as promised, the total cost of the market transaction may exceed what it would cost to perform the activity yourself (Williamson, 1985).

1.1.5 Market Transactions vs. Internal Organization

While market transactions can be costly, organizing activities within a firm is not free either. Internal organization carries its own set of costs. Hiring employees means incurring recruiting expenses, paying salaries and benefits regardless of fluctuations in demand, investing in training, and managing the complexities of human resources. Setting up internal operations requires capital investment in facilities, equipment, and systems. Managing employees requires layers of supervision, coordination, and administration that consume resources.

The decision of whether to organize an activity internally or source it from the market comes down to a comparison of these two sets of costs. When the transaction costs of using the market for a particular activity exceed the costs of performing it internally, the firm should bring that activity in-house. When internal costs exceed market transaction costs, the firm should outsource. This comparison is not static. It changes as firms grow, as markets develop, and as technology evolves. What makes sense to outsource at one stage of a company's development may make sense to bring in-house at another, and vice versa (Williamson, 1985).

It is important to note that transaction costs exist on both sides. External transaction costs are those incurred when dealing with the market: searching for contractors, negotiating contracts, and enforcing agreements. Internal transaction costs are those incurred when organizing activities within the firm: recruiting and retaining employees, coordinating across departments, and managing internal operations. The firm continuously evaluates whether a given activity is more efficiently handled inside or outside its boundaries based on the balance of these costs.

1.1.6 Why Firms Don't Do Everything

If bringing activities inside the firm reduces market transaction costs, why don't firms simply grow to encompass all economic activity? Coase's answer to this question is just as important as his explanation for why firms form in the first place. As a firm grows larger, the internal costs of organization increase. Communication becomes more difficult across a larger hierarchy. Decision-making slows as more layers of management are added. Employees further from the top of the organization may have weaker incentives to perform efficiently than an independent contractor whose livelihood depends on winning and retaining clients. Bureaucracy, coordination failures, and internal politics all add to the cost of running a larger organization (Coase, 1937).

At some point, the internal costs of managing an additional activity exceed the transaction costs of sourcing it from the market. This is the natural limit to the size of the firm. The firm grows to the point where the cost of organizing one more activity internally equals the cost of conducting that activity through a market transaction. Beyond that point, further growth actually destroys value rather than creating it.

This explains why even the largest corporations in the world outsource significant portions of their operations. Apple, for instance, designs its products in-house but contracts with manufacturers like Foxconn to assemble them. For design, the transaction costs of contracting out — protecting proprietary technology, coordinating complex engineering decisions, maintaining secrecy across firm boundaries — exceed the costs of managing the process internally. Conversely, the costs of building and operating massive assembly facilities are higher than the transaction costs of managing a manufacturing contract with a capable partner.

Transaction costs are not fixed quantities that apply uniformly to every firm. They vary from one firm to another and shift within the same firm over time. Two competitors in the same industry can face different transaction costs for the same activity because they differ in managerial expertise, supplier relationships, internal systems, geographic location, or reputation. One firm may find it cheaper to manufacture a component in-house while a rival finds it cheaper to buy from a supplier, and both can be making the right choice given their own circumstances. Transaction costs also change within a firm as it grows, as technology evolves, and as trusted partners emerge or disappear. An activity once cheaper to perform internally may become cheaper to outsource as specialized suppliers develop, and an activity once outsourced may become cheaper to bring in-house as the firm builds scale. Because transaction costs differ across firms and shift over time, the boundaries of the firm are never settled, and reasonable managers facing the same activity can land on different answers.

EX: Jan's Bike Shop

To bring these ideas to life, consider the example of Jan, an avid cyclist who wants to create her own brand of bikes. Jan faces a fundamental choice: should she try to do everything through market transactions, or should she form a firm?

If Jan chooses to operate entirely through the market, she would need to source all materials and components from independent suppliers, hire outside contractors to assemble the bikes, work with wholesalers to distribute and sell them, and use a warranty company to service the bikes after the sale. At every step, Jan and the people she trades with face transaction costs. They have to find each other, research the other's services, negotiate terms, draft contracts, and pay to have those contracts enforced.

Given all of these transaction costs, Jan might discover that she can reduce them, and become more profitable, by hiring someone to assemble the bikes rather than contracting that work out. The search costs of finding reliable assembly contractors, the bargaining costs of negotiating quality standards and delivery timelines, and the enforcement costs of monitoring contractor quality may together exceed the cost of simply employing an assembler directly.

As her business grows, Jan might further discover that transaction costs are reduced if she hires her own salespeople to sell directly to bike stores rather than working through wholesalers. The wholesaler takes a margin, and coordinating with an independent distribution partner involves its own negotiation and monitoring costs. By bringing sales in-house, Jan trades those external transaction costs for the internal costs of managing a sales team, and if the internal costs are lower, she comes out ahead.

Perhaps Jan's bikes become popular enough that the transaction costs associated with working through independent bike shops become high enough that opening her own chain of retail stores and hiring her own sales staff is the most profitable path. Each of these decisions — hiring an assembler, building a sales team, opening retail locations — represents the same fundamental logic: Jan is bringing activities inside her firm because the internal costs of organization are lower than the transaction costs of using the market.

Jan's story illustrates that the decision to form and grow a firm is not a single event but an ongoing process. At each stage, the entrepreneur or manager compares the costs of internal organization against the costs of market exchange and adjusts the boundaries of the firm accordingly. This logic does not only apply to startups. Every firm, from the smallest new venture to the largest multinational corporation, continually makes decisions about what to do internally and what to source from the market. The theory of the firm provides the foundational framework for understanding these decisions.

1.1.7 Looking Ahead

Coase's transaction cost framework gives us a powerful lens for understanding not just why firms exist, but also why they are structured the way they are and why they grow or shrink over time. As we move through this chapter and into the rest of the book, we will build on this foundation. We will map the activities that produce value (the value chain), examine what firms are trying to achieve (vision, mission, and objectives), explore how they create and capture value (business models), and analyze how they compete (competitive advantage). Each of these topics connects back to the fundamental economic logic of the firm: the ongoing effort to organize activities in the way that creates the most value at the lowest cost.

Understanding the theory of the firm also sets the stage for the corporate-level strategy discussions later in this book. When we study vertical integration, diversification, mergers and acquisitions, and strategic alliances, we are essentially studying how firms adjust their boundaries in response to changing transaction costs and organizational capabilities. The logic that explains why Jan hired her first assembler is the same logic that explains why a Fortune 500 company acquires a supplier or spins off a division. The scale changes, but the underlying economics remain the same.

References

Coase, R. H. (1937). The nature of the firm. *Economica, 4*(16), 386–405.

Williamson, O. E. (1985). *The economic institutions of capitalism: Firms, markets, relational contracting.* Free Press.

1.2 The Value Chain — *What do firms actually do?*

We have established that firms exist because they can organize certain activities more efficiently than the market. But what exactly are these activities? When a firm brings work inside its boundaries, it does not perform a single undifferentiated task. It carries out a series of distinct activities: acquiring inputs, transforming them, delivering the resulting product or service to customers, and supporting that entire process with management, hiring, technology, and purchasing. The value chain is a framework that maps these activities, giving us a concrete picture of what happens inside a firm and where value is created along the way (Porter, 1985).

Understanding the value chain at this stage serves a practical purpose. Before we can discuss what firms are trying to achieve, how they create value, or how they compete, we need a shared vocabulary for describing what firms do. The value chain provides that vocabulary. It will reappear throughout this textbook as we examine how different strategic choices lead firms to configure their activities in different ways.

1.2.1 What Is the Value Chain?

The value chain is a framework for breaking down a firm into its strategically relevant activities in order to understand the sources of cost and value creation. Introduced by Porter (1985) in his book *Competitive Advantage*, the value chain describes the full range of activities and processes within a company that add value to the final product or service delivered to the customer. Every firm is essentially a collection of activities: designing, producing, marketing, delivering, and supporting its product. The value chain provides a systematic way to categorize and examine firm activities and how they interact with one another.

The logic is straightforward. A firm earns a margin, which is the difference between the total value it creates for customers and the collective cost of performing its activities (Porter, 1985). If a firm can perform its activities more efficiently than competitors, or perform them in ways that create greater value for customers, it holds an advantage. The value chain gives us the tool to see exactly where that advantage comes from.

This matters because a firm's success rarely stems from one single thing it does. It emerges from the combination of many activities performed well and coordinated effectively (Porter, 1996). A firm might have slightly better purchasing, somewhat more efficient production, and a particularly strong service operation. None of these alone would be decisive, but together they create something that is difficult for competitors to replicate. The value chain allows us to see this full picture.

Porter (1985) divided firm activities into two broad categories: primary activities, which are directly involved in creating and delivering the product, and support activities, which enable and improve the performance of primary activities.

1.2.2 Primary Activities

Primary activities are those directly involved in creating the product or service, delivering it to the customer, and providing after-sale support. Porter (1985) identified five categories of primary activities, and they follow the logical flow of how a product moves through a firm.

Inbound logistics encompasses everything involved in receiving, storing, and distributing inputs to the production process. This includes activities such as receiving raw materials, warehousing, inventory management, and transportation scheduling. For a manufacturer, this might mean managing relationships with parts suppliers and operating a warehouse. For a retailer, it involves receiving merchandise from vendors and distributing it to stores or fulfillment centers. The efficiency of inbound logistics directly affects a firm's cost structure; poor inventory management leads to waste, stockouts, and unnecessary carrying costs.

Operations refers to the activities that transform inputs into the final product or service. In a manufacturing firm, this includes machining, assembling, packing, testing, equipment maintenance, and quality control. In a service firm, operations might involve the actual delivery of the service itself. For a university, the core operation is teaching. For a consulting firm, it is the analytical and advisory work performed for clients. Operations is often where firms invest most heavily in process improvements and efficiency gains, since even small per-unit cost reductions can compound significantly as the firm grows.

Outbound logistics covers the activities required to collect, store, and distribute the finished product to customers. This includes warehousing finished goods, order processing, scheduling delivery, and managing transportation. For companies that sell physical products, outbound logistics can be a major source of advantage or disadvantage. Amazon, for example, has built one of the most sophisticated outbound logistics networks in the world, enabling next-day or same-day delivery that competitors struggle to match.

Marketing and sales includes all activities associated with providing a means for buyers to purchase the product and inducing them to do so (Porter, 1985). This covers advertising, promotion, sales force management, pricing, channel selection, and building relationships with distributors. Marketing and sales activities are where a firm communicates the value it creates to the customer. A firm may have an excellent product, but if its marketing fails to reach the right customers or articulate why the product is worth paying for, that value goes unrealized.

Service refers to activities that maintain or enhance the value of the product after it has been sold. This includes installation, repair, training, parts supply, warranty fulfillment, and customer support. For many firms, service activities are a critical source of differentiation. A company that provides outstanding post-sale support creates loyalty and repeat business, and often commands a price premium. In industries where products are increasingly similar, the quality of after-sale service can become the primary basis of competition.

1.2.3 Support Activities

Support activities do not directly produce or deliver the product, but they enable and improve the performance of primary activities. Porter (1985) identified four categories of support activities, and each one cuts across the entire chain of primary activities rather than being tied to a single stage.

Firm infrastructure includes general management, planning, finance, accounting, legal, government affairs, and quality management. While it is tempting to view infrastructure as mere overhead, it plays a vital role in coordinating all of the firm's activities. Strategic planning, for example, determines which activities the firm invests in and how they are configured. A firm with strong financial management can allocate capital more effectively across its value chain, funding the activities that generate the highest returns.

Human resource management spans the entire value chain and involves recruiting, hiring, training, developing, and compensating employees at every level. The quality of a firm's human resources affects every primary activity. Better-trained manufacturing employees reduce defect rates in operations. More skilled salespeople improve the effectiveness of marketing and sales. Investing in human resource management is investing in the quality of every other activity the firm performs.

Technology development refers to the range of activities related to improving the product and the processes used to make and deliver it. This includes research and development, process automation, and product design. Technology development can affect any activity in the value chain. Advances in logistics technology improve inbound and outbound logistics. New manufacturing processes improve operations. Digital marketing tools improve the effectiveness of marketing and sales. Firms that invest effectively in technology development often find ways to reduce costs or create additional value across multiple activities simultaneously.

Procurement is the function of purchasing the inputs used throughout the value chain. This includes not just raw materials for production, but also supplies, machinery, office equipment, buildings, and professional services. While the cost of procurement itself is usually a small percentage of total costs, the procurement function has an enormous impact on a firm's overall cost and quality (Porter, 1985). Negotiating better prices with suppliers, identifying higher-quality input sources, or developing long-term supplier relationships can improve the performance of every primary activity that uses those inputs.

A note on **information technology**: IT does not fit cleanly into any single support category. Some treatments place it under firm infrastructure alongside finance and general administration, but in practice IT spans both firm infrastructure and technology development. The systems that run accounting, payroll, and enterprise reporting are part of the administrative backbone of the firm, while the systems that enable product design, automate operations, or power digital customer interactions are part of technology development. Rather than forcing IT into one category, it is more accurate to recognize that it cuts across both, and managers should evaluate IT investments based on which activities they support rather than where the IT function sits on an organizational chart.

1.2.3.1 Value Chain Diagram

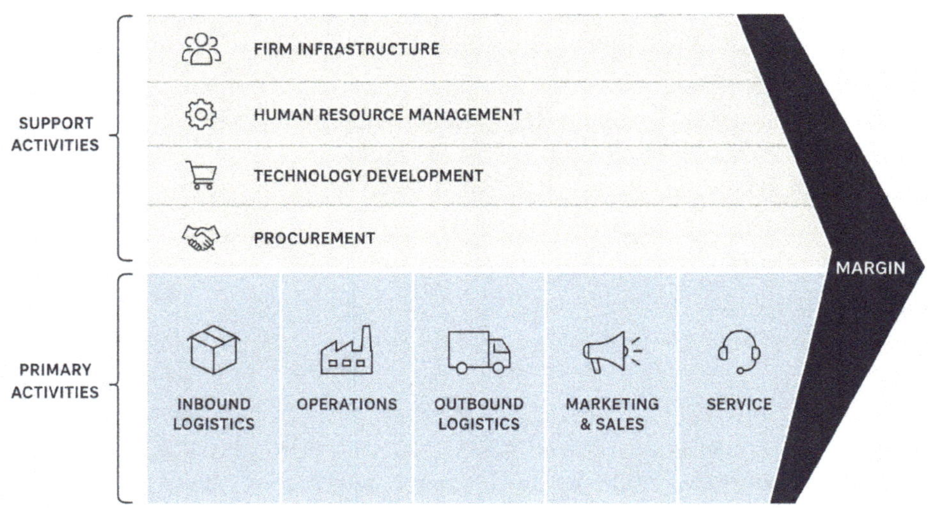

1.2.4 Looking Ahead

The value chain gives us a map of the firm's internal activities, but at this stage we are using it primarily as a descriptive tool to understand what firms do. As we move through the rest of this chapter, we will examine what firms are trying to achieve (vision, mission, and objectives), how they create and capture value (business models), how they compete (competitive advantage), and what strategy means as an integrative concept. Each of these discussions will be grounded in the concrete reality of firm activities that the value chain makes visible.

Later in the book, we will return to the value chain as an analytical tool. We will examine how activities connect and reinforce one another through linkages, how a firm's value chain fits into a broader value system that includes suppliers and distribution partners, and how firms configure their activities differently depending on the strategy they pursue. For now, the value chain provides the foundation: a clear picture of the work that firms actually perform.

References

Porter, M. E. (1985). *Competitive advantage: Creating and sustaining superior performance.* Free Press.
Porter, M. E. (1996). What is strategy? *Harvard Business Review, 74*(6), 61–78.

1.3 Vision, Mission, and Objectives — *What are firms trying to achieve?*

> *If you don't know where you are going, any road will get you there. — Lewis Carroll*

Now that we understand why firms exist, the next logical question is: what are these firms actually trying to accomplish? Every firm needs a sense of direction. Without a clear destination, even the most efficiently organized firm is just wandering. This section introduces three foundational concepts that define a firm's purpose and direction: the vision statement, the mission statement, and strategic objectives.

These three elements form a hierarchy of intent. The vision describes the aspirational future the firm wants to create, the mission defines the firm's current purpose and scope, and objectives translate that purpose into concrete, measurable targets. Together, they provide the framework that guides every strategic decision the firm makes.

1.3.1 Vision Statements

A vision statement describes the future state that a firm aspires to achieve. It is forward-looking, ambitious, and meant to inspire. Think of the vision as the destination on a map; it tells the organization where it ultimately wants to end up, even if the journey to get there will take years or decades.

A well-crafted vision statement should be concise, memorable, and aspirational enough to motivate stakeholders without being so vague that it provides no real guidance (Collins & Porras, 1996). Microsoft's early vision to put "a computer on every desk and in every home" is a classic example. It was ambitious for its time, it was easy to understand, and it gave the entire organization a clear picture of what success looked like.

It is important to recognize, however, that a vision statement is not a strategy. Many companies make the mistake of treating their vision statement as though it were their strategy, often sprinkling in buzzwords like "strategic" or "world-class" to make it sound more substantive. An ambitious or lofty statement has a place in business, providing inspiration and a north star for the organization, but it says nothing about *how* the firm will get there. As we will see later in this chapter, strategy is the plan for how to achieve the vision. The vision is the "where," and the strategy is the "how."

Consider Tesla's vision of accelerating the world's transition to sustainable energy. This is inspiring and directional, but it does not tell us anything about whether Tesla should manufacture its own batteries, license its technology, partner with other automakers, or focus on solar panels versus electric vehicles. Those are strategic decisions, the means by which the vision might be realized. A company can have a compelling vision and still fail spectacularly if its strategy for achieving that vision is poorly conceived or executed.

1.3.2 Mission Statements

While the vision statement looks to the future, the mission statement is grounded in the present. A mission statement defines the firm's current purpose: what it does, who it serves, and how it creates value today. If the vision is the destination, the mission is the vehicle; it describes the core business the firm is in right now and the fundamental reason the organization exists.

Effective mission statements typically address several key elements: the products or services the firm provides, the customers or markets it serves, and the distinctive approach or values that differentiate it from competitors (Collins & Porras, 1996). A hospital's mission might center on providing compassionate, high-quality healthcare to its community. A technology startup's mission might focus on simplifying small business accounting through intuitive software. In each case, the mission clarifies the organization's present-day purpose and scope.

The mission statement serves a practical function beyond inspiration. It helps managers and employees make decisions that are consistent with the firm's core identity. When a new opportunity arises, say, a hospital is offered the chance to invest in a luxury wellness spa, the mission statement provides a reference point. Does this fit who we are and what we do? If the answer is no, the mission statement has done its job by guiding the firm away from a potentially distracting venture.

The distinction between vision and mission matters because firms need both a sense of where they are going and a clear understanding of who they are today. A firm with a vision but no mission lacks grounding; it knows where it wants to be but has no defined starting point. A firm with a mission but no vision risks stagnation; it knows what it does today but has no aspirational future pulling it forward.

1.3.3 SMART Objectives

Vision and mission statements provide direction and purpose, but they are inherently qualitative. To translate aspirations into action, firms need objectives — specific, measurable targets that mark progress toward the vision and fulfillment of the mission. This is where the SMART framework becomes essential (Doran, 1981).

SMART objectives are Specific, Measurable, Achievable, Relevant, and Time-bound. Each criterion addresses a common failure point in organizational goal-setting.

Specific means the objective clearly identifies what is to be accomplished. "Improve customer satisfaction" is vague; "increase our Net Promoter Score from 45 to 60" is specific. Specificity eliminates ambiguity and ensures everyone in the organization understands what success looks like.

Measurable means there is a quantifiable indicator of progress. If you cannot measure it, you cannot manage it, and you certainly cannot know whether you have achieved it. Measurability forces the firm to define success in concrete terms rather than relying on subjective judgment.

Achievable means the objective is realistic given the firm's resources, capabilities, and market conditions. Setting impossibly ambitious targets may seem motivational, but objectives that everyone knows are unattainable tend to be ignored rather than pursued. The goal should stretch the organization without breaking it.

Relevant means the objective aligns with the firm's mission and contributes to the broader vision. Every objective should connect to the larger strategic picture. An objective to expand into luxury fashion would not be relevant for a firm whose mission centers on affordable healthcare.

Time-bound means there is a deadline. Open-ended objectives create no urgency and invite perpetual postponement. A firm that aims to "eventually" grow revenue by 20% will likely never get there. A firm that commits to growing revenue by 20% within 18 months has created accountability.

Consider how these elements work together in practice. A regional coffee chain with a vision to become the leading specialty coffee brand in the Southeast and a mission focused on sourcing ethically grown beans and building community through its cafes might set the following SMART objective: open ten new locations across three states within the next two fiscal years, each achieving positive cash flow within six months of opening. This objective is specific (ten locations, three states), measurable (store count and cash flow), achievable (assuming adequate capital and operational capacity), relevant (directly supports the growth vision), and time-bound (two fiscal years, six-month cash flow target).

1.3.4 Connecting Vision, Mission, and Objectives to Strategy

These three elements — vision, mission, and objectives — do not constitute a strategy on their own. They are necessary preconditions for strategy, not substitutes for it. A firm that knows where it wants to go (vision), what it currently does (mission), and what targets it needs to hit along the way (objectives) has established the foundation for strategic planning. But the critical question remains unanswered: *how* will the firm achieve all of this?

That question, the "how," is the domain of strategy, which we will explore later in this chapter. For now, the key takeaway is that vision, mission, and objectives provide the purpose and direction that strategy serves. Without them, strategy has no anchor. Without strategy, they are just aspirations on a wall.

Sidebar: Your Vision For Your Life

If finding a vision for a company seems too distant, you can apply the same concepts to yourself. As an example, consider a senior-year business student named Priya who has always loved storytelling and wants to write and publish a novel within five years of graduating.

Vision Statement: To become a published fiction author whose work resonates with readers and establishes a foundation for a long-term creative writing career.

This vision is aspirational and forward-looking. It describes a future state Priya wants to reach. It is the destination on the map, not the route.

Mission Statement: To develop disciplined writing habits, craft a compelling manuscript, and build the knowledge of the publishing industry needed to bring a novel from idea to bookshelf.

The mission is grounded in the present. It defines what Priya is doing *now* — honing her craft, producing pages, and learning the business side of publishing.

SMART Objectives:

- Complete a creative writing workshop or online course within six months of graduation to strengthen narrative technique.
- Write a minimum of 1,000 words per day, five days per week, to complete a first draft of at least 80,000 words within 18 months of graduation.
- Finish a revised, polished second draft within two and a half years by completing one full revision cycle every three months.
- Query at least 30 literary agents within three years of graduation, with a completed manuscript and a professional query letter.

Notice how the objectives form stepping stones, with each one building toward the vision and aligning with the mission.

References

Collins, J. C., & Porras, J. I. (1996). Building your company's vision. *Harvard Business Review, 74*(5), 65–77.

Doran, G. T. (1981). There's a S.M.A.R.T. way to write management's goals and objectives. *Management Review, 70*(11), 35–36.

1.4 Business Models and Value Creation — *How do firms operate?*

We have established that firms exist to reduce transaction costs and that they pursue their purpose through a hierarchy of vision, mission, and objectives. The next question is a practical one: how does a firm actually operate on a day-to-day basis to create and capture value? The answer lies in the firm's business model, the underlying logic of how the firm makes money. This section introduces the concepts of value creation and value capture, showing how the gap between cost and customer willingness to pay becomes profit; explains how business models organize around that gap; breaks down the core components of any business model (including a widely used visual framework called the Business Model Canvas); examines how business models can be innovated; and draws a critical distinction between business models and strategy.

1.4.1 How Firms Create and Capture Value

Before we can understand business models, we need to understand the fundamental economic process they are built around: the creation and capture of value. At its core, every firm exists to transform inputs into outputs that are worth more than the inputs themselves. This transformation is the engine of all economic activity, and understanding it is essential to understanding how any business operates.

Inputs are the raw materials, labor, knowledge, capital, and other resources a business acquires. These resources have a certain cost and a certain value in their unconverted state. Steel sitting in a warehouse is worth something, but it is worth far less than what it could become. A skilled engineer's time has market value, but the designs that engineer produces may be worth many times more to the firm than the cost of the engineer's salary.

Transformation is the core act of value creation. The firm combines, configures, and processes these inputs through its operations, applying knowledge, skills, processes, and technology. A furniture maker takes lumber, hardware, fabric, and labor and transforms them into a finished sofa. A consulting firm takes analyst time, industry data, and intellectual frameworks and transforms them into strategic recommendations for a client. The transformation is what makes the firm more than just a collection of purchased resources; it is what turns those resources into something new.

Outputs are the resulting products or services that emerge from this transformation. The critical point is that customers value these outputs more than they would value the individual inputs in their original form. No one walks into a restaurant and offers to pay the chef's salary plus the wholesale cost of ingredients; they pay for the meal and the experience, which are the outputs of the restaurant's transformation processes. The output is greater than the sum of its parts.

The **Value Gap** is the space between what it costs the firm to acquire inputs and perform the transformation (its total costs) and what customers are willing to pay for the output (the value to the customer). This gap represents newly created value (Brandenburger & Stuart, 1996). The firm has not merely moved value from one place to another; it has generated additional value through the transformation process. If a craft brewery spends $3 per six-pack on ingredients and production and a customer is willing to pay $12, the brewery has created $9 of new value.

Value Capture is about how that newly created value gets divided. Creating value is necessary for a firm to exist, but it is not sufficient for the firm to prosper. The firm must also capture a portion of the value it creates, and that captured portion is profit. In the brewery example, the $9 of new value does not automatically flow to the brewer. If the brewery prices the six-pack at $10, it captures $7 as profit and the customer retains $2 as **consumer surplus**, the difference between what the customer was willing to pay ($12) and what they actually paid ($10). If a competitor forces the price down to $6, the brewery captures only $3 while the customer keeps $6. The total value created has not changed, but who captures it has shifted dramatically.

This distinction matters because value creation and value capture are governed by different forces. A firm can be excellent at creating value and still struggle to capture it. Consider a company that develops a breakthrough product but operates in a market with intense price competition. The product generates enormous value for customers, but rivals quickly match the price downward, and most of the value ends up as consumer surplus rather than firm profit. Conversely, a firm with a strong brand or patent protection may capture a large share of the value it creates by maintaining premium prices that competitors cannot easily undercut.

The balance between creation and capture will become a recurring theme throughout this textbook. When we examine competitive advantage in the next section, we will see that advantage is ultimately about creating a larger value gap than competitors and capturing enough of it to generate superior returns. When we explore business-level strategy in Chapter 2, we will see that differentiation and cost leadership represent two fundamentally different approaches to widening and capturing that gap. For now, the key insight is that a viable business requires both: value creation to justify the firm's existence, and value capture to sustain it.

This framework applies not only at the level of the firm but also at the level of individual employees within it. An employee creates value by transforming inputs (their time, tools, training, information, and materials) into outputs that the firm values more than the cost of employing that person. A salesperson who generates $500,000 in revenue but costs $100,000 to employ has created $400,000 in value for the firm. An engineer whose design saves $200,000 annually but costs $120,000 in salary and overhead has created $80,000 in value. If the value of an employee's output does not exceed the cost of their employment, the employee is destroying rather than creating value, an unsustainable situation for both the employee and the firm. Understanding this principle helps clarify why firms make the hiring, compensation, and restructuring decisions they do, and it reinforces the idea that value creation is not an abstraction but a measurable economic reality at every level of the organization.

Without this transformation creating more value than it consumes, no economic value exists, and the firm has no reason to operate. The business model, then, is the architecture that organizes this value creation process, determining what inputs to acquire, how to transform them, who to deliver the outputs to, and how to capture a portion of the value created as profit.

1.4.2 What Is a Business Model?

A business model describes the way a firm creates, delivers, and captures value (Teece, 2010). It is the architecture of the business, the blueprint that explains how all the pieces of the firm fit together to generate revenue and, ultimately, profit. If strategy answers the question "how will we achieve our long-term vision?", the business model answers the more immediate question "how does this business actually work?"

Every firm has a business model, whether its leaders have articulated it or not. A traditional bookstore creates value by curating a selection of books, providing a physical browsing experience, and offering knowledgeable staff recommendations. It delivers that value through its retail locations and captures value by charging a markup on each book sold. A subscription-based e-book service creates value through unlimited access to a large digital library, delivers it through an app, and captures value through monthly subscription fees. Both are in the business of connecting readers with books, but their business models are fundamentally different.

Understanding business models matters because they reveal the logic behind a firm's operations. Two firms can compete in the same industry with the same vision and still operate in completely different ways. The business model is what explains this difference. It forces managers to think clearly about who the customer is, what value the firm offers, how that value reaches the customer, and how the firm earns a return for doing so.

1.4.3 Business Model Components & Canvas

While there are many frameworks for describing business models, most models consist of several core components that together explain the firm's operating logic. These components include the value proposition, the customer segments, customer relationships, the revenue streams, the cost structure, key resources and activities, and channels.

One of the most widely used tools for visualizing and analyzing business models is the **Business Model Canvas**, developed by Alexander Osterwalder and Yves Pigneur (Osterwalder & Pigneur, 2010). The Canvas organizes the components discussed above into a single-page visual framework with nine building blocks, making it easier to see how a business model fits together as a system and to identify where changes or innovations might be needed.

The **value proposition** is the most fundamental component. It defines the specific value the firm offers to its customers, the reason a customer would choose this firm over an alternative. A value proposition might center on price (offering the lowest price option), convenience (making the product easier to access), quality (delivering a superior product), customization (tailoring the offering to individual needs), or some combination of these. Southwest Airlines, for example, built its value proposition around low fares and reliable point-to-point service. It did not try to compete on luxury amenities or global route networks. Its value proposition was clear: affordable, no-frills air travel.

The **customer segments** defines who the firm serves. Not all customers are the same, and business models must be designed around the specific needs, preferences, and willingness to pay of a defined group. A luxury watchmaker and a discount retailer both sell timepieces, but they target entirely different customer segments with different expectations. Clarity about the customer segment shapes every other component of the business model.

The **customer relationships** component describes the kind of ongoing connection the firm establishes and maintains with each customer segment. These relationships range from automated, self-service interactions to dedicated personal assistance, and they may be designed to acquire new customers, retain existing ones, or encourage additional purchases. A budget airline relies on automated booking and minimal direct contact to hold down costs, while a private wealth manager cultivates a high-touch, personal relationship with each client. The form of relationship a firm chooses must fit both its customer segment and its cost structure.

The **revenue streams** describes how the firm earns money from its value proposition. Common revenue models include direct sales, subscriptions, licensing, advertising, freemium (a free basic service with paid premium features), and transaction-based fees. The revenue model must align with the value proposition and customer segment. A business that promises convenience, for example, may find that a subscription model is more natural than a per-transaction model because subscriptions reduce friction for repeat customers.

The **cost structure** identifies the major costs the firm incurs in delivering its value proposition. Some business models are cost-driven, meaning they are designed to minimize costs at every turn (think budget airlines or discount retailers). Others are value-driven, meaning they accept higher costs in exchange for delivering a premium experience or product (think high-end restaurants or luxury fashion brands). Understanding the cost structure is essential because it determines what level of revenue is required for the business to be profitable.

Key resources are the strategic assets the firm needs to deliver on its value proposition. For a pharmaceutical company, key resources include patents, research facilities, and scientific talent. For a logistics company, key resources are warehouses, trucks, and route optimization software. These are the assets (physical, intellectual, human, or financial) without which the business model cannot function.

Key activities are the core tasks the firm must perform to make its business model work. For a pharmaceutical company, key activities include drug development and regulatory approval. For a logistics company, key activities are inventory management and delivery execution. While key resources represent what the firm needs to have, key activities represent what the firm needs to do. Together, they form the operational backbone of the business model.

Key partnerships are the network of suppliers, allies, and other external parties that help the firm operate its business model effectively. Firms form partnerships for many reasons: to access resources they do not own, to reduce risk, to achieve economies of scale, or to focus on their core activities while outsourcing others. A smartphone manufacturer, for example, partners with component suppliers, software developers, and wireless carriers, each contributing something essential that the firm could not efficiently provide on its own. Not every relationship qualifies as a key partnership; the term refers specifically to those external relationships that are critical to delivering the value proposition.

Channels are the mechanisms through which the firm's value proposition reaches the customer. These can be direct (the firm's own stores, website, or sales force) or indirect (distributors, retailers, or platform marketplaces). The choice of channel affects both the customer experience and the cost structure, making it a critical design decision.

Together, these components form an interconnected system. Changing one component typically requires adjustments to others. A firm that shifts from a direct sales revenue model to a subscription model, for example, will likely need to redesign its delivery channels, rethink its cost structure, and possibly redefine its value proposition (Osterwalder & Pigneur, 2010).

EX: Business Model Canvas for Specialty Coffee Shop

To illustrate how these components work together in practice, consider a hypothetical specialty coffee shop opening in an urban college neighborhood. The owner must make deliberate choices about each element of the business model, and those choices must reinforce one another. A decision to serve premium single-origin coffee, for example, implies a particular customer segment, a specific set of supplier partnerships, and a cost structure that looks very different from a budget-focused competitor. The following example walks through each component of the Business Model Canvas for this shop.

Value Proposition: High-quality, locally roasted coffee served in a comfortable workspace environment. The shop differentiates itself from large chains by offering a curated selection of single-origin beans, knowledgeable baristas, and a space designed for remote workers and students who want to linger, not just grab and go.

Customer Segments: Young professionals and college students aged 22–35 in an urban neighborhood who value specialty coffee, seek a productive "third place" outside of home and office, and are willing to pay a modest premium for quality and atmosphere.

Customer Relationships: A personal, community-oriented relationship built on barista familiarity, recognition of repeat visitors, and a loyalty program that rewards regulars. The shop cultivates a sense of belonging through in-person interaction and an active social media presence, rather than the impersonal, transactional contact typical of large chains.

Revenue Streams: Primarily direct sales of beverages and light food items, supplemented by retail sales of whole-bean coffee bags and branded merchandise. The shop also rents its space for private events during evening hours.

Cost Structure: Value-driven rather than cost-driven. Major costs include premium green coffee beans from a local specialty roaster, rent in a high-foot-traffic urban location, barista wages (higher than chain competitors to attract skilled staff), and equipment maintenance for commercial espresso machines and grinders. The willingness to absorb higher ingredient and labor costs is central to delivering the quality experience promised by the value proposition.

Key Resources: A well-designed physical space with ample seating, power outlets, and reliable

Wi-Fi. High-end espresso equipment. Skilled baristas with specialty coffee training. Relationships with local roasters. A recognizable brand identity built through social media presence and community involvement.

Key Activities: Sourcing and curating coffee selections. Training baristas to maintain consistent drink quality. Managing inventory and daily operations. Marketing through social media and local events. Maintaining the physical space to ensure it remains an inviting environment.

Key Partnerships: A local roasting company that supplies freshly roasted beans on a weekly schedule. A regional bakery that provides pastries and light food items, allowing the shop to offer food without operating its own kitchen. A point-of-sale technology provider. Local artists whose rotating work decorates the walls, generating community engagement for both parties.

Channels: Primarily the physical storefront itself, where customers come to the shop for the in-person experience. A secondary channel is a simple online ordering system for pickup orders during peak hours. The shop also uses Instagram and a local presence on Google Maps as awareness channels to drive foot traffic.

1.4.4 Business Model Innovation

Business model innovation occurs when a firm fundamentally changes the way it creates, delivers, or captures value, not by developing a new product, but by rethinking the business model itself. Some of the most transformative competitive moves in business history have not been product innovations but business model innovations (Teece, 2010).

Consider the early days of Amazon in the book industry. Amazon did not invent a new kind of book. It changed the business model. By eliminating physical retail stores and selling directly to customers online, Amazon removed an entire category of costs from its value chain. This allowed it to offer lower prices and a vastly larger selection than any brick-and-mortar bookstore could match. The product was the same; the business model was entirely different. In the language of value creation, Amazon found a way to perform the transformation — connecting readers with books — at dramatically lower cost, widening the value gap and capturing a larger share of it.

Netflix followed a similar pattern in entertainment. It started by disrupting the video rental business model, replacing late fees and store visits with a flat-rate mail subscription. Then it disrupted its own model by shifting to streaming, and later disrupted the content industry by becoming a producer of original programming. Each shift was a business model innovation, not a product innovation.

Business model innovation can take many forms. A firm might change its revenue model, as Adobe did when it shifted from selling software licenses to charging a monthly subscription through Creative Cloud. A firm might reconfigure its value chain, as Dell did in the 1990s by selling computers directly to consumers and building them to order, bypassing traditional retail distribution. A firm might redefine its customer segment, as Airbnb did by turning ordinary homeowners into hospitality providers and ordinary travelers into guests in private homes.

What makes business model innovation strategically powerful is that it is often harder for competitors to imitate than product innovation. A competitor can reverse-engineer a product, but replicating an entirely different way of operating, with its own cost structure, revenue model, delivery channels, and organizational capabilities, is far more difficult (Teece, 2010). This is why business model innovation can be a potent source of competitive advantage, a concept we will explore in the next section.

1.4.5 Business Models vs. Strategy

It is common for business models and strategy to be conflated, but they are distinct concepts that operate at different levels of analysis. A business model describes how the firm operates, the mechanics of value creation and capture. Strategy describes how the firm positions itself relative to competitors to achieve superior performance over time (Teece, 2010).

A business model answers the question: "How does this business work?" Strategy answers the question: "How will this business win?" The business model is primarily an internal description of the firm's operating logic. Strategy is inherently external-facing; it concerns the firm's position in a competitive landscape.

To illustrate the distinction, consider two coffee shops operating with identical business models: both source specialty beans, roast in-house, serve through cozy retail locations, and charge premium prices. Their business models are the same. But one may pursue a strategy of rapid geographic expansion to build brand recognition and achieve economies of scale, while the other pursues a strategy of deep community engagement in a single city, cultivating intense local loyalty. Same business model, different strategies.

Conversely, two firms may have the same strategy, say, competing as the low-cost provider in their industry, but achieve it through very different business models. One might minimize costs through aggressive automation and vertical integration. The other might minimize costs through outsourcing and a lean organizational structure. Same strategy, different business models.

The relationship between business models and strategy is complementary. The business model provides the operating foundation on which strategy is built. For instance, a firm cannot pursue a low-cost strategy if its business model carries a heavy cost structure. The business model must support the strategy, and the strategy must account for the business model's strengths and limitations.

As we move forward in this chapter to discuss competitive advantage and, ultimately, strategy itself, it is important to keep this distinction in mind. The business model is the engine; strategy is the map. You need both to reach your destination, but they serve fundamentally different purposes.

References

Brandenburger, A. M., & Stuart, H. W. (1996). Value-based business strategy. *Journal of Economics & Management Strategy*, *5*(1), 5–24.

Osterwalder, A., & Pigneur, Y. (2010). *Business model generation: A handbook for visionaries, game changers, and challengers.* John Wiley & Sons.

Teece, D. J. (2010). Business models, business strategy and innovation. *Long Range Planning*, *43*(2–3), 172–194.

1.5 Competitive Advantage — *How do firms compete?*

The previous sections established what firms are trying to achieve and how their business models create value. But firms do not operate in isolation. They compete for customers, for resources, for talent, for market position. The central question of strategic management is not simply "how does a firm create value?" but "how does a firm create *more* value than its rivals, and how does it sustain that edge over time?" This is the domain of competitive advantage, one of the most important concepts in all of strategy.

Competitive advantage is what separates firms that thrive from firms that merely survive, and from firms that fail. Understanding what competitive advantage is, where it comes from, how long it can last, and what happens when a firm lacks it provides the conceptual foundation for everything that follows in this book.

1.5.1 What Is Competitive Advantage?

A firm has a competitive advantage when it creates more economic value than its competitors. Building on the value-cost gap introduced in the previous section, a firm holds a competitive advantage when it generates a larger gap between customer willingness to pay and cost than its rivals do (Brandenburger & Stuart, 1996).

This definition has an important implication: competitive advantage is always relative. A firm cannot have a competitive advantage in a vacuum; it can only have one compared to other firms competing in the same market. A restaurant that earns a 15% profit margin might seem successful, but if every other restaurant in its market earns 20%, that firm actually has a competitive disadvantage. Competitive advantage is not about absolute performance; it is about performance relative to rivals.

Competitive advantage typically manifests in one of two ways. A firm may earn higher profit margins than its competitors, meaning it captures more value from each unit sold. Alternatively, a firm may capture greater market share by offering superior value that attracts more customers, even if its per-unit margins are similar to competitors. In many cases, firms with a strong competitive advantage achieve both, higher margins and greater market share, though the emphasis depends on the firm's strategic approach.

It is also important to understand that competitive advantage is not the same thing as simply being profitable. A firm can be profitable without having a competitive advantage if the entire industry is profitable. When an industry is booming, as the smartphone industry was in its early years, nearly every participant can earn healthy returns. That is industry-level profitability, not firm-level competitive advantage. True competitive advantage means outperforming rivals within the same competitive context, not merely riding an industry tailwind.

1.5.2 Sources of Competitive Advantage

Where does competitive advantage come from? Recall from the previous section that a firm creates value by widening the gap between what customers are willing to pay and what it costs the firm to produce. A competitive advantage, then, ultimately works through one of two fundamental levers: a firm can find ways to increase the value it offers customers (raising their willingness to pay), or it can find ways to lower its costs relative to rivals (Brandenburger & Stuart, 1996). Every competitive advantage, however it is achieved, traces back to one or both of these levers: a firm outperforms because its offering is worth more to customers, because it costs less to deliver, or because of some combination of the two.

These two levers describe *what* an advantage does. The harder and more interesting question is *where* the ability to pull those levers comes from. Strategy scholars have offered two broad perspectives on the origins of competitive advantage, and together they organize much of the rest of this book.

The first perspective looks outward, to the firm's **position within its industry**. From this view, advantage stems from how a firm chooses to compete relative to rivals and how it situates itself among the competitive forces of its industry (Porter, 1985). A firm might stake out a position as the premium provider, the low-cost provider, or a specialist serving a narrow niche. Chapter 2 develops these competitive positions in detail, and Chapter 4 examines the industry forces that determine how attractive a given position is. The core idea is that advantage is partly a matter of *choosing where and how to compete.*

The second perspective looks inward, to the firm's **resources and capabilities**, the distinctive assets, skills, knowledge, and organizational processes a firm controls. From this view, advantage arises because a firm possesses something its rivals lack and cannot easily acquire: a powerful brand, proprietary technology, a hard-to-replicate culture, specialized expertise, or privileged access to scarce inputs (Barney, 1991). Two firms competing for the same position will perform differently if one commands superior resources. Chapter 3 develops this resource-based view of the firm. The core idea is that advantage is partly a matter of *what the firm has and can do* that others cannot.

These two perspectives are complementary rather than competing. A strong market position is difficult to defend without distinctive resources to back it, and valuable resources generate little advantage unless they are deployed in a sensible competitive position. Most durable advantages draw on both.

It is also worth dispelling a common oversimplification. Competitive advantage is sometimes reduced to a binary choice between being "different" or being "cheaper." Those are indeed the two most prominent routes, and they receive close attention in the next chapter, but they do not exhaust the possibilities. Advantage can also flow from sources that do not fit neatly into either category: a fundamentally reconfigured business model that removes whole categories of cost, network effects that make a product more valuable as more people adopt it, switching costs that lock in existing customers, economies of scale that smaller rivals cannot reach, accumulated learning that compounds with experience, or the first-mover advantages of entering a market early. The sources of advantage are as varied as the ways firms can create and capture value.

The remainder of this book is, in large part, an extended investigation of these sources: how to identify them, how to build them, and, most importantly, how to make them last.

1.5.3 Temporary vs. Sustainable Competitive Advantage

Not all competitive advantages are created equal. Some last for decades; others evaporate within months. The distinction between temporary and sustainable competitive advantage is critical for understanding why some firms maintain dominant positions while others see their advantages quickly eroded.

A **temporary competitive advantage** exists when a firm outperforms its rivals for a limited period before competitors catch up. This happens when the source of the advantage can be relatively easily imitated, substituted, or made irrelevant by changes in the market. A restaurant that introduces a popular new menu item may enjoy a surge in customers, but if competitors can quickly copy the dish, the advantage is temporary. A tech company that launches an innovative app feature may see a spike in downloads, but if rivals can reverse-engineer the feature within weeks, the advantage is short-lived.

Temporary advantages are common in fast-moving industries where imitation is quick and inexpensive. In the mobile app market, for example, a successful feature introduced by one company is often replicated by dozens of competitors within months. Firms in these environments find themselves in a constant race, where any lead can quickly disappear. The strategic challenge in such industries is not achieving an advantage but continuously generating new ones, staying one step ahead of the imitation cycle.

A **sustainable competitive advantage** exists when a firm's edge persists over an extended period because competitors find it difficult or impossible to imitate, substitute, or neutralize the advantage. Sustainability comes from barriers to imitation, characteristics of the firm's resources, capabilities, or market position that make it hard for rivals to replicate what the firm does (Barney, 1991).

What raises those barriers? In general, an advantage is hardest to copy when its source is difficult for rivals to even identify, difficult to acquire on the open market, or difficult to build quickly even when a competitor knows exactly what to aim for. An advantage rooted in something visible and purchasable tends to be fragile. A piece of equipment any rival can buy, or a price promotion any rival can match, offers little lasting protection. An advantage rooted in something that took years to accumulate and is bound up with how the whole organization works tends to last. A later chapter introduces a formal framework for assessing how well-protected a firm's resources and capabilities are; at this stage, the key idea is simply that the harder an advantage is to imitate, substitute for, or neutralize, the longer it endures.

Corporate culture is a frequently cited example of something that is genuinely hard to copy. Southwest Airlines has long been recognized for its distinctive culture, characterized by employee empowerment, humor, and a strong sense of shared purpose, which contributes to low employee turnover, high customer satisfaction, and operational efficiency. Yet despite Southwest's success being widely studied, competitors have struggled to replicate it. A rival cannot simply instruct its employees to be more engaged; a culture is the product of decades of hiring decisions, leadership behaviors, organizational norms, and shared experiences. It is deeply embedded and inherently difficult to copy, which is precisely why it can support an advantage that lasts.

Other examples follow the same logic. A strong brand built over years of consistent customer experience, proprietary technology protected by patents, a distribution network that would take competitors years and enormous investment to match, and customer relationships locked in by high switching costs all share a common feature: they cannot be replicated quickly or cheaply (Peteraf, 1993). In each case, the advantage endures because the barriers to imitation are high.

It is important to recognize, however, that no competitive advantage is truly permanent. Even the most sustainable advantages can be eroded over time by shifts in technology, changes in customer preferences, regulatory changes, or the emergence of entirely new business models that substitute for the firm's advantage rather than directly imitating it. Barnes & Noble's extensive network of retail stores was a costly-to-imitate advantage, until Amazon found a substitute by selling books online, rendering the physical network far less valuable. Sustainable does not mean eternal; it means the advantage persists long enough to generate above-average returns while the firm continues to adapt.

1.5.4 Competitive Parity and Competitive Disadvantage

Not every firm possesses a competitive advantage, and understanding the alternatives is just as important as understanding advantage itself.

Competitive parity exists when a firm performs at roughly the same level as its competitors; it is neither outperforming nor underperforming relative to rivals. The firm is keeping up, but not pulling ahead. Competitive parity is the default state for many firms in mature industries where competitors have similar resources, similar cost structures, and similar value propositions. In such industries, most participants earn comparable returns, and no single firm holds a meaningful edge.

Competitive parity is not necessarily a bad outcome. In highly competitive industries, simply matching the performance of well-run rivals is a significant achievement. But parity does mean that the firm has not found a way to differentiate itself or achieve a cost position that sets it apart. From a strategic perspective, competitive parity represents a missed opportunity: the firm is surviving but not thriving. When the things a firm relies on to compete are widely available to every rival, they produce parity rather than advantage (Barney, 1991). Having capable employees, functional IT systems, and adequate capital is necessary just to stay in the game, but when every firm in the industry possesses these same things, they become table stakes rather than sources of advantage.

Competitive disadvantage exists when a firm consistently underperforms its rivals. The firm's products are not as valued by customers, its costs are higher than competitors, or both. A firm in competitive disadvantage is losing ground, ceding market share, earning lower margins, or struggling to attract talent and investment.

Competitive disadvantage can arise from many sources. A firm may have failed to invest in capabilities that competitors have developed, leaving it behind in product quality or operational efficiency. It may be burdened by legacy cost structures (outdated facilities, bloated workforces, or inefficient processes) that newer or more agile competitors have avoided. It may have made poor strategic choices, entering markets where it lacks the resources to compete effectively or pursuing a value proposition that customers do not find compelling.

The most dangerous form of competitive disadvantage is the kind that compounds over time. A firm earning below-average returns has fewer resources to reinvest in improvement, which leads to further deterioration in its competitive position, which leads to even lower returns. This downward spiral can be difficult to escape without a fundamental strategic reset, a rethinking of the firm's business model, market position, or organizational capabilities.

1.5.5 The Strategic Imperative

Understanding competitive advantage — what it is, where it comes from, whether it can last, and what the alternatives look like — is essential because it frames the central question of strategic management: *why do some firms outperform others?* Every strategic framework, analytical tool, and managerial decision we will examine in this text is ultimately aimed at helping firms build, sustain, or recover a competitive advantage.

The next sections of this chapter will examine the stakeholders whose interests shape strategic decisions and then bring all of these foundational concepts together into a unified understanding of what strategy actually is. But the concept of competitive advantage will remain at the center of our analysis throughout the entire book. It is the prize that strategy seeks to win.

References

Barney, J. B. (1991). Firm resources and sustained competitive advantage. *Journal of Management, 17*(1), 99–120.

Brandenburger, A. M., & Stuart, H. W. (1996). Value-based business strategy. *Journal of Economics & Management Strategy, 5*(1), 5–24.

Peteraf, M. A. (1993). The cornerstones of competitive advantage: A resource-based view. *Strategic Management Journal, 14*(3), 179–191.

Porter, M. E. (1985). *Competitive advantage: Creating and sustaining superior performance.* Free Press.

1.6 Stakeholders — *Who do they serve?*

> ***"The business of business is people." — Herb Kelleher, Co-founder of Southwest Airlines***

In the previous sections, we established why firms exist, what they aim to achieve, how they create value through their business models, and how they compete for advantage. But there is a critical question we have not yet addressed: who does the firm actually serve? The answer is more complex than it might initially appear, and it has profound implications for how strategy is formulated and executed.

A firm does not operate in isolation. It exists within a web of relationships with individuals and groups who affect, and are affected by, its actions. These are the firm's **stakeholders**, and understanding who they are, what they want, and how much influence they wield is essential to developing a strategy that is both effective and sustainable. A brilliant competitive strategy that ignores the concerns of key stakeholders is a strategy that is likely to fail, not because the market analysis was wrong or the business model was flawed, but because the firm lost the support of the very people and groups it depended on to execute its plans.

1.6.1 What Are Stakeholders?

A **stakeholder** is any individual, group, or organization that can affect or is affected by the achievement of a firm's objectives (Freeman, 1984). This definition deliberately casts a wide net. It includes not only the people who own the firm or work for it, but also the customers who buy from it, the suppliers who provide its inputs, the communities in which it operates, the governments that regulate it, and many others.

This stands in contrast to the older, narrower view that a firm's primary obligation is to its **shareholders**, the owners who have invested capital and bear financial risk. Under this shareholder primacy perspective, most closely associated with the economist Milton Friedman, a business already contributes to society by selling goods and services that customers value above many competing alternatives while operating within the rules of the game (Friedman, 1970). A firm that fails to create sufficient value for its customers will not survive, so the discipline of the market ensures that pursuing profit and serving society are, for the most part, the same activity. Managers, in this view, are agents of shareholders and owe no operational duty beyond that relationship; diverting firm resources toward social goals that do not increase shareholder value amounts to spending other people's money for social ends they did not choose. It also casts managers as unelected arbiters of the public good, substituting their own judgment about worthy causes for that of the shareholders, customers, and employees whose money it is.

The stakeholder perspective does not necessarily reject the importance of shareholders, but it insists that shareholders are just one group among many whose interests must be considered (Freeman, 1984). The logic is practical as much as it is ethical: a firm that consistently ignores the interests of its employees will struggle to attract and retain talent. A firm that mistreats its suppliers will find its supply chain unreliable. A firm that damages its local community may face regulatory backlash or consumer boycotts. In short, firms depend on the cooperation and support of multiple stakeholder groups to survive and prosper, and strategy must account for this reality.

The shift from shareholder primacy to a broader stakeholder orientation has accelerated in recent decades. In 2019, the Business Roundtable, an association of CEOs from many of America's largest corporations, issued a revised statement on the purpose of a corporation, explicitly committing to delivering value to all stakeholders, not just shareholders (Business Roundtable, 2019). Whether this represents a genuine philosophical shift or a public relations exercise remains debated, but it reflects a growing recognition that long-term firm performance depends on maintaining the trust and support of a wide range of constituents.

1.6.2 Categories of Stakeholders

Not all stakeholders are alike. They differ in their relationship to the firm, the nature of their claims, and the urgency of their concerns. A useful starting point is to distinguish between **internal stakeholders** and **external stakeholders**.

Internal stakeholders are those who operate within the boundaries of the firm. They include the firm's owners or shareholders, its managers and executives, and its employees at all levels. These groups have a direct and ongoing relationship with the firm. Shareholders have invested capital and expect financial returns. Managers bear responsibility for strategic and operational decisions and are compensated accordingly. Employees contribute their labor and expertise in exchange for wages, benefits, and working conditions. Each of these groups has distinct interests that may or may not align with one another, a tension we will explore further when we discuss stakeholder conflicts.

External stakeholders exist outside the firm's boundaries but are nonetheless affected by or exert influence over its activities. This is a diverse category that includes customers, suppliers, creditors, competitors, local communities, governments, industry associations, activist groups, the media, and society at large. Customers want quality products at fair prices. Suppliers want reliable purchasing relationships with fair terms. Creditors want assurance that the firm can service its debts. Local communities want jobs, tax revenue, and environmental responsibility. Governments want compliance with laws and regulations. Each of these groups holds a different kind of stake in the firm's behavior and outcomes.

A further distinction is sometimes drawn between **primary stakeholders** and **secondary stakeholders**. Primary stakeholders are those without whose continuing participation the firm cannot survive as a going concern: shareholders, employees, customers, suppliers, and the government (as the entity that provides legal infrastructure and enforces contracts). Secondary stakeholders are those who influence or are influenced by the firm but are not essential for its survival, such as the media, activist groups, or trade associations. This distinction is useful but should be applied carefully: a secondary stakeholder can quickly become a primary concern if, for example, an activist campaign triggers a consumer boycott that threatens revenues.

1.6.3 Stakeholder Power and Interest

Identifying who a firm's stakeholders are is only the first step. The more strategically important question is: which stakeholders matter most, and when? Not all stakeholders deserve equal attention at all times. Some have enormous power to influence the firm's direction, while others have relatively little. Some have intense interest in the firm's decisions, while others are largely indifferent. Effective stakeholder management requires understanding these differences and prioritizing accordingly.

One of the most widely used tools for this purpose is the **stakeholder power-interest matrix** (Mendelow, 1981), which classifies stakeholders along two dimensions: their power to influence the firm and their level of interest in the firm's activities. This produces four categories.

Stakeholders with **high power and high interest** are the firm's key players. These are the groups that demand the most attention because they have both the ability and the motivation to significantly affect the firm's strategy. Major shareholders, key customers, powerful regulators, and senior employees typically fall into this category. The firm must engage closely with these stakeholders, actively managing the relationship and ensuring their concerns are addressed.

Stakeholders with **high power but low interest** must be kept satisfied. They have the ability to cause significant problems for the firm if they become dissatisfied, but they are not normally focused on the firm's day-to-day operations. Government regulators often fall into this category; they may not pay attention to a firm until something goes wrong, but when they do turn their attention to it, they can impose severe consequences. The strategic approach here is to meet their expectations and avoid giving them a reason to become more actively involved.

Stakeholders with **low power but high interest** should be kept informed. These groups care deeply about the firm's activities but lack the ability to directly influence its decisions. Local community groups, individual small shareholders, or lower-level employees may fall here. While they cannot individually force changes, they should not be ignored; they can sometimes mobilize collectively or attract the attention of more powerful stakeholders, amplifying their influence beyond what their individual power would suggest.

Stakeholders with **low power and low interest** require only minimal monitoring. These are groups that are peripherally connected to the firm and unlikely to take action. The firm should remain aware of them but need not invest significant resources in managing these relationships.

It is important to recognize that stakeholder power and interest are not static. They shift over time and in response to events. A community group that was a low-power, high-interest stakeholder might suddenly gain significant power if a firm's environmental violation becomes a national news story and attracts the attention of regulators and politicians. An employee group that was previously content might become highly interested and seek to increase its power through unionization. Effective strategic management requires continuously reassessing the stakeholder landscape rather than treating it as a one-time exercise.

The sources of stakeholder power also vary. Mitchell et al. (1997) identified three key attributes that determine stakeholder salience: **power** (the ability to impose one's will), **legitimacy** (the perceived validity of the stakeholder's claim), and **urgency** (the degree to which the stakeholder's claim demands immediate attention). Stakeholders who possess all three attributes command the greatest managerial attention. Some stakeholders wield **formal or institutional power**, such as the legal authority of a government regulator or the voting rights of a shareholder. Others exercise **economic power**, such as a major customer that accounts for a large share of the firm's revenue or a supplier that provides a critical input with no readily available substitute. Still others possess **social or political power**, such as the ability to shape public opinion through media attention or grassroots organizing. Understanding the source of a stakeholder's power is important because it determines what kinds of actions the firm can take to manage the relationship.

1.6.4 Managing Stakeholder Relationships

Identifying and prioritizing stakeholders is analytically useful, but strategy ultimately requires action. How should firms manage their stakeholder relationships in practice?

The first principle is **alignment**: wherever possible, the firm should seek strategies that create value for multiple stakeholder groups simultaneously. This is not always achievable, but it is more common than one might assume. Investing in employee training, for example, may simultaneously improve employee satisfaction, increase product quality for customers, and drive productivity gains that benefit shareholders. A well-designed sustainability initiative might reduce costs through energy savings, improve brand reputation with customers, satisfy regulatory requirements, and generate positive media coverage. The most effective strategies are often those that find creative ways to align the interests of multiple stakeholders rather than treating stakeholder management as a zero-sum game.

The second principle is **transparency**. Stakeholders who feel informed and included are generally more supportive and forgiving than those who feel blindsided or deceived. Proactive communication about the firm's strategy, performance, and challenges builds trust and social capital that can be drawn upon when difficult decisions must be made. Many corporate crises are not caused by the underlying problem itself but by the perception that the firm was dishonest or secretive in its response. A firm that communicates openly about a product recall, for instance, is likely to recover customer trust far more quickly than one that attempts to minimize or conceal the issue.

The third principle is **engagement**: going beyond one-way communication to actively involve stakeholders in decision-making processes where appropriate. This can take many forms, from customer advisory panels and employee town halls to community impact assessments and supplier partnership programs. The goal is not to give every stakeholder a veto over the firm's strategy but to ensure that their perspectives are heard and considered before decisions are made. This both improves the quality of decisions, because decision-makers have access to more information and perspectives, and increases stakeholder buy-in for the resulting strategy.

The fourth principle is **reciprocity**: the recognition that stakeholder relationships are, at their best, mutually beneficial. A firm that extracts maximum short-term value from its suppliers by squeezing their margins will eventually find that its best suppliers go elsewhere. A firm that demands maximum effort from employees while minimizing compensation and investment in their development will experience high turnover and declining morale. Sustainable stakeholder relationships are built on a foundation of mutual value creation, where each party sees the relationship as worth maintaining over time. This connects directly back to the concept of the value chain introduced earlier in this chapter: the firm exists within a broader value system, and the health of the entire system matters for the firm's long-term success.

1.6.5 Stakeholder Conflicts

Despite the best efforts at alignment, stakeholder conflicts are inevitable. Different stakeholder groups have fundamentally different interests, and satisfying one group often comes at the expense of another. These conflicts are among the most challenging aspects of strategic management, and how a firm navigates them reveals a great deal about its values and strategic priorities.

The most classic stakeholder conflict in business is between **shareholders and employees**. Shareholders generally want to maximize profits, which can mean minimizing labor costs through lower wages, fewer benefits, or workforce reductions. Employees want higher compensation, better working conditions, and job security. A decision to close a factory and move production to a lower-cost country may boost profitability and share price while devastating the local workforce and community. Neither side is wrong in the abstract — each is pursuing legitimate interests — but the firm must decide how to balance these competing claims.

A related tension exists between **shareholders and managers**, which is the core concern of agency theory (Jensen & Meckling, 1976). Because managers are the ones making decisions on behalf of owners, they may sometimes pursue actions that benefit themselves at shareholders' expense. A CEO might pursue an acquisition that increases the firm's size and the CEO's prestige and compensation, even if the acquisition destroys shareholder value. A management team might resist a hostile takeover that would benefit shareholders because it would cost them their jobs. This principal-agent problem is addressed through various corporate governance mechanisms (boards of directors, executive compensation structures, auditing requirements, and the market for corporate control) which we will examine in detail in a later chapter.

Conflicts also arise between **the firm and its customers**. A pharmaceutical company, for example, must decide how to price a life-saving drug. Shareholders expect the firm to maximize revenue. Patients and the public expect access to affordable medicine. Governments and insurers want to control healthcare costs. There is no price point that satisfies all of these stakeholders simultaneously, and the firm's pricing decision will inevitably be criticized by at least some of them.

Short-term versus long-term interests represent another common source of stakeholder conflict, often playing out within a single stakeholder group. Shareholders focused on quarterly earnings may push for cost-cutting measures that undermine the firm's long-term competitive position. A decision to reduce R&D spending will boost this quarter's profits but may leave the firm without the innovations it needs to compete five years from now. One of the most important functions of strategy is to establish a framework for making these tradeoffs, to ensure that short-term pressures do not consistently override long-term value creation.

Firms resolve stakeholder conflicts through a combination of negotiation, prioritization, and compromise. In practice, firms tend to prioritize the stakeholders who have the most power and the most urgent claims, which is not always the same as prioritizing those whose claims are most legitimate (Mitchell et al., 1997). A firm facing a hostile takeover attempt will focus intensely on its shareholders and the acquiring firm, even if its employees are the ones most affected by the outcome. This pragmatic reality does not mean that less powerful stakeholders should be ignored — both ethical obligations and long-term strategic considerations argue for a broader view — but it does mean that strategic managers must be realistic about the dynamics at play.

The key insight for strategic management is that stakeholder analysis is not a standalone exercise. It is embedded in every strategic decision the firm makes. When we discuss competitive strategy, we are implicitly making choices about which stakeholders benefit and which bear costs. When we analyze industry forces, we are examining the power dynamics among firms, customers, suppliers, and potential entrants, all of which are stakeholder relationships. When we consider corporate governance, we are directly confronting the mechanisms through which stakeholder conflicts are managed. Understanding stakeholders is therefore not a separate topic from strategy; it is a lens through which every strategic choice should be evaluated.

References

Business Roundtable. (2019). *Statement on the purpose of a corporation.* https://www.businessroundtable.org/business-roundtable-redefines-the-purpose-of-a-corporation-to-promote-an-economy-that-serves-all-americans

Freeman, R. E. (1984). *Strategic management: A stakeholder approach.* Pitman.

Friedman, M. (1970, September 13). The social responsibility of business is to increase its profits. *The New York Times Magazine.*

Jensen, M. C., & Meckling, W. H. (1976). Theory of the firm: Managerial behavior, agency costs and ownership structure. *Journal of Financial Economics, 3*(4), 305–360.

Mendelow, A. L. (1981). Environmental scanning: The impact of the stakeholder concept. In *Proceedings of the Second International Conference on Information Systems* (pp. 407–417). Cambridge, MA.

Mitchell, R. K., Agle, B. R., & Wood, D. J. (1997). Toward a theory of stakeholder identification and salience: Defining the principle of who and what really counts. *Academy of Management Review, 22*(4), 853–886.

1.7 What Is Strategy? — *Tying it all together*

We have now covered a great deal of ground. We know why firms exist, what they are trying to achieve, how they create value through their business models, how they compete for advantage, and who they serve. With all of these foundational pieces in place, we can now address the central question of this entire book: What is strategy?

1.7.1 Strategy as Competitive Positioning

Despite being one of the most commonly used words in business, "strategy" has no single agreed-upon definition. Scholars and practitioners have debated its meaning for decades (Mintzberg, 1987). Some definitions, however, have proven more useful and enduring than others.

Michael Porter, perhaps the most influential strategy scholar, defined strategy as a broad formula for how a business is going to compete, what its goals should be, and what policies will be needed to carry out those goals (Porter, 1980). At its core, Porter argued, strategy is about the creation and capture of value. A.G. Lafley and Roger Martin offered a complementary definition: strategy is an integrated set of choices that position a business in its industry so as to create sustainable advantage and superior returns (Lafley & Martin, 2013). What both definitions share is an emphasis on **positioning**: strategy is about making deliberate choices that establish where and how a firm will compete.

This positioning view has important implications. First, it means that strategy is fundamentally about **choices**. A firm that tries to be everything to everyone has not made strategic choices; it has avoided them. A good strategy is a decision that makes a thousand other decisions for you. When Southwest Airlines chose to compete as a low-cost, point-to-point carrier, that single strategic choice dictated hundreds of subsequent decisions: no assigned seating, no meals, no hub-and-spoke routing, a single aircraft type, quick gate turnarounds (Porter, 1996). A firm without a clear strategic position, by contrast, faces every operational decision as an isolated choice with no guiding framework.

Second, strategy is not the same thing as a **vision statement**. Many companies confuse the two, producing ambitious declarations filled with words like "innovative," "world-class," and "customer-centric," and calling this their strategy. While a compelling vision provides direction and inspiration, it says nothing about *how* the vision will be achieved. Strategy is precisely that: the plan for how to get from here to the vision. A vision without a strategy is aspiration without a roadmap.

Third, strategy is not the same thing as **tactics**. The key difference is one of scope, time horizon, and reversibility. Strategic decisions take a significant amount of time and resources to implement and therefore cannot be easily reversed; a good rule of thumb is a year or more to execute. Building a new manufacturing facility, entering a new geographic market, or acquiring a competitor are all strategic moves. Tactical decisions, by contrast, are shorter-term actions that can be adjusted relatively quickly: changing a pricing promotion, reassigning sales territories, or adjusting an advertising campaign. The relationship should be hierarchical: tactical decisions should be guided by and consistent with the overarching strategy.

Sidebar: Your Career Strategy

To bring these ideas together with a simple analogy: consider your own career strategy. You could have become an electrician, a path offering high pay, on the job training, and union protection. Instead, you chose *business*, which led to the strategy of attending college, which led to the choice of a specific university. That university choice immediately eliminated all other college options —

one decision that made a thousand others for you. The strategic decision narrowed your path and defined the tactical decisions that followed: which courses to take, which internships to pursue. But notice that the strategy could also fail. A student who chose the right university but then neglected their studies would have a failed strategy; the plan was sound, but the execution fell short. This is why we define strategy as how a firm *plans* to achieve its vision, acknowledging that not every strategy succeeds.

1.7.2 The Three Elements of Good Strategy

If strategy is about positioning through deliberate choices, then **good strategy contains three essential elements** that describe how strategy is actually developed and brought to life. These elements — diagnosis, formulation, and implementation — represent the process by which a firm moves from understanding its situation to taking action (Rumelt, 2011).

The first element is **diagnosis**: analyzing the firm, its industry, and the external environment to identify the core competitive challenge the firm faces. This is the analytical foundation of strategy, understanding the situation as it actually is, not as the firm wishes it were. A good diagnosis cuts through complexity to identify what is really going on. It asks: What is the fundamental challenge or opportunity facing this firm right now? What forces are shaping the competitive landscape? Where are we strong, and where are we vulnerable?

A thorough diagnosis works at three levels. Internally, the firm assesses its own activities, resources, and capabilities to understand where it is genuinely strong and where it is exposed. At the industry level, the firm examines the competitive pressures it faces from rivals, customers, suppliers, and potential new entrants. At the broadest level, the firm considers the macro-environmental trends — technological shifts, regulatory changes, demographic movements — that shape the context in which it operates. Later chapters introduce specific frameworks for each of these levels, but the underlying purpose is the same: build an honest picture of the firm's situation. The quality of the diagnosis determines the quality of everything that follows. A firm that misreads its competitive environment, overestimates its own capabilities, underestimates a rival's determination, or fails to see an emerging technological shift will formulate a strategy built on a flawed foundation.

The second element is **formulation**: developing a guiding policy that addresses the competitive challenge identified in the diagnosis (Rumelt, 2011). This is the creative and intellectual heart of strategy, deciding what the firm will do and, crucially, what it will not do. A guiding policy is not a list of goals or aspirations; it is a specific approach to overcoming the obstacles identified in the diagnosis. It provides direction and coherence, channeling the firm's energy and resources toward a defined competitive position.

Formulation happens at two levels. At the business level, the firm decides how it will compete in a given market — what it will offer, who it will serve, how it will price, and what competitive position it will stake out. At the corporate level, the firm decides what its overall scope will be — which businesses to be in, which markets to enter, and how to allocate resources across them. The guiding policies at these two levels must be coherent with one another. The chapters that follow develop each of these levels in detail.

The third element is **implementation**: executing a set of coherent actions that follow from the guiding policy (Rumelt, 2011). A strategy that exists only on paper or in a boardroom presentation is not a strategy at all. It must be translated into decisions, investments, and organizational changes that are mutually reinforcing. Implementation is where strategy meets reality, and it is often where strategies fail — not because the diagnosis was wrong or the guiding policy was flawed, but because the firm could not or did not execute the required actions.

Implementation involves more than issuing directives. It requires aligning incentives so that managers and employees act in the strategy's interest, building or acquiring the capabilities the strategy demands, and making sure the firm's culture supports rather than resists the changes required. It also involves deciding how to obtain resources and capabilities the firm does not yet have, whether by developing them internally, partnering with other firms, or acquiring them outright. Later chapters return to each of these implementation questions in turn.

Consider how these three elements apply to a firm like Tesla. The diagnostic phase involves analyzing Tesla's position within the automotive industry, the shift toward electric vehicles, regulatory trends favoring emission reduction, the state of battery technology, and the competitive actions of established automakers. The formulation phase involves developing a guiding policy; in Tesla's case, a decision to position as a premium electric vehicle manufacturer that also controls its own distribution and charging infrastructure. The implementation phase involves the specific actions that bring this policy to life: building gigafactories, developing proprietary battery technology, establishing a direct-sales model, and deploying a nationwide supercharger network. Each action is coherent with the others and with the overarching strategy. Critically, Tesla's implementation also involved decisions about what *not* to do (not using franchise dealerships, not relying on existing battery suppliers, not following the traditional automotive playbook) and these deliberate omissions are as much a part of the strategy as the actions taken.

1.7.3 The Strategic Question: Why Do Some Firms Outperform Others?

If there is one question that sits at the heart of strategic management, it is this: **Why do some firms outperform others?** In any industry, firms face broadly similar external conditions: the same macroeconomic environment, the same regulatory landscape, the same pool of potential customers. Yet their performance varies enormously. Southwest Airlines has been consistently profitable for decades while other carriers have cycled in and out of bankruptcy. Some retailers thrive while others with seemingly similar business models collapse. What explains these differences?

The answer is strategy, specifically, the quality and coherence of a firm's strategic choices across multiple dimensions. A good business strategy is the plan by which a company will profitably and sustainably achieve its vision. Two key words deserve emphasis. **Profitably**, because a firm that runs out of money cannot achieve its vision regardless of how noble or innovative that vision may be. **Sustainably**, because a strategy built on a short-term fix, a constant influx of investor capital, or an advantage that competitors can quickly imitate is not a real strategy. If the competition can come in next month and steal all your customers, you do not have a strategic position worth defending.

A good strategy must answer **four fundamental questions**. These questions serve as the organizing logic not only for individual firm strategy, but for the structure of this entire book. Each question opens onto a set of analytical tools and frameworks that we will develop in the chapters ahead, and each connects directly to the diagnostic, formulation, and implementation process described above.

The first question is ***Where do we compete?*** This involves defining the firm's competitive arena: which industries, markets, geographies, and customer segments the firm will operate in, and equally important, which ones it will not. The "where" question may sound straightforward, but it is anything but. Consider a company like Amazon. Does it compete in retail? Cloud computing? Logistics?

Entertainment? Grocery? The answer is all of these, which means Amazon has made a series of corporate-level strategic decisions to extend far beyond its original competitive arena. A local bookstore, by contrast, has answered the "where" question very differently, competing in a single industry, often in a single geographic market, serving a defined customer base.

The "where" question is addressed at multiple levels throughout this book. At the business level, it involves understanding what industry the firm operates in and where the boundaries of that industry lie, questions we take up when we study defining industry boundaries and Porter's Five Forces. At the corporate level, it involves deciding whether to operate in one industry or many, which we address through diversification strategy, vertical and horizontal integration, and the Build/Borrow/Buy framework. The external environment, analyzed through PESTEL and environmental scanning, shapes the attractiveness and viability of different competitive arenas. Even the question of industry life cycles and industry disruption feeds back into the "where" question, because the desirability of competing in a given space changes as industries evolve, mature, and are disrupted by new technologies or business models.

The second question is ***What unique value do we bring?*** This is the question of differentiation in its broadest sense: what does the firm offer that customers cannot easily get elsewhere, and why should customers choose this firm over its competitors? The answer might be a superior product, a lower price, a more convenient experience, a stronger brand, better service, or some combination of these.

This question drives our entire study of business-level strategy. When we examine differentiation strategy, we are asking how firms compete by offering something that customers perceive as uniquely valuable and are willing to pay a premium for. When we examine cost leadership, we are asking how firms compete by delivering acceptable value at a lower cost than rivals, enabling either lower prices or higher margins. When we study focus strategies, we are asking how firms can serve a narrow segment of the market more effectively than broad competitors (Porter, 1985). And when we explore the fundamental tradeoffs inherent in strategy, the tension between differentiation and cost, which opens our business-level strategy unit, we are confronting the reality that firms cannot usually excel at everything simultaneously. The unique value a firm brings is a choice, and that choice has consequences that ripple through every aspect of the business.

The third question is ***What resources and capabilities allow us to deliver this value?*** A firm may identify an attractive market and articulate a compelling value proposition, but none of that matters if the firm lacks the internal assets and skills to execute. This question turns our attention inward, asking what the firm has, and what it can do, that enables its strategic position.

This is the domain of internal analysis, which we explore in depth when we study the resource-based view (RBV) and the VRIO framework. The RBV argues that sustained competitive advantage arises not just from favorable market positioning but from resources and capabilities that are valuable, rare, costly to imitate, and organized to capture value (Barney, 1991). Core competencies, the specific capabilities that are central to a firm's competitive advantage, represent the practical answer to this third question. Path dependence explains why these resources are often difficult for competitors to replicate: they are built over time through a unique sequence of decisions, investments, and experiences that cannot simply be purchased or copied. Organizational culture, which we also examine in the internal analysis unit, is itself a resource, one that can either enable or undermine the firm's ability to deliver on its strategy. Dynamic capabilities address how firms adapt and reconfigure their resources as conditions change, ensuring that today's competitive advantage does not become tomorrow's rigidity.

The value chain, introduced earlier in this chapter as a descriptive map of firm activities, also connects directly to this third question. When we return to it as an analytical tool in Chapter 3, we will see how decomposing the firm into its individual activities reveals where within the firm value is actually being created and where costs are being incurred (Porter, 1985). This granular view helps managers identify which specific activities and capabilities are driving competitive advantage and which are candidates for improvement, outsourcing, or elimination.

The fourth question is ***How do we sustain this unique value over time?*** Identifying a competitive advantage is one thing; protecting it from erosion is another. Competitors will notice a successful strategy and attempt to imitate it, substitute around it, or undercut it. Customers' preferences shift. Technologies evolve. Regulations change. The question of sustainability asks how the firm defends its position against all of these forces over the long term.

This is perhaps the most far-reaching of the four questions, because it draws on nearly every topic in the book. Competitive dynamics, the study of how rivals act and react to each other's competitive moves, is directly about the ongoing battle to sustain advantage in the face of competitive responses. Porter's Five Forces provides a framework for assessing the structural threats to profitability in an industry, including the threat of new entrants who might replicate a firm's strategy and the threat of substitutes that might make it obsolete (Porter, 1980). Industry disruption examines how entirely new technologies or business models can upend established competitive positions. PESTEL analysis identifies macro-environmental forces (political, economic, social, technological, environmental, and legal) that can shift the ground underneath a firm's strategy.

At the corporate level, sustainability is addressed through decisions about growth and scope. The Build/Borrow/Buy framework helps firms decide whether to develop new capabilities internally, access them through alliances and partnerships, or acquire them through mergers and acquisitions, each of which has different implications for the sustainability of the resulting advantage. Diversification strategy addresses whether a firm can sustain value by leveraging its resources across multiple businesses. Corporate governance mechanisms (boards, executive compensation, and shareholder activism) exist in part to ensure that managers make decisions that sustain long-term value rather than pursuing short-term personal interests at the firm's expense.

Taken together, these four questions form a complete strategic logic. A firm that can clearly and coherently answer all four — where it competes, what unique value it delivers, what resources and capabilities underpin that value, and how it will sustain its advantage over time — has the foundation of a sound strategy. A firm that cannot answer one or more of these questions has a gap in its strategic thinking that will eventually manifest as a gap in its performance.

1.7.4 Strategy as a Long-Term Framework

One of the most important characteristics of strategy, and one of the most frequently misunderstood, is that it operates on a **long time horizon**. Strategy is not about winning this quarter or hitting this month's sales target. Those are tactical concerns. Strategy is about building and sustaining a competitive position over years and even decades.

The difficulty is that long-term strategic thinking often conflicts with short-term pressures. Public companies face quarterly earnings expectations. Managers are evaluated on annual performance metrics. In this environment, it is tempting to sacrifice long-term strategic investments (in R&D, in employee development, in brand building) for short-term financial results. This is one of the most common ways firms destroy their own competitive positions. They do not lose to a superior competitor; they erode their own advantages through a series of individually rational but strategically incoherent short-term decisions.

Strategy as a long-term framework serves as a safeguard against this tendency. When a firm has a clearly articulated strategy, every decision can be evaluated against a consistent standard: Does this move strengthen or weaken our strategic position? Without this framework, decisions are made in isolation, driven by whatever pressure feels most urgent at the moment.

This long-term perspective also helps explain why strategy is inherently about **tradeoffs**. Because a firm's resources are finite, committing to one strategic direction means forgoing others. A firm that invests heavily in product innovation is allocating resources away from cost reduction. A firm that pursues premium positioning is choosing not to compete on price. These tradeoffs are uncomfortable, and there is a natural managerial temptation to avoid them, to try to be both the lowest-cost and the most differentiated competitor, to serve every customer segment, to enter every promising market. But attempting to do everything usually results in doing nothing particularly well (Porter, 1996). The essence of strategy is choosing what to do *and what not to do*, and having the discipline to maintain those choices over time.

This brings us full circle to the foundational concepts of this chapter. The theory of the firm tells us that firms exist because they can organize certain activities more efficiently than the market. Vision, mission, and objectives provide direction, but they must be translated into a concrete plan. Business models describe how value is created and captured. Competitive advantage tells us that outperformance requires delivering superior value that must be actively built and defended. Stakeholder analysis reminds us that the firm operates within a network of relationships that constrain and enable its strategic choices.

Strategy is the concept that integrates all of these elements into a coherent whole. It is the plan by which the firm will profitably and sustainably achieve its vision, grounded in a clear-eyed diagnosis of its competitive environment, guided by deliberate choices about where and how to compete, and executed through a set of reinforcing actions that build and protect competitive advantage over time. Every subsequent chapter of this book develops the tools and frameworks needed to craft and execute good strategy.

References

Barney, J. B. (1991). Firm resources and sustained competitive advantage. *Journal of Management, 17*(1), 99–120.

Lafley, A. G., & Martin, R. L. (2013). *Playing to win: How strategy really works.* Harvard Business Review Press.

Mintzberg, H. (1987). The strategy concept I: Five Ps for strategy. *California Management Review, 30*(1), 11–24.

Porter, M. E. (1980). *Competitive strategy: Techniques for analyzing industries and competitors.* Free Press.

Porter, M. E. (1985). *Competitive advantage: Creating and sustaining superior performance.* Free Press.

Porter, M. E. (1996). What is strategy? *Harvard Business Review, 74*(6), 61–78.

Rumelt, R. P. (2011). *Good strategy bad strategy: The difference and why it matters.* Crown Business.

1.8 Assessing Strategic Performance — *Is our strategy working?*

We have now established what strategy is, why it matters, and how it integrates the foundational concepts of this chapter. But defining a strategy is only the beginning. A firm also needs to know whether its strategy is actually working. This requires measurement, and measurement is harder than it sounds. The wrong metrics can lead a firm to believe it is succeeding when it is actually eroding its competitive position, or to panic over short-term numbers when the long-term trajectory is sound. This section introduces the basic financial concepts that underpin performance measurement, explains why financial metrics alone are insufficient, and presents two widely used frameworks for assessing strategic performance: the Balanced Scorecard and Objectives and Key Results (OKRs).

1.8.1 The Financial Foundation

Any assessment of strategic performance begins with financial results. A firm that consistently loses money is not sustaining a viable strategy, regardless of how elegant its positioning may be. Before we can evaluate strategy, students need a working understanding of three core financial statements and the key metrics derived from them.

The **income statement** reports a firm's revenues, costs, and profits over a specific period (typically a quarter or a year). Revenue (also called sales or top line) is the total amount of money the firm earns from selling its products or services. From revenue, the firm subtracts its costs of goods sold (the direct costs of producing what it sells) to arrive at gross profit. It then subtracts operating expenses such as salaries, rent, marketing, and research and development to arrive at operating income. Finally, after accounting for interest, taxes, and other items, the firm arrives at net income (also called the bottom line), which represents what the firm actually earned. The income statement answers a simple question: did the firm make money during this period?

The **balance sheet** provides a snapshot of what the firm owns and what it owes at a single point in time. Assets are everything the firm owns that has economic value, including cash, inventory, equipment, buildings, and intellectual property. Liabilities are the firm's obligations, including loans, accounts payable, and other debts. The difference between assets and liabilities is shareholders' equity — the owners' residual claim on the firm's assets. The balance sheet answers a different question: what is the firm's financial position right now?

The **cash flow statement** tracks the actual movement of cash into and out of the firm during a period. This matters because a firm can report profits on its income statement and still run out of cash. The cash flow statement is divided into three sections: operating activities (cash generated from the firm's core business), investing activities (cash spent on or received from buying and selling long-term assets), and financing activities (cash from borrowing, repaying debt, or issuing stock). The cash flow statement answers a practical question: does the firm have the cash to keep operating?

From these statements, managers and analysts calculate ratios that allow comparison across firms and over time. **Profit margins** (gross margin, operating margin, and net margin) express profitability as a percentage of revenue, revealing how much of each dollar of sales the firm keeps at various stages. **Return on assets (ROA)** measures how efficiently a firm uses its total assets to generate profit. **Return on equity (ROE)** measures the return generated for shareholders specifically. These ratios are how firms benchmark themselves against competitors and track their own performance over time, and they connect directly to the concept of competitive advantage introduced earlier: a firm with a sustained competitive advantage should, over time, generate returns that exceed those of its rivals.

1.8.2 Why Financial Metrics Are Not Enough

Financial statements tell a firm where it has been, but they are imperfect guides to where it is going. This is because most financial metrics are **lagging indicators**: they report the results of decisions made months or years earlier. Revenue this quarter reflects products developed, relationships built, and investments made long before the quarter began. By the time declining financial performance shows up in the numbers, the underlying strategic problems may have been compounding for some time.

Consider a firm that cuts its research and development budget to boost short-term profits. Its income statement will look better immediately. But if those R&D cuts mean the firm has no new products in its pipeline, the financial damage will not appear until years later — when the product line grows stale and customers move to competitors. A manager who evaluates strategy solely through financial metrics might celebrate the cost savings without realizing the firm has traded its future for a better-looking quarter.

This limitation does not mean financial metrics are unimportant. They are essential. But a complete assessment of strategic performance requires supplementing financial measures with **leading indicators**, metrics that signal future performance before it arrives. Customer satisfaction scores, employee retention rates, product development cycle times, and defect rates are all examples of leading indicators. They capture the health of the underlying capabilities and relationships — the things that will eventually drive financial results.

The challenge is organizing these diverse metrics into a coherent system. Two frameworks have emerged as the most widely used approaches to this problem: the Balanced Scorecard and Objectives and Key Results.

1.8.3 The Balanced Scorecard

The Balanced Scorecard (BSC), developed by Robert Kaplan and David Norton, is a strategic performance management framework that supplements financial metrics with measures drawn from three additional perspectives: customers, internal processes, and learning and growth (Kaplan & Norton, 1992). The core insight is that financial performance is the outcome of getting other things right first, and a firm that monitors only outcomes without tracking the drivers of those outcomes is flying blind.

The **financial perspective** asks: how do we look to our shareholders? This perspective includes the traditional financial metrics discussed above, including revenue growth, profit margins, return on assets, return on equity, and cash flow. These remain important, but in the BSC they occupy one quadrant rather than the entire dashboard.

The **customer perspective** asks: how do our customers see us? Metrics here might include customer satisfaction scores, customer retention rates, market share, Net Promoter Score, or the rate of new customer acquisition. The logic is straightforward: financial results depend on customers buying the firm's products, and customer behavior depends on whether the firm is delivering value that meets their needs. A decline in customer satisfaction is a leading indicator of future revenue decline, even if current financial results look healthy.

The **internal process perspective** asks: what must we excel at? This perspective focuses on the operational activities that drive customer value and financial performance. Relevant metrics depend on the firm's strategy but might include production cycle time, defect rates, on-time delivery percentage, inventory turnover, or time to market for new products. This perspective connects directly to the value chain: the firm is measuring the efficiency and effectiveness of the primary and support activities through which it creates value.

The **learning and growth perspective** asks: can we continue to improve and create value? This perspective addresses the firm's capacity to adapt and develop over time. Metrics might include employee satisfaction and retention, training hours per employee, the rate of internal promotion, investment in new technology, or the number of patents filed. The logic is that a firm's ability to improve its internal processes, satisfy its customers, and ultimately deliver financial results depends on the quality and development of its people, systems, and organizational knowledge.

The four perspectives are connected by causal logic. Investments in learning and growth enable better internal processes, which produce greater customer satisfaction, which drives superior financial performance. A firm that tracks all four perspectives can identify problems early and trace their causes through the chain. If financial results are declining, is it because customers are leaving? If customers are leaving, is it because internal quality has slipped? If quality has slipped, is it because the firm underinvested in employee training or technology? The BSC makes these connections visible and manageable.

EX: Balanced Scorecard for a Regional Hospital

A regional hospital implementing a Balanced Scorecard might define metrics across all four perspectives. For the financial perspective, it tracks operating margin, revenue per patient bed, and cost per discharge. For the customer perspective, it measures patient satisfaction scores, average wait times in the emergency department, and patient readmission rates (since readmissions signal that initial care was inadequate). For internal processes, it monitors average length of stay, surgical complication rates, and the percentage of evidence-based treatment protocols followed. For learning and growth, it tracks nurse turnover, continuing education hours per physician, and adoption rates for new electronic health record features.

The causal logic connects these metrics. If nurse turnover rises (learning and growth), surgical preparation may suffer, increasing complication rates (internal processes). Higher complication rates lead to longer stays, higher readmission rates, and declining patient satisfaction (customer). These problems eventually appear as rising costs per discharge and falling operating margins (financial). By monitoring the full scorecard, hospital leadership can identify that the root cause of financial pressure is a staffing problem, not a pricing problem, and respond accordingly.

1.8.4 Objectives and Key Results (OKRs)

While the Balanced Scorecard provides a comprehensive multi-perspective framework, some organizations prefer a simpler, more agile approach. Objectives and Key Results (OKRs) offer exactly that. Originally developed at Intel by Andy Grove and later popularized by its adoption at Google, OKRs have become one of the most widely used goal-setting systems in business (Doerr, 2018).

The structure is deliberately simple. An **objective** is a qualitative statement of what the organization wants to achieve. It should be ambitious, inspiring, and clearly directional. A **key result** is a quantitative measure of progress toward that objective. Each objective typically has two to five key results, and each key result must be specific and measurable. If you cannot put a number on it, it is not a key result.

For example, a software company might set the following OKR:

Objective: Become the preferred platform for small business accounting.

Key Results: 1. Increase monthly active users from 50,000 to 120,000. 2. Achieve a Net Promoter Score of 65 or higher among small business customers. 3. Reduce average customer onboarding time from 14 days to 5 days.

The objective provides direction and motivation; the key results define what success looks like in measurable terms. Together, they create alignment and accountability without the overhead of a full BSC implementation.

OKRs differ from the Balanced Scorecard in several important ways. First, OKRs are typically set on shorter cycles, often quarterly, making them more responsive to changing conditions. Second, OKRs are designed to be ambitious: organizations using OKRs generally expect to achieve about 60 to 70 percent of their key results, with full achievement suggesting the targets were not aggressive enough (Doerr, 2018). Third, OKRs cascade through the organization. Company-level OKRs inform team-level OKRs, which inform individual OKRs, creating vertical alignment from the boardroom to the front line.

The strength of OKRs lies in their simplicity and adaptability. They can be implemented quickly, revised frequently, and applied at any level of the organization. Their limitation is that they do not inherently provide the multi-perspective balance of the BSC. A firm using OKRs must be disciplined about setting objectives across different dimensions of performance; otherwise, the system can drift toward whichever metrics feel most urgent — typically financial ones.

1.8.5 Choosing and Connecting Frameworks

The BSC and OKRs are not mutually exclusive. Some organizations use the BSC to define the overall strategic measurement architecture and then use OKRs to set quarterly targets within that structure. Others choose one framework based on their size, culture, and strategic needs. Larger, more established firms often gravitate toward the BSC because it provides comprehensive coverage across multiple dimensions of performance. Smaller or faster-moving firms often prefer OKRs because they are lighter-weight and easier to iterate.

Regardless of which framework a firm adopts, the underlying principles are the same. Effective strategic performance measurement requires clarity about what the firm is trying to achieve, a mix of leading and lagging indicators, metrics that span multiple dimensions of performance (not just financial results), and a system for reviewing and acting on the data. Without such a system, a firm has no reliable way to know whether its strategy is on track until it is too late to course-correct.

This section completes the foundational arc of Chapter 1. We began by asking why firms exist, then examined what they do, what they are trying to achieve, how they create and capture value, how they compete, who they serve, and what strategy means as an integrative concept. We close by asking how firms know whether their strategy is working. With this foundation in place, we are ready to move into the substance of strategic analysis, beginning with the fundamental strategic choices that define business-level strategy.

References

Doerr, J. (2018). *Measure what matters: How Google, Bono, and the Gates Foundation rock the world with OKRs.* Portfolio/Penguin.

Kaplan, R. S., & Norton, D. P. (1992). The balanced scorecard: Measures that drive performance. *Harvard Business Review, 70*(1), 71–79.

Chapter 2

Business-Level Strategy

2.1 Strategic Choices and Tradeoffs — *Why are tradeoffs unavoidable in strategy?*

> *"There are no solutions, only trade-offs" — Thomas Sowell*

Chapter 1 established that strategy is the plan by which a firm will profitably and sustainably achieve its vision, and that the essence of strategy is choosing what to do *and what not to do*. But this raises an uncomfortable question that most managers would rather avoid: Why must firms choose at all? Why can't a well-managed company simply do everything — offer the highest quality *and* the lowest price, serve every customer segment, invest in innovation *and* maximize short-term profitability? The answer lies in a principle so fundamental to economics that it functions as an axiom, and it is the principle upon which all of business-level strategy ultimately rests: scarcity.

2.1.1 Scarcity: From Economics to Strategy

Every introductory economics course begins with the same insight: resources are scarce. There is never enough of anything to fully satisfy all wants. This is not a temporary condition to be overcome through better technology or smarter management; it is a permanent feature of the human condition. Money, time, talent, attention, production capacity, shelf space, and customer goodwill all exist in finite quantities. The economist Thomas Sowell put it bluntly in *Basic Economics*: the first lesson of economics is scarcity, there is never enough of anything to satisfy everyone completely (Sowell, 2015). This is not a pessimistic view of the world. It is simply an acknowledgment of reality, and it is the starting point for all intelligent resource allocation.

If scarcity defines the economic landscape, then every allocation decision has a cost — not just the direct cost of what you spend, but the *opportunity cost* of what you cannot spend those resources on instead. A dollar invested in a new product line is a dollar that cannot be invested in marketing, employee training, or debt reduction. An hour a CEO spends reviewing an acquisition proposal is an hour not spent visiting customers or developing talent. These opportunity costs are just as real as the line items on a balance sheet, even though they never appear there.

Scarcity, therefore, produces an inescapable consequence: tradeoffs. Every choice a firm makes forecloses alternatives. Every resource committed to one initiative is unavailable for another. This is not a flaw in the system to be engineered away; it is the system. Sowell captured this insight with characteristic directness: "There are no solutions, only trade-offs" (Sowell, 1987). What he meant is that every course of action has costs as well as benefits, and the task of the decision-maker is not to find a costless solution but to determine which set of tradeoffs is most acceptable given the circumstances. This principle applies to personal decisions, public policy, and, with particular force, to business strategy.

For the strategist, the implication is profound. The fundamental question is never "How do we solve this problem?" as though a costless answer exists. The fundamental question is always "Which tradeoff are we willing to accept?" A firm deciding between investing in product quality or investing in cost reduction is not choosing between a good option and a bad one. It is choosing between two valuable uses of scarce resources, each of which precludes the other. The firm that recognizes this reality and makes its tradeoffs deliberately is practicing strategy. The firm that pretends tradeoffs do not exist is not.

2.1.2 Two Mindsets: Recognizing Tradeoffs vs. Wishing Them Away

Sowell's broader intellectual framework offers a useful lens for understanding why tradeoffs are so often ignored in business. In *A Conflict of Visions*, Sowell (1987) described two fundamentally different ways of understanding human institutions and the problems they face. His framework maps neatly onto strategic management: some leaders recognize that tradeoffs are inherent to strategy, while others operate as though tradeoffs can be engineered away with enough effort.

The tradeoff-denying mindset holds that business problems are fully solvable, that with sufficient intelligence, effort, and goodwill, the right leaders can design systems that overcome limitations and produce ideal outcomes. In this view, tradeoffs are obstacles to be eliminated rather than realities to be managed. If a firm is not achieving both the lowest cost *and* the highest quality, this mindset concludes that management simply has not tried hard enough or has not yet found the right approach.

The tradeoff-accepting mindset, by contrast, holds that knowledge is limited, resources are finite, and all choices involve costs. The task is not to eliminate tradeoffs but to navigate them wisely. Perfect outcomes are not available. The best that can be achieved is a thoughtful balancing of competing priorities, with full awareness that every gain comes at a cost somewhere else. Strategies should be judged not by whether they achieve an ideal outcome (they will not) but by whether they produce better results than the available alternatives, all costs considered.

Applied to business strategy, these two mindsets produce strikingly different managerial approaches. The leader who denies tradeoffs believes the firm can be all things to all customers, that with the right innovation, the right processes, or the right culture, the company can offer the cheapest *and* the most differentiated product, serve every market segment, and grow in every direction simultaneously. This view is seductive because it promises that hard choices can be avoided. It is also, in most cases, wrong. Firms that attempt to pursue every opportunity at once typically end up with diffused resources, unclear positioning, and mediocre performance across multiple dimensions rather than excellence in any one.

The leader who accepts tradeoffs acknowledges that the firm operates in a world of finite resources and imperfect information. This acceptance is not defeatist — it is liberating. Once a firm acknowledges that it cannot do everything, it can focus its energy on doing a few things exceptionally well. Accepting tradeoffs does not counsel passivity or low ambition. It counsels clarity. It asks: Given our limited resources, where can we create the most value? What are we willing to give up in order to excel where it matters most? These are the questions that produce genuine strategic positioning.

EX: Denying Tradeoffs in J.C. Penney's Fair and Square Debacle

In 2011, J.C. Penney hired Ron Johnson, the executive who had built Apple's spectacularly successful retail stores, as its new CEO. Johnson arrived with a bold vision that denied the need for tradeoffs: he would reinvent department store retail. He eliminated coupons, ended clearance sales, introduced "everyday low prices," redesigned stores around branded boutique shops, and attempted to attract a younger, more fashion-conscious customer, all at once.

The strategy implicitly assumed that J.C. Penney could simultaneously reposition its brand, change its pricing model, redesign its store experience, and swap its existing customer base for a new one without any of these changes conflicting with the others. In reality, every one of these moves involved painful tradeoffs that the strategy ignored. Eliminating coupons alienated J.C. Penney's core customers, who had been trained over decades to expect promotional pricing. The "everyday low price" approach removed the psychological thrill of getting a deal, which was a primary reason these customers shopped there. The boutique redesign increased costs while failing to attract the aspirational shoppers it targeted, customers who already had plenty of options at genuinely premium retailers. Within seventeen months, J.C. Penney's sales had declined by 25%, the company had lost nearly a billion dollars, and Johnson was fired. The belief that J.C. Penney could reinvent itself along every dimension simultaneously collided with the reality of finite resources, entrenched customer expectations, and the inescapable need to make choices (Denning, 2013; Tuttle, 2013).

2.1.3 Strategic Implications of Tradeoffs

If scarcity is the foundational axiom and tradeoffs are the inevitable consequence, then tradeoffs are not a peripheral concern in strategy — they are the central concern. Several implications follow directly.

Choosing a strategy means choosing what *not* to do. This is perhaps the single most important insight in strategic management, and it is the one that managers most frequently resist. Michael Porter (1996) argued that strategy is fundamentally about being different, about deliberately choosing a different set of activities to deliver a unique mix of value. But being different in some ways necessarily means not being different in others. A firm that chooses to differentiate on product quality is choosing not to compete primarily on price. A firm that focuses on a narrow customer segment is choosing not to serve the broader market. These are not failures of ambition. They are the essence of strategic discipline.

> *"The essence of strategy is choosing what not to do." — Michael Porter*

The reason this principle is so often violated is psychological as much as analytical. Saying "no" to an attractive opportunity feels like leaving money on the table. When a competitor enters a new market, the instinct is to follow. When a customer asks for a feature the firm does not currently offer, the instinct is to add it. Over time, these individually reasonable responses erode the firm's strategic position. The company that once had a clear identity — a defined customer, a specific value proposition, a coherent set of activities — gradually becomes a muddled collection of offerings that tries to compete on every front and excels on none.

Every resource committed to one initiative is unavailable for another. This is the opportunity cost principle applied to strategy. When a firm allocates capital to build a new distribution center, that capital is not available for R&D. When a management team spends six months integrating an acquisition, those are six months not spent developing organic growth opportunities. These opportunity costs are often invisible in strategic planning because they represent paths not taken, but they are no less real for being unseen. The discipline of strategy requires making these costs explicit: not just asking "Is this investment worth making?" but "Is this investment worth making *compared to everything else we could do with these resources*?"

Trying to be all things to all customers is a recipe for mediocrity. A firm that attempts to offer both the lowest price and the most differentiated product is pulling its resources in two directions that fundamentally conflict. Differentiation typically requires investment in design, materials, customer service, branding, and innovation, all of which increase costs. Cost leadership requires stripping away anything that does not contribute to efficiency: standardizing products, minimizing service, leveraging scale. A firm pursuing both simultaneously tends to achieve neither, landing in an uncomfortable middle ground where it is undersold by the cost leader and out-differentiated by the premium competitor. Porter (1980) famously described this position as "stuck in the middle," and warned that it is among the most dangerous places a firm can occupy.

Tradeoffs are a source of strategic clarity and focus. The preceding points might make tradeoffs sound entirely negative, a series of painful sacrifices forced upon the firm by an unforgiving world. But tradeoffs also have a constructive function. They force clarity. A firm that has made clear tradeoffs knows exactly what it is trying to do and for whom. Its employees understand the priorities. Its customers understand the value proposition. Its investors understand the logic. This clarity becomes self-reinforcing: every decision, from hiring to capital allocation to product development, can be evaluated against a consistent strategic framework.

Consider the difference between a firm that has clearly decided to compete as a cost leader and one that vaguely aspires to "offer great value." The cost leader's tradeoffs are explicit: it has chosen efficiency over customization, scale over flexibility, standardized products over personalized service. Every operational decision flows from these choices. The vague "great value" firm, by contrast, has made no real choices at all. Without tradeoffs, there is no strategy — only a wish list.

EX: Tradeoffs as Strategic Discipline: In-N-Out Burger

Few companies illustrate the power of deliberate tradeoffs as clearly as In-N-Out Burger. Since 1948, the chain has maintained a menu of limited items: hamburgers, cheeseburgers, a double-double, and french fries. That is it. No chicken sandwiches, no salads, no breakfast menu, no rotating limited-time offerings. While competitors like McDonald's have expanded their menus to include dozens of items across multiple dayparts, In-N-Out has repeatedly said no.

These are not accidental omissions. They are deliberate tradeoffs that reinforce the entire business model. A limited menu means fewer ingredients to source, simpler supply chains, less waste, and faster kitchen operations. It means employees can be trained quickly and perform their tasks at a high level. It means the company can focus obsessively on the quality of a handful of items rather than spreading its attention across dozens. In-N-Out has also refused to franchise, choosing slower growth in exchange for tighter quality control. It has refused to freeze its beef, choosing higher supply chain costs in exchange for product quality. Each of these "no" decisions has a real cost: forgone revenue, slower expansion, higher input costs. But each also reinforces the firm's strategic position as a fast-food chain that prioritizes quality and simplicity. The tradeoffs produce coherence, and coherence produces competitive advantage.

2.1.4 Setting the Stage for Business-Level Strategy

This chapter will examine the specific strategic positions available to firms, the fundamental ways a business can choose to compete. In the sections that follow, we will explore differentiation strategy, cost leadership, economies of scale, integrated strategies that attempt to combine elements of both, and focus strategies that target narrow market segments. Each of these represents a different answer to the question: How will this firm create and deliver value to its customers?

But every one of these strategies involves tradeoffs. The differentiator trades lower costs for uniqueness. The cost leader trades uniqueness for efficiency. The focused competitor trades market breadth for depth. And the integrated strategist, who attempts to combine differentiation and cost leadership, faces the most complex tradeoff of all — pursuing two objectives that naturally pull in opposite directions. Understanding tradeoffs is not merely helpful preparation for studying these strategies. It is the intellectual foundation upon which all of them rest. The firms that navigate tradeoffs with discipline and clarity are the ones that build sustainable competitive positions. The firms that deny tradeoffs exist are the ones that end up stuck in the middle, doing many things adequately and nothing well.

The tradeoff-accepting mindset teaches us that there are no perfect strategies, only strategies with different costs and benefits. The task of the strategist is not to find the one right answer but to choose wisely among imperfect alternatives, and to have the discipline to live with those choices over time.

References

Denning, S. (2013, February 10). J.C. Penney: Was Ron Johnson's strategy wrong? *Forbes.*

Porter, M. E. (1980). *Competitive strategy: Techniques for analyzing industries and competitors.* Free Press.

Porter, M. E. (1996). What is strategy? *Harvard Business Review, 74*(6), 61–78.

Sowell, T. (1987). *A conflict of visions: Ideological origins of political struggles.* William Morrow.

Sowell, T. (2015). *Basic economics: A common sense guide to the economy* (5th ed.). Basic Books.

Tuttle, B. (2013, April 9). The 5 big mistakes that led to Ron Johnson's ouster at JC Penney. *Time.*

2.2 Differentiation Advantage — *How do firms compete on uniqueness?*

At the most fundamental level, customers choose to buy a product for one of two reasons: it is different (that is, better) than the alternatives, or it costs less than the alternatives. These two reasons correspond to the two foundational business-level strategies: differentiation and cost leadership. We begin with differentiation because it addresses what is arguably the more creative and analytically demanding strategic challenge: how to make customers willing to pay *more* for your product than for a competitor's.

2.2.1 What Is Differentiation Advantage?

> *"In order to be irreplaceable one must always be different."* — *Coco Chanel*

Differentiation is making a product or service different from the competition in one or more ways that increase the value to the customer so that they are willing to pay a higher price, with the goal that the increase in price is more than the cost to create the difference. This definition contains several important elements that deserve emphasis.

First, differentiation is about being *different from the competition*, not simply about being good. A product is not differentiated in a vacuum; it is differentiated relative to the alternatives available to the customer. A restaurant with excellent food is not differentiated if every restaurant in the area also has excellent food. Differentiation requires standing apart.

Second, the difference must *increase value to the customer.* A product that is different in ways customers do not care about is merely unusual, not differentiated. A laptop manufacturer that produces a computer in an unusual color has made a different product, but unless customers value that color enough to pay more for it, there is no differentiation advantage. The difference must matter to the buyer.

Third, and critically, the customer must be *willing to pay a higher price* for the differentiated offering. Differentiation that does not translate into a price premium, or at least into greater market share at the same price, has no strategic value. It is cost without benefit.

The four primary sources of differentiation are superior features, better quality, greater convenience, and brand image. Understanding each is essential for identifying where differentiation opportunities exist.

Superior features enable a product to do a job better, do a unique job, or do more jobs than competing products. Dyson vacuums differentiated themselves through cyclonic separation technology that maintained suction power better than traditional bag-based vacuums, a superior way to do the same job. Build-A-Bear Workshop differentiated by offering a unique job that essentially no competitor offered: the experience of designing and assembling a personalized stuffed animal. The iPhone, at its launch, differentiated by consolidating the jobs of multiple devices (phone, music player, camera, web browser, and GPS) into a single product that replaced a collection of separate gadgets.

Better quality means a product that is more reliable, more durable, and longer lasting than competitors. Toyota and Honda built their reputations in the American market largely on quality. Higher quality translates into customer value through several channels: reliability reduces the risk and inconvenience of breakdowns, durability means fewer replacement purchases over time, reduced repair costs lower the total cost of ownership, and long-lasting products tend to hold higher resale values. Quality differentiation can also provide psychological value, the peace of mind that comes from knowing a product is unlikely to fail.

Convenience means the product or service is easier to find, purchase, or use. Starbucks differentiated partly on coffee quality and brand experience, but also on sheer ubiquity, locating stores so densely that a customer is almost always a short walk from one. Vending machines differentiate a commodity like Coca-Cola by making it available instantly, a few steps away, at the moment of thirst. Convenience reduces the customer's time, effort, and friction, and many customers will pay a premium for that reduction.

Brand image differentiates through association with a lifestyle, a level of status, an emotion, or an identity. Harley-Davidson does not merely sell motorcycles; it sells an identity of freedom and rebellion. Tiffany & Co. does not merely sell jewelry; it sells status and romance, a power so strong that the distinctive blue box itself has become a symbol people will purchase empty. Coca-Cola does not merely sell flavored carbonated water; it sells happiness, nostalgia, and shared experience, spending approximately five billion dollars per year on marketing to sustain that association (Coca-Cola Company, 2024). The power of brand-based differentiation is visible in a simple question: Why do people argue passionately about whether Coke or Pepsi tastes better? The fact that consumers have strong opinions about nearly identical sugar water is itself a testament to the power of brand differentiation.

The more points of differentiation a firm can achieve simultaneously, the stronger its competitive position. Multiple sources of differentiation reinforce one another and make imitation more difficult. A competitor might be able to match one dimension, say convenient locations, but matching convenient locations *and* a powerful brand *and* a perceived taste advantage *and* a positive emotional association is far more challenging. Coca-Cola's strength lies not in any single dimension but in the combination of all of them.

2.2.2 Differentiation Price Premium > Cost of Creating the Difference

The economic logic of differentiation is straightforward but frequently misunderstood (Porter, 1985). Differentiation only works as a strategy when the price premium the firm can charge exceeds the additional cost of creating the differentiation. If it costs a firm $50 per unit more to produce a higher-quality product, and customers are only willing to pay $30 more for that quality, the firm has destroyed value rather than created it. The differentiation is real, but it is unprofitable.

This means that differentiation is not an end in itself; it is a means to superior economic performance. The strategist must always be asking two questions simultaneously: How much additional value does this difference create for the customer? And how much does it cost us to create it? Only when the first answer exceeds the second does differentiation produce competitive advantage.

This logic also explains why differentiation is fundamentally about *perceived* value, not just objective value. A product that is objectively superior in some technical dimension but that customers do not perceive as better provides no differentiation advantage. Conversely, a product that is perceived as better, through branding, design, packaging, or customer experience, holds a differentiation advantage even if its underlying technical specifications are similar to competitors'. The customer pays based on what they believe the product is worth, and perception shapes belief. This is not to say that reality does not matter; products that consistently underperform their perceived quality will eventually lose credibility. But in any given purchase decision, the customer is responding to perceived value, and the gap between perception and reality can be significant.

EX: Perception vs. Reality in Wine Pricing

Consider the wine industry, where the relationship between perceived and actual quality has been studied extensively. In blind taste tests, even experienced wine drinkers frequently cannot distinguish between moderately priced and expensive wines, and in some studies, tasters have rated cheaper wines more highly when they did not know the price (Goldstein et al., 2008). Yet the same consumers, when shown the labels and prices, will consistently rate the expensive wine as superior and will pay a substantial premium for it. The bottle, the label, the price itself, and the reputation of the vineyard all shape perceived value independently of what is actually in the glass. This does not mean that all expensive wines are indistinguishable from cheap ones. It means that a significant portion of the value customers pay for is constructed through branding, signaling, and context rather than through the physical product alone. For the differentiation strategist, this is a crucial insight: investing in how the product is perceived can be as important as investing in the product itself.

2.2.3 Why Differentiation Requires Deeper Customer Knowledge

A cost leadership strategy, as we will see in the next section, can succeed with a relatively general understanding of the market: produce a standardized product as efficiently as possible for the typical customer. Differentiation, by contrast, requires a much deeper understanding of who the customers are, what they value, and why. The differentiator must know *which* differences customers care about, *how much* they are willing to pay for those differences, and *why* those differences matter to them. This knowledge is generated through two primary analytical tools: customer segmentation analysis and consumption chain analysis.

2.2.4 Customer Segmentation Analysis

Customer segmentation is the analysis of customer needs to identify groups of buyers who are similar in the way they discriminate among and value product or service offerings. Not all customers want the same things. A twenty-two-year-old recent graduate shopping for a first car has very different priorities than a fifty-five-year-old executive replacing a luxury sedan. A professional chef evaluating kitchen knives cares about different attributes than a college student outfitting a first apartment. Treating all of these buyers as a single mass market means either over-satisfying some customers or under-satisfying others, and both are costly mistakes.

Over-satisfying a customer segment means providing features, quality, or service that exceed what the segment values and incurring costs that the segment will not pay for. A budget hotel that installs marble countertops and offers pillow menus is spending money on differentiation that its price-sensitive customers did not ask for and will not reward. The investment increases costs without increasing willingness to pay, eroding margins.

Under-satisfying a customer segment means failing to meet the needs the segment cares about most, which costs the firm market share. A business-class airline that does not offer Wi-Fi may lose corporate travelers to competitors who do, not because Wi-Fi is the most important feature in absolute terms, but because it is important *to that segment.* The purpose of segmentation is to calibrate the firm's offering to the specific needs of its target customers, giving them what they value and not spending resources on what they do not.

There are three primary ways to segment a market. **Product attributes** segment customers by the physical or functional characteristics they prioritize, such as speed, battery life, weight, durability, or flavor. A smartphone maker might segment between customers who prioritize camera quality and those who prioritize battery life, designing different models (or marketing the same model differently) to each group. **Customer demographics** segment by characteristics of the buyers themselves: young professionals, retired couples, working parents, college athletes. Each demographic group typically has distinct needs, budgets, and purchase criteria shaped by their life circumstances. **Jobs-to-be-done** segment by the underlying purpose the customer is trying to fulfill: entertainment, transportation, safety, self-expression, social signaling. This third approach, as we will see, offers some of the deepest insights for differentiation strategy.

2.2.5 The Jobs-to-Be-Done Framework

The jobs-to-be-done framework, developed by Clayton Christensen and his collaborators, begins with a deceptively simple insight: customers do not buy products; they hire them to do a job (Christensen et al., 2016). The idea has deep roots. Decades earlier, Levitt (1960) warned that firms falter when they define themselves by their product rather than the customer need it serves, famously observing that the railroads declined because they saw themselves in the railroad business rather than the transportation business. As Theodore Levitt (1983) relayed the point, people do not want to buy a quarter-inch drill; they want a quarter-inch hole. The drill is merely the means to an end. If a firm understands the job the customer is trying to get done, it can design a product that does that job better, and that is the essence of differentiation.

The power of the jobs-to-be-done perspective is that it shifts the focus from the product to the customer's underlying need. When a firm thinks in terms of product features (faster processor, bigger screen, lighter weight), it risks incremental improvements that may not address what the customer actually cares about. When a firm thinks in terms of jobs (help me stay productive while traveling, help me capture and share memorable moments, help me stay connected with my family), it opens up a much broader space for creative differentiation.

Jobs fall into three categories. **Functional jobs** are the practical tasks the customer needs accomplished: getting from point A to point B, keeping food cold, finishing a work project. **Social jobs** relate to how the customer wants to be perceived by others: appearing successful, fitting in with peers, signaling good taste. **Emotional jobs** relate to how the customer wants to feel: safe, excited, relaxed, nostalgic, confident. Most purchase decisions involve all three types of jobs simultaneously, though one may dominate.

The process of identifying jobs-to-be-done requires what Christensen called *customer discovery and empathy*, actually observing and listening to customers to understand not just what they buy but *why* they buy it. This is fundamentally different from asking customers what features they want. Customers are often poor at articulating their own needs in terms of product specifications, but they are excellent at describing the situations in which they struggle, the outcomes they desire, and the frustrations they experience with existing solutions. The strategist's task is to translate those observations into jobs.

The most promising jobs to target are those that are important to the customer, currently unmet or poorly met by existing solutions, and widely held across a significant number of potential buyers. A job that is important but already well-served offers little differentiation opportunity. A job that is unmet but only relevant to a handful of people may not justify the investment. The sweet spot for differentiation is a job that many customers care about deeply and that no competitor is doing well.

EX: The Milkshake That Got Hired

One of Christensen's most famous illustrations of jobs-to-be-done comes from a fast-food chain trying to increase milkshake sales. The company had done extensive traditional market research, surveying customers about flavor preferences, thickness, and price sensitivity, and had made the corresponding product improvements. Sales did not budge.

Christensen's team took a different approach. They observed who bought milkshakes, when, and under what circumstances. A surprising proportion were purchased early in the morning by solo commuters. Through follow-up interviews, the team learned these customers were hiring the milkshake for a specific job: staying occupied during a long, boring commute. The milkshake was thick enough to last the entire drive, could be consumed with one hand, fit in a cupholder, and was more satisfying than the alternatives. A banana was gone in two minutes, a bagel created crumbs, and a candy bar produced guilt. The milkshake's real "competitors" were not other milkshakes but bananas, bagels, donuts, and boredom itself.

Yet the same restaurant sold milkshakes to a completely different group in the afternoon: parents buying them for children after school. These customers were hiring the milkshake for a different job, being the "good parent" who says yes to a treat. For this job, a thick milkshake that took twenty minutes to finish was a liability, not an asset; the parent wanted the child to finish quickly so they could move on with their afternoon.

The same product was being hired for two completely different jobs by two different customer segments. Traditional segmentation by demographics or product attributes would never have revealed this. Only by asking "What job is the customer hiring this product to do?" did the real differentiation opportunities become visible (Christensen et al., 2016).

2.2.6 Consumption Chain Analysis

While segmentation and jobs-to-be-done help identify *who* the customer is and *what* they need, consumption chain analysis examines the customer's *entire experience* with the product, from first awareness to final disposal, looking for differentiation opportunities at every stage. This is valuable not only for established firms seeking to strengthen their competitive position but also for entrepreneurs searching for gaps in existing markets. By systematically considering the customer's entire experience, an entrepreneur can spot stages where a new entrant could create meaningful value.

MacMillan and McGrath (1997) identified more than a dozen questions that map the consumption chain, moving systematically from how customers find your offering, to how they select, order, pay for, and receive it, through how they use, store, and transport it, and finally to how they maintain, repair, and dispose of it. The power of the framework lies not in any single question but in the discipline of examining the full sequence. At each stage, the strategist asks whether the customer's experience could be made easier, faster, less expensive, or more enjoyable, and whether competitors have left that stage underserved.

A few examples illustrate how differentiation can emerge at different stages. Starbucks differentiates at the search stage through sheer physical proximity; by saturating urban areas with locations, the company ensures that a customer who wants coffee rarely has to look for it, and Coca-Cola follows a similar logic by placing vending machines and coolers in virtually every convenience store, gas station, and public venue. Amazon's one-click ordering, free two-day shipping, and frictionless return process are powerful differentiators at the ordering, payment, and delivery stages; the product itself may be identical to what a competitor sells, but the ease of buying it creates meaningful value. Patagonia's repair-and-reuse program differentiates at the end of the chain by allowing customers to extend the life of their products, aligning with both environmental values and economic self-interest.

The value of consumption chain analysis is that it prevents firms from thinking about differentiation too narrowly. Many firms focus exclusively on the product itself, its features, quality, and design, while ignoring the rest of the customer experience. But customers do not evaluate products in isolation; they evaluate the entire process of discovering, buying, using, and disposing of them. A firm that can identify an underserved stage of the consumption chain and improve it has found a differentiation opportunity that product-focused competitors may overlook entirely. For entrepreneurs, this is especially powerful: incumbent firms often optimize the product itself while leaving the surrounding experience full of friction and frustration. The consumption chain gives new entrants a structured way to find those openings.

2.2.7 Barriers to Imitation: Sustaining Differentiation

Differentiation creates competitive advantage, but that advantage will erode over time unless the firm builds barriers that prevent competitors from imitating its points of differentiation. Without barriers to imitation, any successful differentiation will be copied by rivals, the price premium will shrink, and the firm's advantage will dissipate.

The most effective barriers to imitation are built through developing unique resources and capabilities that competitors cannot easily replicate. **Recognized brands** are among the most powerful barriers.

Coca-Cola's brand equity, built over more than a century and sustained by billions of dollars in cumulative marketing investment, cannot be replicated overnight by a new entrant. **R&D-intensive features** create barriers when they require deep technical expertise, specialized equipment, or years of accumulated knowledge. Boeing's composite airframe manufacturing and GE's jet engine designs reflect decades of engineering investment and proprietary know-how that competitors cannot simply reverse-engineer or purchase. **Patents and intellectual property** provide legal protection against imitation, though their duration is limited and their effectiveness varies by industry. **Distribution networks** can serve as barriers when they are difficult or expensive to build; a firm with exclusive access to retail channels or a deeply embedded logistics infrastructure has an advantage that a new competitor cannot simply purchase.

The key insight is that differentiation without barriers to imitation is temporary. A firm may develop a genuinely superior product, but if that superiority can be quickly and cheaply copied, the resulting advantage will be brief. Sustainable differentiation requires not only creating value that customers are willing to pay for, but also developing the resources and capabilities that make that value creation difficult for competitors to replicate. This connection between differentiation and unique resources and capabilities will be discussed further with the resource-based view in Chapter 3.

2.2.8 Risks of a Differentiation Strategy

Like all strategies, differentiation involves tradeoffs and carries significant risks. Four risks deserve particular attention.

First, the firm may fail to create sufficient differentiation. A product that is only marginally different from competitors does not justify a price premium, and customers will default to the cheaper option. The firm incurs the higher costs of attempting to differentiate without capturing the corresponding revenue. This is particularly dangerous when firms invest heavily in features or attributes that customers turn out not to value highly enough to pay for.

Second, customer preferences may shift. A differentiation advantage is built on customers valuing a specific set of attributes, but those valuations are not permanent. Customers may decide that the quality difference between the differentiated product and a cost leader's product is no longer worth the price premium. This can happen when the cost leader improves its quality, when economic conditions make customers more price-sensitive, or simply when tastes change. The luxury watch industry has faced this risk as smartwatches have shifted some customers' definition of "value" from craftsmanship and prestige toward functionality and connectivity.

Third, counterfeit or knockoff products can undermine differentiation by offering a visually or functionally similar product at a fraction of the price. This risk is particularly acute for brand-based differentiation, where the visual signifiers of the brand (logos, designs, packaging) can be copied even when the underlying quality cannot. The global market for counterfeit luxury goods directly erodes the price premium that legitimate differentiators have built over years of investment.

Fourth, the competitive advantage from differentiation will not last without barriers to imitation. As discussed above, any differentiation that can be easily and cheaply copied will be copied. A firm that differentiates through a feature that competitors can quickly replicate (a new restaurant concept, a product design, a service innovation) holds an advantage measured in months, not years. Only differentiation anchored in unique, difficult-to-imitate resources and capabilities produces sustainable competitive advantage.

These risks underscore the central theme of this chapter: every strategy involves tradeoffs. The differentiator trades the simplicity and efficiency of a standardized product for the complexity and cost of creating unique value. When it works, differentiation produces premium pricing, customer loyalty, and sustainable competitive advantage. When it fails, because the difference is insufficient, because customers stop caring, because imitators close the gap, the firm is left with higher costs and no offsetting premium. The discipline of differentiation lies in rigorously ensuring that the value created for customers exceeds the cost of creating it, and in building barriers that protect that value over time.

References

Christensen, C. M., Hall, T., Dillon, K., & Duncan, D. S. (2016). Know your customers' "jobs to be done." *Harvard Business Review, 94*(9), 54–62.

Coca-Cola Company. (2024). *2023 annual report.* The Coca-Cola Company.

Goldstein, R., Almenberg, J., Dreber, A., Emerson, J. W., Herschkowitsch, A., & Katz, J. (2008). Do more expensive wines taste better? Evidence from a large sample of blind tastings. *Journal of Wine Economics, 3*(1), 1–9.

Levitt, T. (1960). Marketing myopia. *Harvard Business Review, 38*(4), 45–56.

Levitt, T. (1983). *The marketing imagination.* Free Press.

MacMillan, I. C., & McGrath, R. G. (1997). Discovering new points of differentiation. *Harvard Business Review, 75*(4), 133–145.

Porter, M. E. (1985). *Competitive advantage: Creating and sustaining superior performance.* Free Press.

2.3 Cost Advantage — *How do firms compete on cost?*

If differentiation asks "How can we make customers willing to pay more?", a cost advantage asks the mirror-image question: "How can we produce at a lower cost than anyone else?" The previous section explored the first fundamental reason customers choose a product, because it is different and better. This section explores the second: because it costs less. A **cost advantage** strategy, also commonly called **cost leadership**, reduces a firm's costs below those of its competitors so that the firm can either beat competitors' prices to gain market share or match competitors' prices and pocket the difference as higher margins.

2.3.1 What Is Cost Advantage?

> *We have never sought to reduce costs by reducing wages; we have always sought to reduce costs by improving methods... To make a product better and cheaper, you must bring your own costs down. — Henry Ford*

A cost advantage exists when a firm can produce and deliver its product or service at a lower cost per unit than its competitors while maintaining a competitive level of quality and features (Porter, 1985). The key phrase is "competitive level." A cost leader does not sell an inferior product; it sells a *good enough* product. The offering must meet the basic expectations of the typical customer. A car manufacturer could dramatically reduce costs by eliminating doors, seatbelts, and a functioning transmission, but the resulting product would not be "good enough" for virtually any customer. A cost advantage is not about producing the cheapest possible product in absolute terms; it is about producing a product that meets acceptable standards of quality and features at the lowest possible cost.

This means that cost leaders typically offer no-frills, standardized products aimed at the typical customer. The focus is on efficiency in every aspect of the operation (production, distribution, administration, marketing) so that the total cost of getting the product to the customer is lower than what any competitor can achieve. Walmart and Amazon are the most prominent examples of this strategy in action. Customers do not shop at Walmart for the store ambiance or curated product selection. They shop at Walmart because prices are consistently low. That consistency is the product of a relentless, company-wide focus on cost reduction that touches every activity in the value chain.

2.3.2 Cost Advantage: Lower Cost → Greater Market Share or Higher Margins

The economic logic of a cost advantage gives the firm a strategic choice. A firm with lower costs than its competitors can deploy that advantage in two ways, and the choice between them depends on the competitive dynamics of the industry.

The first option is to **price below competitors** and capture greater market share. If the cost leader can offer the same basic product at a lower price, price-sensitive customers will switch. In markets where products are relatively undifferentiated and customers comparison-shop actively (groceries, basic apparel, commodity electronics) this approach can rapidly shift market share toward the low-cost firm. The cost leader accepts thinner margins per unit but makes up for it in volume.

The second option is to **match competitors' prices** and earn higher margins on each unit sold. If the cost leader prices at the same level as rivals but produces at a lower cost, the difference flows directly to the bottom line. This approach is less visible to the market (customers may not even realize the firm has a cost advantage) but it produces superior profitability that can be reinvested in further cost reduction, R&D, or strategic expansion.

In practice, most cost leaders use a combination of both approaches, pricing somewhat below competitors to gain volume while still capturing margin advantages. The point is that a cost advantage is versatile: it can be deployed offensively (to take share) or defensively (to build profit reserves), depending on what the competitive situation requires.

2.3.3 Sources of Cost Advantage

Cost advantages do not arise from a single source. They are typically built by combining multiple cost-reduction mechanisms, each contributing to a cumulative advantage that competitors find difficult to match. The five primary sources of cost advantage are economies of scale, learning and experience effects, proprietary knowledge and process savings, lower input costs, and fundamentally different business models.

Economies of scale, the reduction in cost per unit as the volume of production increases, is the most widely recognized source of cost advantage and is important enough to warrant its own dedicated section later in this chapter. For now, the essential point is that scale allows firms to spread fixed costs across more units, specialize their equipment and workforce, and negotiate better terms with suppliers. A factory's rent is the same whether it produces one hundred units or ten thousand; the firm producing ten thousand pays a fraction of the per-unit rent. This logic applies not only to production costs but also to R&D, advertising, distribution, finance, and administrative overhead. The larger the firm's volume, the thinner each of these costs is spread.

Learning and experience effects reduce costs through accumulated practice and knowledge. People get faster with repetition; consider the difference between the first time you tied your shoes and how quickly you do it now. At the organizational level, this principle operates through several mechanisms.

Workers performing the same tasks repeatedly become faster and make fewer errors. Over time, they identify more efficient ways to perform their work, improving processes from the bottom up. Repetitive tasks become candidates for automation, replacing human labor with machines. Engineers and designers discover modifications to the product itself that reduce manufacturing time or material waste. The net result is that the more cumulative output a firm has produced, the lower its per-unit costs tend to be.

Proprietary knowledge and process savings represent a firm's unique operational insights: process innovations, production techniques, or organizational practices that competitors cannot easily observe or replicate. Toyota's production system is the most celebrated example. Toyota developed an interlocking set of practices (pull-based production to avoid overproduction, just-in-time delivery to minimize inventory, visual controls to surface defects immediately, workload leveling to smooth production flow, and systematic bottleneck identification to increase throughput) all embedded within a corporate culture that rewards learning from mistakes rather than punishing them. The system is extraordinarily effective, but its advantage does not come from any single practice. It comes from the *interaction* of dozens of practices reinforced by a culture that took decades to develop. Competitors have studied Toyota's system exhaustively, yet few have replicated its full cost and quality advantages, because the system's effectiveness depends on tacit knowledge, cultural norms, and organizational routines that cannot be copied from a manual.

Lower input costs reduce the firm's total cost by reducing what it pays for the resources (people, raw materials, energy, information, financing) that enter the production process. There are four primary ways to achieve lower input costs. First, a firm can exercise strong *bargaining power over suppliers.* Walmart's enormous purchasing volume gives it leverage that no supplier can ignore; the implicit threat that Walmart could shift orders to a competing supplier extracts pricing concessions that smaller retailers cannot obtain. Second, a firm can *cooperate especially well with suppliers*, creating efficiencies that benefit both parties. Toyota locates many of its suppliers near its assembly plants, reducing transportation costs and enabling just-in-time delivery for both firms. Third, a firm can *source inputs from low-cost locations.* Nike's decision to manufacture shoes in countries with lower labor costs is a straightforward application of this principle. Fourth, a firm can *arrange better access to inputs* than its competitors. De Beers built its dominant position in the diamond industry in part by securing control over a disproportionate share of the world's diamond mines, restricting competitors' access to the fundamental input of the industry.

A fundamentally different business model can create cost advantages by reconfiguring the value chain, eliminating, restructuring, or replacing entire categories of cost that competitors take for granted. This is often the most powerful source of cost advantage because it does not simply do the same activities more efficiently; it changes which activities the firm performs at all.

EX: Amazon vs. Barnes & Noble — Reconfiguring the Value Chain

When Amazon entered the bookselling industry in 1995, Barnes & Noble was the dominant competitor, operating hundreds of retail locations across the United States. Those stores were a source of competitive advantage against other physical bookstores; Barnes & Noble's scale allowed it to negotiate better terms with publishers, spread real estate and staffing costs across enormous sales volume, and offer a browsing experience that smaller bookstores could not match.

Amazon's insight was that the retail store itself, the cornerstone of Barnes & Noble's strategy, was also a massive cost. Every store required rent, utilities, insurance, inventory, fixtures, and dozens of employees. Amazon eliminated this entire category of cost by selling books exclusively online. Without physical stores, Amazon could operate from centralized warehouses, carry a vastly larger inventory without the space constraints of retail shelves, and pass the cost savings on to customers in the form of lower prices. Barnes & Noble's greatest asset, its network of stores, became its greatest liability against a competitor that had simply removed that cost from the equation entirely.

This was not a case of Amazon doing the same thing more efficiently. It was a case of Amazon doing a *fundamentally different thing*, reconfiguring the value chain so that an entire cost category ceased to exist. Barnes & Noble could not easily respond because its stores were the foundation of its existing strategy, its brand identity, and its lease obligations. Matching Amazon's cost structure would have required dismantling the very infrastructure that had made Barnes & Noble successful. This is the power of business model reconfiguration as a source of cost advantage: it creates structural cost differences that competitors with legacy business models find extremely difficult to close.

2.3.4 Law of Experience: Costs Decline as Cumulative Output Doubles

The learning and experience effects described above follow a remarkably consistent empirical pattern known as the law of experience (or the experience curve). The law states that variable and average costs per unit decline by a constant percentage each time cumulative output doubles (Wright, 1936). In the semiconductor industry, for instance, historical data shows approximately a 20 percent cost reduction with each doubling of cumulative production volume. This is not a theoretical prediction; it is an observed regularity across a wide range of industries, from aircraft manufacturing to chemical processing to consumer electronics.

The experience curve has several important strategic implications. First, **first movers in a fast-growing market will secure widening cost advantages**. A firm that enters a market early and grows quickly accumulates experience faster than later entrants, moving further down the cost curve while competitors are still at higher-cost positions. This means that in industries where experience effects are strong, a firm must grow at least as fast as its rivals or accept a persistent cost disadvantage. The longer the firm falls behind in cumulative volume, the wider the cost gap becomes.

Second, the experience curve **provides a basis for predicting future costs and pricing**. If a firm knows its current cost position and the rate at which costs decline with each doubling of output, it can project its future cost per unit at any given production volume. This is valuable for pricing decisions; a firm might price below its current cost in a new market, accepting short-term losses with the knowledge that costs will decline as volume accumulates, and that the low price itself will accelerate the volume growth that drives costs down. It is also valuable for evaluating potential mergers and acquisitions: combining two firms' cumulative volumes can produce cost synergies that are predictable from the shape of the experience curve.

Third, the experience curve **can be used to benchmark cost management**. By plotting a firm's actual costs against the theoretical experience curve, managers can assess whether the firm is capturing the expected cost reductions or falling behind. A firm whose costs are declining more slowly than the curve predicts may have operational inefficiencies, management problems, or aging equipment that is impeding learning. A firm whose costs are declining faster than expected may have found process innovations that are accelerating the curve, a competitive advantage in its own right.

The **experience curve has real limitations** that strategists must keep in mind. First, moving down the curve by buying market share through heavy advertising, price promotions, or acquisitions is not free — the cost of acquiring volume may exceed the savings from gaining it. Second, the curve flattens at high levels of experience: because cost reduction occurs with each doubling of cumulative output, going from one million to two million units produces the same percentage savings as going from one thousand to two thousand, but requires producing an additional million units to get there. The most dramatic improvements happen early, and gains become progressively harder to capture. Third, knowledge spillovers to rivals erode the originator's advantage as employees move between firms, suppliers observe multiple clients' operations, and innovations diffuse through trade publications. Fourth, aging equipment can impede continued cost improvement, allowing newer entrants with state-of-the-art capital investments to leapfrog an incumbent's experience advantage.

2.3.5 Risks of a Cost Advantage Strategy

A cost advantage strategy, like differentiation, involves tradeoffs and carries distinct strategic risks (Porter, 1980).

First, a firm may **lose its cost advantage to competitors deploying newer technology**. A cost position built on scale economies and experience effects can be rendered irrelevant overnight if a competitor introduces a fundamentally more efficient production technology. The incumbent's accumulated experience in the old technology provides no advantage once the basis of competition shifts. This is the risk that digital photography posed to Kodak's film manufacturing cost advantages, and that streaming posed to Blockbuster's retail distribution efficiency.

Second, **competitors may find ways to imitate the cost leader's advantage through their own strategic actions**. If the cost advantage rests on a specific operational practice or supply chain arrangement, a competitor who replicates that practice closes the gap. If the advantage rests on scale, a competitor who grows through acquisition or organic expansion may eventually match the leader's volume. New entrants may also leapfrog the incumbent by investing in state-of-the-art facilities from the start, gaining a comparable cost position without having to traverse the same learning curve. Cost advantages, like differentiation advantages, are only as durable as the barriers that protect them.

Third, **a focus on cost can blind the firm to needed product or marketing changes**. A cost advantage strategy directs management attention toward efficiency, standardization, and process improvement. That focus can become a liability when customer preferences shift or when the market begins to value features the firm has chosen not to provide. The cost leader, oriented toward squeezing cost out of the existing product, may be slow to recognize that the product itself needs to change. By the time the shift is acknowledged, competitors who were paying closer attention to the customer have already established stronger positions.

Fourth, **cost inflation can narrow the price differential** that makes a cost advantage strategically valuable. The cost leader's position depends on maintaining a price gap wide enough that price-sensitive customers will accept a more basic product in exchange for the savings. When industry-wide input costs rise, every firm's prices rise with them, and the cost leader's absolute price advantage becomes a smaller percentage of the total price. A \$2 advantage on a \$10 product is a 20% discount; the same \$2 advantage on a \$20 product is only a 10% discount. The cost leader can be executing flawlessly, maintaining all its operational advantages, and still find its strategic position eroding as the price gap loses its decisiveness in customer decision-making.

EX: The Vulnerability of a Cost Advantage — Kodak and the Shift to Digital

For most of the twentieth century, Kodak was the dominant cost leader in photographic film. The company's scale was unmatched: it produced more film than any competitor, operated the most efficient manufacturing facilities in the industry, and had moved further down the experience curve than anyone else. Its cost per roll of film was lower than any rival could achieve, and it used that advantage to maintain dominant market share and healthy margins for decades.

But Kodak's cost advantage was specific to the production of *film*, a physical, chemical product. When digital photography emerged, the entire cost structure of the industry shifted. Digital cameras eliminated the need for film entirely. Kodak's vast manufacturing experience, its highly optimized chemical processes, and its billions of dollars in specialized production equipment became irrelevant. The company's cost advantage did not erode gradually — it became structurally obsolete. A firm with zero experience in film manufacturing but competence in digital sensors and software could enter the market with a fundamentally lower cost structure because the most expensive input, film itself, had been removed from the equation.

Kodak recognized the digital threat early (it actually invented the first digital camera in 1975) but was reluctant to cannibalize its highly profitable film business. By the time it committed to the digital transition, competitors with no legacy film infrastructure had established strong positions. Kodak's story illustrates a critical risk of a cost advantage: the advantage is always tied to a specific production technology and business model. When the underlying technology shifts, the accumulated cost advantages of the old model can become worthless, and the scale and experience that were once strengths become anchors that slow the firm's adaptation.

2.3.6 The Tradeoff at the Heart of a Cost Advantage

The cost leader makes a deliberate tradeoff: it sacrifices product uniqueness for operational efficiency. It offers fewer features, less customization, simpler design, and a more standardized experience than differentiators, and it accepts that some customers will choose the differentiated alternative. In exchange, the cost leader gains the ability to serve price-sensitive customers profitably, to survive price wars that would destroy higher-cost competitors, and to generate margins that can be reinvested in further cost reduction.

This tradeoff connects directly to the theme established in the first section of this chapter. The cost leader has made a clear strategic choice about what it will and will not do. It will not try to offer the best product, the most innovative features, or the most personalized service. It will try to offer a good-enough product at a price no competitor can match. That clarity of purpose, that willingness to accept what the strategy cannot do in order to excel at what it can, is what separates a genuine cost leader from a firm that is simply cheap.

References

Porter, M. E. (1980). *Competitive strategy: Techniques for analyzing industries and competitors.* Free Press.

Porter, M. E. (1985). *Competitive advantage: Creating and sustaining superior performance.* Free Press.

Wright, T. P. (1936). Factors affecting the cost of airplanes. *Journal of the Aeronautical Sciences, 3*(4), 122–128.

2.4 Economies of Scale — *What drives cost advantages?*

> *"Cheapness is in proportion to the scale of production." — Andrew Carnegie*

The previous section identified economies of scale as a primary source of cost advantage. Because it is a concept that students frequently misunderstand, it deserves a more thorough treatment. Economies of scale do not simply mean "bigger is better." They describe a specific economic relationship: as the scale of operations increases, firms gain access to efficiencies that lower their cost per unit.

Economies of scale are defined as lower costs per unit due to additional efficiencies possible through greater scale of operations. Scale here refers to the volume of output over a consistent time period, for instance, units produced per month or cases sold per year. The key insight is that certain costs do not increase proportionally with output. As a firm produces more, it can spread these costs across a larger number of units, driving down the average cost per unit. This cost reduction is not automatic or unlimited, but within certain ranges, it provides a powerful advantage to firms that can achieve sufficient volume.

Economies of scale arise from four primary sources: spreading fixed production costs, spreading non-production costs, specialization of tasks and people, and specialization of equipment.

2.4.1 Spreading Fixed Production Costs Across More Units

The most intuitive source of economies of scale is the spreading of fixed production costs. A factory's rent, a production line's lease payment, and the cost of manufacturing equipment are all fixed; they remain the same whether the firm produces one unit or ten thousand units. When these fixed costs are divided across a larger number of units, the cost attributable to each individual unit falls. A factory that costs $100,000 per month to operate adds $100 to the cost of each unit if the firm produces 1,000 units, but only $10 per unit if it produces 10,000. The factory itself has not changed. The equipment has not improved. The only difference is volume.

This relationship has an important implication: to justify the purchase of production equipment, a firm must reach a minimum scale. If a piece of machinery costs $50,000 but reduces per-unit labor costs by $2, the firm needs to produce at least 25,000 units before the investment breaks even. A firm producing only 5,000 units per year cannot economically justify the purchase, and is therefore stuck with higher per-unit costs. The smaller firm is not less intelligent or less well-managed; it simply lacks the volume to take advantage of production technology available to its larger competitors.

Production investment is also characteristically "lumpy." Equipment is not available in infinitely divisible increments. A machine might be economical for producing between 5,000 and 50,000 units per month, but once a firm exceeds that capacity, it must invest in a larger, more expensive machine suited to the next range of production volume. This creates a staircase pattern of investment, and between these steps, the firm is either underutilizing expensive capacity or constrained by insufficient capacity.

EX: The Lemonade Stand and Production Technology

Consider a simple lemonade stand. Producing one gallon by hand requires squeezing twenty lemons (about twenty minutes of labor) and heating water to dissolve sugar (ten minutes), plus ingredients. At $15 per hour labor and $5.50 in ingredients, each gallon costs about $13 to produce and sells for $16, yielding $3 in profit. At this scale, profit is perfectly linear: ten gallons yields $30, one hundred gallons yields $300. There is no advantage to being bigger.

Now introduce a $100 juicer that squeezes lemons in half the time. At one gallon, total costs jump to $111, producing a loss of $95. But at one hundred gallons, the labor savings more than offset the juicer's cost, generating $450 in profit compared to $300 from hand squeezing. At one thousand gallons, profits rise to $5,400 versus $3,000 by hand.

Take this further with a commercial-grade "mega juicer" costing $800 but processing lemons five times faster. At one gallon, the loss is catastrophic: negative $793. At one hundred gallons, the firm is still losing $100, while the $100 juicer earns $450. But at one thousand gallons, the mega juicer yields $6,200 against the smaller juicer's $5,400. The lesson is clear: at every scale level, there is an optimal production technology. Equipment that is ruinously expensive at low volumes becomes enormously profitable at high volumes.

This example simplifies by charging the equipment's full price against total production. In practice, a production technology is paid for across its useful life, and the firm compares output *per period* to the equipment's cost *per period.* The logic is unchanged: a fixed cost is spread across volume.

2.4.2 Spreading Non-Production Costs

The logic of spreading fixed costs extends well beyond the factory floor. Research and development, advertising, distribution networks, financing costs, and administrative overhead do not scale proportionally with output. A pharmaceutical company that spends $1 billion developing a new drug faces the same R&D cost whether it sells one million doses or one hundred million. A software company's development costs are identical whether the application is downloaded by one thousand users or one hundred million. In each case, higher volume dramatically reduces the per-unit burden of these fixed investments.

EX: Beer Advertising Scale

Anheuser-Busch InBev's marketing budget dwarfs that of smaller competitors in absolute terms. The company reported $7.2 billion in sales and marketing investment in fiscal year 2024. By contrast, the Boston Beer Company, maker of Samuel Adams, Twisted Tea, and Truly, spent approximately $448 million on advertising, promotional, and selling expenses the same year. However, Anheuser-Busch's global volume was approximately 491 million barrels or approximately $14.68 in marketing cost per barrel. Whereas, Boston Beer Company had ~7.5 million barrels of shipment volume, or about $59.70 per barrel (Anheuser-Busch InBev, 2025; Boston Beer Company, 2025). Despite Anheuser-Busch spending 16 times Boston Beer's marketing budget, they only pay 1/4 as much per beer to do it.

The smaller firm is not overspending on advertising. It is simply unable to spread its advertising investment across enough units to achieve the same per-unit efficiency. The scale advantage is self-reinforcing: Anheuser-Busch can afford Super Bowl commercials, global sponsorship deals, and year-round media campaigns while still paying far less per unit sold than a competitor spending a fraction of the total. This dynamic repeats across virtually every non-production cost category: the firm with greater volume can spread out expenses more.

2.4.3 Specialization of Tasks and People

Adam Smith observed in *The Wealth of Nations* that the division of labor is limited by the extent of the market (Smith, 1776). This insight applies directly to economies of scale. A small firm with limited volume cannot support high levels of employee specialization. The owner of a small business might simultaneously handle production, marketing, sales, accounting, and customer service. No single person can be expert in all of these functions, so each is performed adequately but not optimally.

The alternative is equally problematic. The small firm can hire specialists, but without enough work to keep them fully occupied, it pays specialist wages for generalist-level utilization.

Scale resolves this tension. A firm with sufficient volume can hire dedicated specialists and keep them fully employed. The marketing department has enough campaigns to run, the accounting team has enough transactions to process, and the production managers have enough output to oversee. Each employee focuses on a narrower range of tasks, develops deeper expertise through repetition and training, and performs at a higher level than a generalist juggling multiple responsibilities. The larger firm thus achieves both task efficiency (each function performed by an expert) and payroll efficiency (each expert fully utilized).

This effect extends to professional development. A firm large enough to employ a full-time data analyst can hire someone with a degree in statistics and years of experience. A small firm that needs occasional data analysis must either train an existing employee (who will never develop the same depth of expertise) or outsource the work (which introduces its own costs and coordination challenges). Scale does not merely allow a firm to do the same things more efficiently — it allows the firm to do things that smaller competitors literally cannot do at all.

2.4.4 Specialization of Equipment

The logic that applies to people also applies to machinery and technology. Specialized equipment, designed to perform one task extremely well, is typically faster, more precise, and cheaper per unit of output than general-purpose equipment. However, specialized equipment is expensive, and its cost can only be justified at high volumes. A commercial bakery producing ten thousand loaves per day can invest in a dedicated dough-mixing system, automated shaping machines, and a continuous-flow oven. But a bakery producing two hundred loaves per day cannot justify the expense; the specialized equipment would sit idle most of the time, and the cost per loaf would actually increase.

This creates a compounding advantage for larger firms. Not only can they spread fixed costs across more units and employ specialized people, but they can also deploy specialized tools that further reduce per-unit costs. The small competitor faces a fundamentally different cost structure, not because it is less capable, but because its volume does not permit the same investments. In industries where specialized equipment offers significant efficiency gains (semiconductor manufacturing, automobile production, large-scale logistics) this source of economies of scale can create formidable barriers to entry.

2.4.5 The Long-Run Cost Curve and Diminishing Returns

The four sources of economies of scale combine to produce the classic long-run average cost curve taught in microeconomics. As output increases from low levels, average costs fall, sometimes steeply, as fixed costs are spread, specialists are utilized, and specialized equipment is deployed. This is the region of increasing returns to scale, where each additional unit of output costs less than the last.

However, this decline does not continue indefinitely. At some point, the major efficiencies have been captured. Fixed costs have been spread as thinly as they will go. Specialists are fully employed. The best available equipment is already in use. Beyond this point, the cost curve flattens into a region of constant returns to scale, where additional output does not meaningfully reduce per-unit costs.

Eventually, if the firm continues to grow, it may encounter *diseconomies* of scale — rising per-unit costs caused by the increasing complexity of managing a very large organization. Communication becomes slower, bureaucracy multiplies, coordination costs rise, and the firm loses the agility that smaller competitors enjoy. The long-run cost curve thus has a characteristic U-shape, and the strategically relevant question for any firm is where on this curve it currently operates.

2.4.6 Diseconomies of Scale in Economic Downturns

Scale advantages depend critically on volume. When demand is strong and production runs at or near capacity, fixed costs are spread efficiently and the large firm enjoys its structural cost advantage. But when demand drops, as it inevitably does during economic downturns, the mathematics reverse. Fixed costs do not disappear when production slows. The factory rent is still due. The specialized equipment is still depreciating. The salaried specialists are still on the payroll. With fewer units to absorb these costs, the per-unit burden rises sharply. The very scale that was an advantage in good times becomes a liability in bad times.

EX: U.S. Airlines 2002-2006

The U.S. airline industry following the September 11 attacks provides a stark illustration. Between 2002 and 2006, the large legacy carriers suffered catastrophic losses. Aircraft leases and loan payments continued regardless of how many seats were filled, airport gate contracts remained in force, and labor agreements prevented rapid workforce adjustments. The large carriers could not shrink their cost structures quickly enough to match the drop in demand.

Smaller airlines, by contrast, had far less fixed infrastructure. Their fleets were smaller, their route networks leaner, and their cost structures more variable. While they also suffered, their losses were dramatically smaller. The scale that had given legacy carriers cost advantages during strong demand became a crushing burden when passengers stopped flying.

Firms can respond to this vulnerability by lowering prices to maintain volume, restructuring their cost base from fixed to variable (e.g., outsourcing functions previously performed in-house), or diversifying into counter-cyclical businesses. None of these responses eliminates the fundamental vulnerability, but each can mitigate it.

2.4.7 Why Scale Matters Even for Small Businesses

A common reaction to the discussion of economies of scale is that it applies only to large corporations. This view is mistaken. Even if a small firm does not itself operate at the scale necessary to capture significant economies, it is affected by scale economies at every turn.

Economies of scale are fundamentally how volume discounts work. When a supplier offers a lower price for larger orders, it is passing along some portion of its own scale economies. A small retailer ordering fifty units pays more per unit than a large chain ordering fifty thousand, not because the supplier dislikes small businesses but because the supplier's own costs are higher on a per-unit basis at lower volumes. The small firm therefore faces a structural cost disadvantage in its input prices.

The same dynamic works in reverse with buyers. A small firm's customers may demand volume discounts that the firm cannot profitably provide because it lacks the scale to reduce its own per-unit costs sufficiently. The firm is squeezed from both sides, paying more for inputs than larger competitors and unable to offer comparable pricing to volume buyers.

This is a large part of the reason that crowdfunding platforms like Kickstarter and Indiegogo exist. These platforms allow new ventures to aggregate pre-orders, achieving committed demand that justifies production at a scale sufficient to reach competitive per-unit costs. The crowdfunding model is, in essence, a mechanism for overcoming the chicken-and-egg problem of scale: you need volume to achieve low costs, but you need low costs to attract volume.

Understanding economies of scale is therefore relevant for any business, regardless of size. It shapes the cost of inputs, the pricing expectations of customers, the competitive dynamics of the industry, and the minimum viable scale at which a new venture can profitably operate. A small business owner who ignores economies of scale is not exempt from its effects; they are simply unaware of the forces acting upon their firm.

References

Anheuser-Busch InBev. (2025, February 26). *AB InBev reports full year and fourth quarter 2024 results* [Press release]. Business Wire.

Boston Beer Company. (2025, February 25). *Boston Beer reports fourth quarter financial results* [Press release]. GlobeNewsWire.

Smith, A. (1776). *An inquiry into the nature and causes of the wealth of nations.* W. Strahan and T. Cadell.

2.5 Integrated Cost/Differentiation Strategy — *Can firms overcome the tradeoff?*

Chapter 2.1 established that strategy is built on tradeoffs, that scarcity forces firms to choose between competing uses of limited resources. Chapters 2.2 and 2.3 then presented the two foundational strategies that follow from this logic: differentiation (competing on uniqueness) and cost leadership (competing on price). These two strategies pull in fundamentally different directions. Differentiation demands investment in design, quality, branding, service, and innovation, all of which increase costs. Cost leadership demands stripping away anything that does not contribute to efficiency: standardizing products, minimizing service, and leveraging scale. A natural question arises: Is it possible to pursue both at the same time? Can a firm offer meaningful differentiation *and* maintain a cost advantage?

The answer is a qualified yes, qualified because the integrated strategy is more difficult to execute, more vulnerable to competitive pressure, and more likely to result in strategic failure than either pure strategy. But under certain conditions, firms can successfully position themselves between the cost leader and the differentiator, creating genuine value for customers who want something better than the cheapest option but are not willing to pay for the most differentiated one.

2.5.1 What Is the Integrated (Hybrid) Strategy?

The **integrated cost leadership/differentiation strategy**, often called a **hybrid strategy**, is a strategic position in which a firm combines elements of both cost advantage and differentiation advantage (Porter, 1985). Rather than committing fully to one end of the spectrum, the hybrid strategist seeks to deliver a product that offers *enough* differentiation to justify a price above the cost leader's, while maintaining *enough* cost discipline to price below the differentiator's. The firm occupies the space between the two poles, offering what might be described as good value: a reasonable combination of quality and price that appeals to customers who find the cost leader's product too basic and the differentiator's product too expensive.

This is not the same as being mediocre at both cost and differentiation. A successful hybrid strategy requires genuine competence on both dimensions, real cost efficiencies and real differentiated features. The firm must actually be lower cost than the differentiation leaders and actually offer meaningfully better features or experience than the cost leaders. If it fails on either dimension, it does not occupy a strategic middle ground; it occupies no ground at all.

2.5.2 Two Forms of the Hybrid Strategy

The hybrid strategy manifests in two distinct forms, each of which approaches the cost-differentiation spectrum from a different direction.

The first form starts from the cost side: the firm provides a **relatively lower-cost product with some valued differentiation features** over the cheapest products in the market. The starting point is efficiency and low cost, but the firm invests selectively in features, quality, or experience that elevate its offering above the bare-bones products of the pure cost leader. The firm does not attempt to match the differentiator on every dimension; it chooses a few areas where modest investment yields meaningful customer value and focuses its differentiation efforts there.

The second form starts from the differentiation side: the firm produces an **"almost as good" differentiated product at lower cost** than the comparison differentiated products. Here the starting point is a premium product, but the firm finds ways to deliver most of the differentiated value at a significantly lower price. The customer gets an experience that is close to, though not quite equal to, the full premium offering, at a price that makes the remaining gap feel unimportant. This form often appeals to customers who aspire to the premium category but find the price of the true differentiator difficult to justify.

Both forms share the same underlying logic: the firm creates value by occupying a position that neither the cost leader nor the differentiator is well-suited to attack. The cost leader would have to add features and increase costs to match the hybrid's offering. The differentiator would have to reduce prices and potentially dilute its brand to compete on price. If the hybrid firm has executed well, it occupies a defensible position precisely because it would require competitors on both sides to move away from their own strategic strengths.

EX: Target — Positioned Between Walmart and Macy's

The U.S. retail landscape offers a clean illustration of the hybrid strategy in action. Walmart is the quintessential cost leader: massive scale, relentless efficiency, everyday low prices, and a no-frills shopping environment. Its entire operation is built around minimizing cost and passing those savings to the customer. At the other end sits Macy's, a department store that competes on differentiation: curated brand assortments, a more pleasant shopping atmosphere, seasonal fashion, and in-store services that justify higher prices.

Target positions itself deliberately between these two extremes. Its prices are higher than Walmart's but meaningfully lower than Macy's. Its stores are cleaner, better organized, and more visually appealing than a typical Walmart, but they do not approach the staffing levels or service experience of a full-service department store. Target invests selectively in differentiation: designer collaborations with brands like Hearth & Hand by Chip and Joanna Gaines, a curated private-label apparel line, and a store design aesthetic that feels more upscale than its prices would suggest. At the same time, Target maintains cost discipline through efficient supply chain management, large-format stores, and significant purchasing scale.

The result is a value proposition that appeals to a specific and sizable customer segment: shoppers who want a better experience and more stylish products than Walmart offers, but who are not willing to pay Macy's prices for everyday purchases. Target's strategy works because it delivers genuine differentiation (not merely the *perception* of differentiation) while maintaining genuine cost efficiency (not merely hoping costs will work out). It is a deliberate strategic choice, not an accident of being unable to commit to either pure strategy.

EX: Hyundai Genesis — Affordable Luxury

The automobile industry provides another instructive example. The BMW 5 Series has long been a benchmark for the luxury sedan segment, a differentiated product with premium engineering, brand prestige, and a price tag to match. Hyundai's Genesis line (now a standalone Genesis brand) entered this space not by attempting to out-differentiate BMW, but by offering a vehicle that delivered much of the luxury experience (refined interiors, powerful engines, advanced technology, strong build quality) at a substantially lower price point.

The Genesis does not claim to be a *better* car than the BMW 5 Series. Its strategy is more nuanced: it claims to be *nearly as good* at a significantly lower cost. For the customer who values luxury features and driving experience but finds the BMW's price premium difficult to justify, or who simply prefers to allocate that money elsewhere, the Genesis offers a compelling alternative. It is differentiated relative to mainstream sedans (a Honda Accord or Toyota Camry), but it is less expensive than the premium players it most closely resembles. This is the second form of the hybrid strategy in action: an "almost as good" differentiated product at a lower price than the comparison differentiators.

Genesis's success has depended on genuine execution on both dimensions. The vehicles must actually deliver a luxury-caliber experience; if they felt like rebranded Hyundais with leather seats, the strategy would fail. And the pricing must actually be lower; if the Genesis crept toward BMW pricing, customers would simply buy the BMW. The strategic position only works as long as the firm maintains credibility on both cost and differentiation simultaneously.

2.5.3 Risks of an Integrated Strategy

The hybrid strategy carries all of the risks associated with both differentiation and cost leadership strategies individually: the risks of shifting customer preferences, technological disruption, imitation, and the experience curve effects discussed in previous sections all apply. But the integrated strategy adds two risks that are unique to its middle position, and together they constitute the most serious danger facing the hybrid firm.

The cost leader's product may improve, eroding the hybrid firm's differentiation advantage. If Walmart invests in cleaner stores, better private-label brands, or a more pleasant shopping experience, it narrows the gap between itself and Target. Customers who were choosing Target specifically because of its superior atmosphere and product selection may find that Walmart now offers "good enough" versions of those features at a lower price. The hybrid firm's differentiation advantage — the primary reason customers were willing to pay its higher prices — shrinks. The firm has not done anything wrong. The cost leader has simply gotten better, and in doing so has pulled the rug out from underneath the hybrid's value proposition from below.

The differentiation leader's product may become cheaper, eroding the hybrid firm's cost advantage. If BMW offers aggressive financing, loyalty discounts, or lower-priced entry models, it narrows the gap between itself and Genesis from the other direction. Customers who were choosing Genesis specifically because of the price difference may find that a BMW is now attainable for only marginally more money, and if the gap is small enough, most will choose the brand with greater prestige. The hybrid firm's cost advantage — the primary reason price-sensitive customers were willing to accept a less prestigious brand — evaporates. Again, the firm itself has not changed. The differentiator has simply become more affordable, and the hybrid is squeezed from above.

2.5.4 The Danger of Being Stuck in the Middle

These two risks converge on what Porter (1980) described as the danger of being "stuck in the middle." When the cost leader improves its product from below and the differentiator lowers its prices from above, the hybrid firm's strategic space narrows, potentially to the point of disappearing entirely. The firm finds itself undersold by the cost leader (who now offers comparable features at a lower price) *and* out-differentiated by the premium competitor (who is now close enough in price that customers see no reason to compromise). The middle position that once seemed like an attractive compromise becomes a no-man's-land where the firm has no compelling answer to the question, "Why should I buy from you instead of them?"

This is not merely a theoretical concern. Industries are littered with firms that attempted a hybrid strategy, failed to maintain sufficient advantage on either dimension, and found themselves trapped between more committed competitors. The key lesson is that the integrated strategy demands exceptional execution and constant vigilance. The pure cost leader can focus all of its energy on efficiency. The pure differentiator can focus all of its energy on uniqueness. The hybrid firm must do both well enough to maintain a credible position against each, and it must do so while competitors on both sides are actively working to close the gaps that define the hybrid's strategic space.

The integrated strategy is not inherently flawed. Firms like Target and Genesis have demonstrated that it can be executed profitably and sustained over time. But it is the most demanding of the fundamental strategies, and the one most likely to produce strategic failure when execution falters. The tradeoff between cost and differentiation does not disappear simply because a firm chooses to pursue both; it becomes more complex, more difficult to manage, and more punishing when it is mishandled.

References

Porter, M. E. (1980). *Competitive strategy: Techniques for analyzing industries and competitors.* Free Press.
Porter, M. E. (1985). *Competitive advantage: Creating and sustaining superior performance.* Free Press.

2.6 Focus Strategies — *How do niche strategies work?*

The strategies examined so far (differentiation, cost leadership, and the integrated hybrid) all assume that the firm competes across the broad market. The differentiator seeks to serve a wide range of customers with a uniquely valuable product. The cost leader targets the mass market with efficient, standardized offerings. The hybrid strategist positions between these two poles for the broad middle. But not every firm needs to, or should, compete for the entire market. Some of the most profitable strategic positions involve serving not the most customers, but the *right* customers. This is the logic of the focus strategy (Porter, 1980).

2.6.1 What Is a Focus Strategy?

A **focus strategy** is a business-level strategy in which a firm concentrates its efforts on serving the needs of a specific customer segment or industry segment rather than the market as a whole (Porter, 1980). The focused firm does not attempt to appeal to everyone. Instead, it deliberately narrows its target market and directs all of its resources, capabilities, and attention toward understanding and serving that segment better than any broad-market competitor can.

The focus strategy is not a third alternative to differentiation and cost leadership; it is a *modifier* that can be applied to either one (Porter, 1985). A focused firm still competes on the basis of either uniqueness or cost. The difference is that it does so within a defined segment rather than across the entire industry. This distinction is critical: focus is about *where* the firm competes, while differentiation and cost leadership are about *how* it competes. A firm can pursue focused differentiation (offering a uniquely valuable product to a specific segment), focused cost leadership (offering the lowest-cost product to a specific segment), or even a focused hybrid strategy. The narrowing of the target market is what makes it a focus strategy; the basis of competitive advantage within that market is what determines which type.

2.6.2 How Focus Creates Value: Increased Differentiation and/or Lower Costs for a Specific Segment

The fundamental mechanism of a focus strategy is that narrowing the target market allows the firm to achieve levels of differentiation or cost efficiency that would be impossible, or at least impractical, when serving the broad market (Porter, 1985). A firm trying to serve everyone must make compromises. Its products must be general enough to appeal to diverse tastes. Its operations must be flexible enough to handle varied demands. Its marketing must speak to multiple audiences. Every one of these compromises comes at a cost: the product is a little less perfect for any individual customer, the operations are a little less efficient for any particular task, and the marketing is a little less compelling to any specific audience.

The focused firm makes the opposite tradeoff. By choosing a narrow segment, it can tailor its product precisely to the needs, preferences, and expectations of that group. It can design its operations specifically around the requirements of that segment. It can craft its marketing to speak directly to those customers in language they find resonant. The result is either greater differentiation (the product is more perfectly suited to the segment's needs than any broad-market offering could be) or lower costs (the operations are more efficient because they are optimized for a narrow, predictable set of demands), or, in some cases, both (Porter, 1985).

This is not merely a theoretical possibility. It is the reason that specialty retailers coexist with department stores, that boutique consulting firms coexist with McKinsey, and that craft breweries coexist with

Anheuser-Busch. Each of these focused competitors has found a segment whose needs are sufficiently distinct from the broader market that a tailored offering creates meaningful additional value.

2.6.3 Types of Focus Segments

Firms can define their focus along three primary dimensions, each of which narrows the target market in a different way (Porter, 1980).

A particular buyer group. The firm targets a specific demographic, psychographic, or behavioral segment of customers. A financial advisory firm that serves exclusively physicians has chosen a buyer-group focus. So has a clothing brand that designs exclusively for petite women, or a travel agency that specializes in adventure vacations for retirees. In each case, the firm has identified a group of customers whose needs are distinct enough from the general population that a tailored offering creates superior value. The key requirement is that the buyer group's needs must genuinely differ from those of the broader market; if the segment wants essentially the same thing as everyone else, there is no advantage to focusing on it.

A particular product line segment. The firm targets a specific category or grade within a broader product market. Consider the paint industry: Sherwin-Williams serves the broad market with products for homeowners, contractors, industrial applications, and automotive uses. A focused competitor might choose to serve only professional painters, offering premium-grade products with specialized formulations, selling through contractor supply channels, and providing technical support that do-it-yourself customers neither need nor would pay for. The focused firm does not offer a full product line. It offers a deep product line within a narrow category, and it knows that category better than any generalist ever could.

A particular geographic market. The firm targets a specific region, city, or locality. A regional grocery chain that understands local food preferences, sources from nearby farms, and builds relationships with the community is pursuing a geographic focus. So is a law firm that specializes in the regulatory environment of a particular state or municipality. Geographic focus works when local conditions (customer preferences, regulatory requirements, supply chain logistics, cultural factors) are sufficiently different from those in other regions that a locally tailored approach creates meaningful advantages over national or global competitors that must standardize across diverse markets.

These three dimensions are not mutually exclusive. A firm can combine them, for example, a company that sells high-end cycling equipment (product line segment) to competitive amateur cyclists (buyer group) in the Pacific Northwest (geographic market). The more dimensions along which the firm narrows its focus, the smaller its addressable market but the greater its potential depth of advantage within that market.

2.6.4 Focused Differentiation vs. Focused Cost Leadership

Once a firm has selected its target segment, it must still choose its basis of competitive advantage within that segment. This choice produces two distinct focus strategies (Porter, 1980).

Focused differentiation involves offering a product that is uniquely suited to the needs of the target segment, more specialized, more tailored, or more valuable to those customers than any broad-market offering (Porter, 1985). A boutique hotel that caters exclusively to business travelers, offering amenities like private meeting rooms, 24-hour room service, and express check-in, is pursuing focused differentiation. It does not compete on price; it competes on the depth of its understanding of what business travelers actually want and its willingness to deliver exactly that. The broad-market hotel chain, which must also accommodate families, tourists, and conference groups, cannot match this level of segment-specific tailoring without fundamentally restructuring its operations.

Focused cost leadership involves offering the lowest-cost product within the target segment, not across the entire market, but within the specific niche the firm serves (Porter, 1985). This is possible when the segment's needs are simpler or more predictable than those of the broad market, allowing the firm to strip away costs associated with features, services, or capabilities that the segment does not value. A no-frills airline that serves only short-haul routes between secondary cities is pursuing focused cost leadership. Its operating costs are lower because it avoids the hub infrastructure, long-haul fleet complexity, and premium services that full-service carriers must maintain. Within its narrow geographic and route focus, it can offer the lowest fares, not because it is a more efficient version of a major airline, but because it has structured its entire business around a narrower, less expensive set of operational requirements.

EX: Focused Cruise Lines — Young Singles vs. Seniors

The cruise industry provides a clear illustration of how focus strategies work and why they create value. A major cruise line like Royal Caribbean or Carnival operates broadly, attempting to appeal to families, couples, retirees, young adults, and group travelers simultaneously. This requires the ship to accommodate diverse and sometimes conflicting preferences: a family-friendly pool deck and a late-night dance club, early-bird dining and midnight buffets, children's programming and quiet reading lounges. The result is a product that serves many segments adequately but no single segment perfectly.

Now consider a cruise line that focuses exclusively on young single adults. Every design decision, from the ship's layout to the entertainment programming to the dining options, can be optimized for that segment. The onboard experience might feature high-energy nightlife venues, social mixer events, adventure excursions at ports of call, and a contemporary aesthetic throughout. There is no need to allocate deck space to a children's play area or to hire staff for a kids' club. Every dollar of investment and every square foot of ship space is directed toward what the target customer values most. The result is a differentiated experience that the broad-market cruise line simply cannot replicate without alienating its other customer segments. This is focused differentiation: the narrowing of the target market enables a level of tailoring that creates genuine additional value.

Alternatively, consider a cruise line focused on seniors. This segment may value tranquility, early dining times, accessible ship design, enrichment programming such as lectures and cooking classes, and a more relaxed pace of activities. A senior-focused cruise line could potentially achieve cost savings as well: entertainment could wind down earlier in the evening, reducing staffing costs for late-night operations. The bar and beverage program might be simpler. Shore excursion partnerships could be tailored to lower-intensity options. These are not enormous cost savings individually, but collectively they allow the focused firm to operate more efficiently for its segment than a broad-market competitor that must maintain a full range of offerings around the clock. This illustrates how focus can create both differentiation advantages (a product more perfectly suited to the segment) and cost advantages (operations streamlined for the segment's specific demands).

2.6.5 Risks of a Focus Strategy

Like all strategies, the focus approach carries risks that are inherent to the position it occupies. Three risks are particularly important.

A competitor may focus on an even narrower segment. If a firm can gain advantage by narrowing its focus from the broad market to a specific segment, then a rival can potentially gain further advantage by narrowing its focus even more (Porter, 1980). The cruise line focused on young singles might find itself challenged by a competitor focused specifically on young single professionals aged 25–35 who are interested in wellness and fitness travel. The more narrowly defined competitor can tailor its offering even more precisely, potentially out-differentiating the original focused firm within a sub-segment. This is the same logic that gave the focused firm its advantage in the first place; it simply works against it when applied recursively.

An industry-wide competitor may expand its product line into the segment. One of the greatest threats to a focused firm is that a broad-market competitor decides the segment is attractive enough to warrant dedicated attention (Porter, 1980). If Royal Caribbean launches a dedicated sub-brand for young adult cruises, it brings to that effort the financial resources, brand recognition, fleet assets, and marketing reach of a global corporation. The focused firm's advantages (deeper segment knowledge, tighter customer relationships) may not be sufficient to withstand an attack from a competitor with vastly greater resources. This risk is especially acute when the segment grows large enough to attract attention from major players who previously considered it too small to bother with.

The differences between the focused segment and the broader market may diminish. A focus strategy is only valuable when the target segment has needs that are meaningfully distinct from those of the general market (Porter, 1980). If those differences narrow, because customer preferences converge, because technology makes mass customization feasible, or because broader social trends homogenize tastes, the focused firm's advantage erodes. The product that was once uniquely suited to a distinct segment becomes merely one of many adequate offerings in an increasingly undifferentiated market. The firm's specialization, which was once its greatest asset, becomes a constraint that limits its ability to compete on equal footing with larger, more diversified rivals.

2.6.6 Summary: The Fundamental Strategies of Business Framework

The strategies examined across this chapter (differentiation, cost leadership, integrated cost/differentiation, focused differentiation, and focused cost leadership) constitute the fundamental strategies of business (Porter, 1980, 1985). Every firm that competes in a market, whether it recognizes it or not, occupies a position within this framework. The framework can be understood along two dimensions.

The first dimension is the **breadth of the target market**: broad or narrow. Firms competing across the entire industry are pursuing broad-market strategies (differentiation, cost leadership, or the integrated hybrid). Firms concentrating on a specific segment are pursuing focus strategies (focused differentiation or focused cost leadership).

The second dimension is the **basis for customer value**: distinctiveness or cost. Firms that compete by offering a product that is different from and better than competitors' are pursuing differentiation-based strategies (broad differentiation or focused differentiation). Firms that compete by offering a product at a lower cost than competitors are pursuing cost-based strategies (broad cost leadership or focused cost leadership). Firms that attempt to combine elements of both are pursuing the integrated hybrid strategy.

Together, these two dimensions produce five fundamental strategic positions:

Differentiation: competing on uniqueness across the broad market. **Cost leadership**: competing on low cost across the broad market. **Focused differentiation**: competing on uniqueness within a specific segment. **Focused cost leadership**: competing on low cost within a specific segment. **Integrated cost/differentiation**: combining elements of both across the broad market.

Each position involves distinct tradeoffs, requires different resources and capabilities, and carries its own set of risks (Porter, 1996). No position is inherently superior to the others; the right strategy depends on the firm's resources, the structure of the industry, the needs of customers, and the positions already occupied by competitors. What matters is that the firm makes a deliberate choice, commits to it with discipline, and understands the tradeoffs it has accepted. As Chapter 2.1 established, strategy without tradeoffs is not strategy at all. The fundamental strategies of business are the specific tradeoffs available to every firm — the choices that define how it will create and capture value in a competitive market.

References

Porter, M. E. (1980). *Competitive strategy: Techniques for analyzing industries and competitors.* Free Press.
Porter, M. E. (1985). *Competitive advantage: Creating and sustaining superior performance.* Free Press.
Porter, M. E. (1996). What is strategy? *Harvard Business Review, 74*(6), 61–78.

Chapter 3

Internal Analysis

3.1 Resource-Based View — *What makes resources strategically valuable?*

In the previous chapter, we established that firms compete through business-level strategies: differentiation, cost leadership, and their variants. We explored how firms create value by being different or being cheaper, and how strategic tradeoffs force firms to choose among these approaches. But we left a critical question largely unanswered: what determines whether a particular firm can actually execute a given strategy? Two firms in the same industry may both pursue differentiation, yet one earns extraordinary returns while the other struggles to break even. Two cost leaders may have access to the same suppliers and technologies, yet one achieves consistently lower costs than the other. What explains these differences?

The answer is that firms are not identical collections of interchangeable parts. Each firm possesses a unique bundle of resources and capabilities that shape what it can and cannot do. The strategic question is not just "what strategy should we pursue?" but "what do we have, and what can we do, that allows us to pursue that strategy better than anyone else?" This is the domain of the resource-based view, the theoretical lens that turns our analysis inward and examines the firm itself as the primary source of competitive advantage.

3.1.1 Why Internal Analysis Matters

External analysis, which we will cover in Chapter 4, examines the industry and broader environment in which a firm competes. It answers important questions about industry attractiveness, competitive forces, and macroeconomic trends. But external analysis cannot explain why firms within the same industry perform so differently.

Consider two industries with very different reputations. Pharmaceuticals is widely regarded as attractive, while steel is not. In recent years, U.S. pharmaceutical firms earned an average return on invested capital of roughly 29% while steel producers averaged about 7% (Damodaran, 2026). Yet firms within each industry vary widely around those averages, and the ranges overlap: the strongest steel producers can outearn pharmaceutical firms. Industry membership sets a backdrop. It does not determine the outcome.

Three decades of empirical work confirm the pattern. Researchers decompose the variance in firm profitability into the portion attributable to industry membership, to the corporate parent, and to the individual business itself. Rumelt (1991) found business-unit effects dwarfing industry effects, though his estimates varied with method. McGahan and Porter (1997) assigned industry a larger share but still found business-specific effects to be the dominant influence. Misangyi, Elms, Greckhamer, and LePine (2006), using a multilevel technique that accounts for businesses being nested within both corporations and industries, estimated business segment effects at roughly twice the relative importance of either industry or corporate effects, with industry and corporate effects almost identical to each other.

This shows managers are not passive beneficiaries of industry conditions — they are active architects of firm performance. Thus, management majors reading this text (or those aspiring toward entrepreneurship) can smile at the knowledge that they will have a real impact in their future careers.

While choosing the right industry matters, what a firm does with its resources and capabilities matters considerably more. Internal analysis is the set of tools and frameworks that help managers understand what is happening inside the firm that either creates or destroys competitive advantage.

3.1.2 The Resource-Based View (RBV)

The resource-based view is the dominant framework for conducting internal analysis in strategic management. Its central premise is deceptively simple: each firm is a collection of unique resources and capabilities, and this uniqueness is the basis for differing firm performance (Barney, 1991). Firms that develop superior resources and capabilities, relative to their competitors, are the ones that achieve sustained competitive advantage and above-average profits.

This perspective represents a fundamentally different way of thinking about competitive advantage than industry-level analysis. Rather than asking "what industry should we be in?" the resource-based view asks "what do we have, and what can we do, that our competitors cannot easily replicate?" The RBV directs managerial attention inward, toward the assets, skills, and organizational processes that make the firm distinctive.

The RBV has its roots in the work of economist Edith Penrose (1959), who argued that a firm is essentially a bundle of productive resources and that its growth depends on how effectively it deploys and develops those resources over time. Wernerfelt (1984) later coined the term "resource-based view" and reframed Penrose's insight as a basis for strategy. The framework was formalized as a theory of competitive advantage by Jay Barney in his seminal 1991 article, which established the criteria for determining which resources are strategically significant, criteria we will explore in detail in later sections of this chapter when we discuss the VRIO framework.

3.1.3 Two Key Assumptions of the Resource-Based View

The resource-based view rests on two foundational assumptions that distinguish it from other approaches to strategy. If either assumption does not hold, the RBV loses its explanatory power, so understanding them clearly is essential.

The first assumption is **resource heterogeneity**, the idea that resources and capabilities differ across firms. This may seem obvious, but many economic models treat firms as essentially interchangeable, differing only in size or market position. The RBV rejects this view. People are not interchangeable widgets. The software engineers at Apple possess different knowledge, skills, and creative abilities than the software engineers at Google, even though both groups hold similar job titles and work in the same industry. The manufacturing processes at Toyota differ from those at General Motors. The brand reputation of Nike is not the same as the brand reputation of Under Armour. Every firm's resource endowment is at least somewhat unique, and these differences are not trivial; they are the raw material from which competitive advantage is built.

The second assumption is **imperfect resource mobility**, the idea that some resources are difficult or impossible to transfer from one firm to another. If every resource could be freely bought, sold, and moved between firms, then any competitive advantage based on superior resources would be short-lived. A competitor could simply purchase whatever it was missing. But many of the most strategically important resources do not work this way. Corporate culture, for instance, cannot be purchased in a marketplace. It is embedded in the daily interactions, shared values, and accumulated history of a specific group of people working within a specific organization. An employee's individual skills might be mobile (they can leave and join a competitor) but the collective capability that emerges from the interactions among many employees within a particular organizational context is far less portable. Imperfect resource mobility is what allows resource-based advantages to persist over time.

Together, these two assumptions establish the logical foundation for the RBV: firms differ in what they have and what they can do (heterogeneity), and these differences can persist because the underlying resources are not easily transferred between firms (imperfect mobility). Without heterogeneity, there is nothing to differentiate one firm from another. Without imperfect mobility, any differences would be quickly arbitraged away.

3.1.4 Categories of Resources

Resources are the inputs that firms use to create goods and services. This is a deliberately broad definition, one that is regarded as both a strength and a weakness of the resource-based view. It is a strength because it allows the framework to encompass virtually anything that contributes to a firm's competitive position. It is a weakness because, without further structure, the concept of a "resource" is so expansive that it risks becoming analytically unwieldy.

To bring greater precision to internal analysis, Robert Grant (1991) proposed a classification that identifies six categories of resources, offering managers a practical checklist for systematically inventorying what a firm actually possesses.

Financial resources include the firm's cash, securities, borrowing capacity, and retained earnings. Financial resources determine a firm's ability to invest in new opportunities, weather downturns, fund research and development, and respond to competitive threats. Firms with strong financial resources have strategic flexibility that cash-strapped competitors lack. However, financial resources alone rarely constitute a competitive advantage because capital markets are generally efficient; firms with strong business prospects can usually raise capital. The advantage lies not in having money per se, but in the strategic options that financial reserves make possible.

Physical resources include the firm's plant, equipment, land, natural resource holdings, and geographic location. Because physical resources are visible and quantifiable, competitors can often acquire comparable assets; they are important but rarely the primary basis for sustained advantage unless they involve inherently scarce or unique assets.

Human resources encompass the skills, knowledge, experience, and capacity for communication and collaboration of the firm's employees. Their value lies not only in individual expertise but in employees' capacity to work together effectively. A team of individually talented people who cannot collaborate is far less valuable than a team whose members' skills complement and reinforce one another.

Human resources occupy a unique position because they are simultaneously indispensable and inherently mobile. Unlike a factory or a patent, an employee can choose to leave. When key employees depart, they take their knowledge and capabilities with them, potentially diminishing the firm's competitive position. This creates a fundamental tension: firms must invest in developing their human capital to build competitive advantage, but they must also work to retain it, since the advantage can walk out the door.

Technological resources include intellectual property such as patents, copyrights, and trade secrets, as well as proprietary production processes, research facilities, and the firm's accumulated technical knowledge and expertise. In technology-intensive industries, these resources can be decisive. A strong patent portfolio can provide years of legally protected competitive advantage, and proprietary production know-how can enable cost or quality advantages that competitors cannot reverse-engineer. Technological resources often overlap with both human and organizational resources, since much technical knowledge resides in the expertise of employees and the routines through which that expertise is applied.

Organizational resources include the firm's structure, management systems, planning processes, culture, and the internal coordination mechanisms that enable the firm to function as a coherent whole. Because they are embedded in the everyday routines and relationships of the organization rather than residing in any single asset, organizational resources are difficult to observe from outside the firm and difficult to replicate. A competitor can copy a reporting structure or a planning process on paper, but the tacit understanding and accumulated coordination that make those systems actually work develop only through years of shared experience. This is what makes organizational resources among the most strategically significant a firm can develop.

Reputational resources include the firm's brand names, its relationships with customers and suppliers, and the overall perception of the firm's products and conduct among external stakeholders. Grant treats reputation as a distinct category because it operates differently from other resources. Reputation is built incrementally through consistent behavior over time and can be destroyed rapidly by a single misstep. It influences customer purchasing decisions, supplier willingness to extend favorable terms, and the firm's ability to attract talent. A strong reputation acts as a signal that reduces uncertainty for those who interact with the firm, creating an advantage that is both valuable and slow to replicate.

3.1.5 Capabilities

While resources are the building blocks of competitive advantage, they rarely create value on their own. A pile of lumber, a set of power tools, and a team of workers do not automatically produce a house. Someone must organize these resources, coordinate their use, and direct them toward a productive outcome. This is the role of capabilities.

Capabilities are the combinations of procedures and expertise that a firm relies on to produce goods and services from its resources (Grant, 1991). Put more simply, capabilities represent what the firm *does* with what it *has*. They are the organizational routines, processes, and skills through which resources are deployed and coordinated to create value. If resources are the nouns of strategy, the things a firm possesses, capabilities are the verbs, the actions a firm can perform.

Management plays the central role in forming capabilities by bundling resources together in ways that produce coordinated action. A capability is not located in any single resource; it emerges from the interaction and integration of multiple resources under managerial direction. This is an important distinction because it means capabilities are inherently organizational; they belong to the firm as a whole, not to any individual person or asset within it.

EX: Chick-fil-A's Customer Service Capability

Chick-fil-A provides an instructive example of how resources are bundled into a capability. The company is widely recognized for its exceptional customer service, consistently ranking at or near the top of customer satisfaction surveys in the fast-food industry. But this service quality does not arise from any single resource. It is the product of a deliberate capability built from multiple integrated elements.

Chick-fil-A's hiring practices emphasize selecting employees who are naturally friendly and service-oriented. Its training programs instill specific behavioral standards, including the well-known practice of responding to customer thanks with "my pleasure" rather than the more casual "you're welcome" or "no problem." The company's franchise model selects owner-operators who are deeply invested in their individual locations, creating accountability and personal commitment to service quality that is difficult to achieve in a corporate-managed structure. Cultural reinforcement through leadership modeling, peer expectations, and organizational values sustains these behaviors over time.

No single element — the hiring criteria, the training scripts, the franchise model, or the cultural norms — constitutes the capability by itself. The capability emerges from their integration. A competitor could adopt the phrase "my pleasure," but without the supporting infrastructure of hiring practices, training systems, franchise incentives, and cultural reinforcement, the phrase would be hollow imitation rather than genuine capability.

This example illustrates a broader principle: capabilities are difficult to decompose into their individual components and even more difficult to reassemble from scratch. This complexity is one reason why capabilities, rather than individual resources, are often the more durable source of competitive advantage.

3.1.6 From Resources and Capabilities to Competitive Advantage

The resource-based view provides a clear conceptual progression. Firms possess resources of various kinds. Management bundles these resources together to form capabilities, the organizational processes and routines through which the firm creates value. When a capability is not only effective but superior relative to the competition, it becomes a core competency, a concept we will develop fully in the next sections of this chapter. Core competencies, in turn, are the foundation of sustained competitive advantage.

This progression — resources → capabilities → core competencies → competitive advantage — is the central logic of internal analysis. It explains why two firms in the same industry, facing the same external conditions, can produce dramatically different financial results. The firm with superior resources, organized into superior capabilities, which are deployed as core competencies aligned with its business-level strategy, will outperform the firm that lacks these internal advantages.

The remaining sections of this chapter develop this logic further. The value chain framework provides a structured way to identify *where* within the firm resources and capabilities create value. The VRIO framework provides the criteria for determining *which* capabilities qualify as core competencies. Path dependence and organizational culture explain *why* some capabilities are so difficult for competitors to replicate. And dynamic capabilities address how firms must continuously adapt their resource base as competitive conditions evolve.

References

Barney, J. B. (1991). Firm resources and sustained competitive advantage. *Journal of Management, 17*(1), 99–120.

Damodaran, A. (2026). *Margin/ROIC by sector (US)* [Data set]. New York University, Stern School of Business. https://pages.stern.nyu.edu/~adamodar/New_Home_Page/datafile/mgnroc.html

Grant, R. M. (1991). The resource-based theory of competitive advantage: Implications for strategy formulation. *California Management Review, 33*(3), 114–135.

McGahan, A. M., & Porter, M. E. (1997). How much does industry matter, really? *Strategic Management Journal, 18*(S1), 15–30.

Misangyi, V. F., Elms, H., Greckhamer, T., & LePine, J. A. (2006). A new perspective on a fundamental debate: A multilevel approach to industry, corporate, and business unit effects. *Strategic Management Journal, 27*(6), 571–590.

Penrose, E. T. (1959). *The theory of the growth of the firm.* John Wiley & Sons.

Rumelt, R. P. (1991). How much does industry matter? *Strategic Management Journal, 12*(3), 167–185.

Wernerfelt, B. (1984). A resource-based view of the firm. *Strategic Management Journal, 5*(2), 171–180.

3.2 Value Chain Analysis — *How do we use the value chain strategically?*

In Chapter 1, we introduced the value chain as a descriptive framework, a map of the primary and support activities that make up a firm's operations. That introduction gave us a shared vocabulary for understanding what firms do: inbound logistics, operations, outbound logistics, marketing and sales, service, and the support functions that enable them. Now, with the resource-based view and our understanding of competitive advantage in hand, we can use the value chain as an analytical tool.

The resource-based view tells us that competitive advantage stems from a firm's unique bundle of resources and capabilities, but it does not tell us where within the firm those resources and capabilities are deployed. A firm may know that it possesses a valuable and rare capability, yet still struggle to pinpoint exactly which activities that capability supports or how it translates into lower costs or greater customer value. Value chain analysis bridges this gap. By examining how activities connect, how they fit into a broader system of suppliers and partners, and how they can be configured to support different strategies, the value chain provides a map for locating precisely where value is created and where costs are incurred (Porter, 1985). If the resource-based view answers the question *what do we have?*, the value chain answers the question *where does it matter?*

3.2.1 Linkages and Coordination

One of the most important and often overlooked aspects of the value chain is the concept of linkages, the relationships and coordination between different activities (Porter, 1985). Competitive advantage frequently arises not from performing individual activities well in isolation, but from the way activities are connected and reinforce one another.

A linkage exists when the way one activity is performed affects the cost or effectiveness of another activity (Porter, 1985). For example, investing more in procurement to source higher-quality raw materials may reduce costs in operations by lowering defect rates and rework. Spending more on product design (technology development) may reduce after-sale service costs by creating a product that is more reliable and requires less repair. These tradeoffs are not visible if you examine each activity in isolation; they only become apparent when you analyze how the activities connect.

Coordination across activities is also critical. A firm that tightly integrates its demand forecasting (firm infrastructure) with its inbound logistics and operations can reduce inventory costs and improve responsiveness. Just-in-time manufacturing systems, for example, depend on precise coordination between procurement, inbound logistics, and operations. The competitive advantage of these systems comes not from any single activity but from the linkage between them.

Linkages also create barriers to imitation. A competitor can observe that a firm has excellent customer service or efficient operations, but it is much harder to see and replicate the specific way that dozens of activities are coordinated and optimized together (Porter, 1996). This is one reason why competitive advantages rooted in value chain coordination tend to be more sustainable than advantages based on any single activity.

3.2.2 The Value System

The value chain does not exist in isolation. Every firm's value chain is embedded in a larger stream of activities that Porter (1985) called the value system. The value system includes the value chains of suppliers (who provide inputs to the firm), the firm itself, distribution channel partners (who help deliver the product to customers), and ultimately the buyers.

Understanding the value system is important because a firm's competitive position is affected not only by its own activities, but by how well it coordinates with the activities of others in the system. Consider the coffee industry as an example. The value system for a cup of coffee includes farm production, exporters and traders, processing and roasting, retail distribution, and the coffee shop that serves the final product. Each stage adds value, and each stage captures a different share of the total profit available in the system.

This leads to the concept of a **profit pool**, the total profit earned across all stages of the value system (Gadiesh & Gilbert, 1998). Profit is not distributed equally across the value system. In the coffee industry, for instance, farm producers and exporters capture relatively thin margins, while processors and coffee shops capture significantly larger shares. Understanding where profit pools are deepest in the value system can inform strategic decisions about where to compete and whether to integrate vertically into adjacent stages, a topic we will explore in greater depth when we turn to industry and external environment analysis.

3.2.3 Using Value Chain Analysis

Value chain analysis is a practical tool that managers use to diagnose competitive advantage and identify opportunities for improvement. The process typically involves several steps. First, the firm identifies its primary and support activities, being as specific as possible about what it actually does. Second, it analyzes the cost and value contribution of each activity, looking for activities that are disproportionately expensive or that create disproportionate value. Third, it examines linkages between activities to identify coordination opportunities. Finally, it compares its value chain to those of competitors to identify where differences exist and whether those differences are sources of advantage or disadvantage.

EX: Starbucks' Value Chain

In its inbound logistics, Starbucks purchases beans directly from farmers, maintaining a roasting plant and close partnerships with conservation organizations. Its operations emphasize consistent quality across thousands of locations through standardized processes. Outbound logistics includes global distribution channels along with delivery and pick-up options. Marketing and sales leverages its rewards program, social media presence, and brand partnerships. And its service extends beyond the product itself to include the in-store experience, mobile ordering, and community involvement. On the support side, Starbucks invests heavily in environmentally sustainable infrastructure, extensive employee training and development programs, mobile and digital technology, and ethical sourcing through its direct trade procurement program. The competitive advantage of Starbucks comes not from any one of these activities alone, but from how they are all configured and coordinated to deliver a consistent, premium coffee experience.

3.2.4 Strategic Implications

Value chain analysis connects directly to the strategic concepts we covered in the previous chapter. A firm pursuing a cost advantage will configure its value chain to minimize costs across activities, investing in efficient operations, streamlining logistics, and leveraging economies of scale in procurement (Porter, 1985). A firm pursuing differentiation will configure its value chain to maximize the unique value it delivers, investing in product design, superior service, and marketing that communicates its distinctive qualities.

The value chain also helps explain why firms within the same industry can follow very different strategies and still be successful. Two airlines may have similar primary activities (they both fly planes from one city to another) but their value chains can look very different. One might invest heavily in service, comfortable seating, and in-flight amenities, configuring its value chain around differentiation. The other might strip out every unnecessary cost, optimize turnaround times, and automate as many processes as possible, configuring its value chain around cost leadership. The value chain framework makes these strategic differences visible and analyzable (Porter, 1996).

Finally, value chain analysis provides the foundation for many of the more advanced strategic frameworks explored later in this chapter and beyond. The VRIO framework (Chapter 3.3) tests whether the capabilities behind a firm's activities are valuable, rare, costly to imitate, and organized to be exploited. Decisions about vertical integration, whether to bring supplier or distributor activities inside the firm, are fundamentally questions about reconfiguring the value chain. Industry analysis through Porter's Five Forces considers how forces like supplier power and buyer power affect the profitability of activities across the value system (Porter, 1980). In each case, the value chain provides the underlying map of firm activities that makes deeper strategic analysis possible.

References

Gadiesh, O., & Gilbert, J. L. (1998). Profit pools: A fresh look at strategy. *Harvard Business Review, 76*(3), 139–147.

Porter, M. E. (1980). *Competitive strategy: Techniques for analyzing industries and competitors.* Free Press.

Porter, M. E. (1985). *Competitive advantage: Creating and sustaining superior performance.* Free Press.

Porter, M. E. (1996). What is strategy? *Harvard Business Review, 74*(6), 61–78.

3.3 Core Competencies — *What are a firm's critical capabilities?*

The previous sections established that firms possess unique bundles of resources and capabilities, and that the value chain reveals where those resources and capabilities are deployed. But not all capabilities are created equal. Every firm has dozens, perhaps hundreds, of capabilities, from processing payroll to answering customer phone calls to managing supply contracts. Most of these are necessary for the firm to function, but they do not set the firm apart from its competitors. The strategic question is: which of a firm's capabilities are so superior, so distinctive, and so difficult to replicate that they serve as the foundation for sustained competitive advantage? These are the firm's core competencies.

3.3.1 The Progression: Resources → Capabilities → Core Competencies

Core competencies are best understood as the culmination of the conceptual progression introduced in Chapter 3.1. Firms begin with resources, the financial, physical, human, technological, organizational, and reputational inputs available to them. Management bundles these resources together to form capabilities, the organizational routines and processes through which the firm creates value. When a capability is not merely functional but genuinely superior relative to what competitors can do, it rises to the level of a core competency. Core competencies are, in essence, the capabilities that matter most, the ones that differentiate the firm and drive its competitive advantage (Grant, 1991; Prahalad & Hamel, 1990).

This distinction matters because it prevents managers from treating every competent activity as a strategic asset. A firm may be perfectly adequate at accounting, facilities maintenance, and employee scheduling without any of these constituting a core competency. Core competencies are reserved for the capabilities that meet a more demanding standard, one that determines whether the capability can sustain competitive advantage over time. That standard is the VRIO framework.

3.3.2 The VRIN → VRIO Framework

The criteria for identifying core competencies were originally articulated by Jay Barney (1991) in his foundational resource-based view article. Barney proposed that for a resource or capability to be a source of sustained competitive advantage, it must be valuable, rare, and difficult to imitate, with no strategically equivalent substitutes, a framework commonly abbreviated as VRIN.

Over time, the non-substitutability criterion was folded into the broader concept of inimitability, on the logic that if a capability can be effectively substituted, it is, in practical terms, imitable in its competitive effect. Simultaneously, scholars recognized that possessing a valuable, rare, and inimitable capability is insufficient if the firm is not structured to capture value from it, leading to the addition of an "organized to exploit" criterion. The result is VRIN evolved into VRIO: Valuable, Rare, costly to Imitate, and Organized to exploit (Barney, 1995).

These four criteria are the standard by which a capability is judged a core competency. Barney presented them in the order the acronym preserves, valuable first and organized last, as a sequential test that begins with the broadest question and narrows from there. What follows examines each criterion in depth, but reaches them by a different route, one that begins where managers and students naturally begin: with what the firm already does well.

3.3.3 The Core Competency Method

> *"The diversified corporation is a large tree... The root system that provides nourishment, sustenance, and stability is the core competence." — C.K. Prahalad & Gary Hamel*

Applied in its original order, VRIO begins with the broadest question, is it valuable?, and narrows from there. That first step is where managers and students tend to stall. Facing everything a firm owns and does, they either weigh resources too generic to matter ("our computers," "our employees") or leap to capabilities they already assume are important, skipping the very screen the framework exists to provide.

The core competency method begins somewhere more natural: with what the firm plainly does well. Ask "what is this firm good at?" and people readily name places where it beats its rivals, and in doing so they have already, if roughly, filtered for something valuable and something rare. Nobody lists a strength that is irrelevant or that every competitor shares. The method works with that instinct instead of against it.

The traditional approach builds from the bottom up: start with resources, decide which are valuable, then which are rare, and so on. The core competency method runs the other way. It starts at the top, with a visible strength, and works down to the capabilities and resources that produce it, applying the VRIO tests only once the source of the advantage is clear. The bottom-up approach still has its place: when a firm wants to inventory its resources comprehensively and surface assets it has not yet recognized as competencies, working upward is the more systematic sweep, a backstop to the core competency method rather than a rival to it.

The method runs in six steps: two to locate the competency and its sources, and four to test it.

Step 1: Identify the core competency. Start with the question the method is built on: what does the firm do better than its competitors? This roots the analysis in something observable, a strength the firm and its stakeholders would recognize on their own, rather than in a theoretical list of assets.

Starting from a known strength carries one hazard: survivorship bias, the temptation to assume that because a capability looks like a strength, it must be valuable and rare. The four tests exist to check that assumption rather than take it on faith, and the first two, value and rarity, meet it head-on.

Step 2: Trace the core competency to its sources. Then ask: how does the firm do it better? As we saw in Chapter 3.1, core competencies are built from capabilities, which are themselves bundles of resources.

Finding the how is the hardest part of the method, because the strength you started with is a result, and results rarely announce their causes. The honest first answer is usually too vague to test: "great service," "a strong brand," "products people love." Each just restates the outcome instead of naming the machinery that produces it. The work of this step is to keep asking what would have to be true for that outcome to hold, peeling back one layer at a time until you reach something concrete enough to examine.

Separate the two layers deliberately. First name the capability: the repeatable activity the firm performs unusually well, how it designs, sources, sells, or serves. Then name the resources that activity draws on: the particular assets, relationships, knowledge, and people that make it work. The value chain from Chapter 3.2 is a natural map here, because it pushes you to point at the activities that actually generate the advantage rather than settling for a general sense that the firm is "good."

Expect the answer to be a system, not a single thing. A strength that holds up under scrutiny usually rests on several capabilities and resources reinforcing one another, which is part of why rivals struggle to copy it. Pinning them down now is what makes the rest of the method work: whether the advantage is rare, durable, or fully exploited depends on these specific sources, not on the name of the strength.

Step 3: Is it (still) Valuable? Value comes first, but because the analysis began with a recognized strength, it is largely a given: a capability the firm and its customers already treat as an advantage is valuable now. The real question is whether it will stay that way.

Value is defined relative to the competitive environment. A capability is valuable only while it helps the firm seize an opportunity or fend off a threat that still matters in its market. The same test screens out traits that are distinctive but strategically inert: a firm may employ an unusual number of left-handed people, but unless that helps it serve customers, cut costs, or counter a threat, it is not an advantage.

Asking about value first, and framing it around the future, guards against a specific trap: excelling at something the market is leaving behind. A firm that is the world's best maker of film cameras might pass every other test, rare, hard to imitate, fully exploited, and still fail this one, because demand has collapsed. The diagnosis is *obsolescent strength.*

Step 4: Is it Rare? With value confirmed, the next question is whether the capability is scarce among competitors. A capability can be genuinely valuable yet still fail to produce competitive advantage if every competitor possesses it. In that case, the capability is simply a requirement for competing, an industry norm rather than a differentiating strength. The result is competitive parity: the firm matches its competitors but does not surpass them.

In some cases, rarity rests on an underlying absolute scarcity, such as a firm that controls one of the world's few commercially viable diamond mines. In others the scarcity is local, as when a quarry sits beside a growing city while competitors' deposits lie too far away to haul profitably. Such cases rarely cause confusion in practice.

More often, rarity is misjudged because it is not simply a question of whether competitors have the resource at all, but of nature and degree. Consider reputation. Nearly every established firm has a reputation, so asking whether competitors have reputations is the wrong question. The right question is whether many competitors have a reputation similar to the one held by the firm being analyzed. Framed this way, rarity becomes a matter of how the resource compares, not merely whether it exists elsewhere.

The degree or quality of a resource is therefore central to assessing its rarity. A manufacturer recognized as the highest-quality producer in its field holds a rare reputation for quality, even though many competitors also have reputations for quality. The reputation is rare not because quality reputations are uncommon but because being regarded as the best is uncommon. The same logic applies broadly: a resource that many firms possess in ordinary measure can still be rare for the firm that holds it at an exceptional level.

Whether rarity stems from absolute scarcity, local scarcity, or exceptional degree, the competitive implication is the same: a capability that is widely available at a comparable level cannot be the basis for above-average performance.

Step 5: Can competition Imitate it? A valuable, rare capability produces an advantage, but that advantage endures only if competitors cannot easily copy it. If they can, the lead is temporary: the capability spreads, becomes an industry best practice, and the advantage dissipates.

Some capabilities resist imitation because they are inherently complex, depend on a firm's particular history, or work for reasons even the firm cannot fully articulate. We take up these mechanisms, path dependence, causal ambiguity, and social complexity, later in the chapter. The point here is simply that how long an advantage lasts tracks how hard its source is to reproduce.

This step also absorbs non-substitutability, the "N" of the original VRIN framework. A competitor need not copy a capability directly; it can neutralize the advantage by reaching the same result another way. Barnes & Noble's national network of stores was costly to replicate, so Amazon did not try. It substituted an online platform that reached more customers at a fraction of the cost. Substitutes are dangerous precisely because they arrive from unexpected directions, and a firm guarding against direct imitation may not see them coming.

If the capability can be readily copied or substituted, the diagnosis is *temporary advantage*: the firm leads for now, but the lead is exposed.

Step 6: Organized to capture? The last test asks whether the firm is organized to turn the competency into results. A capability that is valuable, rare, and hard to copy still yields nothing if the firm is not built to use it. McDonald's owns one of the world's most recognizable brands, but the brand does not print money on its own. The company captures its value by placing restaurants where travelers, unsure of local options, reach for a name they trust: airports, highway exits, tourist districts. The location strategy is what turns brand recognition into profit.

Organization is more than strategy. It is management systems, incentives, reporting lines, and everyday routines. A drug company may hire brilliant scientists yet let bureaucracy stall its best candidates. A tech firm may build a breakthrough algorithm its salespeople cannot explain to customers. In each case the advantage exists but goes unused.

If the firm is not organized to exploit the competency, the diagnosis is *underexploited potential*: a real strength the firm fails to convert into results. Because this is usually within management's direct control, it is often the most immediately actionable finding in a strategic analysis.

When a competency clears all four tests, still valuable, rare, costly to imitate, and fully exploited, the diagnosis is *sustainable competitive advantage*: it can support above-average performance over time.

3.3.3.1 Applying the Core Competency Method

Valuable?	Rare?	Difficult/Costly to Imitate?	Organized to Exploit?	Competitive Implication
No	No	—	—	No competitive advantage
No	Yes	—	—	Obsolescent strength
Yes	No	—	—	Competitive parity
Yes	Yes	No	—	Temporary competitive advantage
Yes	Yes	Yes	No	Underexploited potential
Yes	Yes	Yes	Yes	Sustainable competitive advantage

EX: Applying the Core Competency Method to Trader Joe's

Trader Joe's competes in the grocery business, an industry defined by thin margins and intense price competition, yet it earns some of the highest sales per square foot of any retailer in the country. An outside observer might name several strengths: low prices, an unusually friendly and helpful staff, famously loyal customers, and a lineup of distinctive products shoppers love. A full analysis would test each of these, but the process is the same for every one, so this example works through just one: its distinctive products.

Step 1: Identify the core competency. Start with: what does Trader Joe's do better than its competitors? Ask a regular shopper and the answer comes back fast — the products. Trader Joe's offers a lineup of distinctive, high-quality items that customers love, from seasonal snacks to frozen meals to pantry staples they cannot find at an ordinary grocer. Shoppers do not merely tolerate the selection; they seek it out, treating specific items as a reason to make the trip and recommending them to friends. That enthusiasm is visible and widely recognized, which is exactly what this step is looking for: a strength the firm clearly holds relative to rivals, the kind a shopper or a competitor would name without hesitation. Offering products customers love is the claim the rest of the method will examine, beginning by tracing where that strength comes from.

Step 2: Trace the core competency to its sources. How does Trader Joe's offer products customers love? The capability is developing and curating its own lineup of distinctive items rather than reselling the same national brands every grocer carries. That capability draws on a specific set of resources: decades of direct relationships with suppliers, an in-house product-development operation, and a deliberately small, frequently rotating assortment of only a few thousand items, tied together by a private-label model under which roughly four of five items carry the Trader Joe's name. No single one of these produces the strength; they work as a system, which is part of why rivals struggle to copy it. The tests that follow judge that system, not the phrase "products customers love."

Step 3: Is it (still) Valuable? Largely a given, because the analysis began with a strength customers already reward: the products drive industry-leading sales per square foot and unusually strong loyalty. The real question is whether that will hold. Demand for distinctive, discovery-oriented grocery products shows no sign of collapsing, and because the items are exclusive, the competency insulates Trader Joe's from the direct price comparisons that pressure conventional grocers. This is not an obsolescent strength; the market still rewards it.

Step 4: Is it Rare? Yes, though the rarity is a matter of degree rather than simple presence. Nearly every grocer stocks a few interesting or exclusive items, so asking whether competitors carry any distinctive products is the wrong question; almost all of them do. The right question is whether any competitor offers distinctive products at Trader Joe's level, and here few come close. For most chains, the distinctive items are a small accent on a sprawling, national-brand-dominated shelf, a specialty aisle a shopper might browse but would rarely make the trip for. At Trader Joe's the distinctive products are not an accent but the entire assortment, curated and rotated so that the store itself becomes the destination. A resource many firms hold in ordinary measure can still be rare for the firm that holds it at an exceptional level, and that is the case here: it is not that rivals lack distinctive products, but that none has built its whole identity around them the way Trader Joe's has.

Step 5: Can competitors Imitate it? Largely no. A rival cannot simply decide to offer distinctive products; doing so requires the supplier relationships and own-label operation Trader Joe's has built over decades, costly to replicate and tied to the firm's history. The deliberately small assortment reinforces the barrier: because Trader Joe's concentrates its entire volume across only a few thousand items, it buys each in far larger quantities than a conventional grocer, earning leverage with suppliers and lower per-unit costs. A competitor who wanted to match that buying power would have to drop the national-brand variety that draws much of its own traffic, along with the slotting-fee revenue that comes with it. Substitution is the subtler threat: Aldi and Costco's Kirkland line show that heavy own-label assortments can be built by other routes. What neither has matched is the combination of distinctiveness and discovery, a small, rotating selection customers treat as a destination rather than a stock-up trip. A genuine substitute would need some other way to generate that loyalty, and none has done so at scale.

Step 6: Organized to exploit it? Yes. Distinctive products only pay off if the firm keeps the value they create rather than handing it to rivals, and Trader Joe's is structured to do exactly that. Because the items are own-label, a customer who wants them has to shop at Trader Joe's, and that exclusivity converts enthusiasm directly into loyalty and margin. The organization is aligned behind this: products developed in-house, sourcing direct from suppliers, and a refusal to pay the slotting fees national brands charge for shelf space. A grocer organized around stocking every national brand could not capture the same value.

Passing all four tests, Trader Joe's ability to offer distinctive products customers love yields a *sustainable competitive advantage*, which is why a chain with small stores and a fraction of a normal grocer's selection continues to outperform far larger competitors.

3.3.4 Core Competencies and Business-Level Strategy

The relationship between core competencies and business-level strategy is direct and consequential. The business-level strategies examined in Chapter 2 (differentiation, cost leadership, and their focus variants) each require different types of core competencies to execute effectively.

Firms pursuing a cost leadership strategy need core competencies that drive efficiency and cost reduction. These competencies tend to reside in operations, logistics, and procurement, the value chain activities most directly responsible for producing and delivering the product at the lowest possible cost (Porter, 1985). Walmart's legendary inventory management system, Toyota's lean manufacturing processes, and Amazon's fulfillment logistics infrastructure are all core competencies that support cost leadership by enabling these firms to operate at lower cost than their competitors.

Firms pursuing a differentiation strategy need core competencies that create unique value for customers. These competencies are more likely to be found in research and development, marketing, service, and product design, the value chain activities that shape the customer's perception of the product's distinctiveness. Apple's design capability, Ritz-Carlton's service culture, and Nike's brand management are core competencies that support differentiation by making these firms' products worth paying more for.

Firms pursuing focus strategies need core competencies that are specifically aligned with the needs of their target segment. A focused differentiator serving high-end audiophiles needs deep expertise in acoustic engineering and premium materials sourcing. A focused cost leader serving budget-conscious college students needs streamlined operations and aggressive procurement tailored to that segment's price sensitivity. The core competency must be not just generally strong but specifically relevant to the narrow market the firm has chosen to serve.

This alignment between core competencies and business-level strategy is not coincidental; it is a strategic imperative. A firm whose core competencies do not match its chosen strategy faces an uncomfortable reality: either it must build new competencies to support its strategy (a lengthy and uncertain process), or it must shift its strategy to one that its existing competencies can support. Misalignment between strategy and competencies is one of the most common causes of strategic failure.

3.3.5 Protecting and Leveraging Core Competencies

Identifying and developing core competencies is only half the challenge. Firms must also protect them from erosion and leverage them for continued advantage. Several principles guide this effort.

Human capital as a critical, and vulnerable, core competency. Employee knowledge, skills, and expertise are frequently at the heart of a firm's competitive advantage. A law firm's reputation rests on the talent of its partners. A technology company's innovation pipeline depends on the creativity of its engineers. A consulting firm's value proposition is built on the intellectual capital of its consultants. In each case, the firm's core competency is embodied in people — and people, unlike patents or factories, can leave.

The departure of key employees represents one of the most direct threats to a firm's competitive position. When a senior engineer leaves a technology firm and joins a competitor, they take with them not only their individual expertise but also their knowledge of the firm's processes, projects, and strategic direction. Firms must therefore invest not only in developing human capital but also in retaining it, through competitive compensation, meaningful work, career development opportunities, and an organizational culture that makes talented people want to stay. The most sophisticated firms also work to distribute critical knowledge across multiple employees and embed it in organizational routines and systems, reducing their vulnerability to any single departure.

Reinvesting above-average profits. Core competencies generate above-average profits, and those profits create the opportunity for reinvestment. Firms that channel above-average returns back into the resources and capabilities that produced them create a virtuous cycle: superior capabilities generate superior profits, which fund further capability development, which sustains the competitive advantage over time. Firms that instead divert profits to unrelated activities or distribute them entirely to shareholders risk starving the very capabilities that made the profits possible in the first place.

Building complementary assets. Core competencies are strengthened when they are surrounded by complementary assets, supporting resources and capabilities that enhance the competency's effectiveness and make it harder for competitors to replicate the overall system (Teece, Pisano, & Shuen, 1997). A pharmaceutical company's drug development competency is complemented by its regulatory expertise, clinical trial management capabilities, and relationships with physicians and hospitals. An e-commerce company's logistics competency is complemented by its data analytics capabilities, customer interface design, and supplier network. Each complementary asset reinforces the core competency and adds another layer of complexity that competitors must overcome to match the firm's overall capability.

Together, these protective measures — retaining human capital, reinvesting profits, and building complementary assets — help ensure that core competencies remain a source of sustained competitive advantage rather than a temporary lead that erodes over time. As the following sections will discuss, the mechanisms that make competencies difficult to imitate (path dependence, social complexity, and organizational culture) provide additional layers of protection. But these mechanisms are not self-sustaining. They require deliberate managerial attention and continued investment to remain effective as competitive conditions evolve.

References

Barney, J. B. (1991). Firm resources and sustained competitive advantage. *Journal of Management, 17*(1), 99–120.

Barney, J. B. (1995). Looking inside for competitive advantage. *Academy of Management Executive, 9*(4), 49–61.

Grant, R. M. (1991). The resource-based theory of competitive advantage: Implications for strategy formulation. *California Management Review, 33*(3), 114–135.

Porter, M. E. (1985). *Competitive advantage: Creating and sustaining superior performance.* Free Press.

Prahalad, C. K., & Hamel, G. (1990). The core competence of the corporation. *Harvard Business Review, 68*(3), 79–91.

Teece, D. J., Pisano, G., & Shuen, A. (1997). Dynamic capabilities and strategic management. *Strategic Management Journal, 18*(7), 509–533.

3.4 Path Dependence — *Why can't resources be easily imitated?*

The previous section introduced the "costly to imitate" criterion as the decisive test separating temporary competitive advantages from sustainable ones. A capability that is valuable, rare, and easy to copy will generate an advantage that competitors quickly erode. A capability that is valuable, rare, and genuinely difficult to replicate can sustain above-average performance for years or even decades. But this raises a question that the VRIO framework itself does not fully answer: *why* are some capabilities so difficult to imitate? What is it about certain resources and organizational processes that makes them resistant to replication, even when competitors can clearly see the advantage and are motivated to copy it?

The answer lies in the concept of path dependence, the idea that competitive advantages are built over time through a unique sequence of decisions, investments, experiences, and circumstances that cannot simply be purchased or reproduced. Path dependence explains why two firms can start with similar ambitions, operate in the same industry, and observe each other's strategies, yet end up with profoundly different capabilities. The advantage held by the leading firm is not merely a collection of assets that could be assembled from a catalog; it is the accumulated product of a specific journey that unfolded over time, one step building on the last, in ways that no competitor can retrace.

3.4.1 What Is Path Dependence?

> *History matters. We cannot understand today's choices without looking at the path that led us here. — Douglass North, Nobel Economist*

Path dependence, in its simplest form, means that where you end up depends on how you got there. A firm's current capabilities are not just a function of what it decides to do today; they are shaped by every decision, investment, accident, and adaptation that preceded this moment. The firm's history constrains and enables its present options in ways that cannot be separated from the sequence of events that produced them.

Consider an analogy. Two people may both be fluent in Mandarin, but the person who grew up speaking it at home possesses a different kind of fluency (deeper, more intuitive, more culturally embedded) than the person who learned it in a classroom at age thirty. The end result might appear similar on a proficiency test, but the underlying capability is qualitatively different, produced by a fundamentally different path. The same logic applies to firms. Two companies may both have strong customer service, but the firm that built its service culture over twenty years of careful hiring, training, and cultural reinforcement possesses a capability that is qualitatively different from, and more resilient than, the one assembled through a rapid initiative launched last quarter.

The strategic implication is that capabilities shaped by path dependence cannot simply be purchased or replicated on demand. A competitor cannot write a check to acquire twenty years of organizational learning. It cannot compress a decade of trust-building between employees and managers into a six-month program. The time, sequence, and context in which a capability developed are inseparable from the capability itself.

3.4.2 Sources of Path Dependence

Scholars have identified three primary mechanisms through which path dependence creates barriers to imitation: unique historical conditions, causal ambiguity, and social complexity (Barney, 1991; Dierickx & Cool, 1989). Each operates differently, but all share the common feature of making a firm's capabilities resistant to replication.

Unique historical conditions. Some competitive advantages originate in circumstances that were specific to a particular time and place and that no longer exist for others to exploit. Being in the right place at the right time, and making the right decisions given those circumstances, can create advantages that competitors who arrived later simply cannot access.

> **EX: Coca-Cola's Historical Advantage**
>
> Coca-Cola's brand was established in the late nineteenth century, during a period when national advertising was just emerging and consumer brand loyalty in soft drinks was being formed for the first time. A company entering the soft drink market today faces an entirely different competitive landscape, one in which consumer attention is fragmented across thousands of brands, advertising is exponentially more expensive relative to its reach, and shelf space is fiercely contested. Coca-Cola's brand recognition was built under historical conditions that no longer exist, and no amount of investment can recreate those conditions. The advantage is real, visible, and well-understood by competitors, yet it cannot be replicated because the historical window in which it was formed has closed.

Unique historical conditions also encompass geographic advantages (a firm that secured a prime location before the area became desirable), regulatory advantages (a firm that obtained licenses or patents under a previous regulatory regime), and relational advantages (a firm that forged partnerships with key suppliers or distributors when those partners were still small and available). In each case, the advantage derives not from a decision that was inherently brilliant but from the fact that the decision was made at a specific moment that is no longer available to others.

Causal ambiguity. Some competitive advantages are difficult to imitate because competitors, and sometimes even the firm itself, cannot clearly identify what causes the advantage. The link between the firm's resources and its superior performance is ambiguous, making it impossible to determine which specific factors to replicate (Lippman & Rumelt, 1982; Reed & DeFillippi, 1990).

Causal ambiguity arises most often when a competitive advantage results from the interaction of many factors working together in complex ways. A firm may have superior product quality, but the quality may depend on an intricate combination of supplier relationships, production processes, quality control routines, employee expertise, and managerial oversight. An outside observer can see the result (the product is better) but cannot disentangle which elements are essential and which are incidental. Even insiders may disagree about what drives the advantage. Is it the raw materials? The equipment calibration? The experience of the floor supervisor? The informal communication patterns between the design team and the production line? When no one can confidently specify the causal mechanism, imitation becomes a matter of guesswork.

This ambiguity is a powerful barrier to imitation precisely because it denies competitors a blueprint. A firm attempting to replicate an ambiguous advantage must essentially guess which resources and processes matter, invest in building or acquiring them, and hope that the combination produces a similar result. The probability of getting this right, of reconstructing the exact combination of factors from the outside, is extremely low, particularly when the factors interact in non-obvious ways.

Social complexity. The third source of path dependence involves competitive advantages that are rooted in complex social phenomena: interpersonal relationships, trust, shared norms, organizational culture, and the accumulated routines that govern how people work together within the firm. These phenomena are inherently difficult to imitate because they emerge organically from human interaction over time and cannot be engineered on command.

Trust between employees and management, for example, is built through years of consistent behavior: keeping promises, treating people fairly, communicating transparently, and following through on commitments even when it is costly. A competitor cannot manufacture this trust by issuing a memo or revising its employee handbook. The informal knowledge-sharing networks that develop when employees have worked together for years (knowing who has expertise in which areas, who can be relied on in a crisis, who works well together on cross-functional teams) cannot be replicated by redesigning an organizational chart. These social structures are real, they create tangible value, and they are extraordinarily resistant to imitation because they are the product of countless small interactions accumulated over time.

Social complexity is closely related to organizational culture, which we will examine in detail in the next section. For now, the essential point is that when a competitive advantage is embedded in the social fabric of an organization, in the way people relate to each other, collaborate, resolve conflicts, and coordinate their efforts, it is protected by a barrier that no amount of money or managerial initiative can easily breach. This is why culture is the most commonly cited example of a difficult-to-imitate resource in the strategic management literature.

3.4.3 Why Path Dependence Matters for Strategy

Path dependence provides the theoretical foundation for the "costly to imitate" criterion in the VRIO framework. Without path dependence, the VRIO framework would have difficulty explaining why imitation is costly. After all, if a competitor can observe a firm's advantage and has the financial resources to invest in replicating it, what prevents them from doing so? The answer is that the advantage is not a static asset that can be copied; it is the product of a historical process that cannot be repeated.

This insight has several practical implications. First, it explains why competitive advantages can persist even in industries with intense competition and well-resourced rivals. Google's competitors can see that Google has a superior search algorithm, but the algorithm's superiority is the product of more than two decades of continuous development, user feedback integration, and data accumulation that cannot be compressed into a shorter timeline. Second, path dependence explains why acquisitions do not always transfer capabilities successfully. Buying a company gives you its assets, but it does not guarantee that the capabilities embedded in that company's unique history, culture, and social relationships will survive the transition to new ownership. Third, path dependence reinforces a central message of internal analysis: competitive advantage is deeply embedded in the firm's history and social fabric, which makes it both more durable and more difficult to build from scratch than external analysis alone might suggest.

3.4.4 Resource Stocks: Inflows and Outflows

A firm's resource base is not static; it is constantly in flux. Firms continuously acquire new resources: they hire employees, purchase equipment, develop intellectual property, and build relationships with customers and suppliers. At the same time, firms lose resources through turnover, depreciation, obsolescence, and organizational forgetting. Employees leave and take their knowledge with them. Skills that are not practiced atrophy. Customer relationships that are not actively maintained weaken over time.

A useful way to think about this dynamic is the metaphor of a leaky bucket. A firm's stock of resources is like a bucket of water that is simultaneously being filled and drained. Maintaining the level of water requires continuous investment. The moment a firm stops filling the bucket, the water level begins to drop.

This metaphor carries an important strategic implication: a firm cannot simply build a capability and then stop investing in it. The firm that developed an outstanding customer service culture ten years ago will not automatically retain that culture today if it has stopped investing in the hiring practices, training programs, and cultural reinforcement that built it. Path dependence is not a one-time phenomenon but a continuous process. The firm's current capabilities are the result of past path-dependent investments, and its future capabilities will depend on the investments it makes today.

3.4.5 Competitive Advantages Are Not Permanent

Path dependence helps explain why some competitive advantages are durable, but it does not make them permanent. Even the most deeply embedded advantages can erode over time.

Competitors may catch up. Although path dependence makes rapid imitation difficult, it does not make imitation impossible. A determined competitor with sufficient resources and patience can, over years or decades, develop capabilities that approximate the leader's advantage. An advantage that was rare and inimitable ten years ago may become an industry standard if enough competitors invest long enough in developing similar capabilities.

The external environment may shift what is strategically important. A capability that is valuable today may become irrelevant if customer preferences change, new technologies emerge, or regulatory conditions evolve. Path dependence protects the capability from imitation, but it does not protect it from obsolescence. As discussed in Chapter 3.3, a firm can be perfectly organized to exploit a rare, difficult-to-imitate capability that the market no longer cares about. Path dependence can make this problem worse: the very investments that made the capability strong can make the firm reluctant to abandon it even when the strategic landscape has shifted.

Because competitive advantages are not permanently sustainable, firms must pursue a dual mandate: exploit current advantages while simultaneously developing new ones (March, 1991).

EX: Walmart and Apple — Exploitation and Exploration

Walmart illustrates the exploitation side of this equation. Its inventory management system — built over decades through continuous investment in logistics technology, supplier integration, and data analytics — is a path-dependent capability that has sustained its cost leadership position for years. But Walmart has not rested on this advantage. It has continuously improved its inventory management, incorporating new technologies such as RFID tracking and predictive analytics as they became available. Each improvement builds on the previous one, extending the firm's advantage incrementally while making it more difficult for competitors to replicate the entire accumulated system. This is exploitation: making a strong capability even stronger over time.

Apple illustrates the exploration side. Apple built its initial competitive advantage around personal computing, developing design and user-experience capabilities that were genuinely path-dependent. But rather than defining itself permanently by that original advantage, Apple applied its core design capability to entirely new product categories: first the iPod and music distribution through iTunes, then the iPhone and the mobile computing ecosystem, then services like Apple Music and Apple TV+. Each move into a new domain represented an exploration, the development of new capabilities and the entry into new markets, while still leveraging the design and brand resources that Apple had built along its path-dependent history. Apple's willingness to explore new areas, even at the risk of cannibalizing its existing products, has allowed it to remain competitively relevant across multiple industry shifts.

The lesson from both examples is the same: firms must manage the tension between exploiting what they have and exploring what they might become. Path dependence gives current advantages their durability, but the same historical commitments that protect those advantages can also create rigidity if the firm becomes too attached to capabilities that the market is outgrowing. The dynamic capabilities framework, which we will examine in Chapter 3.6, addresses this tension directly by asking how firms can systematically sense, seize, and reconfigure resources as competitive conditions evolve (Teece, Pisano, & Shuen, 1997).

References

Barney, J. B. (1991). Firm resources and sustained competitive advantage. *Journal of Management, 17*(1), 99–120.

Dierickx, I., & Cool, K. (1989). Asset stock accumulation and sustainability of competitive advantage. *Management Science, 35*(12), 1504–1511.

Lippman, S. A., & Rumelt, R. P. (1982). Uncertain imitability: An analysis of interfirm differences in efficiency under competition. *The Bell Journal of Economics, 13*(2), 418–438.

March, J. G. (1991). Exploration and exploitation in organizational learning. *Organization Science, 2*(1), 71–87.

Reed, R., & DeFillippi, R. J. (1990). Causal ambiguity, barriers to imitation, and sustainable competitive advantage. *Academy of Management Review, 15*(1), 88–102.

Teece, D. J., Pisano, G., & Shuen, A. (1997). Dynamic capabilities and strategic management. *Strategic Management Journal, 18*(7), 509–533.

3.5 Culture — *How does culture create competitive advantage?*

The previous section identified social complexity as one of the three primary sources of path dependence. Organizational culture is the most pervasive and strategically significant expression of social complexity within a firm. This section examines culture not merely as an example of inimitability but as a strategic resource in its own right, one that can powerfully reinforce a firm's strategy, protect its competitive position, and, under certain conditions, undermine its ability to adapt.

3.5.1 Organizational Culture as a Strategic Resource

Organizational culture refers to the shared values, beliefs, norms, and assumptions that shape how people within a firm think, behave, and make decisions. It is the largely unwritten set of rules that governs daily conduct, the things that employees instinctively understand about "how we do things here" even when no formal policy dictates them. It operates as an intangible resource that profoundly shapes firm behavior and performance.

From the perspective of the resource-based view, culture is strategically significant because it tends to satisfy all four VRIO criteria simultaneously. A strong culture is **valuable** because it aligns employee behavior with strategic objectives and reduces coordination costs. It is **rare** because no two firms develop identical cultures. It is **costly to imitate** because culture is socially complex, causally ambiguous, and path dependent. And when the firm's systems and structures are aligned with its culture, the firm is **organized to exploit** the value that culture creates (Barney, 1986; Barney, 1991). Few resources satisfy all four criteria as naturally as organizational culture.

3.5.2 How Culture Supports Strategy

Culture matters for competitive advantage because it directly affects a firm's ability to execute its chosen business-level strategy. A firm can articulate a brilliant strategy in a boardroom presentation, but strategy is ultimately implemented by people, and how those people behave daily is shaped far more by culture than by strategic plans or policy manuals.

Culture reinforces or undermines strategy execution. When culture and strategy are aligned, employees naturally behave in ways that support strategic objectives, not because they are told to but because cultural norms point them in the right direction. When culture and strategy are misaligned, employees may resist changes that conflict with deeply held norms, even when those changes are strategically necessary. A firm competing on cost leadership benefits from a culture that values efficiency, discipline, and waste reduction. A firm competing on differentiation benefits from a culture that values creativity, customer responsiveness, and innovation. When the culture matches the strategy, execution becomes more natural and less dependent on constant managerial oversight.

Culture as a coordination mechanism. One of culture's most valuable functions is its ability to coordinate behavior without relying on formal controls (Barney, 1986; O'Reilly & Chatman, 1996). In any firm of meaningful size, managers cannot supervise every decision. Rules help but cannot anticipate every situation. Culture fills this gap by providing a shared framework for decision-making. A customer service representative who internalizes a culture of putting the customer first does not need to consult a manual to handle an unusual complaint. Culture functions as a decentralized coordination system that aligns thousands of individual decisions without requiring centralized control over each one.

3.5.3 Culture as a Barrier to Imitation

EX: Southwest Airlines' Culture

Southwest Airlines has long been recognized for a distinctive culture characterized by humor, informality, employee empowerment, and shared purpose. This culture contributes directly to competitive advantage by driving low employee turnover, high customer satisfaction, and operational efficiency. Southwest's culture has been studied extensively and its characteristics are no secret, yet competitors have found it virtually impossible to replicate. The reason is that Southwest's culture is not a policy that can be adopted. It is the accumulated product of decades of deliberate choices, beginning with co-founder Herb Kelleher's leadership philosophy and extending through every hiring decision, training program, promotion, celebration, and crisis response that followed. A competitor would need to replicate not just the visible manifestations of the culture but the entire infrastructure that produces and sustains them.

3.5.4 How Culture Is Built

Culture develops over time through four primary mechanisms that interact and reinforce one another (Schein, 2010).

Hiring. Culture begins with who is allowed through the door. Firms with strong cultures are deliberate about hiring people who fit the existing cultural values, not just people with the right technical qualifications. Southwest famously hires for attitude and trains for skill. This selectivity ensures that new employees are predisposed to embrace the culture rather than resist it.

Socialization. Once hired, new employees must learn "how things work here." Socialization happens through formal training programs and through informal channels: observing experienced colleagues, learning which behaviors are praised, hearing the stories that carry cultural values, and gradually internalizing the organization's way of doing things.

Leadership. Culture is shaped by the behavior of leaders at every level. Employees watch what leaders do far more carefully than they listen to what leaders say. A CEO who espouses innovation but punishes risk-taking sends a cultural message that contradicts the official narrative. Leaders serve as cultural role models whose behavior sets the tone for what is valued throughout the organization.

Reinforcement. Culture persists because it is continuously reinforced through formal mechanisms (recognition programs, promotion criteria, compensation structures) and informal ones (peer expectations, social approval, storytelling). Together, these create a self-reinforcing cycle: the culture shapes behavior, the behavior reinforces the culture, and the culture becomes increasingly embedded and resistant to change.

3.5.5 Culture as a Potential Rigidity

The very characteristics that make culture a powerful source of competitive advantage — its embeddedness, its self-reinforcing nature, its resistance to imitation — can also make it a liability when the competitive environment changes (Leonard-Barton, 1992). A strong culture is, by definition, resistant to change. This resistance is an asset when culture is aligned with strategic needs, but it becomes a liability when those needs shift and the culture does not shift with them.

When a firm's external environment evolves, the firm may need to adopt new strategies or abandon practices that once served it well. But deeply embedded cultural norms can make these transitions extraordinarily difficult. Consider a firm with a long-standing culture of engineering perfectionism. If the industry shifts toward rapid iteration and minimum viable products, the same culture that once produced excellence may now produce paralysis. Engineers rewarded for getting things perfect may resist shipping products that are merely good enough.

This transformation from asset to liability is one of the most dangerous dynamics in strategic management (Sørensen, 2002). It is dangerous because it is subtle: the culture does not change, the world around it does. This is the internal equivalent of the "obsolescent strength" diagnosis from the VRIO discussion in Chapter 3.3. The most successful firms find ways to preserve the core elements of their culture — the foundational values that define who they are — while adapting specific practices and priorities to reflect changing competitive conditions. This capacity for cultural adaptation without cultural abandonment is itself a rare and valuable capability, one that connects directly to the concept of dynamic capabilities examined in the next section.

References

Barney, J. B. (1986). Organizational culture: Can it be a source of sustained competitive advantage? *Academy of Management Review*, *11*(3), 656–665.

Barney, J. B. (1991). Firm resources and sustained competitive advantage. *Journal of Management*, *17*(1), 99–120.

Leonard-Barton, D. (1992). Core capabilities and core rigidities: A paradox in managing new product development. *Strategic Management Journal*, *13*(S1), 111–125.

O'Reilly, C. A., & Chatman, J. A. (1996). Culture as social control: Corporations, cults, and commitment. *Research in Organizational Behavior, 18*, 157–200.

Schein, E. H. (2010). *Organizational culture and leadership* (4th ed.). Jossey-Bass.

Sørensen, J. B. (2002). The strength of corporate culture and the reliability of firm performance. *Administrative Science Quarterly, 47*(1), 70–91.

3.6 Dynamic Capabilities — *How do firms adapt resources over time?*

The preceding sections of this chapter have developed a comprehensive framework for internal analysis. The resource-based view established that competitive advantage originates in a firm's unique bundle of resources and capabilities. The value chain revealed where within the firm those resources are deployed to create value. The VRIO framework provided criteria for distinguishing ordinary capabilities from core competencies. Path dependence explained why some capabilities are so resistant to imitation. And organizational culture illustrated both the power and the peril of deeply embedded social resources: powerful because they coordinate behavior and resist imitation, perilous because they can resist necessary change with equal force.

Running through each of these discussions has been an uncomfortable truth: the resources and capabilities that drive today's competitive advantage may not drive tomorrow's. Industries evolve. Customer preferences shift. Technologies disrupt established business models. Regulations change the rules of competition. A firm that excels in a stable environment may find its carefully cultivated competencies rendered irrelevant by forces beyond its control. The previous section's discussion of culture as a potential rigidity made this danger vivid; a firm can be perfectly organized to exploit a rare, inimitable capability that the market no longer values. Path dependence, the very mechanism that protects competitive advantage, can also lock firms into strategic positions that become progressively less viable as conditions change.

This creates a fundamental problem for the resource-based view as presented so far. If competitive advantage is built through slow, path-dependent accumulation of resources, and if the value of those resources can be eroded by environmental change, then how does a firm sustain its competitive position over the long term? The answer cannot simply be "build better resources," because even the best resources are vulnerable to shifts in what the market rewards. The answer must involve something more: the capacity to change the resource base itself, to sense when the environment is shifting, to reconfigure capabilities in response, and to build new advantages even as old ones are being exploited (Helfat & Peteraf, 2003). This is the domain of dynamic capabilities.

3.6.1 What Are Dynamic Capabilities?

> *"It is not the strongest of the species that survives... but the species that survives is the one that is able best to adapt and adjust to the changing environment in which it finds itself."* — *Leon C. Megginson*

Dynamic capabilities are the firm's ability to integrate, build, and reconfigure internal and external competencies to address rapidly changing environments (Teece, Pisano, & Shuen, 1997). This definition requires careful unpacking, because the term is easily confused with the ordinary capabilities discussed throughout this chapter.

The critical distinction is that dynamic capabilities are not capabilities in the usual sense; they are not the routines and processes through which a firm produces its current products or delivers its current services. Those are operational or ordinary capabilities. Dynamic capabilities operate at a higher level: they are the organizational processes through which the firm changes its ordinary capabilities. If ordinary capabilities determine how well a firm performs its current activities, dynamic capabilities determine how effectively a firm adapts those activities when circumstances demand it. Dynamic capabilities are, in essence, the capacity to change and renew capabilities, the ability to alter what the firm does and how it does it.

This distinction matters because a firm can possess excellent ordinary capabilities and still lack dynamic capabilities. A firm may be extraordinarily efficient at manufacturing a particular product using a particular process, yet be completely unable to reconfigure its operations when a new technology makes that process obsolete. The ordinary capability is strong; the dynamic capability is absent. Conversely, a firm may not be the absolute best at any single activity yet possess a superior ability to sense changing conditions, reallocate resources, and adapt its operations in response, making it more durable over the long run than a more capable but more rigid competitor.

3.6.2 Types of Dynamic Capabilities

David Teece (2007), building on his earlier work, identified three categories of dynamic capabilities that together describe how firms sense environmental changes, respond to them, and transform themselves accordingly. These three categories (sensing, seizing, and reconfiguring) provide a useful framework for understanding how dynamic capabilities operate in practice.

Sensing refers to the firm's ability to identify and assess opportunities and threats in the external environment. This is the scanning and interpretive function, the organizational equivalent of peripheral vision. Sensing capabilities include activities such as monitoring technological developments, tracking shifts in customer behavior, analyzing competitor actions, identifying emerging market segments, and interpreting regulatory trends. Sensing is fundamentally about awareness: knowing that something important is changing before the change has fully materialized.

Sensing is not simply a matter of gathering information. Every firm has access to industry reports, market data, and competitive intelligence. The dynamic capability lies in the firm's ability to interpret that information accurately, to distinguish genuine signals from noise, and to recognize the strategic implications of what it observes. Many firms that failed in the face of industry disruption did not fail because they lacked information; they failed because they failed to interpret the information correctly or to appreciate its significance until it was too late. Kodak's engineers invented digital photography technology in the 1970s, but the company's leadership did not sense, or did not accept, that digital imaging would fundamentally transform its industry until competitors had already seized the opportunity.

Seizing refers to the firm's ability to mobilize resources to capture value from the opportunities that sensing has identified. Where sensing is about awareness, seizing is about action: committing resources, making investments, designing products, entering markets, and building the organizational structures needed to exploit a recognized opportunity. Seizing requires decisiveness, because opportunities in rapidly changing environments are often time-sensitive. A firm that senses an opportunity but deliberates too long may find that competitors have moved first.

Seizing also involves making strategic choices under uncertainty. When a new technology or market shift is detected, the firm must decide how much to invest, which approach to take, and how to balance the new opportunity against its existing commitments. These are difficult decisions because they require the firm to allocate scarce resources toward uncertain outcomes while still maintaining the operations that generate current revenue. Firms with strong seizing capabilities are able to make these commitments quickly and effectively, structuring investments in ways that manage risk while preserving the ability to scale up rapidly if the opportunity proves viable.

Reconfiguring refers to the firm's ability to continuously renew and transform its organizational assets, structures, and routines. This is the most demanding of the three dynamic capabilities because it involves changing the firm itself, not just what the firm does, but how it is organized to do it. Reconfiguring includes activities such as reorganizing business units, reallocating resources across divisions, redesigning processes, integrating acquisitions, shedding assets that are no longer strategically relevant, and reshaping the firm's culture to align with new strategic directions.

Reconfiguring is where the tension between exploitation and exploration, introduced in Chapter 3.4, becomes most acute. The firm must dismantle or modify routines and structures that are currently generating value in order to build new ones that will generate value in the future. This is inherently risky, because the existing routines are proven while the new ones are not. It also generates organizational resistance, because employees whose roles, skills, and identities are tied to the existing way of doing things will naturally resist changes that threaten their position. Successful reconfiguring requires not only strategic vision but also the managerial skill to navigate the human and organizational complexities of transformation.

3.6.3 Dynamic Capabilities and Sustained Competitive Advantage

The relationship between dynamic capabilities and sustained competitive advantage is best understood through the exploitation-exploration framework introduced in Chapter 3.4 (March, 1991). As discussed there, firms must simultaneously exploit their current advantages, refining and extending the capabilities that generate today's profits, and explore new opportunities, developing the capabilities that will generate tomorrow's profits. Dynamic capabilities are the organizational mechanisms through which this dual mandate is executed.

The Walmart and Apple examples discussed in Chapter 3.4 illustrate this relationship clearly. Walmart's continuous improvement of its inventory management system represents exploitation enabled by dynamic capabilities: the firm senses incremental opportunities for efficiency gains, seizes them through targeted technology investments, and reconfigures its logistics operations to incorporate each improvement. Each cycle of sensing, seizing, and reconfiguring makes the existing advantage stronger and more deeply embedded. Apple's successive entries into music, smartphones, and services represent exploration enabled by dynamic capabilities: the firm sensed shifts in consumer behavior and technology, seized those opportunities by committing resources to entirely new product categories, and reconfigured its organizational structure and business model to support each new venture.

What makes dynamic capabilities a source of sustained competitive advantage is that they enable the firm to adapt its resource base over time rather than relying on any single set of resources to remain valuable indefinitely. A firm with strong dynamic capabilities is not dependent on any particular product, technology, or market position for its long-term success. Instead, it possesses the higher-order ability to sense when change is needed, seize new opportunities as they arise, and reconfigure its organization to deliver on those opportunities. This adaptability is itself a form of competitive advantage, one that is particularly valuable in industries characterized by rapid technological change, shifting customer preferences, and unpredictable competitive dynamics.

EX: Netflix's Sequential Transformations

Netflix provides a compelling illustration of dynamic capabilities in action. The company began in 1997 as a DVD-by-mail rental service, competing against Blockbuster's network of physical stores. This initial business model was itself an act of sensing and seizing; founder Reed Hastings recognized that the internet could be used to manage a rental queue and that the U.S. Postal Service could deliver DVDs more conveniently than a trip to the video store. Netflix built operational capabilities around warehouse logistics, recommendation algorithms, and subscription billing that gave it a cost and convenience advantage over traditional rental stores.

But Netflix did not define itself by its DVD logistics capability. As broadband internet penetration increased in the mid-2000s, the company sensed that streaming video would eventually replace physical media. Rather than waiting for the transition to threaten its existing business, Netflix seized the opportunity by investing heavily in streaming technology and licensing content for digital delivery, even though doing so cannibalized its profitable DVD business. This required significant reconfiguring: the company shifted engineering talent, renegotiated content deals, redesigned its user interface, and gradually reoriented its entire business model around streaming.

Then, as competition in the streaming market intensified and content licensing costs rose, Netflix sensed another shift, the need to own its content rather than merely license it. The company seized this opportunity by investing billions in original programming, beginning with *House of Cards* in 2013. This again required reconfiguring: Netflix had to build entirely new capabilities in content development, production management, and creative talent acquisition, capabilities that had nothing to do with the logistics and recommendation systems that had defined its earlier competitive advantage.

Each of these transitions — from DVD-by-mail to streaming to original content production — represents a complete cycle of sensing, seizing, and reconfiguring. At each stage, Netflix voluntarily disrupted its own existing business model before competitors could do so. The dynamic capabilities that enabled these transitions — the organizational willingness to cannibalize current revenue streams, the ability to reallocate resources toward uncertain but promising opportunities, and the managerial skill to reconfigure the organization around fundamentally new activities — are as much a source of Netflix's sustained competitive advantage as any individual product or technology.

3.6.4 Limits of Dynamic Capabilities

Dynamic capabilities are valuable, but they are not unlimited or cost-free. Several important constraints affect a firm's ability to sense, seize, and reconfigure effectively.

Organizational inertia and resistance to change. The same path dependence and cultural embeddedness that protect a firm's current advantages also resist efforts to change them (Leonard-Barton, 1992). Employees, managers, and even executives develop cognitive frameworks, routines, and identities that are tied to existing ways of doing things. Reconfiguring the firm's resource base means disrupting these established patterns, which generates friction and resistance. The stronger the firm's existing culture and the more successful its current strategy, the greater the inertia that dynamic capabilities must overcome. This is the paradox identified in Chapter 3.5: the very cultural strength that coordinates and motivates employees in service of the current strategy can become the primary obstacle to the strategic adaptation that dynamic capabilities are supposed to enable.

The cost and risk of reconfiguring established routines. Reconfiguration is not merely an organizational challenge; it is a financial one. Dismantling proven processes and building new ones requires investment with uncertain returns. A firm that reconfigures prematurely may abandon a profitable capability before its useful life has ended. A firm that reconfigures in the wrong direction may invest heavily in capabilities that turn out to be strategically irrelevant. The act of reconfiguring is itself a strategic bet, and not all bets pay off. Even Netflix's successful transformations involved enormous financial risk; the company took on billions in debt to fund its content investments, a gamble that could have failed if subscribers had not materialized in sufficient numbers.

Not all firms possess strong dynamic capabilities. Dynamic capabilities are themselves unevenly distributed across firms (Eisenhardt & Martin, 2000). Some firms have deeply embedded routines for scanning the environment, making bold investment decisions, and reorganizing their operations. Others lack these routines entirely, either because their leadership is risk-averse, because their organizational structures are too rigid, because their cultures resist experimentation, or because they have simply never needed to adapt in the past and have not developed the capacity to do so. Firms in stable industries, where competitive conditions change slowly, may have little experience with reconfiguration and may find themselves completely unprepared when disruption finally arrives. The assumption that any firm can develop dynamic capabilities on demand is incorrect; like ordinary capabilities, dynamic capabilities must be built over time, and firms that have not invested in building them will struggle to develop them under pressure.

3.6.5 Dynamic Capabilities and the Internal Analysis Framework

Dynamic capabilities represent the final piece of the internal analysis framework developed throughout this chapter. The resource-based view explains that competitive advantage originates in a firm's unique resources and capabilities. The value chain shows where those resources create value. Core competencies and the VRIO framework identify which capabilities are strategically significant. Path dependence and culture explain why those capabilities are durable. And dynamic capabilities explain how firms can adapt their resource base over time to sustain advantage in a changing world.

Together, these concepts form a coherent logic for understanding what happens inside the firm that determines competitive success or failure. The firm that possesses superior resources, organized into superior capabilities, evaluated through the VRIO framework as genuine core competencies, protected by path dependence and a supportive culture, and continuously renewed through dynamic capabilities, is the firm best positioned to achieve sustained competitive advantage — not as a permanent state, but as an ongoing process of building, exploiting, protecting, and adapting the internal foundations of strategic success.

References

Eisenhardt, K. M., & Martin, J. A. (2000). Dynamic capabilities: What are they? *Strategic Management Journal, 21*(10–11), 1105–1121.

Helfat, C. E., & Peteraf, M. A. (2003). The dynamic resource-based view: Capability lifecycles. *Strategic Management Journal, 24*(10), 997–1010.

Leonard-Barton, D. (1992). Core capabilities and core rigidities: A paradox in managing new product development. *Strategic Management Journal, 13*(S1), 111–125.

March, J. G. (1991). Exploration and exploitation in organizational learning. *Organization Science, 2*(1), 71–87.

Teece, D. J. (2007). Explicating dynamic capabilities: The nature and microfoundations of (sustainable) enterprise performance. *Strategic Management Journal, 28*(13), 1319–1350.

Teece, D. J., Pisano, G., & Shuen, A. (1997). Dynamic capabilities and strategic management. *Strategic Management Journal, 18*(7), 509–533.

Chapter 4

Industry & External Environment Analysis

4.1 Environmental Scanning, Monitoring, and Competitive Intelligence — *How do we gather external information?*

> *"The goal is to turn data into information, and information into insight." — Carly Fiorina, CEO of HP*

The first three chapters of this text have progressively built a toolkit for understanding strategy from the inside out. Chapter 1 established what firms are, why they exist, and what strategy means. Chapter 2 introduced the fundamental business-level strategies (differentiation, cost leadership, and their variants) through which firms compete. Chapter 3 turned inward, developing frameworks for analyzing the resources, capabilities, and competencies that determine whether a firm can actually execute its chosen strategy. Together, these chapters explain why some firms outperform others *within the same industry*. But they leave an equally important question unanswered: why are some industries far more profitable than others?

Consider the contrast between the soft drink industry and the steel industry. The soft drink industry has been extraordinarily profitable for decades, with dominant firms earning margins that most businesses would envy. The steel industry, by contrast, has been characterized by razor-thin margins, brutal price competition, and periodic waves of bankruptcy. The firms in these industries may each possess valuable resources and execute competent strategies, yet the average firm in soft drinks vastly outperforms the average firm in steel. The internal analysis tools from Chapter 3 cannot explain this difference; it has nothing to do with one steel company's culture being better than another's. The explanation lies outside the firm, in the structure of the industry and the broader environment in which it operates.

This chapter shifts the lens from internal to external analysis. Where Chapter 3 asked "what do we have, and what can we do?", Chapter 4 asks "what is happening around us, and how does it affect our ability to earn profits?" The two perspectives are complementary. Internal analysis explains performance differences between firms within an industry; external analysis explains performance differences between industries. A complete strategic diagnosis requires both. The most brilliantly managed firm in a structurally unattractive industry may still struggle, and even a mediocre firm in a highly attractive industry may earn comfortable returns. Understanding the external environment is therefore essential, not as a replacement for internal analysis, but as its necessary counterpart.

Before we can analyze industry structure and external forces, however, we must address a more fundamental question: what industry are we actually in? The answer is far less obvious than it appears, and getting it wrong can lead to strategic blind spots that no amount of internal excellence can overcome.

4.1.1 Defining the Industry Boundary

An industry is a group of firms producing products or services that are close substitutes for one another. This definition sounds straightforward, but in practice, drawing the boundary around an industry requires judgment, and the boundary a firm chooses has profound implications for its strategic analysis.

The key criterion for determining industry boundaries is **substitutability**, which operates on two dimensions. Demand-side substitutability asks how willing buyers are to switch between products. If customers readily substitute one product for another, choosing Pepsi instead of Coca-Cola, for instance, those products are in the same industry. Supply-side substitutability asks how easily producers can switch their production from one product to another. If a manufacturer of luxury sedans can retool its factories to produce SUVs with modest investment, those products may belong to the same industry even if customers view them somewhat differently.

The challenge is that substitutability is not binary; it exists on a continuum, and where one draws the line determines the scope of the competitive analysis that follows. Consider BMW. Is BMW in the luxury car industry? The automotive industry? The transportation industry? Each definition is defensible, and each leads to a fundamentally different strategic analysis.

If BMW defines its industry narrowly as luxury automobiles, its competitive set includes Mercedes-Benz, Lexus, and Audi. The analysis focuses on brand prestige, driving experience, and premium features. If BMW broadens the definition to the automotive industry, the competitive set expands to include Toyota, Ford, Hyundai, and dozens of others, and the strategic questions shift toward manufacturing efficiency, global supply chains, and mass-market positioning. If BMW takes the broadest view (transportation) then competitors include Uber, Lyft, public transit systems, and even bicycle-sharing programs, and the strategic landscape changes dramatically.

None of these definitions is universally correct. The appropriate industry boundary depends on the strategic question being asked. When BMW evaluates the threat of Lexus developing superior battery technology for electric vehicles, a narrow industry definition centered on luxury automobiles is most useful. When BMW considers the threat of Uber developing autonomous vehicles that could reduce car ownership altogether, a broader transportation industry definition becomes necessary. When BMW assesses the opportunity created by government regulations that increase the cost of ride-sharing services, the broadest definition captures the relevant competitive dynamics. The industry boundary is not a fixed fact to be discovered — it is a strategic choice that shapes what the firm sees and what it misses.

4.1.2 Narrow vs. Broad Industry Definitions

The choice between narrow and broad industry definitions involves real tradeoffs. A narrow definition identifies fewer competitors and allows for more focused competitive analysis. It makes rivalry more concrete and specific: you know exactly who you are fighting and over what. However, a narrow definition may cause a firm to overlook threats emerging from outside the defined boundary, threats that are no less real for being invisible in the analysis.

A broad definition captures a larger total addressable market and reveals more potential threats and substitutes. It provides a wider field of vision, making it harder for unexpected competitors to arrive undetected. However, a broad definition can make the competitive analysis unwieldy; if everyone is a competitor, the term loses analytical precision.

This tradeoff is particularly visible in entrepreneurship. When entrepreneurs discuss the total addressable market (TAM) for their ventures, they tend to use broad industry definitions ("the global transportation market is $7 trillion") because maximizing the perceived profit potential of the market makes the opportunity appear more attractive to investors. When those same entrepreneurs discuss their competitive landscape, they pivot to narrow definitions ("there are only two other companies offering electric scooter subscriptions in mid-sized cities") because minimizing the number of visible competitors makes the venture appear more defensible. Both framings can be legitimate, but the shift between them is worth recognizing.

Where the industry boundary is drawn determines what counts as rivalry among existing competitors versus what counts as substitution. Rival products are within the industry; substitute products come from outside it. If McDonald's defines its industry as fast food, then a fast casual chain like Chipotle is a substitute — a different product serving a similar customer need. If McDonald's defines its industry as quick-service restaurants, then Chipotle is a direct rival. The underlying forces are identical; the boundary determines how they are categorized, and that shapes the strategic conclusions drawn.

4.1.3 Strategic Groups

Within any industry boundary, firms do not all compete in the same way. A strategic group is a collection of firms within the same industry that follow similar strategies along similar dimensions (Hunt, 1972; Porter, 1980). Firms within a strategic group tend to target similar customers, offer comparable products, and compete on similar bases.

Consider the retail industry. Walmart, Costco, and Dollar General form one strategic group, competing primarily on low prices and operational efficiency. Nordstrom, Neiman Marcus, and Saks Fifth Avenue form another, competing on premium service, curated selection, and brand prestige. Both groups operate within the retail industry, but they follow fundamentally different strategies and largely serve different customer segments.

Competitive rivalry is typically more intense within a strategic group than between groups, because firms within the same group are fighting for the same customers with similar offerings (Porter, 1980). Walmart's most direct competitive threat comes from Costco and Target, not from Neiman Marcus. This means that identifying which strategic group a firm belongs to, and understanding the dynamics within that group, is an important step in competitive analysis.

Strategic groups are often depicted visually by plotting firms along two key strategic dimensions, such as price and product breadth, or geographic coverage and level of service. While any two-dimensional depiction necessarily oversimplifies strategy (real strategies are multidimensional), these visual maps can effectively illustrate how firms cluster within an industry and where competitive intensity is greatest.

4.1.3.1 Strategic Groups: Automobile Industry Illustrative Example

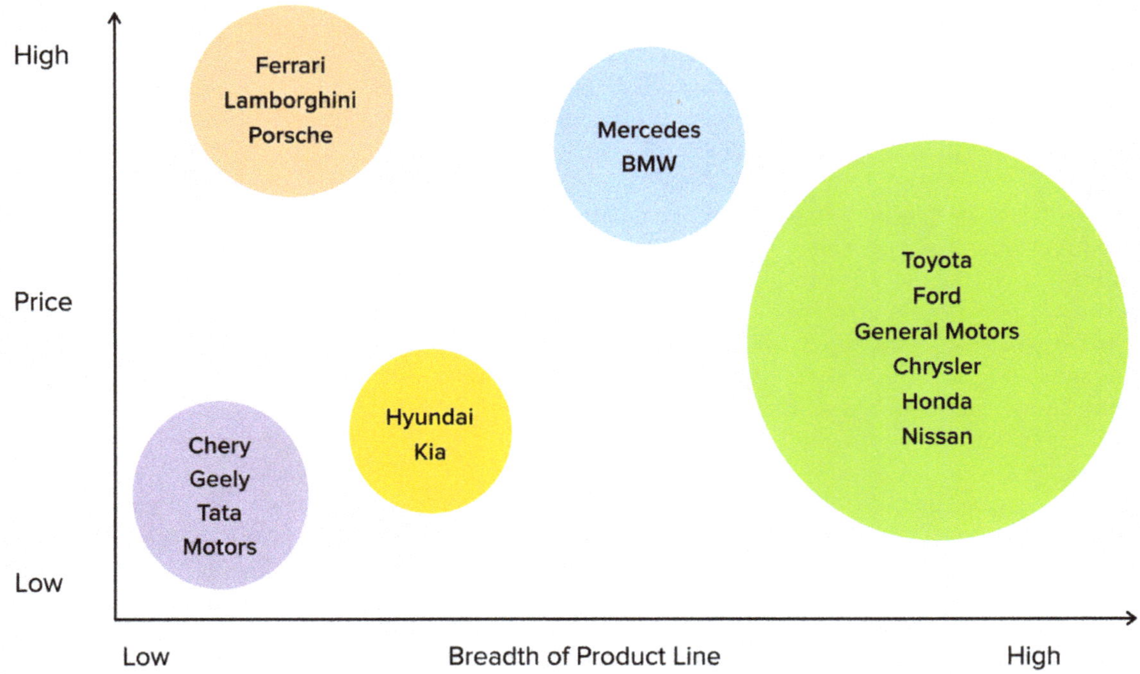

4.1.4 Industry Concentration

Not all industries have the same number and size distribution of firms, and this matters enormously for competitive dynamics and profitability. Industry concentration refers to how market share is distributed among firms in the industry, and it ranges along a spectrum from perfect competition to monopoly.

At one extreme, **perfect competition** features many small firms selling essentially identical (commodity) products with low barriers to entry. In this structure, no individual firm has pricing power, and competitive forces drive profits toward zero. Agriculture provides a classic example: thousands of small wheat farmers sell a commodity product, and no single farmer can influence the market price. At the other extreme, a **monopoly** features a single firm that, absent government regulation, can charge whatever the market will bear because customers have no alternative suppliers.

Most industries fall between these extremes. **Monopolistic competition** features many firms, some small, some large, selling differentiated products with moderate barriers to entry. Restaurants, clothing retailers, and hair salons exemplify this structure. **Oligopoly** features a few large firms that collectively dominate the market. The commercial aircraft industry (Boeing and Airbus), wireless carriers in the United States (AT&T, Verizon, T-Mobile), and major credit card networks (Visa, Mastercard, American Express) are oligopolies where a handful of firms control the vast majority of market share.

Industry concentration is commonly measured using the **Herfindahl-Hirschman Index (HHI)**, calculated by squaring each firm's market share (expressed as a percentage) and summing the results. The index ranges from near zero in a market of many tiny competitors to 10,000 in a pure monopoly (a single firm with 100% market share, since $100^2 = 10{,}000$). Higher values indicate greater concentration. The U.S. Department of Justice and Federal Trade Commission use the HHI to evaluate whether a proposed merger would create an unacceptable level of market concentration, generally treating markets with an HHI above 1,000 as concentrated and those above 1,800 as highly concentrated (U.S. Department of Justice & Federal Trade Commission, 2023).

The contrast between concentrated and competitive industries is stark. Consider U.S. wireless carriers, an oligopoly dominated by three national networks. Using approximate subscriber shares of 35% (T-Mobile), 34% (Verizon), and 27% (AT&T), the HHI is $35^2 + 34^2 + 27^2 = 1{,}225 + 1{,}156 + 729 = 3{,}110$, far above the threshold for a highly concentrated market (TeleGeography, 2025). This is precisely why the 2020 Sprint–T-Mobile merger drew intense regulatory scrutiny: combining two of the four national carriers raised the index substantially in an already-concentrated market.

Now consider U.S. homebuilding, long regarded as one of the most fragmented industries in the economy. Using 2024 shares of new single-family home closings (D.R. Horton 13.6%, Lennar 11.7%, PulteGroup 4.6%, NVR 3.3%, and Meritage 2.3%), these five largest builders contribute only $13.6^2 + 11.7^2 + 4.6^2 + 3.3^2 + 2.3^2 = 359$ to the index (National Association of Home Builders, 2025). Adding the remaining national builders and a long tail of thousands of small and regional firms, each holding a fraction of a percent, leaves the industry's HHI around 400, comfortably within the unconcentrated range. The same arithmetic that flags wireless as highly concentrated confirms that no homebuilder commands meaningful pricing power over the industry as a whole.

Critically, industry concentration is not static. Industries can shift dramatically along the concentration spectrum over time, which raises the importance of dynamic strategic analysis. The pineapple industry provides a vivid illustration. Before the 1990s, the fresh pineapple market closely resembled perfect competition: many small growers selling a commodity product with minimal differentiation and thin margins. Then Del Monte introduced the "Gold Extra Sweet" pineapple, a variety bred for brighter color, sweeter taste, and longer shelf life. Customers overwhelmingly preferred it. Within years, Del Monte captured approximately 70% of the global fresh pineapple market, transforming an industry that had operated near perfect competition into something approaching oligopoly (Herath & Vink, 2018). Many smaller growers who could not access the new variety were driven from the market entirely. A single product innovation reshaped the entire competitive structure of an industry.

4.1.5 Environmental Scanning, Monitoring, and Competitive Intelligence

Having established that industries are defined by boundaries, populated by strategic groups, and characterized by varying levels of concentration, and that all of these can change, we arrive at the practical question: how does a firm stay informed about what is happening in its external environment? The answer involves three related but distinct activities.

Environmental scanning is the broad study of all segments of the external environment to detect early signals of change (Hambrick, 1982). Scanning is wide-angle: the firm is not looking for anything specific but rather surveying the landscape for anything that might eventually matter. A pharmaceutical company scanning the environment might notice shifting demographic patterns, emerging regulatory proposals, advances in gene therapy technology, and changing public attitudes toward drug pricing, all at once, without knowing in advance which of these will prove most consequential.

Environmental monitoring is more focused. Once scanning has identified a potentially important trend or change, monitoring involves tracking that development over time to determine whether it is growing in significance and how it might affect the industry (Daft, Sormunen, & Parks, 1988). If scanning reveals that a new regulatory proposal has been introduced, monitoring tracks its progress through the legislative process, assesses the likelihood of passage, and evaluates its potential impact on the firm and its competitors.

Competitive intelligence is the systematic gathering and interpretation of information about competitors: their strategies, capabilities, intentions, and likely responses to competitive moves (Chen, 1996). Competitive intelligence goes beyond general environmental awareness to focus specifically on the firms that a company competes against directly. It asks questions like: What are our competitors investing in? How might they respond if we lower prices? Are they planning to enter a new market segment? Effective competitive intelligence draws on publicly available information (financial filings, patent applications, job postings, press releases, executive speeches, and industry reports) and synthesizes it into actionable strategic insight.

The goal of all three activities is the same: to identify opportunities and threats before they fully materialize. A firm that detects an emerging technological shift early has time to adapt its strategy. A firm that learns of a competitor's expansion plans before the formal announcement has time to prepare a response. A firm that recognizes a regulatory threat while it is still a proposal, rather than after it becomes law, can lobby against it, build coalitions, or begin adapting its operations in advance. Environmental scanning, monitoring, and competitive intelligence are not peripheral activities — they are the information foundation upon which all external strategic analysis rests.

The sections that follow in this chapter will provide specific frameworks for conducting that analysis. Competitive dynamics (Ch 4.2) examines how firms interact with rivals through competitive actions and responses. Porter's Five Forces (Ch 4.3) provides a structured framework for assessing overall industry attractiveness. Subsequent sections address vertical integration, complementors, industry evolution, and the broader macro-environment through PESTEL analysis. Each of these frameworks depends on the firm having done the foundational work described in this section: defining its industry boundary, understanding its strategic group, and continuously gathering intelligence about the competitive and environmental landscape in which it operates.

References

Chen, M.-J. (1996). Competitor analysis and interfirm rivalry: Toward a theoretical integration. *Academy of Management Review*, *21*(1), 100–134.

Daft, R. L., Sormunen, J., & Parks, D. (1988). Chief executive scanning, environmental characteristics, and company performance: An empirical study. *Strategic Management Journal*, *9*(2), 123–139.

Hambrick, D. C. (1982). Environmental scanning and organizational strategy. *Strategic Management Journal*, *3*(2), 159–174.

Herath, H. M. U. N., & Vink, M. (2018). The diffusion and impact of the MD-2 "Super Sweet" pineapple variety. In N. Ferrara (Ed.), *Pineapple: Production, Nutritional Properties, and Health Effects* (pp. 25–48). Nova Science Publishers.

Hunt, M. S. (1972). *Competition in the major home appliance industry, 1960–1970* [Doctoral dissertation, Harvard University].

National Association of Home Builders. (2025, July 8). *Top ten builder share rises again in 2024*. Eye on Housing. https://eyeonhousing.org/2025/07/top-ten-builder-share-rises-again-in-2024/

Porter, M. E. (1980). *Competitive strategy: Techniques for analyzing industries and competitors*. Free Press.

TeleGeography. (2025). *2025 mobile market summary*. https://resources.telegeography.com/2025-mobile-market-summary

U.S. Department of Justice & Federal Trade Commission. (2023). *Merger guidelines*. https://www.ftc.gov/system/files/ftc_gov/pdf/2023_merger_guidelines_final_12.18.2023.pdf

4.2 Competitive Dynamics — *How do firms compete and respond to rivals?*

The previous section established the foundations of external analysis: how firms define their industry boundaries, identify strategic groups, and gather competitive intelligence through environmental scanning and monitoring. These activities provide the informational raw material for understanding the competitive landscape. But understanding the landscape is not the same as understanding how competition actually unfolds within it. Industries are not static structures that firms passively inhabit. They are arenas in which firms continuously take actions against one another, respond to those actions, and adjust their strategies based on the results. This section examines the dynamics of that ongoing competitive interaction: how firms analyze their competitors, what drives competitive behavior, and what determines whether a firm will act first or respond to a rival's move.

4.2.1 Competitive Rivalry vs. Competitive Dynamics

Before diving into the mechanisms of competitive interaction, it is important to distinguish between two related but distinct concepts that are often conflated.

Competitive rivalry is the ongoing set of competitive actions and responses occurring between two individual competitors (Chen, 1996). Rivalry is always analyzed at the firm-pair level; it describes the relationship between a specific firm and a specific competitor. When Southwest Airlines launches service on a new route that United Airlines already serves, and United responds by lowering its fares on that route, the action-response sequence constitutes competitive rivalry between those two firms. Even though Southwest's route expansion may affect multiple airlines, rivalry as a concept focuses on the dyadic interaction between two firms at a time.

Competitive dynamics is the broader, industry-level phenomenon, the total set of actions and responses taken by all firms competing within a market (Smith, Ferrier, & Ndofor, 2001). While rivalry zooms in on individual pairs of competitors, competitive dynamics zooms out to capture the aggregate pattern of competitive interaction across the entire industry. The competitive dynamics of the U.S. airline industry, for instance, reflect the combined effect of thousands of individual rivalries playing out simultaneously across hundreds of routes. Industry-level outcomes (pricing trends, consolidation patterns, the pace of innovation) emerge from the accumulation of these individual rivalries.

The distinction matters because the factors that drive firm-level rivalry are not identical to those that shape industry-level dynamics. A particular pair of firms may engage in intense rivalry even within an industry that is relatively stable overall, and an industry can be characterized by aggressive competitive dynamics even if no single rivalry dominates the landscape. Understanding competition requires both levels of analysis.

4.2.2 Competitor Analysis

Effective competition begins with understanding one's competitors. Competitor analysis is the process of studying a rival's future objectives, current strategies, underlying assumptions, and capabilities in order to predict its behavior and inform one's own competitive actions and responses (Porter, 1980). Without this understanding, competitive actions are essentially taken blind; the firm does not know how rivals are likely to react, and it cannot anticipate moves that competitors might initiate.

Two dimensions are particularly useful for structuring competitor analysis: market commonality and resource similarity.

Market commonality refers to the number of markets in which a firm and a competitor both compete, as well as the importance of each shared market to each firm (Chen, 1996). Two firms that overlap in many markets are engaged in multi-market competition, and this overlap has a counterintuitive effect on competitive behavior. Firms with greater multi-market contact are actually *less* likely to initiate aggressive competitive actions against one another, but they are *more* likely to respond aggressively when attacked (Gimeno & Woo, 1996). The logic is one of mutual deterrence: if Delta Airlines launches a fare war against American Airlines on the Dallas–New York route, American can retaliate not just on that route but on every other route where the two airlines compete. Both firms understand this dynamic, so they tend to exercise restraint in initiating attacks but respond forcefully to attacks in order to protect their positions across the full portfolio of shared markets.

EX: Multi-Market Competition in Airlines

Consider a simplified scenario. Delta and American both operate routes between Dallas and New York, Chicago and Miami, and Los Angeles and Atlanta. Each route is a distinct market, and the two airlines overlap in all three. If Delta decides to undercut American's fares on the Dallas–New York route, American can retaliate not just on that route but across all three shared markets, launching promotions, adding capacity, or matching fares in Chicago–Miami and Los Angeles–Atlanta as well. Because both airlines understand that aggression in one market can trigger responses across all shared markets, neither has a strong incentive to be the first mover. The result is a kind of competitive equilibrium that would not exist if the two firms competed in only a single market.

Resource similarity refers to how comparable the firm's tangible and intangible resources are to a competitor's in terms of both type and amount (Chen, 1996). Firms with similar resource profiles are likely to have similar strengths and weaknesses, pursue similar strategies, and be capable of responding to each other's competitive moves in kind. Assessing resource similarity is straightforward when the critical resources are tangible, comparing manufacturing capacity, financial reserves, or distribution networks is relatively objective. It becomes considerably more difficult when the critical resources are intangible, comparing brand reputation, organizational culture, or proprietary knowledge requires judgment and inference.

Together, market commonality and resource similarity form a two-dimensional framework for competitor analysis. Firms that are high on both dimensions, competing in many of the same markets and possessing similar resource endowments, will tend to experience the highest levels of rivalry. These are firms that are fighting over the same customers with similar weapons. Conversely, firms that are low on both dimensions, operating in different markets with fundamentally different resource bases, will experience the least rivalry. They may technically be in the same broadly defined industry, but their paths rarely cross in meaningful ways.

4.2.3 Drivers of Competitive Behavior

Understanding who your competitors are is a necessary first step, but competitor analysis alone does not explain why firms act or refrain from acting. The drivers of competitive behavior, the factors that determine whether a firm will initiate a competitive action or respond to a rival's move, can be organized into three categories: awareness, motivation, and capability (Chen, 1996).

Awareness is the extent to which competitors recognize their mutual interdependence, that is, the degree to which each firm understands that its actions affect, and are affected by, the other firm's actions. Awareness is a function of the market commonality and resource similarity discussed above. When two firms compete in many of the same markets and possess similar resources, each is acutely aware of the other as a competitive threat. When firms operate in different market segments with dissimilar resource profiles, each may barely register the other's existence. Awareness is the precondition for competitive action; a firm cannot respond to a threat it does not perceive.

Motivation is the firm's incentive to take a competitive action or to respond to a competitor's move. Motivation relates to perceived gains and losses. A firm is more likely to act when the potential gains from action are high, entering a lucrative new market segment, for instance, and more likely to respond when the potential losses from inaction are severe, losing a major customer group to a rival's new product. Motivation explains why firms sometimes tolerate competitive provocations without responding: if the threatened market is small or strategically unimportant, the motivation to mount a costly response may simply not be there.

Capability refers to the firm's resources and the flexibility those resources provide. Without adequate resources, a firm lacks the ability to either attack a competitor or respond to a competitor's actions, regardless of its awareness and motivation. A small regional airline may be fully aware that a major carrier is encroaching on its most profitable route (high awareness) and deeply motivated to defend its market position (high motivation), but if it lacks the fleet, the financial reserves, and the gate access to mount an effective response, awareness and motivation alone are insufficient.

An important dynamic emerges from the interaction of capability and competitive response. The greater the resource advantage between the acting firm and its competitors, the greater the expected delay in the competitor's response (Smith et al., 2001). A well-resourced firm can launch competitive actions with some confidence that smaller, less capable rivals will need considerable time to formulate and execute a response, if they can respond at all. However, even firms facing resource disadvantages should eventually respond to competitive threats, because the cost of inaction, continued erosion of market position, typically outweighs the cost of a delayed or imperfect response.

4.2.4 Competitive Actions and Responses

The core unit of analysis in competitive dynamics is the competitive action, a strategic or tactical move that a firm takes to build or defend its competitive advantages or improve its market position, and the competitive response, a strategic or tactical move taken to counter a competitor's action (Smith et al., 2001).

The distinction between strategic and tactical actions is important because each type generates different competitive dynamics.

Strategic actions are market-based moves that involve a significant commitment of organizational resources and are difficult to reverse. Building a new manufacturing facility, acquiring a competitor, launching an entirely new product line, or entering a foreign market for the first time are all strategic actions. These moves require substantial capital, organizational restructuring, and long planning horizons. Because they are so resource-intensive and difficult to undo, strategic actions signal serious competitive intent and tend to reshape the competitive landscape in lasting ways.

Tactical actions are market-based moves taken to fine-tune an existing strategy. They involve fewer resources and are relatively easy to reverse. Adjusting pricing, launching a promotional campaign, modifying product features, or altering distribution arrangements are tactical actions. These moves are part of the ongoing day-to-day competitive maneuvering that occurs within a broader strategic framework.

The type of action shapes the type of response it provokes. Strategic actions tend to elicit strategic responses, and tactical actions tend to elicit tactical responses. However, the response patterns differ in timing and frequency. Strategic actions elicit fewer competitive responses, and those responses tend to be slower; rivals need time to assess the implications of a major strategic move and to mobilize the resources required for an adequate response. A competitor that observes a rival building a billion-dollar semiconductor fabrication facility cannot respond overnight; it must evaluate whether to match the investment, pursue an alternative strategy, or accept a diminished competitive position. Tactical actions, by contrast, typically receive quick responses. When one airline drops fares on a popular route, competing airlines often match the reduction within hours or days. The resources required are minimal, the decision is straightforward, and the cost of failing to respond (losing customers immediately) is tangible and immediate.

4.2.5 Likelihood of Action

Not all firms are equally likely to initiate competitive action. Two factors are particularly influential in determining whether a firm will be the one to make the first move: the advantages of being a first mover and the effect of organizational size.

A **first mover** is a firm that takes an initial competitive action to build or defend its competitive advantage or improve its market position (Lieberman & Montgomery, 1988). First movers invest in product innovation and development, aggressive advertising, and advanced research and development. The potential rewards are significant: first movers can capture early demand, establish brand loyalty before competitors enter, and build switching costs that lock in customers. Customers who develop a commitment to the first mover's product may be difficult for later entrants to pry away, giving the first mover a durable market share advantage.

However, first-mover status also carries risks. A **second mover** responds to the first mover's action, typically through imitation. The second mover studies customer reactions to the first mover's innovation, identifies any mistakes the pioneer made, and avoids both those errors and the enormous research and development expense that the first mover absorbed. Second movers may also develop more efficient processes and technologies by learning from the first mover's experience. A **late mover** responds only after considerable time has elapsed. Late movers typically earn only average returns and may permanently lag behind in understanding how to create value for customers in that product space.

Organizational size affects competitive behavior in predictable ways, though these are tendencies rather than iron laws. Small firms tend to be nimble and flexible competitors. They rely on speed and surprise, have the organizational flexibility to launch a greater variety of competitive actions, and can execute those actions faster than their larger counterparts. Large firms, by contrast, are likely to initiate more total competitive actions during a given period due to their slack, the extra, unused resources available for competitive initiatives. However, large firms are typically slower to respond to strategic actions because of greater bureaucratic complexity, more layers of decision-making, and larger organizational inertia.

These are tendencies, not destiny. Large firms can deliberately cultivate the speed and flexibility of small firms through decentralized decision-making, autonomous business units, and cultures that reward initiative. Small firms can attempt to build the resource advantages of large firms through strategic alliances, focused investment, and efficient resource deployment. The best competitors in any industry tend to combine the strengths of both — the agility of the small with the resources of the large.

4.2.6 Likelihood of Response

When a competitor takes action, the targeted firm must decide whether and how to respond. Three factors are particularly important in determining the likelihood and nature of competitive response: the type of action, the actor's reputation, and market dependence.

Type of competitive action. As discussed above, strategic actions tend to provoke slower, more deliberate responses because of the time and resources required to assess and counter a major competitive move. Tactical actions provoke quicker responses because they are simpler to evaluate and less expensive to match. This asymmetry creates a strategic implication: firms that wish to act without provoking immediate retaliation may favor strategic actions, which buy time before competitors can respond effectively. Firms that want to test the competitive waters or make incremental adjustments use tactical actions, knowing that responses will come quickly but will also be incremental.

Actor's reputation. Competitors do not evaluate each competitive action in isolation; they interpret it through the lens of the acting firm's history and reputation. A firm will study how a competitor has responded to attacks in the past in order to predict its likely future responses. A firm known for aggressive retaliation (matching every price cut, countering every product launch, and fighting for every point of market share) establishes a reputation that deters rivals from attacking in the first place. Competitors think twice before provoking a firm they believe will respond forcefully. Conversely, a firm with a reputation for passive responses may invite increasingly aggressive competitive actions from rivals who expect to act without consequence.

EX: Reputation as Deterrence in Consumer Electronics

Consider how Samsung's reputation for rapid competitive response affects its rivals' behavior. When a competitor introduces a new feature in its smartphone lineup, Samsung has historically responded within months, sometimes weeks, with a comparable or superior offering. This pattern of aggressive, fast response is well known throughout the industry. As a result, competitors planning to launch innovative features must factor in the near-certainty of a Samsung countermove when calculating the expected return on their investment. Some firms may delay or abandon planned actions that would otherwise be profitable, simply because Samsung's reputation makes the expected competitive response too costly to absorb. The reputation itself functions as a competitive weapon, deterring action before it occurs.

Market dependence. The extent to which a firm's revenues or profits are derived from a particular market powerfully influences how vigorously it responds to competitive threats in that market. A firm that earns 80% of its revenue from a single market will respond far more aggressively to an attack on that market than a diversified firm for which the same market represents only 10% of revenue. Market dependence raises the stakes of inaction; losing ground in a market that the firm depends upon threatens the entire enterprise, not just one business segment.

4.2.7 Number of Competitors and Competitive Intensity

The dynamics described so far play out among a given set of rivals, but the number of those rivals is itself a powerful determinant of how intensely they compete. The intuitive expectation is that competition grows steadily fiercer as more firms enter, yet the relationship is far from linear. Studying geographically isolated local markets for retail and professional services such as physicians, druggists, and tire dealers, Bresnahan and Reiss (1991) found that competitive conduct changes most sharply with the entry of the second and third firms. Almost all of the movement away from monopoly-style behavior toward genuinely competitive conduct occurs by the time a market contains three competitors, and once a market has between three and five firms, an additional entrant has little further effect. A market need not be crowded to behave as though it were; a mere handful of rivals can be enough to push prices and margins close to competitive levels.

This result carries an important qualification rooted in the markets studied. The services Bresnahan and Reiss examined were relatively undifferentiated, where one provider's offering closely resembled another's. When firms can differentiate their products (Chapter 2), each competes in a somewhat distinct space, which dampens rivalry and can allow even markets with five or more firms to sustain above-competitive margins. Firm count and differentiation therefore work together: numerous undifferentiated rivals produce intense competition, while meaningful differentiation can preserve profitability even as the number of competitors rises.

4.2.8 Market Cycle Speed and Competitive Dynamics

The competitive dynamics discussed throughout this section do not unfold at the same pace in every industry. The speed at which competitive advantages are built, eroded, and rebuilt varies dramatically depending on the industry's market cycle speed, the rate at which competitive advantages can be imitated (Williams, 1992).

Slow-cycle markets are markets where imitation is costly and takes long periods of time. Utilities provide a classic example: the infrastructure required to generate and distribute electricity creates advantages that competitors cannot replicate quickly or cheaply. Pharmaceutical companies with patent-protected drugs operate in slow-cycle conditions during the patent period. In slow-cycle markets, firms concentrate their competitive actions on protecting, maintaining, and extending their proprietary competitive advantages. The pace of competitive interaction is measured and deliberate because the advantages at stake are durable.

Standard-cycle markets are markets where imitation takes a moderate amount of time and involves moderate cost. The automotive industry exemplifies this category, as does most of the consumer packaged goods industry. Firms in standard-cycle markets seek large market shares, invest in building brand loyalty through sustained marketing, and carefully control their operations to maintain efficiency. Competitive advantages in these markets are meaningful but not permanent; a rival with sufficient resources and commitment can eventually replicate most advantages, though the process takes years rather than weeks.

Fast-cycle markets are markets where imitation happens quickly and at relatively low cost. Mobile applications, fashion apparel, and many technology-driven consumer products operate in fast-cycle conditions. Competitors can use reverse engineering, benchmarking, or parallel development to quickly imitate or improve upon successful products. In fast-cycle markets, firms are in a constant race; competitive leads can appear and disappear within months. The emphasis shifts from protecting existing advantages to continuously creating new ones. Speed, innovation, and the ability to rapidly iterate on products and business models become the most important competitive capabilities.

The market cycle speed of an industry has direct implications for which competitive strategies are viable and how firms should allocate their resources between exploitation of current advantages and exploration of new ones. In slow-cycle markets, the priority is defense, protecting the advantages that take so long to build. In fast-cycle markets, defense is largely futile because advantages are inherently short-lived; the priority is offense, constantly innovating and staying ahead of the imitation curve. Standard-cycle markets require a balance of both. This connects directly to the dynamic capabilities framework introduced in Chapter 3.6: sensing, seizing, and reconfiguring are progressively more important as market cycle speed increases.

4.2.9 Competitive Rivalry and Business-Level Strategy

Competitive rivalry affects all types of strategy, but it most directly influences business-level strategy — the differentiation, cost leadership, and focus strategies examined in Chapter 2. The success of any business-level strategy is determined not only by the firm's initial competitive actions but also by how well it anticipates competitors' responses and how effectively it responds to competitors' moves in return. A differentiation strategy is only as durable as the firm's ability to maintain its uniqueness in the face of imitative competitive responses. A cost leadership strategy is only sustainable as long as the firm can defend its cost position against rivals pursuing similar efficiencies.

The frameworks in this section (competitor analysis, the drivers of competitive behavior, the likelihood of action and response, and market cycle speed) provide the tools for making these assessments. They transform the study of competition from an abstract concept into a structured analytical exercise, enabling managers to think systematically about who their competitors are, what those competitors are likely to do, and how the firm should position itself in anticipation. The next section builds on this foundation by examining the broader structural forces that determine overall industry profitability, Porter's Five Forces framework.

References

Bresnahan, T. F., & Reiss, P. C. (1991). Entry and competition in concentrated markets. *Journal of Political Economy, 99*(5), 977–1009.

Chen, M.-J. (1996). Competitor analysis and interfirm rivalry: Toward a theoretical integration. *Academy of Management Review, 21*(1), 100–134.

Gimeno, J., & Woo, C. Y. (1996). Hypercompetition in a multimarket context: The role of strategic similarity and multimarket contact in competitive de-escalation. *Organization Science, 7*(3), 322–341.

Lieberman, M. B., & Montgomery, D. B. (1988). First-mover advantages. *Strategic Management Journal, 9*(S1), 41–58.

Porter, M. E. (1980). *Competitive strategy: Techniques for analyzing industries and competitors.* Free Press.

Smith, K. G., Ferrier, W. J., & Ndofor, H. (2001). Competitive dynamics research: Critique and future directions. In M. A. Hitt, R. E. Freeman, & J. S. Harrison (Eds.), *The Blackwell handbook of strategic management* (pp. 315–361). Blackwell Publishers.

Williams, J. R. (1992). How sustainable is your competitive advantage? *California Management Review, 34*(3), 29–51.

4.3 Porter's Five Forces — *What determines industry profitability?*

The previous section examined how individual firms compete through actions and responses, the micro-level dynamics of rivalry between specific competitors. But competitive dynamics alone cannot explain why some industries are consistently more profitable than others. The airline industry has been notoriously unprofitable for decades, despite containing firms with excellent management teams, strong brands, and sophisticated operational capabilities. The soft drink industry, by contrast, has generated extraordinary profits for its major players over the same period, even though its core product (flavored sugar water) is technologically simple and easily replicated. If firm-level factors like resources and capabilities were the only determinants of profitability, we would expect talented managers to earn high returns regardless of which industry they chose. The persistent profitability differences between industries tell us that something beyond firm-level strategy is at work.

Michael Porter's Five Forces framework provides the answer. First published in his landmark 1980 book *Competitive Strategy*, the framework identifies five structural forces that collectively determine the profit potential of an industry, that is, the degree to which an average firm in that industry can earn good returns (Porter, 1979, 1980). The framework does not predict any individual firm's performance; a brilliant firm can outperform its industry average, and a poorly managed firm can underperform. But it reveals the structural ceiling on profitability that the industry imposes on all participants. A firm in a structurally attractive industry begins with a significant advantage: the competitive environment is working in its favor. A firm in a structurally unattractive industry faces an uphill battle: the competitive environment actively erodes profitability, and even strong execution may produce only modest returns.

The five forces are: rivalry among existing competitors, bargaining power of suppliers, bargaining power of buyers, threat of new entrants, and threat of substitute products or services. Each force represents a distinct source of competitive pressure that can extract value from industry participants. The stronger the forces, the more difficult it is for firms to earn attractive profits. The weaker the forces, the more profit the industry allows firms to retain. Understanding each force, what drives it, how to assess it, and how it interacts with the others, is the core task of industry-level external analysis.

4.3.1 Understanding the Framework's Logic

Porter's framework descends from the structure–conduct–performance (SCP) paradigm developed in industrial organization economics (Mason, 1939; Bain, 1956). SCP proposed a causal chain: an industry's structure (concentration, entry barriers, product differentiation) shapes how firms behave, or conduct (pricing, investment, rivalry), which in turn determines performance (profitability). Economists used SCP to identify industries earning excess profits at consumers' expense, a concern for regulators. Porter inverted that logic for managers, asking how a firm can find or position itself within industries whose structure permits attractive profits. The five forces describe the structural conditions that drive this variation in industry profitability.

The economic logic that unifies the forces can be seen as a division of value. In any industry, there is a finite pool of value created by the products or services firms produce and sell. The five forces determine how that value is divided among the various players: the industry's firms, their suppliers, their buyers, potential entrants, and providers of substitute products (Porter, 2008). Each force represents a different party's ability to capture a larger share of that value pool at the expense of the industry's firms.

When suppliers have strong bargaining power, they capture value by charging higher input prices. When buyers have strong bargaining power, they capture value by demanding lower prices or better terms. When the threat of new entrants is high, incumbents must invest in deterrence (lower prices, increased marketing, capacity expansion) that consumes profits. When substitute products are readily available, they cap the prices that industry firms can charge. And when rivalry among existing competitors is intense, firms compete away their own profits through price wars, advertising battles, and costly innovation races. In every case, the force operates by redistributing value away from the industry's firms and toward some other party, or by destroying value through wasteful competition.

This logic also reveals an important point about the direction of each force. When analyzing the Five Forces, students sometimes struggle with the question: "good for whom?" The answer is always the same. The analysis is conducted from the perspective of the focal industry, the industry whose attractiveness is being assessed. A condition that is "good" strengthens the position of firms within that industry. A condition that is "bad" weakens it. For each of the five forces, a *low* force is favorable to industry profitability, and a *high* force is unfavorable. This consistency holds across all five forces without exception.

4.3.2 Force 1: Rivalry Among Existing Competitors

Rivalry is the most visible of the five forces and often the first that comes to mind when people think about competition. It refers to the competitive pressure that firms within the same industry exert on one another, the ongoing battle for customers, market share, and competitive position. High rivalry erodes profitability by forcing firms to compete on price, increase spending on marketing and innovation, or make other costly moves to attract and retain customers.

A common error is to conclude that rivalry is high in every industry. The reasoning usually runs: the firms compete on price, features, advertising, and service, so rivalry must be intense. But listing the dimensions along which firms compete says nothing about intensity. Nearly every firm in nearly every industry competes along several dimensions and responds to its rivals' moves; competitive response of some kind is close to universal. What separates high rivalry from low is not whether firms respond to one another, nor how many dimensions they compete on, but how far they must go in those responses, and in particular how much of their own profit they surrender in the process. Two industries can compete on the exact same dimensions and yet reach opposite outcomes: one erodes its margins to near zero in a chronic price war, while the other settles into a stable equilibrium in which no firm finds it worthwhile to break ranks. The structural factors below determine which outcome prevails.

Several structural factors determine the intensity of rivalry within an industry.

Number of competitors. Industries with many competitors tend to experience higher rivalry than those with few. When many firms are vying for the same customers, each firm's actions affect the others, and the probability of aggressive competitive moves increases. A concentrated industry, one dominated by a handful of large players, often exhibits more restrained competition, because each firm's actions are highly visible and the consequences of aggression are predictable. This connects to the industry concentration concepts introduced in Chapter 4.1: industries closer to the oligopoly end of the spectrum tend to have lower rivalry than those closer to perfect competition.

Industry growth rate. Rivalry is more intense in flat or declining markets than in growing ones. When the overall market is expanding, firms can grow simply by capturing new demand; they do not need to steal customers from competitors. In a stagnant or shrinking market, the only way to grow is to take market share from rivals, which intensifies competition and often triggers price wars. This is one reason why firms in mature industries frequently face more brutal competitive conditions than firms in rapidly growing ones.

Fixed costs relative to variable costs. Industries with high fixed costs and relatively low variable costs create intense pressure to maintain volume. If most of a firm's costs are fixed (factory leases, equipment depreciation, salaried workforce) then each additional unit sold contributes disproportionately to covering those fixed costs. When demand softens, firms in high-fixed-cost industries face a painful choice: cut prices to maintain volume (eroding margins but covering fixed costs) or maintain prices and risk catastrophic underutilization of expensive capacity. The result is that firms in high-fixed-cost industries often compete aggressively on price during downturns, even when doing so drives industry-wide profitability to near zero. The steel industry, airlines, and hotels all exhibit this pattern.

Exit barriers. When firms cannot easily exit an unprofitable industry, they remain and fight, even when rational economic analysis would suggest that exit is the better option. Exit barriers arise when firms have made significant investments in non-redeployable assets, assets that cannot be repurposed for another use or sold at a reasonable price. A steel foundry represents an enormous capital investment that has virtually no alternative use. A firm that has invested hundreds of millions of dollars in such a facility will continue operating and competing even at thin or negative margins, because the alternative (shutting down and writing off the entire investment) is even worse. Exit barriers trap competitors in the industry, sustaining rivalry long past the point where it would otherwise subside through natural exit.

Product differentiation. When products are largely undifferentiated, when customers perceive few meaningful differences between offerings, competition tends to collapse into price wars. If every firm's product serves the same function equally well, the only remaining basis for competition is price, and price competition directly destroys profitability. Product differentiation reduces rivalry by giving each firm a basis for competition other than price. Customers who perceive genuine differences between products are less likely to switch based solely on a small price difference, which allows firms to maintain margins even in the face of competitive pressure. This is why, as discussed in Chapter 2, differentiation strategy is one of the fundamental approaches to achieving competitive advantage; it changes the nature of the competitive game from "who is cheapest?" to "who offers the most valued product?"

Switching costs. When switching costs are low, customers can easily move from one firm to another, and firms are constantly at risk of losing their customer base to a competitor's slightly better offer. Low switching costs make customer poaching easy and profitable, which encourages aggressive competitive behavior. When switching costs are high, because customers have made learning investments, signed contracts, integrated their systems with a particular supplier, or built workflows around a specific product, rivalry is dampened. Customers locked in by switching costs are less responsive to competitive moves, which reduces the incentive for firms to engage in costly battles for each other's customers.

EX: Rivalry in the U.S. Airline Industry

The U.S. airline industry illustrates how multiple rivalry factors can compound to create an intensely competitive environment. The industry has a large number of competitors, ranging from major carriers like Delta, United, and American to low-cost carriers like Southwest, Spirit, and Frontier. The overall market growth rate for domestic air travel has been modest for years; the industry is mature, not rapidly expanding. Fixed costs are enormous: aircraft leases, airport gate fees, maintenance facilities, and crew salaries represent massive investments that must be covered regardless of passenger volume. Exit barriers are high because aircraft and airport infrastructure are specialized assets with limited alternative uses. Product differentiation in economy class is minimal; for most travelers, a seat from Dallas to Chicago is functionally identical regardless of which airline provides it. And switching costs are low: frequent flyer programs create some loyalty, but travelers regularly book based on price and schedule rather than airline affiliation. The result of all these factors converging is an industry notorious for intense rivalry and chronically poor profitability, despite carrying hundreds of millions of passengers each year. Airlines do not compete along more dimensions than firms in other industries. What makes their rivalry intense is that the structural factors push each concession, whether lower fares, added capacity, or costlier perks, further until little profit remains.

4.3.3 Force 2: Bargaining Power of Suppliers

Suppliers provide the inputs (raw materials, components, labor, services, technology) that industry firms need to produce their products. When suppliers have strong bargaining power, they can charge higher prices, reduce the quality of inputs, or impose unfavorable terms, all of which reduce the profitability of the firms they supply. Supplier power, in essence, captures value that would otherwise remain with the industry's firms.

Several factors determine the bargaining power of suppliers.

Supplier concentration relative to the industry. When a few suppliers dominate the market for a critical input and the buying industry is fragmented, suppliers hold significant power. The semiconductor industry provides a telling example: a small number of chip fabricators (most notably TSMC) supply the vast majority of advanced chips to a wide range of industries, giving them substantial leverage over their customers. Conversely, when many suppliers compete to serve the industry, no individual supplier can exert meaningful pricing power.

Availability of substitute inputs. If the industry can switch to alternative inputs without significant cost or quality degradation, supplier power is limited. A food manufacturer that can substitute one type of vegetable oil for another depending on price has reduced the bargaining power of any single oil supplier. When no substitutes exist for a critical input, the supplier's power increases substantially.

Importance of the industry to the supplier. Suppliers are more accommodating when the focal industry represents a significant portion of their sales. A steel supplier that sells 40% of its output to the automotive industry has a strong incentive to maintain good relationships and competitive pricing, because losing automotive customers would be devastating. If the industry represents only a trivial portion of the supplier's business, the supplier has less incentive to offer favorable terms.

Switching costs for changing suppliers. When firms in the industry have invested in processes, training, or systems that are tailored to a specific supplier's inputs, switching to a different supplier becomes costly and disruptive. These switching costs give the incumbent supplier leverage, because the buyer cannot credibly threaten to take its business elsewhere without incurring significant expense. High switching costs between suppliers increase supplier power; low switching costs diminish it.

Threat of forward integration by suppliers. If a supplier can credibly threaten to enter the focal industry, to bypass its current customers and sell directly to end consumers, this threat increases the supplier's bargaining power. The supplier is effectively saying: "give me better terms, or I will become your competitor." The credibility of this threat depends on the supplier's resources, capabilities, and track record. We will examine vertical integration threats in greater detail in the next section.

Threat of backward integration by the industry. Supplier power also falls when firms in the focal industry can credibly threaten to produce a critical input themselves rather than buy it. This reverses the leverage of the forward-integration threat above: the industry is now saying, "offer better terms, or we will make this input in-house and stop buying from you." A firm with the capital and technical capability to bring production in-house can extract concessions from suppliers without ever acting on the threat. Its credibility depends on the industry's resources, the scale at which its firms operate, and whether internal production is economically feasible.

4.3.4 Force 3: Bargaining Power of Buyers

Buyers are the customers, whether individual consumers or other businesses, that purchase the industry's products. When buyers have strong bargaining power, they can negotiate lower prices, demand higher quality or more services, and play competitors against each other, all of which reduce industry profitability. Buyer power captures value for the customer at the expense of the industry's firms.

It is important to keep the focal industry framework firmly in mind when analyzing buyer power. The buyers in a Five Forces analysis are the customers of the focal industry; they may be end consumers, or they may be firms in a downstream industry. The same factors that determine bargaining power apply regardless, but the specific dynamics differ depending on whether the buyer is Walmart negotiating with consumer goods manufacturers or an individual consumer choosing between brands of toothpaste.

Buyer concentration and purchase volume. When a small number of buyers account for a large proportion of the industry's sales, those buyers wield significant power. In the grocery industry, a handful of large retailers (Walmart, Kroger, Costco) account for a substantial share of total food purchases, giving them enormous leverage over food manufacturers. Each buyer's potential defection represents a meaningful revenue loss for the supplier, which strengthens the buyer's negotiating position. Conversely, when the industry sells to a large number of small, fragmented buyers, no single buyer has significant leverage. Individual retail consumers are the clearest case: because they are so numerous and fragmented, any one customer's purchase is trivial to the seller, and end consumers as individuals therefore wield almost no bargaining power no matter how price-sensitive they feel. Their influence emerges only when it is aggregated by a concentrated intermediary, such as a large retailer negotiating on the strength of the millions of purchases it represents.

Product standardization. When the industry's product is standardized or perceived as a commodity, buyer power increases because buyers can easily switch between suppliers. If one firm's product is functionally interchangeable with another's, the buyer has no reason to accept a higher price; there is always an equivalent alternative available. Product differentiation is the primary countermeasure: buyers have less power when the product offers something unique that is not available from competitors. This is another reason why differentiation strategy, as discussed in Chapter 2, is so strategically important; it does not merely create a basis for premium pricing; it fundamentally shifts the power dynamic between the firm and its customers.

Buyer switching costs. When buyers face high costs to switch from one supplier to another, because of contractual obligations, learning investments, integration of systems, or the disruption of changing workflows, their bargaining power is diminished. They cannot credibly threaten to take their business elsewhere because doing so would be too costly. When switching costs are low, buyers can and do play suppliers against each other, driving down prices and demanding better terms.

Buyer price sensitivity. Buyers who are highly price-sensitive exert more downward pressure on industry prices. Price sensitivity is influenced by several factors: how large the purchase is relative to the buyer's total costs, how much the quality of the input affects the quality of the buyer's own product, and how profitable the buyer's own business is. A construction company purchasing commodity steel is likely to be price-sensitive because steel is a major cost component. A luxury watchmaker purchasing a tiny sapphire crystal for a $10,000 watch is far less price-sensitive regarding that specific input because it represents a negligible fraction of the product's final cost.

Threat of backward integration by buyers. If a buyer can credibly threaten to produce the industry's product internally, to make rather than buy, this threat increases the buyer's bargaining power. The buyer is essentially telling the supplier: "lower your prices, or I will supply myself." As with forward integration threats, the credibility of this threat depends on the buyer's resources, capabilities, and the economic feasibility of internal production.

Threat of forward integration by the industry. Just as a buyer's threat to integrate backward raises buyer power, the industry's ability to integrate forward lowers it. If firms in the focal industry can credibly threaten to bypass their current buyers and reach end customers directly, whether by opening their own stores, selling online, or acquiring a distributor, buyers lose leverage. A manufacturer able to sell straight to consumers is less dependent on any single retailer, which weakens that retailer's ability to demand price concessions. The credibility of the threat depends on the industry's resources, capabilities, and the economic feasibility of reaching customers without the buyer.

EX: Bargaining Power Across a Value Chain — Farmers, Frozen Entrée Makers, and Food Retailers

The relationship between buyer power and supplier power becomes especially clear when examining adjacent industries in a value chain. Consider three linked industries: farmers, frozen entrée makers, and food retailers.

Farmers sell commodity agricultural products (potatoes, chicken, vegetables) to frozen entrée manufacturers. There are many small farmers, the products are largely undifferentiated, and switching between suppliers is easy for the manufacturers. The farmers, in this analysis, are the suppliers, and the frozen entrée makers are their buyers. The result is low supplier power and high buyer power: the entrée makers can negotiate favorable prices because they are fewer and larger, and the products they purchase are commodities.

Now shift the focal industry one step downstream. The frozen entrée makers are selling to food retailers. Here, the entrée makers become the suppliers and the retailers become the buyers. The dynamics change. The entrée makers are relatively concentrated; a few large firms like Nestlé and Conagra dominate the market, and they sell differentiated products. Consumers may have strong brand preferences for a particular frozen dinner, which means that a retailer who stops carrying that brand risks losing customers. This product differentiation gives the entrée makers more leverage than the farmers had, even though both are in the supplier role. The retailer cannot as easily substitute one brand for another without affecting its own sales.

The lesson is that the same Five Forces principles apply at every link in the value chain, but the specific factors (concentration, differentiation, switching costs) shift as you change which industry is the focal one. Keeping the focal industry clearly identified is essential for conducting an accurate analysis.

4.3.5 Force 4: Threat of New Entrants

New entrants bring additional capacity, the desire to gain market share, and often substantial resources. Their entry increases competition and puts downward pressure on prices, which erodes the profitability of incumbent firms. The threat of new entrants therefore depends on the barriers to entry that protect the industry, structural obstacles that make it difficult or costly for outsiders to enter.

An important conceptual point that frequently confuses students: the factors discussed below are **barriers to entry**, and they have an **inverse relationship** with the threat of entry. As barriers go higher, the threat of new entrants goes lower. When we say that a factor "increases barriers," that is favorable to incumbents; it protects their profitability by discouraging new competitors from entering. The analysis is always conducted from the perspective of firms already inside the industry.

Capital requirements. Some industries require enormous upfront investment simply to begin competing. Entering the aerospace industry, for instance, requires billions of dollars in manufacturing facilities, engineering talent, certification processes, and supply chain development. These capital requirements alone exclude all but the most well-funded potential entrants. By contrast, starting a local landscaping business requires minimal capital: a truck, some equipment, and a willingness to work. Capital requirements vary enormously across industries and represent one of the most straightforward barriers to entry.

Scale requirements. In industries where economies of scale are significant, a concept explored in depth in Chapter 2.4, new entrants face a difficult choice. They can enter at a large scale, which requires massive upfront investment and creates the risk of excess capacity if demand does not materialize, or they can enter at a small scale and accept a cost disadvantage relative to incumbents who have already achieved efficient volume. In commodity markets like steel, cement, or commodity chemicals, the minimum efficient scale of production is so large that a new entrant must immediately capture significant market share just to be cost-competitive. This creates a substantial barrier.

Scope economies. Related to but distinct from scale economies, scope economies arise when a firm can share resources across multiple products or services. Large retailers like Walmart or Amazon benefit from scope economies: they can spread the costs of their distribution infrastructure, technology platforms, store operations, and brand marketing across thousands of product categories. Adding one more product category to a Walmart store is marginally very inexpensive. A new entrant attempting to compete in just one product category does not enjoy these economies, putting it at a structural disadvantage.

Switching costs. When customers in the industry have already invested in learning, integration, or relationships with incumbent firms, new entrants must not only offer a competitive product; they must also compensate customers for the cost of switching. The technology industry provides many examples: businesses that have built their operations around Microsoft's software ecosystem face enormous switching costs if they want to move to an alternative. A new entrant in enterprise software must offer something dramatically better to overcome the inertia created by those switching costs. This barrier protects incumbents even when their products are not objectively superior to what a new entrant might offer.

Access to scarce resources. Some industries are protected by limited access to critical resources. De Beers historically controlled access to the world's major diamond mines, making it extremely difficult for a new firm to enter the diamond industry regardless of how much capital it possessed. Coca-Cola's distribution network, built over more than a century and reaching virtually every retail location on earth, represents a resource that no new entrant could easily replicate. When the most important inputs to an industry are scarce and already controlled by incumbents, the barrier to entry is formidable.

Learning curve advantages. As firms produce more of a product over time, they accumulate knowledge and experience that improve efficiency, quality, and reliability. This learning curve effect means that incumbents who have been producing for years or decades possess operational know-how that new entrants must develop from scratch. A motorcycle manufacturer with decades of experience producing millions of units has achieved a level of reliability and manufacturing precision that a new entrant simply cannot match on day one. The learning curve is a time-dependent barrier; it cannot be overcome with money alone; it requires accumulated experience.

Product complexity. When the industry's product is technically complex, the pool of potential entrants shrinks dramatically. The x86 microprocessor industry is dominated by Intel and AMD not because other firms lack ambition, but because designing and manufacturing advanced semiconductors requires a depth of specialized expertise that very few organizations possess. Product complexity creates a natural barrier by limiting the number of firms with the technical capability to compete.

Entry-deterring regulations. Government regulations can create substantial barriers to entry. Tariffs increase the cost for foreign firms to enter a domestic market. Licensing requirements, in industries such as banking, telecommunications, healthcare, and energy, require new entrants to navigate complex regulatory processes before they can begin operating. Environmental regulations impose compliance costs that must be absorbed before a single unit is sold. While regulation is often discussed as a burden on existing firms, it is equally, and often more, burdensome for potential entrants who must meet the same requirements without the revenue base or organizational infrastructure that incumbents already possess. Therefore, regulations tend to help incumbent firms, and especially larger firms, because they possess the resources to manage regulatory compliance more efficiently.

4.3.6 Force 5: Threat of Substitute Products or Services

Substitutes are fundamentally different products from outside the industry that serve the same function or purpose for the end consumer. The critical distinction between substitutes and rivals is that rivals compete within the industry by offering similar products, while substitutes compete from outside the industry by offering different products that solve the same customer problem. As discussed in Chapter 4.1, this distinction is directly tied to how the industry boundary is drawn; where that boundary falls determines what is classified as rivalry and what is classified as substitution.

Streaming services are substitutes for cable television, fundamentally different delivery mechanisms and business models serving the same customer need for entertainment content. Ride-sharing services like Uber and Lyft are substitutes for car ownership, different products that solve the same transportation problem. A drinking fountain in a hallway is a substitute for a vending machine drink, a fundamentally different way to satisfy thirst. In each case, the substitute product is not a slightly different version of the industry's product; it is an entirely different product that happens to fulfill a similar need.

Substitutes exert competitive pressure by acting as a cap on profitability. If firms in the industry charge too much, if prices rise beyond a certain threshold relative to the value delivered, customers will switch to the substitute product. The industry cannot raise prices indefinitely because at some point, the substitute becomes the more attractive option. This cap operates even if no substitute product is currently taking significant market share; the mere availability of an affordable substitute constrains the industry's pricing power.

The strength of the substitution threat depends on the **price-performance tradeoff** of the substitute relative to the industry's product (Porter, 2008). If the substitute offers comparable performance at a significantly lower price, or dramatically better performance at a comparable price, the threat is high. If the substitute is inferior in performance and not significantly cheaper, the threat is low. Customers make this tradeoff calculation, consciously or unconsciously, whenever they choose between an industry's product and an available substitute.

EX: Substitution in the Taxi Industry

Before the emergence of ride-sharing platforms, the taxi industry in most major cities operated with limited substitution threats. Public transit served as a partial substitute, but it lacked the convenience and door-to-door service that taxis provided. Private car ownership was an alternative, but it involved fixed costs (insurance, parking, maintenance) that made it a poor substitute for occasional transportation needs. Taxis held significant pricing power as a result.

The launch of Uber and Lyft introduced a fundamentally different product — on-demand transportation coordinated through a mobile platform, with dynamic pricing, driver ratings, and cashless payment. This substitute matched or exceeded the performance of traditional taxis on nearly every dimension that customers valued (convenience, reliability, cleanliness, price transparency) while often being cheaper. The price-performance tradeoff shifted dramatically against the taxi industry. Customers defected in enormous numbers, taxi medallion values collapsed in cities like New York (where they fell from over $1 million to under $200,000), and the industry was permanently transformed. The substitution threat that had been low for decades became overwhelming in the span of a few years.

4.3.6.1 Porter's Five Forces Diagram

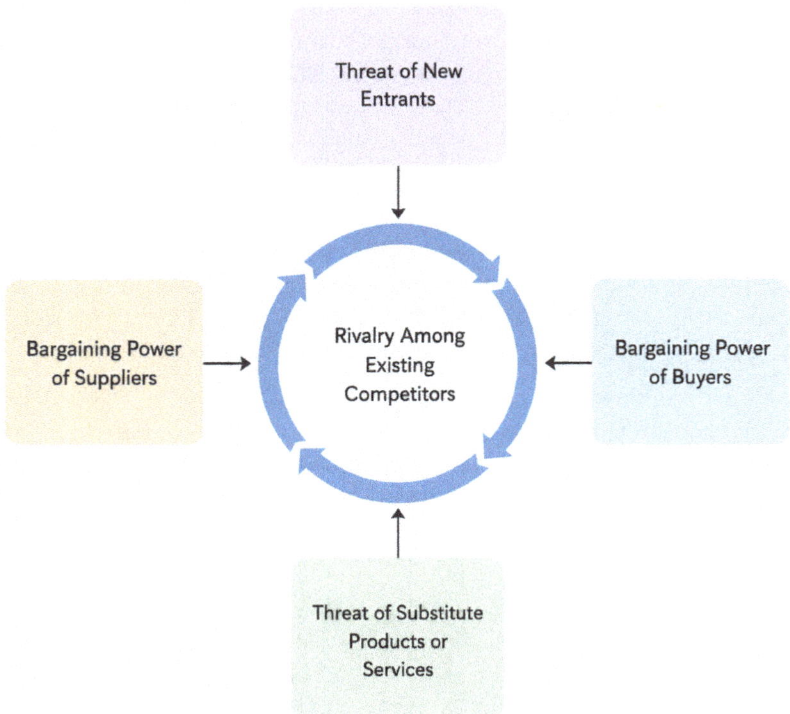

4.3.7 Applying the Five Forces

Conducting a Five Forces analysis requires applying the framework systematically rather than impressionistically. The process involves four steps.

First, **analyze each force individually**, identifying the specific factors that drive that force in the industry being examined. This means going beyond vague assessments like "rivalry seems high" to specify *why*: is it because there are many competitors? Because the industry growth rate is low? Because fixed costs are high? The specific factors matter because they point toward different strategic responses.

Second, **assess each force as high, medium, or low**. This assessment is necessarily a judgment call; there is no formula that converts individual factors into a definitive rating. But the assessment should be grounded in specific evidence rather than intuition alone. A force is high when its underlying factors collectively create strong competitive pressure on industry profitability. A force is low when those factors are weak or absent.

Third, **evaluate the combined strength of the five forces** to determine overall industry attractiveness. An industry where all five forces are low is highly attractive; firms face minimal competitive pressure and can expect to earn strong profits. An industry where all five forces are high is unattractive; competitive pressure comes from every direction, and even well-managed firms may struggle to earn adequate returns. Most industries fall somewhere in between, with some forces favorable and others unfavorable. The overall assessment requires weighing the combined effect.

Fourth, **remember the connection to industry boundary**. As established in Chapter 4.1, where the industry boundary is drawn determines what counts as rivalry among existing competitors versus what counts as substitution. It also affects how suppliers and buyers are identified. A Five Forces analysis is only as accurate as the industry definition it is based upon. Analysts should be explicit about the boundary they are using and consider whether alternative definitions would materially change the conclusions.

EX: Five Forces Analysis of the Soft Drink Industry

The soft drink industry illustrates how the Five Forces framework can explain an industry's profitability. The **threat of new entrants is low**. The industry has moderate to high capital requirements for large-scale production, significant economies of scale and scope, high product differentiation driven by decades of brand investment, and distribution network advantages that incumbents like Coca-Cola and PepsiCo have built over generations. A craft or artisanal soda company can enter on a small scale, but competing at the national or global level against incumbents is extraordinarily difficult.

Rivalry is medium. There are only a few large competitors, which tends to reduce rivalry. However, because the core product is essentially flavored sugar water, differentiation is almost entirely a function of branding and marketing rather than product attributes. This means the firms must invest heavily in advertising to maintain the perceived differences that justify their prices. The rivalry is real but tempered by the oligopolistic structure; Coca-Cola and PepsiCo have a well-established competitive equilibrium and generally avoid destructive price wars.

Supplier power is low. The primary ingredients (water, sugar, flavorings, packaging materials) are commodities available from many suppliers. No individual supplier has meaningful bargaining leverage over firms as large as Coca-Cola or PepsiCo.

Buyer power is medium. The direct buyers are large retailers like Walmart and grocery chains, not individual consumers, who purchase from the retailer rather than the manufacturer. Retailers have some leverage: switching costs at the retail level are low, and a store can shift shelf space toward whichever brand offers better terms or promote its own private-label alternatives. That leverage is checked, however, by consumer brand loyalty. Shoppers expect to find Coca-Cola and Pepsi on the shelf, so a retailer that replaced the major brands with a private label would risk losing customers, which limits how hard it can push the manufacturers. Consumers' low price sensitivity reinforces this: because shoppers are not very responsive to soft drink prices, retailers have little reason to negotiate aggressively over wholesale costs.

The threat of substitutes is high. Consumers do not need to drink soft drinks; they have an enormous range of alternatives, including water, juice, tea, coffee, energy drinks, sparkling water, sports drinks, and alcoholic beverages. Many of these substitutes are perceived as healthier, which in a socio-cultural environment increasingly concerned about sugar consumption and obesity, makes them increasingly attractive.

The overall assessment: the soft drink industry is attractive. Three of the five forces (new entrants, supplier power, and rivalry) are low to medium, which supports strong profitability. Buyer power is moderate and manageable. The one genuinely threatening force is substitution, but the industry has managed this threat through brand investment, product line expansion (diet, zero-sugar, flavored water), and acquiring brands in substitute categories. The structural conditions explain why this industry has been extraordinarily profitable for decades.

References

Bain, J. S. (1956). *Barriers to new competition.* Harvard University Press.

Mason, E. S. (1939). Price and production policies of large-scale enterprise. *The American Economic Review, 29*(1), 61–74.

Porter, M. E. (1979). How competitive forces shape strategy. *Harvard Business Review, 57*(2), 137–145.

Porter, M. E. (1980). *Competitive strategy: Techniques for analyzing industries and competitors.* Free Press.

Porter, M. E. (2008). The five competitive forces that shape strategy. *Harvard Business Review, 86*(1), 78–93.

4.4 (Threat of) Forward/Backward Vertical Integration — *How does integration threat affect bargaining power?*

The Five Forces analysis in the previous section identified supplier and buyer bargaining power as two structural forces that determine industry profitability. When suppliers are powerful, they charge higher prices for inputs. When buyers are powerful, they demand lower prices or better terms. In both cases, the focal industry loses profitability to parties on the other side of a transaction.

But what if a firm could change the terms entirely — not by negotiating harder, but by eliminating the need for the transaction? What if a buyer produced the input itself, or a supplier distributed its product directly to end customers? This is the logic of vertical integration: extending the firm's operations upstream (toward suppliers) or downstream (toward buyers) along the value chain. Critically, a firm does not always need to actually integrate. The credible *threat* of integration alone can shift bargaining dynamics in the firm's favor.

Vertical integration connects several concepts we have already covered. In Chapter 1, we examined Coase's (1937) theory of the firm and transaction costs in determining the boundary between internal production and market procurement. In Chapter 3, we explored the value chain and how firms reconfigure activities through outsourcing. Here, vertical integration enters the analysis as a force that directly affects bargaining power dynamics within Porter's (1980) Five Forces.

4.4.1 Vertical Integration as a Force Within the Five Forces

Vertical integration affects both supplier power and buyer power through the same mechanism: it gives one party a credible alternative to the transaction, shifting bargaining leverage.

The **credible threat of backward integration reduces supplier bargaining power**. Backward integration means moving upstream, producing inputs rather than purchasing them from suppliers. If a buyer can make the supplier's product itself, the supplier must offer better terms to retain the business. Even if the buyer has not yet integrated, the supplier must factor in the possibility that it could.

The **credible threat of forward integration reduces buyer bargaining power**. Forward integration means moving downstream, selling products directly to end customers rather than relying on intermediary buyers. If the supplier can bypass the buyer entirely, the buyer must offer better terms to remain a valuable distribution partner.

In both cases, the integration threat functions as a countervailing force. It does not eliminate supplier or buyer power — concentration, switching costs, and product differentiation still apply — but it provides a structural counterweight that limits how aggressively the powerful party can exercise its leverage.

4.4.2 Backward Integration

Backward integration involves producing inputs that the firm previously purchased from suppliers. The firm becomes its own supplier for one or more critical inputs, reducing dependence on external suppliers and gaining greater control over input quality and cost.

Backward integration is not always feasible. It requires capabilities outside the firm's traditional domain, significant capital investment, and management of unfamiliar activities. The decision depends on whether reduced supplier dependence outweighs the costs and complexities of internal production — a calculus directly related to the transaction cost framework from Chapter 1 (Williamson, 1985). Apple's move to design its own processors, announced in 2020 and completed across the Mac lineup by 2023, illustrates the bargaining consequence: every remaining supplier now knows Apple can bring critical components in-house when external terms become unfavorable (examined further in Ch 5.5).

4.4.3 Forward Integration

Forward integration involves moving downstream to control distribution, retail, or direct customer relationships. Instead of relying on intermediary buyers, the firm sells directly to end customers, capturing a larger share of the value it creates.

Forward integration carries risks. Building distribution capabilities requires significant investment and new organizational skills. But by controlling the downstream relationship with customers, the firm reduces dependence on powerful buyers and captures value that would otherwise be extracted by intermediaries. Disney's 2019 launch of Disney+ shows the effect on buyer power: once Disney could reach audiences directly, every remaining distribution partner faced the reality that Disney could pull its content for exclusive distribution through its own platform (examined further in Ch 5.5).

4.4.4 Why "Threat" Matters More Than Actual Integration

One of the most important insights about vertical integration is that **the threat of integration can be as powerful as integration itself**. A firm does not always need to spend billions building upstream capacity or launching a direct-to-consumer platform. If suppliers and buyers believe the firm *could* integrate and *would* do so if pushed too far, the mere possibility reshapes the negotiation.

This is a matter of credibility, which depends on three factors: the firm's resource base, its organizational capabilities, and its track record. A small startup threatening to manufacture semiconductor chips is not credible. Apple making the same threat is extremely credible because it has demonstrated the capability repeatedly (Porter, 1980).

When the threat is credible, it functions as a standing negotiation lever. Suppliers moderate pricing because they know that excessive margins will eventually trigger the buyer to produce the input internally. Buyers moderate demands because they know that pushing too hard will lead the supplier to bypass them. The threat creates an invisible ceiling on how much bargaining power the other party can exercise.

This also means firms can invest strategically in building integration *capability* even without intending to fully integrate. A firm that develops small-scale internal production of a critical input — enough to demonstrate technical feasibility — has established the credibility of the threat. The investment pays for itself through improved bargaining terms, even if the capability is never scaled to full production.

Full vertical integration is not the only option. Alternatives such as taper integration (partial integration that preserves external sourcing) and strategic outsourcing allow firms to capture some bargaining power benefits without bearing the full costs and risks. These alternatives are examined in detail in Chapter 5.5, where vertical integration is revisited as a corporate-level strategy decision.

4.4.5 Connecting Vertical Integration to the Five Forces

Vertical integration does not operate in isolation from the other forces. A firm that integrates backward may raise barriers to entry, because new entrants face a competitor that controls its own supply chain. A firm that integrates forward may increase rivalry at the downstream level by entering a market where it was previously only a supplier. Integration can also create new substitution dynamics: Disney+ did not just change Disney's bargaining position but introduced a new competitor into streaming, intensifying rivalry for consumers choosing between cable and streaming.

These interactions remind us that industry structure is not fixed. The most effective strategists do not merely analyze the current forces; they consider how their actions can change the forces in their favor. The next section continues this theme by examining complementors and ecosystems — industry participants not captured in Porter's original framework but that significantly influence the value available to the focal industry.

References

Coase, R. H. (1937). The nature of the firm. *Economica, 4*(16), 386–405.

Porter, M. E. (1980). *Competitive strategy: Techniques for analyzing industries and competitors.* Free Press.

Williamson, O. E. (1985). *The economic institutions of capitalism: Firms, markets, relational contracting.* Free Press.

4.5 Complementors & Ecosystems — *Who else creates value in our industry?*

The previous three sections have developed a comprehensive framework for analyzing industry structure. Porter's Five Forces identifies the competitive pressures that determine industry profitability. Vertical integration — actual or threatened — reveals how firms can reshape bargaining dynamics within the Five Forces. Together, these tools provide a powerful lens for understanding the competitive environment. But they share a common limitation: they focus almost exclusively on adversarial relationships. Every force in Porter's framework describes a party that is trying to capture value at the expense of the focal industry's firms: rivals fighting for market share, suppliers and buyers extracting favorable terms, new entrants threatening to increase competition, and substitutes luring customers away.

This adversarial focus misses an important category of industry participant: firms whose success *increases* the value of the focal firm's products. Not every relationship in an industry is zero-sum. Some firms create value that spills over and benefits others, often without any direct competitive interaction. These are complementors, and the networks of interdependent relationships they form constitute industry ecosystems. Understanding complementors and ecosystems is essential for a complete picture of the external environment, because they can be just as consequential for a firm's profitability as the five competitive forces, sometimes more so.

4.5.1 The Sixth Force: Complementors

A complementor is a firm that produces a product or service that increases the value of the focal firm's offering when the two are used together (Brandenburger & Nalebuff, 1996). The relationship is one of mutual value creation: the complementor's product makes the focal firm's product more valuable to customers, and the focal firm's product makes the complementor's product more valuable in return.

The concept is intuitive when illustrated with examples. Software applications are complementors to computer hardware: a laptop without software is an expensive paperweight, and software without hardware is a set of instructions with nothing to execute them. The value of each product depends critically on the existence and quality of the other. Similarly, the network of gas stations across a country complements the automobile industry. Cars are far more valuable to customers when they can refuel conveniently, and gas stations are only viable businesses because millions of people own cars. Neither industry created the other, but each depends on the other for a substantial portion of its value.

Complementors are not captured within Porter's original Five Forces framework (Porter, 1980), which is one of the most frequently cited limitations of the model. Porter's forces describe competitive and adversarial relationships, parties trying to take value from the focal industry. Complementors represent the opposite: parties that add value to the focal industry. Brandenburger and Nalebuff (1996) proposed complementors as a "sixth force," arguing that any complete analysis of an industry's competitive environment must account for the firms whose products or services enhance, rather than diminish, the focal industry's profit potential.

The distinction between complementors and the existing five forces is worth emphasizing. A supplier provides inputs that the firm needs to produce its product; the relationship is transactional, and the supplier's bargaining power determines how much value the supplier extracts. A complementor provides a separate product that makes the firm's product more attractive to customers; the relationship is symbiotic, and the complementor's success directly benefits the firm. A substitute draws customers away from the firm's product by offering an alternative way to satisfy the same need. A complementor draws customers *toward* the firm's product by increasing the total value the customer receives.

EX: Video Game Consoles and Game Developers

The video game industry provides one of the clearest illustrations of how complementors create value. A gaming console — whether a PlayStation, Xbox, or Nintendo Switch — is essentially worthless without games to play on it. The console manufacturer invests billions in hardware development, but the device's value to consumers depends almost entirely on the quality and variety of games available. Game developers are the console's complementors: every great game released for a platform increases the platform's attractiveness to consumers, which drives hardware sales, which in turn attracts more game developers, creating a virtuous cycle.

This dynamic explains why console manufacturers invest so heavily in nurturing their complementor ecosystems. Sony, Microsoft, and Nintendo provide development tools, technical support, marketing assistance, and sometimes direct funding to game studios. They host developer conferences, maintain certification programs, and create storefront platforms that make it easy for developers to distribute and sell their games. These investments are not acts of charity — they are strategic actions designed to strengthen the complementor ecosystem and, by extension, the value of the console itself. A console with a thriving library of high-quality games commands premium pricing and earns customer loyalty; a console with a sparse game library, regardless of its hardware specifications, struggles to attract buyers.

4.5.2 Industry Ecosystems

The concept of complementors extends naturally into the broader idea of an industry ecosystem, a network of interdependent firms that collectively create value that no single firm could create alone (Adner, 2006). In an ecosystem, firms are linked not through simple buyer-seller transactions but through complex webs of complementary products, shared platforms, common standards, and mutual dependence.

Platform businesses and multi-sided markets represent perhaps the most important contemporary expression of the ecosystem concept. A platform is a product or service that connects two or more distinct groups of users, creating value by enabling interactions between them (Eisenmann, Parker, & Van Alstyne, 2006). Apple's App Store is a platform that connects application developers with iPhone users. Uber is a platform that connects drivers with riders. Airbnb is a platform that connects property owners with travelers. In each case, the platform's value depends on having participants on both sides: an app store with no apps attracts no users, and an app store with no users attracts no developers. Each side is a complementor to the other, and the platform orchestrates the ecosystem that brings them together.

Network effects are the engine that drives ecosystem value. A network effect exists when the value of a product or service increases as more people use it (Katz & Shapiro, 1985). Economists distinguish two forms. *Direct* (or same-side) network effects arise when additional users on the same side make the product more valuable to others on that side: a telephone is useless with one subscriber and indispensable when everyone owns one. *Indirect* (or cross-side) network effects arise in multi-sided markets when growth on one side makes the platform more valuable to the other side: as more developers create apps for the iPhone, the iPhone becomes more attractive to consumers, and as more consumers buy iPhones, the platform becomes a more lucrative target for developers. These reinforcing dynamics can produce winner-take-all or winner-take-most outcomes, where the platform with the largest network dominates and late entrants struggle to attract either side. The same dynamics create a barrier to entry: a new platform must reach critical mass on both sides at once — the "chicken-and-egg" problem — before its network is valuable enough to sustain itself. Network effects can also turn negative when congestion or declining quality sets in, as when a social platform fills with spam or a road network clogs with traffic.

Ecosystem health affects individual firm performance. A firm does not operate in isolation from the health of its broader ecosystem. If a console manufacturer's key game studios go bankrupt, or if a platform's developer community migrates to a competing platform, the focal firm suffers, not because of anything it did wrong in its own operations, but because the ecosystem on which its value depends has deteriorated. Conversely, a thriving ecosystem amplifies the firm's competitive position. Apple's competitive advantage in smartphones is not solely a function of its hardware design, brand reputation, or operating system; it is inseparable from the vast ecosystem of apps, accessories, services, and content that exists around the iPhone. That ecosystem creates switching costs, reinforces customer loyalty, and increases the total value proposition in ways that Apple's own products alone could not achieve.

This ecosystem perspective reveals a form of competitive advantage that the resource-based view (Chapter 3) does not fully capture. Ecosystem-based advantages are not located entirely within the firm; they emerge from the relationships, interdependencies, and collective capabilities of the network. They are extraordinarily difficult for competitors to replicate, because a competitor cannot simply copy the firm's internal resources; it must replicate or build an equivalent ecosystem, which requires attracting and coordinating the independent choices of thousands of complementors, developers, content creators, and other participants.

4.5.3 Strategic Implications

The existence of complementors and ecosystems has several important strategic implications that go beyond the purely analytical.

Firms can increase demand by nurturing complementors. Rather than viewing all external parties as threats or adversaries, firms that recognize the role of complementors can take active steps to cultivate them. This might involve providing technical resources and developer tools (as Apple and Google do for app developers), offering favorable economic terms to attract early participants (as video game console makers do during platform launches), or investing directly in complementor firms through venture capital or strategic partnerships. The goal is to strengthen the complementor ecosystem, which in turn strengthens demand for the firm's own product. Every dollar invested in nurturing complementors can yield returns that exceed what the same dollar would produce if invested in the firm's own product development, because the complementor's contribution amplifies the firm's value proposition beyond what the firm could create alone.

Alliance and cooperative strategies with complementors represent a distinct category of strategic action that we will explore in greater depth in Chapter 5. Unlike the adversarial relationships that dominate the Five Forces framework, complementor relationships are fundamentally cooperative, as both parties benefit from the other's success. This cooperative dynamic creates opportunities for strategic alliances, joint ventures, co-development agreements, and other partnership structures that formalize and deepen the complementary relationship. Starbucks placing its coffee in Barnes & Noble bookstores, Nike producing officially licensed NFL uniforms, and Cargill partnering with Coca-Cola to create Truvia are all examples of firms leveraging complementary assets through cooperative strategy. In each case, the combined offering is more valuable to customers than either firm's product alone.

Standard-setting and ecosystem coordination as competitive tools. In technology-intensive industries, establishing a dominant standard can be one of the most powerful competitive moves available. A standard, whether a technical specification, a file format, a communication protocol, or a platform architecture, defines the rules by which complementors create compatible products. The firm that controls the standard controls the ecosystem. Apple's iOS illustrates the dynamic clearly. iOS retains its dominant position in premium smartphones not primarily because the operating system is technically superior to Android — many reviewers argue the technical gap has narrowed or reversed on specific dimensions — but because the iOS ecosystem of apps, accessories, services, and payment integrations creates switching costs that competing platforms cannot easily overcome. Once developers prioritize iOS, consumers face a more valuable platform; once consumers buy iPhones, developers face a more lucrative target. The standard reinforces itself.

Google's Android offers a revealing counterpoint. Recognizing that Apple's head start in iOS would be impossible to overcome through superior product alone, Google made Android free and open to handset manufacturers, deliberately sacrificing direct OS revenue in order to win the ecosystem battle on volume. By giving Samsung, HTC, Xiaomi, and dozens of other manufacturers a platform they could customize and ship at scale, Google attracted the global majority of smartphone buyers and, with them, the developer attention required to sustain a competitive app ecosystem. The strategic choice was not about which OS was better but about which ecosystem could be assembled fastest and most broadly. Both iOS and Android demonstrate that competition in platform industries is fought through complementor recruitment, not just product features.

Standard-setting battles are often fought through ecosystem alliances. When two or more competing standards vie for dominance, firms align themselves with one standard or the other and recruit complementors to their side. The recent battle over electric vehicle charging standards in North America provides a vivid illustration. For years, the Combined Charging System (CCS) was the consensus standard backed by most major automakers, while Tesla operated a proprietary connector and its own Supercharger network. Despite CCS having broader automaker support on paper, Tesla's Supercharger network had grown into the most reliable, widely deployed, and well-maintained fast-charging ecosystem in the United States. In 2023, Ford announced that it would adopt Tesla's connector — rebranded as the North American Charging Standard (NACS) — for its future EVs. Within months, GM, Rivian, Volvo, Hyundai, and most other major manufacturers followed. CCS, despite its earlier coalition support, effectively lost the standards battle. The standard with the more developed complementor ecosystem (the charging network itself) prevailed, illustrating that competitive success in ecosystem-driven industries depends not only on the quality of a firm's own product but on its ability to coordinate, attract, and retain a network of complementors that collectively outperforms the competing ecosystem.

4.5.4 Complementors and the Five Forces

Recognizing complementors does not invalidate Porter's Five Forces; it supplements the framework with a dimension that the original model omitted. A comprehensive industry analysis should assess both the competitive forces that erode profitability (the five forces) and the complementary relationships that enhance it (the sixth force). In some industries, complementors are a minor consideration: the profitability of a cement manufacturer is shaped almost entirely by rivalry, buyer power, supplier power, entry barriers, and substitution. In other industries, particularly technology platforms, entertainment, and multi-sided markets, complementors are the central strategic reality, and an analysis that ignores them will miss the most important dynamics shaping the industry.

The preceding sections of this chapter have built an increasingly complete picture of industry structure: the competitive forces that constrain profitability, the integration strategies that reshape bargaining power, and the complementary relationships that create new value. But this picture has been largely static, a snapshot of industry conditions at a single point in time. The next section addresses a critical limitation of all static frameworks: industries change. The forces that define an industry's structure today may look very different tomorrow, and firms that fail to anticipate those changes risk being caught flat-footed by shifting competitive conditions.

References

Adner, R. (2006). Match your innovation strategy to your innovation ecosystem. *Harvard Business Review*, *84*(4), 98–107.

Brandenburger, A. M., & Nalebuff, B. J. (1996). *Co-opetition.* Currency Doubleday.

Eisenmann, T., Parker, G., & Van Alstyne, M. W. (2006). Strategies for two-sided markets. *Harvard Business Review, 84*(10), 92–101.

Katz, M. L., & Shapiro, C. (1985). Network externalities, competition, and compatibility. *The American Economic Review, 75*(3), 424–440.

Porter, M. E. (1980). *Competitive strategy: Techniques for analyzing industries and competitors.* Free Press.

4.6 Industry Dynamics — *How do industries change and evolve?*

> *"Every success story is a tale of constant adaption, revision and change. A company that stands still will soon be forgotten."* — *Richard Branson*

The preceding sections developed a rich set of tools for analyzing industry structure: the Five Forces, vertical integration threats, and complementor ecosystems. These frameworks are powerful, but they share a common limitation: they tend to produce a snapshot of industry conditions at a single point in time (McGahan, 2004). A Five Forces analysis conducted today tells us about today's rivalry, today's barriers to entry, today's supplier and buyer power. It does not tell us what those forces will look like in five years.

An industry that is highly attractive today may become unattractive tomorrow. The pineapple industry example from Chapter 4.1 illustrated this vividly: a single product innovation transformed a near-perfect-competition commodity market into something approaching oligopoly within years. Industry structure is not fate. It is the current expression of forces that are themselves in motion (Porter, 1980).

This section examines the sources of industry change and how those changes ripple through the Five Forces framework. The goal is not to predict the future but to equip students with the conceptual tools to recognize when industry conditions are shifting. This connects directly to the environmental scanning activities introduced in Chapter 4.1: firms that continuously scan for signals of industry change are better positioned to respond, or to drive the change themselves (Hambrick, 1982).

4.6.1 Industries Are Not Static

The temptation when conducting industry analysis is to treat the results as fixed. But every factor that drives the Five Forces is itself subject to change (Porter, 1980). The number of competitors rises and falls as firms enter, exit, merge, and fail. Growth rates accelerate during innovation and decelerate as markets mature. Switching costs can be undermined by new technologies. Regulations that protected incumbents can be repealed. Supplier and buyer power shift as upstream and downstream industries consolidate or fragment.

The implication is that industry analysis must be treated as an ongoing process, not a one-time exercise. Firms that treat their industry analysis as permanently settled risk making strategic commitments based on conditions that no longer exist. The most strategically aware firms build industry monitoring into their regular management processes, revisiting their analysis periodically and tracking the specific factors that could shift each force.

This dynamic perspective also affects how firms should interpret current attractiveness. A currently attractive industry showing signs of structural erosion may be less appealing than it appears. Conversely, a currently unattractive industry undergoing structural improvement may represent a strategic opportunity that a static analysis would miss entirely (McGahan, 2004).

4.6.2 Sources of Industry Change

Industry change does not happen randomly. While specific timing and magnitude are difficult to predict, the sources from which change emerges are identifiable (McGahan, 2004). Five sources account for the vast majority of industry structural change.

Technological innovation is perhaps the most potent source of industry change (Christensen, 1997). New technologies can create entirely new products, render existing ones obsolete, transform production processes, and redefine the basis of competition. Digital photography did not merely create a new product; it destroyed the film photography industry and shifted competition from optical engineering and chemical science to semiconductor technology and software.

Technology affects industry structure through multiple channels simultaneously (Porter, 1980). A new technology can lower barriers to entry (cloud computing enabled software startups without server infrastructure), create new substitutes (streaming services replacing cable and physical media), shift bargaining power (e-commerce gave consumers unprecedented price comparison ability), and alter rivalry (social media created competitive arenas that did not previously exist).

Regulatory shifts alter industry structure by changing the rules of competition (McGahan, 2004). New regulations can raise barriers to entry, as environmental compliance requirements impose costs that established firms absorb more easily than entrants. Deregulation can lower barriers, as the Airline Deregulation Act of 1978 demonstrated when new carriers entered previously protected routes, dramatically increasing rivalry. Trade policy changes expand or contract the competitor set by affecting foreign firms' market access. Because regulation is a product of political processes, it is subject to change whenever political priorities shift, making it an inherently dynamic element of industry structure.

Changes in customer preferences and demographics alter the demand side of competition (McGahan, 2004). Shifting consumer values can redirect spending away from some industries and toward others. The growing preference for plant-based foods has created new entrants and substitutes in the meat industry. Demographic shifts such as aging populations and urbanization alter the size and composition of customer segments, affecting industry growth rates and buyer behavior. When preferences shift toward substitutes, the focal industry faces both stronger substitution and declining growth, intensifying rivalry as firms fight over a shrinking pool of demand (Porter, 1980).

Globalization expands or redefines industry boundaries by introducing new competitors, suppliers, and markets (McGahan, 2004). When trade barriers fall or communication costs decline, firms that competed only nationally suddenly face global competition. The globalization of the steel industry transformed national markets into a global one where low-cost producers compete directly with established steelmakers, increasing rivalry and reducing domestic suppliers' bargaining power.

Convergence of previously separate industries occurs when technological or market developments blur the boundaries between industries that were once distinct (McGahan, 2004). The convergence of telecommunications, computing, and media into a single digital ecosystem is perhaps the most consequential example of the past three decades. Apple is simultaneously a computer manufacturer, phone maker, media distributor, financial services provider, and advertising platform. Industry convergence creates strategic confusion because frameworks designed for clearly bounded industries lose precision when boundaries dissolve (Porter, 1980). Firms that recognize convergence early can position themselves at the intersection of merging industries, while firms clinging to traditional definitions risk being blindsided by unrecognized rivals.

4.6.3 How Industry Change Affects the Five Forces

Each of the five competitive forces is dynamic, not fixed (Porter, 1980). The strategic payoff of understanding industry dynamics comes from connecting sources of change to specific shifts in the forces that determine profitability.

New technologies can lower barriers to entry or create new substitutes. Cloud computing dramatically lowered the capital requirements for entering the software industry, while cloud-based SaaS models created substitutes for traditional licensed software at a fraction of the upfront cost. Both shifts eroded the structural protections that had made the traditional software industry highly profitable (Christensen, 1997).

Regulatory changes can increase or decrease supplier and buyer power. The EU's General Data Protection Regulation gave consumers greater control over personal data, effectively increasing buyer power relative to data-dependent firms. When governments require generic drug production after patent expiration, they increase supplier competition and reduce patent-holders' bargaining power.

Shifts in demand growth rate affect the intensity of rivalry. This is one of the most predictable dynamics in industry analysis (Porter, 1980). When growth declines, firms can no longer grow by capturing new demand and must instead take market share from competitors, which provokes competitive responses and often triggers price wars. The transition from a growth industry to a mature one is frequently the most dangerous period for firm profitability.

Each force is a variable, not a constant. The central lesson of industry dynamics is that every element of a Five Forces analysis is subject to change (McGahan, 2004). A strategically literate manager does not merely analyze the current state of each force but considers the trajectory of each force and the factors that might accelerate or reverse it.

This dynamic perspective connects directly to the dynamic capabilities framework from Chapter 3.6. Sensing is the ability to detect when industry forces are shifting; seizing enables the firm to act on those shifts before competitors do; and reconfiguring allows the firm to adapt its internal operations to match evolving industry structure (Teece, 2007). Firms with strong dynamic capabilities do not merely react to industry change; they anticipate it, prepare for it, and sometimes initiate it themselves.

The next section builds on this foundation by examining one of the most well-documented patterns of industry change: the industry life cycle.

References

Christensen, C. M. (1997). *The innovator's dilemma: When new technologies cause great firms to fail.* Harvard Business School Press.

Hambrick, D. C. (1982). Environmental scanning and organizational strategy. *Strategic Management Journal, 3*(2), 159–174.

McGahan, A. M. (2004). How industries change. *Harvard Business Review, 82*(10), 86–94.

Porter, M. E. (1980). *Competitive strategy: Techniques for analyzing industries and competitors.* Free Press.

Teece, D. J. (2007). Explicating dynamic capabilities: The nature and microfoundations of (sustainable) enterprise performance. *Strategic Management Journal, 28*(13), 1319–1350.

4.7 Industry Life Cycles — *What are predictable patterns of industry evolution?*

The previous section established that industries are dynamic, with forces shaping competition constantly in motion. But acknowledging that industries change does not mean that change is entirely unpredictable. While specific timing and magnitude are difficult to forecast, most industries follow a broadly recognizable pattern of evolution from birth through growth, maturity, and eventual decline (Klepper, 1997). This pattern is the industry life cycle.

The industry life cycle model provides a temporal framework for understanding how competitive conditions, strategic priorities, and firm behavior evolve as an industry ages (Klepper, 1997). Where the Five Forces framework (Ch 4.3) offers a structural snapshot at a given moment, and the industry dynamics discussion (Ch 4.6) explains the sources of change, the life cycle model maps the predictable trajectory of that change across time. It answers a question the Five Forces alone cannot: not just *what* are the competitive conditions, but *where is this industry heading*?

Understanding the life cycle matters because the strategies that succeed in one stage frequently fail in another (Anderson & Zeithaml, 1984). A firm that thrives during growth by investing heavily in product innovation may find itself outcompeted in maturity if it cannot transition to cost discipline. Conversely, a firm optimized for mature-market competition will struggle in an embryonic industry where the product itself is still being defined.

4.7.1 The Industry Life Cycle Model

Industries tend to pass through four distinct stages: embryonic (introduction), growth, maturity, and decline (Klepper, 1997). Each stage is characterized by a different combination of market growth rate, competitive intensity, number of market segments, emphasis on product versus process design, and dominant functional priorities (Utterback & Abernathy, 1975). The transitions between stages are not always clean; some industries move through stages quickly, others linger for decades, and some cycle back from decline to growth through innovation (Moon, 2005). But the general pattern is consistent enough to serve as a reliable strategic planning tool.

4.7.1.1 Industry Life Cycle Diagram

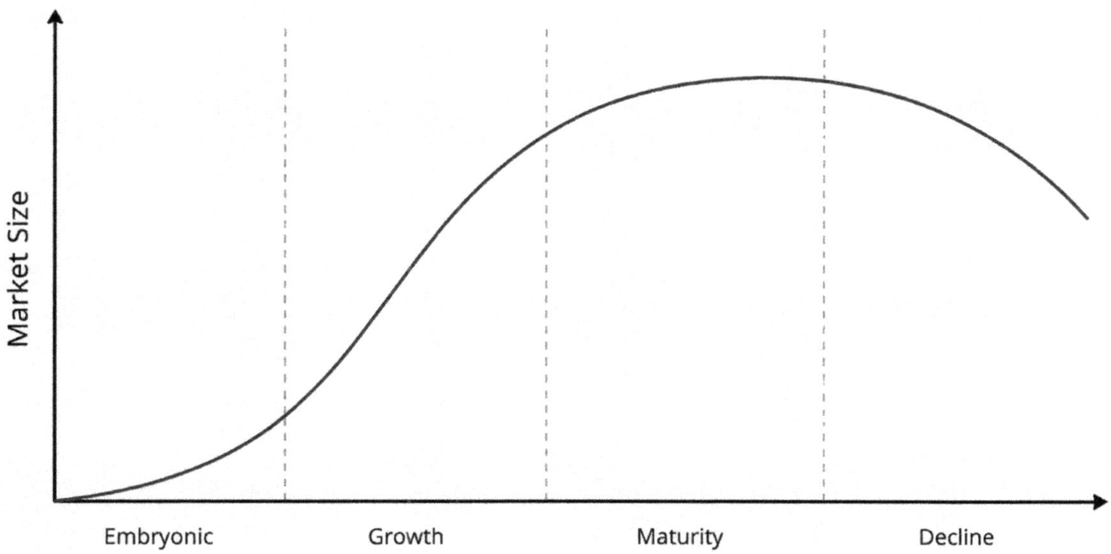

4.7.2 Embryonic Stage

The embryonic stage marks the birth of an industry. A new technology or business model has been developed, but the market barely exists (Moore, 1991). Demand is small and uncertain. The product is often rudimentary, with significant uncertainty about which design approach will ultimately prevail. Customers are early adopters willing to tolerate imperfection in exchange for novelty or a solution to a previously unmet need.

Competition is low simply because few firms are in the market (Klepper, 1997). Because the product is still being defined, the primary functional emphasis is on research and development. The strategic priority is not efficiency or scale but problem-solving: firms are trying to figure out what the product should be, how it should work, and who will buy it. Emphasis on product design is very high as firms experiment with features and configurations, while emphasis on process design is low because volume does not yet justify investment in production optimization (Utterback & Abernathy, 1975).

The overall strategic objective is to create and increase consumer demand (Utterback & Abernathy, 1975). The fundamental challenge is not beating competitors but convincing potential customers that this new category is worth their attention. The dominant generic strategy is differentiation, because success depends on creating something sufficiently novel and valuable to pull customers into a market that did not previously exist.

4.7.3 Growth Stage

The growth stage begins when embryonic uncertainty starts to resolve. Customers become better informed, and the market expands beyond early adopters as mainstream customers begin purchasing (Klepper, 1997). This expansion attracts new competitors seeking to capture growing demand.

Competitive intensity is moderate (Klepper, 1997). Although more competitors have entered, the rapidly expanding pie means firms can grow without necessarily taking share from one another. This relatively benign environment can mask strategic weaknesses that will become devastating once growth slows. Firms growing rapidly may confuse revenue growth with strategic strength, failing to recognize that their growth is driven by the expanding market rather than by any sustainable competitive advantage.

The functional emphasis shifts from R&D to sales and marketing. Building brand recognition and customer loyalty during this stage is critical because the relationships established now carry forward into more competitive stages ahead (Anderson & Zeithaml, 1984). The dominant strategy remains differentiation, but cost consciousness begins to matter as firms build infrastructure for scaling production.

4.7.4 Maturity Stage

The maturity stage is the longest and most strategically complex phase (Klepper, 1997). It begins when aggregate demand slows as the market becomes saturated, with few new adopters remaining. Growth comes primarily from replacement purchases, upgrades, or incremental expansion rather than new customer acquisition. The transition from growth to maturity is one of the most dangerous periods in an industry's evolution because it fundamentally changes the nature of competition (Porter, 1980).

In the growth stage, firms prospered by capturing expanding demand. In maturity, growth becomes zero-sum: one firm's gain is another's loss. This shift transforms competition from market expansion to market share warfare. Marginal competitors begin to exit, and the industry consolidates as stronger firms acquire weaker ones (Klepper, 1997).

Competitive intensity is very high, typically the highest at any point in the industry's life (Porter, 1980). Customers have become knowledgeable and demanding, with the leverage to negotiate aggressively because multiple competitors fight for their business. The functional emphasis shifts decisively from product design to process design and production efficiency (Utterback & Abernathy, 1975). The primary question shifts from "What should we build?" to "How can we build it better and cheaper?"

Where differentiation dominated earlier stages, cost leadership becomes critical in maturity (Porter, 1980). Differentiation does not disappear — firms that maintain meaningful differentiation in a mature market often earn premium returns — but the cost discipline required to survive intensifies dramatically.

Two repositioning approaches are particularly relevant in mature markets (Moon, 2005). **Reverse positioning** strips away features that the industry has accumulated but that some customers do not value, offering a simplified, lower-cost product. **Breakaway positioning** redefines the product's category entirely, reigniting growth by creating a new value proposition.

EX: The U.S. Airline Industry

The U.S. airline industry has been mature for decades, illustrating virtually every characteristic of mature-market competition. Growth is slow, driven by population growth rather than new adoption. Competition is intense, with legacy and low-cost carriers battling over the same routes. Customer power is high because online booking makes comparison effortless. The functional emphasis is overwhelmingly on operational efficiency: fuel management, fleet utilization, route optimization, and yield management.

4.7.5 Decline Stage

The decline stage begins when industry sales and profits enter a sustained fall (Klepper, 1997). The market contracts because the product is being displaced by substitutes, customer preferences have permanently shifted, or the need the product serves has diminished.

Competition in decline takes on a distinctive character. If firms accept decline and exit in an orderly fashion, competitive intensity may decrease as the market shrinks to a size supporting remaining players profitably. But if firms refuse to exit due to high exit barriers or emotional attachment, competition can become brutal as firms slash prices in a shrinking market (Porter, 1980).

Managers must decide among four strategic options (Harrigan & Porter, 1983):

Maintain by continuing to invest enough to keep the product competitive, betting that competitors will exit first, leaving the firm as a profitable survivor.

Harvest by deliberately reducing investment and extracting maximum cash flow while allowing market position to erode gradually.

Consolidate by acquiring competitors as they exit, betting that the declining industry will stabilize at a level supporting fewer, larger players.

Exit by divesting or shutting down entirely, recognizing that the industry's decline is irreversible and resources are better deployed elsewhere.

Not all declining industries follow a straight path to extinction. Some experience renewal through technological innovation, regulatory changes, or cultural shifts (Moon, 2005). Vinyl records appeared to be in terminal decline throughout the 1990s and 2000s, but a cultural resurgence of interest in analog sound reversed the trend.

4.7.6 Strategic Implications Across the Life Cycle

The life cycle model's greatest strategic value lies in mapping the alignment between generic strategy and industry stage (Anderson & Zeithaml, 1984).

Differentiation dominates in the embryonic and growth stages. When the product is still being defined and the market expanding, creating something uniquely valuable is the primary source of advantage (Porter, 1980).

Cost leadership becomes critical in maturity. As growth slows, producing and delivering efficiently becomes a survival requirement (Porter, 1980). This is the stage where the economies of scale discussed in Chapter 2.4 become most strategically important.

Integrated strategies may be necessary in mature markets. The maturity stage often rewards firms combining meaningful differentiation with cost discipline, as described in the hybrid strategy from Chapter 2.5.

The decline stage requires strategic discipline. The choices available each require clear-eyed assessment of competitive position, industry trajectory, and the opportunity cost of continued investment (Harrigan & Porter, 1983).

4.7.7 Connecting the Life Cycle to Other Frameworks

The industry life cycle complements the other analytical tools in this chapter. A Five Forces analysis tells you current structural conditions; the life cycle model tells you the direction those conditions are likely to move. Together they provide not just a snapshot but a moving picture of industry evolution.

The life cycle connects to competitive dynamics (Ch 4.2). In growth, competitive actions tend to be strategic, involving investments in brand-building and capacity expansion. In maturity, tactical actions like pricing adjustments and promotional campaigns become more frequent as firms battle over market share. In decline, actions shift toward consolidation, cost-cutting, and exit decisions.

Finally, the life cycle connects to dynamic capabilities from Chapter 3.6. The transition from one stage to the next requires firms to reconfigure resources, routines, and strategies (Teece, 2007). Firms with strong dynamic capabilities can sense transitions, seize opportunities to adapt, and reconfigure their organizations accordingly. Firms without these capabilities often continue executing strategies appropriate to the previous stage until it is too late.

The next section examines what happens when industry change is neither gradual nor predictable — when disruption rewrites the rules entirely.

References

Anderson, C. R., & Zeithaml, C. P. (1984). Stage of the product life cycle, business strategy, and business performance. *Academy of Management Journal, 27*(1), 5–24.

Harrigan, K. R., & Porter, M. E. (1983). End-game strategies for declining industries. *Harvard Business Review, 61*(4), 111–120.

Klepper, S. (1997). Industry life cycles. *Industrial and Corporate Change, 6*(1), 145–182.

Moon, Y. (2005). Break free from the product life cycle. *Harvard Business Review, 83*(5), 86–94.

Moore, G. A. (1991). *Crossing the chasm: Marketing and selling high-tech products to mainstream customers.* HarperBusiness.

Porter, M. E. (1980). *Competitive strategy: Techniques for analyzing industries and competitors.* Free Press.

Teece, D. J. (2007). Explicating dynamic capabilities: The nature and microfoundations of (sustainable) enterprise performance. *Strategic Management Journal, 28*(13), 1319–1350.

Utterback, J. M., & Abernathy, W. J. (1975). A dynamic model of process and product innovation. *Omega, 3*(6), 639–656.

4.8 Industry Disruption — *What drives unpredictable industry change?*

The previous two sections examined how industries evolve. Chapter 4.6 identified sources of industry change and how they ripple through the Five Forces. Chapter 4.7 introduced the industry life cycle, a model of predictable evolution through embryonic, growth, maturity, and decline stages. Together, these sections described industry change as something that, while not perfectly foreseeable, follows recognizable patterns.

This section addresses a fundamentally different kind of change: disruption. Disruption does not follow the life cycle's orderly progression. It rewrites the rules of an industry, sometimes abruptly, sometimes through a process invisible to incumbents until it is too late (Christensen, 1997). Understanding disruption matters because it explains why dominant firms with vast resources, loyal customers, and deep expertise can be displaced by smaller, weaker competitors offering seemingly inferior products.

4.8.1 Disruption vs. Predictable Industry Evolution

The industry life cycle assumes continuous, directional change. Firms can observe transitions and adjust. The signals are readable: slowing growth, intensifying rivalry, increasing price sensitivity.

Disruption operates on a different logic (Christensen, 1997). Rather than intensifying existing competitive forces, disruption changes the forces themselves. A disruptive shift can redefine what the industry is, who the competitors are, and how value is created. The shift from physical retail to e-commerce was not simply intensified rivalry among retailers; it transformed the retail industry's entire value chain, cost structure, and basis of competition.

The distinction matters because predictable life cycle transitions call for strategic adjustment, while disruption calls for strategic reinvention (Tushman & Anderson, 1986). The firm may need to abandon the very capabilities that made it successful. This is why disruption is so dangerous — not because incumbents lack resources to respond, but because responding effectively often requires them to act against everything their experience and organizational structures have taught them.

4.8.2 Types of Disruption

Disruption takes distinct forms, each with its own mechanisms and strategic implications (Danneels, 2004).

Disruptive innovation is the form most closely associated with Christensen (1997), who identified a pattern in which new entrants offering simpler, cheaper, and initially inferior products enter at the low end, serving customers whom incumbents consider unprofitable, and then progressively improve until they displace established firms. The disruptive product does not need to be better than the incumbent's at the time of entry. It needs only to be good enough for an underserved segment and then improve faster than incumbents expect.

Christensen's framework explains why incumbents so often dismiss disruptive entrants. The new product is initially worse on the dimensions that the incumbent's best customers care about. A rational incumbent will conclude it is irrelevant. But the disruptive entrant competes on simplicity, affordability, or convenience, attracting customers who were previously priced out of the market. As the disruptive product improves, it eventually reaches a performance threshold that satisfies mainstream customers, at which point the incumbent's advantages evaporate (Christensen & Raynor, 2003).

Technological disruption involves a breakthrough that fundamentally changes how value is created and delivered, independent of the low-end entry pattern (Tushman & Anderson, 1986). Digital photography illustrates this: the disruption was driven not by low-end entry but by the fundamental superiority of the underlying technology once it crossed a quality threshold. Digital images could be stored, edited, and shared at near-zero marginal cost, eliminating the need for film processing infrastructure entirely.

Business model disruption occurs when a new way of capturing value undermines incumbents' revenue models, even when the underlying product or technology remains similar (Markides, 2006). The newspaper industry was disrupted less by technology than by a business model shift. The internet did not make news reporting obsolete, but it unbundled the revenue streams on which newspapers depended: classified advertising went to Craigslist, search advertising to Google, display advertising attention to social media. Each component was picked off by a specialist that served that function more efficiently.

4.8.3 Why Incumbents Struggle with Disruption

If disruption were simply a matter of recognizing a new technology and investing in it, large incumbents would win every time. Yet incumbents fail with remarkable regularity (Christensen, 1997). Several organizational mechanisms explain why.

Core competencies can become core rigidities (Leonard-Barton, 1992). This concept, introduced in Chapter 3.5, is central to understanding incumbent failure. When disruption shifts the basis of competition, the capabilities that defined the firm's advantage may become irrelevant. This is the "obsolescent strength" diagnosis from the VRIO discussion in Chapter 3.3: the firm is superbly organized to exploit a rare capability that has ceased to be valuable.

Existing investments and organizational inertia compound the rigidity problem (Tushman & Anderson, 1986). Incumbents have massive sunk costs in physical assets, supply chains, and human capital optimized for the existing way of doing business. Organizational inertia extends beyond physical assets to routines, incentive structures, and managerial mindsets that are designed for the world as it was, not the world as it is becoming (Hannan & Freeman, 1984).

Customer feedback loops reinforce existing trajectories. One of Christensen's (1997) most counterintuitive insights was that incumbents fail partly *because* they listen to their customers. Their most profitable customers want better versions of the existing product, not simpler, cheaper alternatives. By faithfully serving these customers, incumbents invest in sustaining innovations that move upmarket, opening the low end to disruptive entrants (Christensen & Raynor, 2003).

The innovator's dilemma synthesizes these mechanisms into a single strategic paradox (Christensen, 1997). The very practices that make a firm successful — investing in R&D to serve demanding customers, protecting profitable business lines, making rational resource allocation decisions — are the practices that leave it vulnerable to disruption. The disruptive opportunity looks smaller, less profitable, and more uncertain than the existing business, making it perpetually difficult to justify investment against the incumbent's standard financial metrics.

4.8.4 Strategic Responses to Disruption

Can incumbents defend against disruption? The answer is a qualified yes, but doing so requires organizational capabilities and managerial discipline that are rare (Christensen & Raynor, 2003).

Sensing and monitoring through environmental scanning is the first line of defense. Disruptive threats frequently emerge at the periphery of an industry — in underserved segments, adjacent industries, or among non-consumers — rather than from the established competitors that firms typically monitor most closely (Christensen, 1997). Effective disruption scanning requires deliberate attention to weak signals: entrants with unconventional business models, technologies that are currently inferior but improving rapidly, and customer segments completely unserved by existing products.

Building dynamic capabilities is the organizational foundation for response (Teece, 2007). As discussed in Chapter 3.6, sensing means recognizing the threat early; seizing means committing resources before the financial case is fully clear; reconfiguring means transforming the organization to support the new reality. Netflix's sequential transformations — from DVD-by-mail to streaming to original content — represent dynamic capabilities at their highest level. The willingness to cannibalize one's own current model is perhaps the rarest and most important capability in responding to disruption.

Creating an autonomous organization was Christensen's central prescription (Christensen, 1997). Because a disruptive business looks too small and too unprofitable to compete for resources or attention inside the core firm, incumbents should pursue it through a separate, independent unit — small enough to be excited by a small opportunity, with its own cost structure, customers, and resource-allocation process. Insulating the new venture from the parent's most demanding customers and standard financial metrics allows it to serve the low end without being starved of investment or judged against the core business's margins. IBM's decision to develop its personal computer through an autonomous unit in Boca Raton, Florida, far from its mainframe organization, is the classic example.

Strategic alliances and acquisitions offer an alternative for incumbents that cannot develop disruptive capabilities internally (Capron & Mitchell, 2012). This approach, examined in detail in Chapter 5, provides faster access to the disruptive capability than internal development, though acquisitions carry risks of overpaying and destroying the acquired firm's entrepreneurial culture.

4.8.5 Disruption Limits

While disruption is powerful and widely applicable, it is important to recognize its boundaries (Danneels, 2004). Not every competitive threat is a disruption. Some changes are better understood as sustaining innovations — improvements along dimensions current customers already value (Christensen, 1997). Flat-screen television was transformative but not disruptive; incumbents like Samsung and LG led the transition. The distinction matters because sustaining innovations favor incumbents with resources to invest, while disruptive innovations favor entrants targeting underserved markets (Christensen & Raynor, 2003).

The next section moves from industry-level analysis to the broadest level of environmental assessment: the macro-environmental forces that shape the context in which all industries operate.

References

Capron, L., & Mitchell, W. (2012). *Build, borrow, or buy: Solving the growth dilemma.* Harvard Business Review Press.

Christensen, C. M. (1997). *The innovator's dilemma: When new technologies cause great firms to fail.* Harvard Business School Press.

Christensen, C. M., & Raynor, M. E. (2003). *The innovator's solution: Creating and sustaining successful growth.* Harvard Business School Press.

Danneels, E. (2004). Disruptive technology reconsidered: A critique and research agenda. *Journal of Product Innovation Management, 21*(4), 246–258.

Hannan, M. T., & Freeman, J. (1984). Structural inertia and organizational change. *American Sociological Review, 49*(2), 149–164.

Leonard-Barton, D. (1992). Core capabilities and core rigidities: A paradox in managing new product development. *Strategic Management Journal, 13*(S1), 111–125.

Markides, C. (2006). Disruptive innovation: In need of better theory. *Journal of Product Innovation Management, 23*(1), 19–25.

Teece, D. J. (2007). Explicating dynamic capabilities: The nature and microfoundations of (sustainable) enterprise performance. *Strategic Management Journal, 28*(13), 1319–1350.

Tushman, M. L., & Anderson, P. (1986). Technological discontinuities and organizational environments. *Administrative Science Quarterly, 31*(3), 439–465.

4.9 PESTEL — *What macro-environmental forces affect industries?*

The preceding sections of this chapter have progressively widened the lens of external analysis. We began with competitive dynamics between individual firms (Ch 4.2), moved to the structural forces that shape entire industries (Ch 4.3–5), examined how those structures evolve over time (Ch 4.6–7), and explored how disruption can overturn established conditions entirely (Ch 4.8). Each of these frameworks operates at the industry level. But industries do not exist in isolation. They operate within a broader macro-environment, a set of political, economic, social, technological, environmental, and legal forces that shape the context in which all industries function (Fahey & Narayanan, 1986). PESTEL analysis is the framework for identifying and assessing these forces.

PESTEL is both the broadest and, in many ways, the most fundamental level of external analysis. The forces it identifies are not specific to any single industry; they affect multiple industries simultaneously, often in different ways (Fahey & Narayanan, 1986). A change in interest rates affects housing, automotive, banking, and retail industries differently. Population aging creates opportunities for healthcare companies while threatening industries dependent on younger consumers. A new environmental regulation may impose costs on one industry while creating a new market for another. The power of PESTEL lies in its systematic approach to scanning this macro-environment, ensuring that strategists consider the full range of external forces rather than focusing narrowly on competitive dynamics within their own industry.

It is worth noting that PESTEL is sometimes rendered as PEST (folding the Legal and Environmental categories into the Political category). These variations are less important than the underlying discipline: systematically scanning the macro-environment across multiple dimensions to identify forces that create opportunities or threats for the firm and its industry.

4.9.1 Political Factors

Political factors encompass the ways in which governments influence the economy, specific industries, and individual firms (Fahey & Narayanan, 1986). These include tax policies, trade policies, government spending priorities, monetary policy, business regulation, environmental regulation, and the overall political stability of the environments in which a firm operates. Political factors are among the most consequential macro-environmental forces because governments possess the unique power to change the rules of the game — to create new markets, destroy existing ones, redirect capital flows, and alter the competitive landscape through legislation, regulation, and executive action.

Tax policy directly affects firm profitability and investment decisions. Changes in corporate tax rates influence where firms locate operations, how they structure financing, and how much they invest in growth. Tax incentives targeted at specific industries can redirect capital toward favored sectors. Trade policy, including tariffs, quotas, trade agreements, and sanctions, determines the degree to which foreign competitors can access domestic markets and the costs domestic firms face when sourcing inputs internationally (Porter, 1980). A tariff on imported steel protects domestic producers but simultaneously increases costs for every industry that uses steel as an input.

Government spending is a major source of demand for many industries. Defense contractors, infrastructure firms, healthcare providers, and technology companies derive significant revenue from government contracts. When spending priorities shift, the industries receiving funding experience growth while those losing funding may contract. In many industries, the government is the single largest customer.

Political factors can create both opportunities and threats, often simultaneously (Fahey & Narayanan, 1986). Government incentives for electric vehicles create opportunities for battery manufacturers while threatening traditional automotive parts suppliers. Trade agreements opening new export markets create opportunities while exposing domestic industries to foreign competition. The strategic challenge is not merely to identify political factors but to assess how each one affects the specific industry and firm in question.

EX: The U.S.-China Trade War and the Agricultural Industry

The escalation of tariffs between the United States and China beginning in 2018 illustrates how political factors can reshape industry dynamics. When China imposed retaliatory tariffs on U.S. agricultural exports, American soybean farmers — who had depended on China as their largest export market — faced a sudden and dramatic decline in demand. The political factor did not change anything about the product itself, the production technology, or the underlying consumer need for soybeans. But it fundamentally altered the economic equation by increasing the effective price of American soybeans in the Chinese market, redirecting Chinese purchases to Brazilian producers and leaving American farmers with oversupply and depressed prices. The same political shift that threatened American farmers created an opportunity for Brazilian agricultural firms, illustrating PESTEL's central insight: a single macro-environmental force can be an opportunity for one firm or industry and a threat for another.

4.9.2 Economic Factors

Economic factors are the macroeconomic conditions that directly affect an economy's performance and, by extension, the industries and firms that operate within it (Fahey & Narayanan, 1986). Key economic factors include GDP growth rates, inflation, interest rates, foreign exchange rates, unemployment levels, consumer purchasing power, and the overall business cycle. These factors shape the demand environment in which firms compete and influence the cost structures they face.

GDP growth reflects the overall expansion or contraction of economic activity. In periods of strong growth, consumer and business spending rise, demand expands across most industries, and firms find it easier to grow revenue and maintain margins. In periods of stagnation or recession, demand contracts, competition for a shrinking pool of spending intensifies, and firms face pressure on both revenue and costs. Importantly, economic conditions do not affect all industries equally (Fahey & Narayanan, 1986). Recessions disproportionately impact discretionary industries such as travel, luxury goods, entertainment, and restaurants, where consumers can defer or eliminate spending. Industries providing necessities, including utilities, healthcare, and basic food staples, are relatively insulated because demand for their products is less sensitive to economic fluctuations.

Inflation affects both the revenue and cost sides of the income statement. Rising inflation increases nominal prices but also increases input costs. The net effect depends on the firm's pricing power relative to its cost exposure. Firms with strong differentiation can pass cost increases through to buyers; cost leaders on thin margins may find that inflation compresses profitability. Interest rates influence the cost of capital, affecting investment decisions and the financial viability of leveraged firms. Low interest rates encourage borrowing and investment, stimulating growth-oriented industries like real estate and construction. Rising rates increase the cost of debt, slowing investment and reducing demand in rate-sensitive sectors.

Foreign exchange rates matter for any firm that operates internationally or competes against foreign firms (Fahey & Narayanan, 1986). A strong domestic currency makes exports more expensive in foreign markets (threatening export-dependent industries) while making imports cheaper (benefiting firms that source inputs internationally). A weak domestic currency has the opposite effects. For multinational firms, exchange rate fluctuations can dramatically affect reported earnings, making foreign revenue more or less valuable when converted back to the home currency.

Consumer purchasing power, the real income available for spending after accounting for taxes and inflation, is the ultimate driver of demand in consumer-facing industries. When purchasing power rises, consumers trade up to higher-quality products, explore new categories, and spend more freely. When purchasing power declines, they trade down, delay purchases, and become more price-sensitive, shifting the competitive dynamics within industries toward cost leadership and value-oriented positioning.

A common misconception is that industry costs and competition are themselves part of the macro-environment. They are not. Competitive rivalry and the cost of inputs operate at the industry level, addressed by the Five Forces and the earlier sections of this chapter; the macro-environment sits above the industry and acts upon it. Interest rates, inflation, and exchange rates do not compete with the firm directly, but they shape the industry conditions that determine its costs and demand. The purpose of economic analysis within PESTEL is therefore not to inventory the firm's costs or its rivals, but to identify the macroeconomic forces influencing those industry-level factors and to trace each one forward to its specific industry effect.

4.9.3 Socio-Cultural Factors

Socio-cultural factors encompass the demographics, cultural trends, lifestyle changes, social attitudes, and consumer preferences that shape market demand and workforce characteristics (Fahey & Narayanan, 1986). These forces evolve gradually, often over years or decades, but their cumulative impact on industry structure and firm strategy can be profound.

Demographic shifts alter the size, composition, and behavior of customer segments (Fahey & Narayanan, 1986). Population aging is among the most consequential demographic trends in developed economies. As populations age, demand grows for healthcare, pharmaceuticals, retirement services, and accessibility-oriented products, while demand may decline for products associated with younger demographics. An aging population creates opportunity for a firm like Walgreens, which can sell more prescriptions and health-related products to a growing elderly customer base. Urbanization, the migration of populations from rural to urban areas, reshapes demand for housing, transportation, food delivery, and entertainment. Changing household structures, including smaller families, more single-person households, and later marriage, alter spending patterns in industries from real estate to food packaging to automotive.

Cultural trends and shifting consumer values create some of the most powerful opportunities and threats in the macro-environment (Fahey & Narayanan, 1986). The growing consumer preference for sustainable and eco-friendly products has reshaped competition in industries from fashion to food to energy. Firms that recognized this trend early and invested in sustainable practices, materials, and messaging gained a differentiation advantage; firms that dismissed it as a passing fad have found themselves losing market share to more responsive competitors. The increasing demand for health and wellness products, from organic food to fitness technology to mental health services, has created entirely new market segments and redirected consumer spending. The rise of remote work, accelerated by the COVID-19 pandemic, has restructured demand for commercial real estate, commuter transportation, home office equipment, and collaborative software.

Workforce characteristics are the supply-side complement to consumer demand trends. Labor market conditions, including the availability of skilled workers, prevailing wages, expectations about work-life balance, and attitudes toward employer loyalty, affect firm cost structures, operational capabilities, and competitive strategies. Labor shortages in specific skill areas can constrain an industry's growth potential; demographic decline in working-age populations can create economy-wide labor scarcity. Changing workforce expectations, such as greater demand for flexibility, purpose-driven work, and diversity, require firms to adapt their human resource practices to attract and retain talent.

EX: The Gluten-Free Food Industry

The rapid growth of the gluten-free food segment illustrates how socio-cultural shifts can create entirely new markets. The percentage of the population diagnosed with celiac disease did not change dramatically in the 2010s, yet the gluten-free food market exploded in size. The growth was driven primarily by a cultural trend: a widespread consumer perception, reinforced by media coverage, wellness influencers, and dietary fads, that gluten-free diets are healthier. This socio-cultural shift had nothing to do with political regulation, economic conditions, or technological innovation. It was a change in consumer attitudes and preferences that created a massive new market segment. Food manufacturers that recognized the trend early and developed gluten-free product lines captured significant revenue; those that dismissed it as a niche concern missed a multi-billion-dollar opportunity. The example also illustrates PESTEL's practical value: it forces strategists to systematically consider socio-cultural factors that might otherwise be overlooked in an analysis focused exclusively on industry structure and competitive dynamics.

4.9.4 Technological Factors

Technological factors encompass innovations that affect the operations, products, and competitive dynamics of industries (Fahey & Narayanan, 1986). Technology is unique among PESTEL categories in that it can simultaneously reshape multiple other categories, altering economic productivity, enabling new regulatory approaches, transforming social behaviors, and creating environmental impacts. Technological factors include both the opportunities that new technologies create and the threats they pose to firms that cannot adapt.

On the opportunity side, automation and artificial intelligence are improving efficiency and cost structures across virtually every industry. Manufacturing firms use robotic assembly to reduce labor costs; logistics firms use AI-driven route optimization to reduce fuel consumption; retailers use machine learning to personalize recommendations and predict demand. Amazon's AI-controlled fulfillment center robots have dramatically increased order processing capacity while reducing per-unit costs. These capabilities can fundamentally alter the cost structures and competitive positions of firms that adopt them, creating advantages that less technologically capable competitors cannot easily match.

Digital transformation is creating entirely new product lines and customer engagement channels. Companies that once sold physical products now sell digitally enhanced versions: automobiles with software-defined features, appliances connected to the Internet of Things, fitness equipment integrated with streaming content. These digital layers create new revenue streams (subscription services, software updates, data monetization) and new sources of differentiation that were not available a decade ago. The growth of cybersecurity and data-driven services represents a technological factor that is simultaneously an opportunity (creating new markets worth hundreds of billions of dollars) and a response to a technological threat (the proliferation of cyberattacks and data breaches).

On the threat side, technological change creates the risk of obsolescence for firms whose products, processes, or business models are rendered irrelevant by new technology — the disruption dynamics discussed in Chapter 4.8. The pace of technological change also imposes escalating R&D costs, as firms must invest continuously to keep pace with innovation or risk falling behind. Dependence on a few key technology providers, a situation common in industries that rely on proprietary platforms, cloud infrastructure, or semiconductor supply, creates strategic vulnerability. When a firm's critical capabilities depend on a technology partner's continued cooperation, pricing decisions, or operational reliability, that dependence is itself a macro-environmental risk.

A related misconception is that a firm's own choices are part of the macro-environment. They are not. The technology a firm selects to run its operations or embed in its products is a firm-level choice, not a technological factor of the macro-environment. What the macro-environment supplies is the set of options: the technologies available for firms to adopt, and the pace at which that set expands or contracts. Macro-environmental technological forces limit or enlarge the menu of choices; the firm's decision about which items on that menu to use belongs to strategy, not to PESTEL. The role of technological analysis within PESTEL is therefore to assess how macro-level innovation is reshaping the options available to the industry, not to catalog the choices any single firm has already made.

4.9.5 Environmental (Ecological) Factors

Environmental factors relate to the physical and ecological conditions that affect industries, including climate, weather patterns, geographical location, global climate change, natural resource availability, and environmental regulations (Fahey & Narayanan, 1986). While environmental factors have always mattered for industries directly dependent on natural resources such as agriculture, energy, mining, and fishing, their relevance has expanded dramatically as environmental awareness, regulation, and consumer expectations have increased.

Climate and weather directly affect the operations, costs, and demand patterns of numerous industries. Agricultural yields depend on rainfall and temperature. Energy consumption varies with seasonal weather patterns. Supply chains are vulnerable to extreme weather events like hurricanes, floods, and droughts that can disrupt production and distribution networks. As climate change increases the frequency and severity of extreme weather, these operational risks intensify across a widening range of industries.

Environmental regulations have expanded well beyond traditional industries associated with environmental impact (Fahey & Narayanan, 1986). Carbon taxes and emissions trading systems are designed to internalize the environmental costs of economic activity, but their reach extends further than many firms expect. Digital firms operating large server farms consume enormous electricity with significant carbon footprints. As governments consider broadly defined carbon taxes, even firms producing purely digital products may face environmental compliance costs. This expansion of environmental regulation beyond traditional smokestack industries is one of the most strategically significant PESTEL trends of recent decades.

Environmental factors can go so far as to ban a firm's product entirely. The phaseout of incandescent light bulbs in the United States eliminated an entire product category, threatening firms built around that technology while creating enormous opportunity for LED manufacturers. Several jurisdictions have set targets to ban the sale of new gasoline-powered vehicles, a shift that would fundamentally restructure the automotive value chain. For firms in affected industries, these are existential strategic events that demand proactive response.

On the opportunity side, the expansion of green industries, including renewable energy, carbon credits, sustainable materials, and circular economy business models, represents one of the largest market-creation events of the current era. Consumer and investor preference for sustainable business practices has become a meaningful source of differentiation, particularly in industries where products are otherwise difficult to distinguish.

4.9.6 Legal Factors

Legal factors focus on the existing laws and legal frameworks that govern business activity, with the recognition that laws can vary significantly by country, state, and municipality (Fahey & Narayanan, 1986). Key legal factors include employment law, consumer protection law, intellectual property law, health and safety regulations, antitrust and competition law, and data privacy regulations.

The distinction between legal and political factors is sometimes confusing but strategically important. Legal factors refer to the laws that are currently in effect, the existing legal framework within which firms must operate. Political factors include the potential for new legislation, regulatory change, and shifts in government policy that have not yet been enacted (Fahey & Narayanan, 1986). A firm conducting a PESTEL analysis treats current employment law (minimum wage requirements, overtime rules, anti-discrimination statutes) as a legal factor and proposed changes to that law (a pending bill to raise the minimum wage) as a political factor. This distinction matters because the strategic implications differ: legal factors represent constraints that must be managed now, while political factors represent possible future constraints that must be monitored and anticipated.

Employment law affects firm cost structures, workforce flexibility, and human resource practices. Minimum wage laws set a floor on labor costs. Overtime regulations determine when firms must pay premium wages. Anti-discrimination and workplace safety requirements impose compliance costs and shape hiring, promotion, and termination decisions. These laws vary dramatically across jurisdictions, and a firm operating in multiple countries or states must navigate a patchwork of different legal requirements where the compliance burden itself becomes a significant operational consideration.

Consumer protection law governs how firms can market, sell, and service their products. Truth-in-advertising requirements, product liability standards, warranty obligations, and recall procedures all affect the cost and risk of serving consumer markets. In industries where consumer safety is paramount, such as pharmaceuticals, food, automotive, and children's products, regulatory compliance is not merely a legal obligation but a critical component of the firm's license to operate.

Intellectual property law determines how effectively firms can protect their innovations from imitation (Fahey & Narayanan, 1986). Strong IP protections, including patents, copyrights, trademarks, and trade secrets, allow innovators to capture the returns from their investments in R&D and creative work. Weak IP protections reduce the incentive to innovate by making it easier for competitors to free-ride on the innovator's efforts. The strength and enforcement of IP law varies significantly across countries, creating strategic considerations for firms that operate internationally or compete against foreign firms with different levels of IP protection.

Antitrust and competition law constrains how firms can compete, grow, and consolidate (Stigler, 1971). Merger reviews can block acquisitions that would reduce competition. Price-fixing and market allocation agreements are prohibited. Dominant firms may face restrictions on pricing practices, exclusive dealing arrangements, or bundling strategies that could exclude competitors. For firms pursuing growth through acquisition (a topic to be examined in Chapter 5), antitrust law represents a binding constraint on strategic options; a planned merger that would create significant competitive advantage may be prohibited if it would substantially reduce competition in the relevant market.

4.9.7 Identifying Opportunities and Threats Through PESTEL

The ultimate purpose of PESTEL analysis is not to catalog macro-environmental forces for their own sake but to translate those forces into strategically actionable assessments of opportunities and threats (Aguilar, 1967). Each PESTEL factor can represent an opportunity, a threat, or both simultaneously, depending on the industry in question, the firm's competitive position, and its existing resources and capabilities.

This is where PESTEL analysis connects to the broader analytical framework of this chapter. The opportunities and threats identified through PESTEL feed directly into the external dimension of SWOT analysis (Ch 4.10), providing the macro-environmental inputs that complement the industry-level inputs from the Five Forces, competitive dynamics, and industry life cycle analyses (Andrews, 1971). A comprehensive external analysis draws on all of these frameworks: the Five Forces identify structural threats and opportunities within the industry, competitive dynamics reveal firm-level competitive threats and opportunities, life cycle analysis highlights stage-specific strategic challenges, and PESTEL ensures that the broadest macro-environmental forces are not overlooked.

The practical discipline of PESTEL is to force systematic scanning across all six categories (Fahey & Narayanan, 1986). Without a structured framework, strategists tend to focus on the most visible forces, typically economic and technological, while underweighting political, socio-cultural, environmental, and legal forces that may be equally consequential. At the same time, PESTEL is most valuable when focused rather than exhaustive (Aguilar, 1967). The goal is not to identify every conceivable factor but to identify those most likely to materially affect the industry and firm in question, assess whether each represents an opportunity or threat, and evaluate the magnitude and timeline of the expected impact. A well-executed PESTEL analysis is selective, prioritized, and connected to strategic decision-making.

This connection between PESTEL and strategic action highlights the importance of environmental scanning from Chapter 4.1. PESTEL is not a one-time exercise. Macro-environmental forces are constantly evolving: political administrations change, economic cycles turn, social attitudes shift, technologies advance, and laws are enacted, amended, or repealed (Aguilar, 1967). Firms that treat PESTEL as a periodic checklist rather than an ongoing scanning discipline risk being surprised by shifts that a more vigilant approach would have detected early.

The next and final section of this chapter introduces SWOT analysis, the synthesizing framework that pulls together the internal analysis of Chapter 3 with the external analysis of Chapter 4, translating the full range of analytical insights into a foundation for strategy formulation.

References

Aguilar, F. J. (1967). *Scanning the business environment.* Macmillan.

Andrews, K. R. (1971). *The concept of corporate strategy.* Dow Jones-Irwin.

Fahey, L., & Narayanan, V. K. (1986). *Macroenvironmental analysis for strategic management.* West Publishing.

Porter, M. E. (1980). *Competitive strategy: Techniques for analyzing industries and competitors.* Free Press.

Stigler, G. J. (1971). The theory of economic regulation. *Bell Journal of Economics and Management Science, 2*(1), 3–21.

4.10 SWOT — *How do we synthesize internal and external analysis?*

> *"If you know the enemy and know yourself, you need not fear the result of a hundred battles."* — *Sun Tzu*

This chapter has developed a comprehensive set of tools for analyzing the external environment, from competitive dynamics (Ch 4.2), to industry structure (Ch 4.3–5), to industry evolution and disruption (Ch 4.6–8), to the macro-environmental forces captured by PESTEL (Ch 4.9). Chapter 3 did the same for the internal environment, developing frameworks for analyzing resources and capabilities, mapping where value is created, identifying core competencies, understanding path dependence and culture, and explaining how firms adapt through dynamic capabilities.

Each of these frameworks produces valuable insights on its own. But strategy does not emerge from internal analysis alone, nor from external analysis alone. It emerges from the intersection of the two, from understanding what the firm can do in the context of what the environment demands (Learned et al., 1965). SWOT analysis is the synthesizing framework that bridges this gap. It pulls together the internal and external dimensions of strategic analysis into a single integrated assessment, translating the full range of analytical insights into a foundation for strategic decision-making.

4.10.1 What Is SWOT Analysis?

SWOT stands for Strengths, Weaknesses, Opportunities, and Threats. It is a framework that organizes the outputs of internal and external analysis into four categories that, taken together, provide a comprehensive snapshot of the firm's strategic position (Learned et al., 1965).

Strengths and Weaknesses are drawn from internal analysis, the frameworks developed in Chapter 3. They describe the firm's internal capabilities and limitations relative to competitors. Strengths are the internal resources, capabilities, and activities in which the firm excels; weaknesses are the areas where the firm falls short.

Opportunities and Threats are drawn from external analysis, the frameworks developed in Chapter 4. They describe the external conditions that could help or harm the firm's competitive position. Opportunities are favorable external conditions the firm could exploit; threats are unfavorable conditions that could undermine its performance.

The deceptive simplicity of this two-by-two structure is both SWOT's greatest asset and its greatest liability (Hill & Westbrook, 1997). Its asset is accessibility: virtually anyone can understand the categories, and the framework requires no specialized technical knowledge to populate. Its liability is that simplicity can breed superficiality — a risk that this section addresses directly in the discussion of SWOT's limitations.

4.10.2 Purpose of SWOT

SWOT analysis serves a specific purpose in the strategic analysis process: it bridges the gap between analysis and strategy formulation (Learned et al., 1965). The frameworks in Chapters 3 and 4 are diagnostic tools that help the firm understand its current situation. SWOT takes their outputs and organizes them in a way that points toward strategic action. It does not, by itself, generate strategy. It creates the synthesized understanding from which strategy can be developed.

This distinction is critical. SWOT is a synthesis tool, not an analytical tool. It does not produce new information; it organizes information already produced by other frameworks. The resource-based view identifies resources and capabilities. The value chain reveals where value is created. VRIO determines which capabilities constitute genuine advantages (Barney, 1991). Porter's Five Forces assesses structural attractiveness (Porter, 1980). PESTEL scans the macro-environment. SWOT pulls all of this into a single integrated picture.

As discussed in Chapter 1.7, good strategy contains three elements: diagnosis, formulation, and implementation (Rumelt, 2011). SWOT sits at the boundary between diagnosis and formulation. It is the final diagnostic act — the moment where the strategist says, "Given everything we know about our internal capabilities and the external environment, what is our strategic position?" and the first step toward formulation: "Given this position, what should we do?"

4.10.3 Strengths

Strengths are internal capabilities that give the firm a competitive advantage. In the language of the frameworks developed in Chapter 3, strengths are the capabilities that pass the VRIO test, meaning they are valuable, rare, difficult to imitate, and the firm is organized to exploit them (Barney, 1991). They are the core competencies that enable the firm to create value in ways that competitors cannot easily match.

Strengths can be identified at multiple levels of analysis (Grant, 1991). At the resource level, a strength might be a proprietary technology, a strong brand, or a uniquely talented workforce. At the capability level, it might be operational excellence in manufacturing or a highly effective product development pipeline. At the value chain level, a strength is an activity where the firm performs significantly better than competitors.

The key discipline in identifying strengths is distinguishing genuine competitive advantages from mere competencies (Prahalad & Hamel, 1990). A firm may be competent at many things without any of those competencies being a strength in the SWOT sense. A strength is a capability that is superior relative to competition and contributes meaningfully to value creation and capture. The VRIO framework from Chapter 3.3 provides the filter: if a capability is valuable but not rare, it is a competitive necessity. If it is valuable and rare but easy to imitate, it is a temporary advantage. Only capabilities that survive the full VRIO assessment qualify as genuine strengths (Barney, 1991).

A crucial discipline in identifying strengths is tracing each one to its root cause. Many observers would call Walmart's low prices its greatest strength, but low prices are an outcome, not a strength in themselves. They result from underlying capabilities: logistics and distribution efficiency, scale-driven purchasing power, and disciplined cost control. Listing "low prices" as a strength stops at the symptom; identifying the capabilities that produce those prices reaches the actual source of advantage. A good SWOT analysis digs beneath surface-level outcomes to find the root cause of each item, because it is the root cause, not the visible result, that the firm must protect, extend, or defend.

4.10.4 Weaknesses

Weaknesses are internal limitations or deficiencies that hinder the firm's competitive performance. They are the mirror image of strengths: areas where the firm's capabilities fall short of what the competitive environment demands or where the firm underperforms relative to its rivals.

Weaknesses can be identified through the same frameworks used to identify strengths, applied in reverse. At the resource level, a weakness might be insufficient capital, an outdated technology infrastructure, or a weak brand reputation in key markets. At the capability level, a weakness might be slow product development cycles, poor quality control, or ineffective marketing. At the value chain level, a weakness is an activity where the firm underperforms competitors, whether through higher production costs, less efficient logistics, or weaker after-sales service.

The VRIO framework is useful here as well, though in an inverted sense (Barney, 1991). Capabilities that fail VRIO criteria are not necessarily weaknesses; they may simply be areas of competitive parity.

A weakness is something more specific: a capability below the industry norm, or an absence of a capability that competitors possess and the environment rewards. The VRIO discussion in Chapter 3.3 is particularly instructive. A capability that the firm is not organized to exploit represents underexploited potential. A capability that was once valuable but is no longer, the "obsolescent strength" diagnosis, is a weakness masquerading as a strength.

Identifying weaknesses requires intellectual honesty and organizational courage. Firms naturally prefer to focus on their strengths, and organizational cultures often resist acknowledging areas of genuine deficiency. But an honest accounting of weaknesses is essential for effective strategy formulation. A strategy that assumes capabilities the firm does not possess, or that ignores critical deficiencies, is a strategy built on wishful thinking rather than strategic reality.

4.10.5 Opportunities

Opportunities are external conditions that the firm could exploit to create or enhance its competitive advantage. They are drawn from the external analysis frameworks developed throughout this chapter, including conditions in the competitive environment, the industry structure, or the macro-environment that favor the firm or that the firm could turn to its advantage (Learned et al., 1965).

At the industry level, opportunities can emerge from any of the Five Forces (Ch 4.3). Weakening supplier power creates an opportunity to negotiate better terms. A decline in the threat of substitutes may increase the focal industry's pricing power. The exit of a major competitor reduces rivalry and creates market share available for capture. Changes in entry barriers create different types of opportunities depending on whether the firm is defending its position or seeking new territory (Porter, 1980).

At the macro-environmental level, PESTEL analysis (Ch 4.9) is the primary source of opportunity identification. Favorable political shifts, economic growth, technological innovation, socio-cultural changes, environmental trends, and legal developments can all create opportunities for firms positioned to benefit.

Opportunities also emerge from industry dynamics (Ch 4.6) and the industry life cycle (Ch 4.7). A maturing industry that is beginning to consolidate creates acquisition opportunities for well-capitalized firms. An embryonic industry entering its growth phase creates opportunities for early movers to establish brand recognition and customer loyalty. A declining industry may present opportunities for firms willing to acquire the assets of exiting competitors at distressed prices.

The critical insight about opportunities is that they are external to the firm but not external to the firm's strategic calculus (Learned et al., 1965). An opportunity that the firm lacks the resources or capabilities to exploit is not, strategically speaking, a meaningful opportunity. This is where SWOT's synthesizing power becomes apparent: opportunities must be evaluated in conjunction with strengths and weaknesses. The question is never simply "Does this opportunity exist?" but rather "Does this opportunity exist, and do we have the internal capabilities to capitalize on it?"

4.10.6 Threats

Threats are external conditions that could undermine the firm's competitive position or reduce its profitability. Like opportunities, they are drawn from the external analysis frameworks, including competitive dynamics, Five Forces analysis, industry life cycle assessment, disruption analysis, and PESTEL scanning (Learned et al., 1965).

At the industry level, threats include the strengthening of any of the Five Forces: increasing rivalry as new competitors enter or growth slows, rising supplier or buyer power, growing threat of substitutes, or lowering of entry barriers that invite new competition (Porter, 1980). The competitive dynamics framework (Ch 4.2) identifies firm-specific threats: a competitor's strategic action that targets the firm's market position, a rival's resource investments that could erode the firm's advantage, or aggressive pricing moves that pressure margins.

At the macro-environmental level, PESTEL threats include adverse regulatory changes, economic downturns, technological shifts that render products or processes obsolete, socio-cultural changes that redirect consumer preferences, environmental regulations that increase costs, and legal developments that constrain strategic options.

Disruptive threats (Ch 4.8) deserve special attention because they are often the most dangerous and most easily overlooked. A disruptive entrant operating in a different segment with a different business model may not appear on a conventional threat assessment focused on direct competitors. Yet as the disruption discussion demonstrated, these indirect threats can be existential. A thorough threat assessment must look beyond the current competitive set to consider entrants, substitutes, and business model innovations that could reshape fundamental industry dynamics.

As with opportunities, threats must be evaluated in context. A threat that the firm's existing strengths can neutralize is a manageable challenge; a threat that targets a known weakness is a strategic emergency. This contextual evaluation is the essence of SWOT's synthesizing function (Learned et al., 1965).

4.10.7 Limitations of SWOT

SWOT is one of the most widely used frameworks in strategic management. It is also one of the most frequently criticized, and the criticisms warrant serious attention (Hill & Westbrook, 1997).

SWOT tends to produce long, undifferentiated lists without prioritization. A typical SWOT exercise generates extensive lists with each item presented as equally important (Hill & Westbrook, 1997). But some strengths are far more significant than others, some threats more urgent, some opportunities more valuable. A SWOT analysis that lists twenty strengths without distinguishing the one or two that truly drive competitive advantage provides the illusion of comprehensiveness without strategic insight. Effective SWOT requires ruthless prioritization: identifying the critical few factors most consequential for decision-making.

SWOT is a static snapshot that does not capture dynamic changes over time. As the frameworks in Chapters 4.6–4.8 emphasize, competitive conditions are constantly evolving. A strength today may become irrelevant tomorrow if the basis of competition shifts; an opportunity that appears favorable now may evaporate as industry conditions change. SWOT captures the strategic position at a moment in time but does not inherently account for the trajectory of change (Hill & Westbrook, 1997). To mitigate this limitation, SWOT should be conducted periodically and supplemented with dynamic frameworks, not treated as a one-time exercise.

SWOT is only as good as the analysis that feeds into it. SWOT is a synthesis framework, not an analytical one (Learned et al., 1965). If the internal analysis is superficial, lacking rigorous VRIO application, thorough value chain analysis, or honest capability assessment, then the SWOT output will be superficial. If the external analysis is incomplete, the resulting assessment will have blind spots. The principle is straightforward: garbage in, garbage out.

SWOT does not by itself generate strategy. It is a common mistake to treat the completion of a SWOT analysis as the completion of strategic analysis (Hill & Westbrook, 1997). SWOT identifies the strategic position; it does not prescribe the strategic response. Two firms could produce identical

SWOT analyses and pursue completely different strategies depending on their risk tolerance, strategic ambitions, and interpretation of how the quadrants interact. SWOT informs strategic decision-making; it is not a substitute for strategic thinking.

4.10.8 Connecting SWOT to Strategy Formulation

Despite its limitations, SWOT provides a structured foundation for the strategic thinking that follows (Learned et al., 1965). The four quadrants interact in ways that suggest different types of strategic action.

Match strengths to opportunities. The most favorable strategic position is one where the firm's internal strengths align with external opportunities (Weihrich, 1982). A firm with a core competency in data analytics operating in an industry where data-driven decision-making is becoming the basis of competition is positioned to leverage that strength. Strategic formulation in this quadrant asks: how can we deploy our strongest capabilities to capitalize on the most promising environmental conditions?

Convert weaknesses into strengths. When the firm identifies a weakness in an area where the competitive environment demands strength, the strategic question becomes one of investment: where should we build capability to close the gap? This may involve internal development through R&D, hiring, or process redesign, or it may involve acquiring missing capabilities through partnerships or acquisitions (Chapter 5). Not every weakness needs conversion; the challenge is determining which weaknesses are strategically critical and which are merely inconvenient. Some apparent weaknesses are not deficiencies at all but the deliberate consequences of strategic tradeoffs. A cost leader that offers fewer features, or a focused firm that declines to serve segments outside its niche, will register "weaknesses" relative to broad-line rivals. These are the price of a coherent position (Chapter 2), not problems to be fixed; attempting to eliminate them would blur the very tradeoffs that make the strategy work. Such weaknesses should be acknowledged and accounted for rather than addressed directly.

Mitigate threats using strengths. When external threats target areas where the firm is internally strong, the firm is in a defensible position (Weihrich, 1982). A firm with a powerful brand facing new entrants can leverage customer loyalty to defend market share. A firm with a strong balance sheet facing an economic downturn can weather the storm and acquire distressed competitors. Strategic formulation here asks: how can our advantages serve as a shield against external pressures?

Avoid the worst case. The most dangerous position is one where a significant threat targets an area of internal weakness. A firm with weak digital capabilities facing rapid technological disruption, or a firm with high fixed costs facing severe recession, is in strategic peril. These intersections require immediate attention: either the weakness must be urgently addressed, exposure to the threat reduced, or the firm must consider whether exit is the most rational response.

These four strategic logics — leverage, develop, defend, and avoid — do not constitute a complete strategy (Rumelt, 2011). They are starting points that must be developed through subsequent frameworks: corporate-level decisions about scope and growth (Chapter 5), and governance mechanisms that ensure strategic decisions serve stakeholder interests (Chapter 6). But they provide the critical bridge between where the firm is (diagnosis) and what the firm should do (formulation).

4.10.9 SWOT as the Capstone of Internal and External Analysis

SWOT analysis occupies a unique position in this textbook's analytical sequence. It is not a new analytical tool in the way that the Five Forces, VRIO, or PESTEL are. It is the framework that makes all of those tools strategically useful by integrating their outputs into a coherent picture (Learned et al., 1965). Without SWOT or something like it, a firm might conduct brilliant internal and external analyses and still fail to connect the insights to strategic action. Next we turn to strategies specific to larger firms with corporate-level strategy in Chapter 5.

References

Barney, J. B. (1991). Firm resources and sustained competitive advantage. *Journal of Management, 17*(1), 99–120.

Grant, R. M. (1991). The resource-based theory of competitive advantage: Implications for strategy formulation. *California Management Review, 33*(3), 114–135.

Hill, T., & Westbrook, R. (1997). SWOT analysis: It's time for a product recall. *Long Range Planning, 30*(1), 46–52.

Learned, E. P., Christensen, C. R., Andrews, K. R., & Guth, W. D. (1965). *Business policy: Text and cases.* Irwin.

Porter, M. E. (1980). *Competitive strategy: Techniques for analyzing industries and competitors.* Free Press.

Prahalad, C. K., & Hamel, G. (1990). The core competence of the corporation. *Harvard Business Review, 68*(3), 79–91.

Rumelt, R. P. (2011). *Good strategy bad strategy: The difference and why it matters.* Crown Business.

Weihrich, H. (1982). The TOWS matrix — A tool for situational analysis. *Long Range Planning, 15*(2), 54–66.

Chapter 5

Corporate-Level Strategy

5.1 Build, Borrow, Buy — *How should firms grow: make, partner, or acquire?*

5.1.1 The Shift from Business-Level to Corporate-Level Strategy

The first four chapters of this book focused on how firms compete within a single industry. Business-level strategy asks a deceptively focused question: *How do we compete in this business?* The answer involves choosing a strategic position, whether differentiation, cost leadership, or a focused variant, and assembling the resources, capabilities, and value chain activities needed to execute it effectively. Whether a firm competes on product uniqueness, operational efficiency, or a combination of both, business-level strategy is concerned with winning in the competitive arena the firm currently occupies.

Corporate-level strategy asks a fundamentally different question: *Which businesses should we be in, and how do we manage them?* This is the domain of multi-business strategy, encompassing decisions about scope, growth, and resource allocation across a portfolio of businesses, products, or markets. While business-level strategy looks inward at competitive positioning within a single industry, corporate-level strategy looks outward and upward, asking whether the firm can create additional value by participating in multiple industries or markets simultaneously.

The distinction matters because the logic of value creation changes. At the business level, value comes from delivering a product or service that customers prefer over alternatives, through superior differentiation, lower costs, or both. At the corporate level, value must come from the combination of businesses itself. A diversified firm must be worth more than the sum of its parts, or there is no strategic rationale for corporate-level strategy at all. If each business unit would perform just as well, or better, as an independent company, then the corporate parent is not creating value; it is destroying it through overhead, bureaucracy, and distraction.

This is a high bar to clear, and many firms fail. Research consistently shows that a large proportion of acquisitions destroy shareholder value (King et al., 2004), that many diversification efforts lead to corporate bloat rather than synergy (Berger & Ofek, 1995), and that the complexity of managing multiple businesses introduces costs that can overwhelm the benefits. The corporate-level strategy topics in this chapter — organic growth, strategic alliances, mergers and acquisitions, integration, and diversification

— are therefore not just a menu of growth options. They are decisions that, if made poorly, can undermine everything the firm has built at the business level.

The key insight connecting these two levels of strategy is this: growth requires resources and capabilities. A firm that wants to enter a new market, develop a new product line, or expand geographically needs specific resources it may not currently possess. The central question of corporate-level strategy is how to close that gap, and the Build, Borrow, Buy framework provides a structured approach to making that decision.

5.1.2 The Strategic Resource Gap

Every growth strategy begins with a recognition that the firm's current resource base is insufficient for the opportunity it wants to pursue. This insufficiency is the **strategic resource gap** — the difference between the resources and capabilities the firm currently possesses and those it needs to achieve its growth objectives (Capron & Mitchell, 2012).

The concept builds directly on the resource-based view introduced in Chapter 3. The RBV establishes that competitive advantage is rooted in a firm's unique bundle of resources and capabilities, but it is primarily a static framework that explains why a firm has an advantage at a given point in time. The strategic resource gap adds a dynamic dimension: the resources a firm needs tomorrow may differ from those it has today, and closing that gap is the central challenge of corporate growth.

Resource gaps take many forms. A pharmaceutical company may have deep expertise in drug discovery but lack the regulatory knowledge to enter the European market. A technology startup may have a revolutionary product but lack the manufacturing capacity to scale. A consumer goods company may have a powerful brand in one category but lack the formulation expertise to extend into adjacent categories. In each case, the firm faces the same fundamental question: how should it acquire the resources and capabilities it lacks? The Build, Borrow, Buy framework provides a systematic decision tree for answering this question, guiding managers through a series of sequential decisions that match the characteristics of the resource gap to the most appropriate growth strategy (Capron & Mitchell, 2012). The framework asks four key questions, each of which narrows the range of appropriate options.

5.1.3 Decision 1: How Relevant Are the Firm's Existing Internal Resources?

The first decision point asks whether the firm's current resources and capabilities are relevant to the growth opportunity. Internal resources are considered relevant when two conditions are met: they are similar to the resources needed for the new opportunity, and they are superior to those of competitors in the targeted area (Capron & Mitchell, 2012).

When internal resources are highly relevant, the firm's best option is to **build**, developing the needed capabilities internally through organic growth. If a firm already has a strong technology platform and the opportunity requires an extension of that platform, existing knowledge, organizational routines, and employee skills provide a foundation that can be adapted and expanded without needing to look outside the firm.

When internal resources have low relevance, internal development becomes risky and slow. A firm attempting to build capabilities in a domain where it has no experience is essentially starting from scratch, competing against firms with years of accumulated knowledge and path-dependent advantages (Ch 3). In these cases, the firm should look externally, either borrowing resources through alliances or buying them through acquisition.

Consider the difference between a software company expanding into a related enterprise market versus expanding into biotechnology. In the first case, the firm's existing engineering talent, development processes, and customer relationships are highly relevant, so it can build. In the second case, those resources have almost no relevance to pharmaceutical R&D, and the firm must borrow or buy.

5.1.4 Decision 2: How Tradable Are the Targeted External Resources?

If the firm must look externally, the next question concerns the tradability of the resources it needs. Highly tradable resources can be clearly defined, separated from their organizational context, and transferred through contracts. Intellectual property is often highly tradable; a firm can license a patent or brand without acquiring the entire organization. Lucasfilm's licensing of *Star Wars* IP to toy manufacturers, game developers, and theme park operators illustrates this well.

Other resources are far less tradable. A firm's reputation for quality is deeply embedded in its culture, employee behaviors, and routines. Tacit knowledge — expertise that employees carry but cannot easily codify — is similarly difficult to trade. Toyota's production system, for example, involves deeply embedded routines and a culture of continuous improvement that cannot simply be licensed.

Tradability also depends on the contract itself: whether the two firms can spell out the deal in writing and hold each other to it. No contract can capture every detail or foresee everything that might happen, so every contract is incomplete to some degree (Williamson, 1985). When a resource is simple and easy to inspect, the parties can write a clear agreement and confirm that both sides deliver, so the resource changes hands easily. When the resource is complex, its quality is hard to judge, or its value depends on effort the contract cannot pin down in advance, the agreement is harder to write and harder to enforce. Those gaps give each side room to cut corners or take advantage of the other, and the greater that risk, the harder the resource is to trade through a simple market deal. A trade involves promises on both sides: the seller commits to deliver the resource as described, and the buyer commits to pay and to use it within agreed limits. Tradability therefore depends not only on the resource but on how easily those mutual promises can be put in writing and enforced: a resource that looks well-defined may still resist a straightforward purchase if the deal cannot be captured in an enforceable contract.

When targeted resources are highly tradable, the firm can **borrow** them through a contractual alliance or licensing agreement, gaining access without the cost of deeper integration. When they are not easily tradable, embedded in the partner's organization, culture, or tacit knowledge, a simple contract is insufficient, and the firm must consider deeper partnerships or acquisition.

5.1.5 Decision 3: How Close Do You Need to Be to the Resource Partner?

When resources are not highly tradable, the firm must determine the degree of organizational closeness it needs with the resource partner, including the depth of coordination, knowledge sharing, and mutual adaptation required to effectively utilize the partner's resources.

When **low closeness** is sufficient, a contractual alliance remains appropriate. The firms can share specific resources through detailed agreements governing the scope and terms of cooperation. When **high closeness** is needed, requiring significant coordination, shared decision-making, or workflow integration, the firm should consider an equity alliance or joint venture. In an equity alliance, one firm takes a partial ownership stake in another, aligning financial incentives. In a joint venture, the partners create an entirely new entity with shared ownership and governance, enabling deep collaboration on activities that require substantial mutual investment. When **extreme closeness** is needed, when resources are so deeply embedded they can only be fully accessed through ownership, the firm should consider acquisition, which provides full ownership and control, enabling the acquiring firm to direct the target's resources, restructure its operations, and integrate capabilities directly.

5.1.6 Decision 4: How Well Can You Integrate the Target Firm?

If the analysis points to acquisition, the framework requires one final assessment: can the firm actually integrate the target successfully? Integration is where many acquisitions fail, and the Build, Borrow, Buy framework wisely positions this as a gating decision rather than an afterthought.

Successful integration requires several conditions. The resource gap must be vital enough to justify the cost and disruption. The acquiring firm must have the organizational capacity to absorb the target, including compatible cultures, experienced integration teams, and sufficient managerial attention. Key employees — often the carriers of the very capabilities that made the acquisition attractive — must be willing to stay under new ownership.

If integration conditions are favorable, the firm proceeds. If they are not, if cultural incompatibility is severe, if key personnel are likely to depart, or if the firm lacks acquisition experience, the framework directs managers back to reconsider building or borrowing, or to reformulate the growth strategy entirely. This is a critical feature: it recognizes that a strategically logical acquisition can still be a terrible decision if integration is unlikely to succeed.

EX: Disney's Sequential Use of Build, Borrow, and Buy

The Walt Disney Company illustrates how a single firm can employ all three growth modes depending on the resource gap it faces. When Disney expanded its theme park operations from Disneyland to Walt Disney World, it was building, leveraging its existing capabilities in park design, entertainment, and hospitality management to develop a new property internally. Disney's existing resources were highly relevant to this growth opportunity, making organic development the natural choice.

When Disney wanted to enter the Japanese market, it initially chose to borrow. Tokyo Disneyland, which opened in 1983, was operated through a licensing agreement with the Oriental Land Company. Disney licensed its intellectual property, brand, and park design expertise, all highly tradable resources, while the Japanese partner provided local market knowledge, real estate, and operational management. Disney did not need extreme closeness to make this work; a contractual relationship was sufficient.

But when Disney determined that it needed to fundamentally expand its creative capabilities in computer-generated animation, a resource gap that could not be filled internally (Disney's own CGI capabilities lagged behind the industry) and that was not easily tradable (Pixar's creative culture and talent could not be separated from the organization), it chose to buy. Disney acquired Pixar in 2006 for $7.4 billion, gaining not just Pixar's technology but its creative leadership, organizational culture, and storytelling methodology. The high integration requirements and the embedded nature of Pixar's capabilities made acquisition the appropriate choice under the Build, Borrow, Buy logic.

Disney's subsequent acquisitions of Marvel Entertainment (2009) and Lucasfilm (2012) followed a similar rationale. In each case, the targeted resources, including iconic intellectual property portfolios, creative talent, and established franchise ecosystems, were deeply embedded in their respective organizations and required ownership-level closeness to fully leverage across Disney's platform of theme parks, consumer products, and media distribution.

5.1.7 Connection to Transaction Cost Economics

The Build, Borrow, Buy framework connects directly to the transaction cost economics introduced in Chapter 1.1. Coase (1937) explained the existence of firms by pointing to the costs of using the market, and Williamson (1985) extended this logic, arguing that the boundary of the firm is determined by the relative costs of internal organization versus market exchange. Chapter 1.1 framed that boundary as a comparison between the cost of organizing an activity internally and the transaction costs of sourcing it from the market. Build, Borrow, Buy applies the same comparison to the resources a firm needs but does not yet possess.

The transaction cost logic explains why firms choose one growth mode over another. Three conditions drive transaction costs upward: asset specificity, uncertainty, and the risk of partner opportunism. Asset specificity is the degree to which a resource is valuable within a particular relationship and worth far less outside of it, as when a supplier builds tooling that fits only one customer's product. When resources are highly specific, uncertainty is high, and opportunism is a real risk, transaction costs rise, pushing the firm toward ownership through building or buying. When resources are more generic, uncertainty is manageable, and trust can be established, transaction costs are lower, and the firm can rely effectively on borrowing. This grounding in economic theory means the framework does not just describe options; it explains the underlying forces that make one option superior to another in a given situation. A firm that understands transaction cost logic can anticipate when alliances are likely to fail (when partner opportunism is difficult to control), when acquisitions are likely to succeed (when integration achieves cost savings that offset the acquisition premium), and when internal development is the safest path (when existing capabilities are directly relevant and the risk of market exchange is unacceptably high).

5.1.8 The Road Ahead: Corporate Growth Strategies in Detail

The Build, Borrow, Buy framework provides the organizing logic for the remainder of this chapter. Each of the three growth modes raises its own set of strategic questions, presents its own advantages and risks, and requires its own analytical tools. Chapter 5.2 explores organic growth (build), examining when internal development is most effective and how firms can leverage existing resources to enter new markets. Chapter 5.3 examines strategic alliances and joint ventures (borrow), exploring the different partnership structures available, why firms choose to cooperate, and the competitive risks that alliances create. Chapter 5.4 covers mergers and acquisitions (buy), analyzing why firms acquire, how the acquisition process works, and why so many acquisitions fail to deliver the value they promise. Subsequent sections address horizontal and vertical integration, diversification strategy, internal capital markets, and portfolio management, all building on the foundational logic introduced here.

Together, these topics form the core of corporate-level strategy: the decisions that determine not just how a firm competes, but where it competes, how it grows, and how it manages the complexity that growth inevitably brings.

References

Berger, P. G., & Ofek, E. (1995). Diversification's effect on firm value. *Journal of Financial Economics, 37*(1), 39–65.

Capron, L., & Mitchell, W. (2012). *Build, borrow, or buy: Solving the growth dilemma.* Harvard Business Review Press.

Coase, R. H. (1937). The nature of the firm. *Economica, 4*(16), 386–405.
King, D. R., Dalton, D. R., Daily, C. M., & Covin, J. G. (2004). Meta-analyses of post-acquisition performance: Indications of unidentified moderators. *Strategic Management Journal, 25*(2), 187–200.
Williamson, O. E. (1985). *The economic institutions of capitalism: Firms, markets, relational contracting.* Free Press.

5.2 Organic Growth (Build) — *When should firms develop capabilities internally?*

5.2.1 What Is Organic Growth?

The Build, Borrow, Buy framework introduced in Chapter 5.1 established that when a firm's existing internal resources are highly relevant to a growth opportunity, the preferred strategy is to build, developing the needed capabilities internally rather than acquiring them from outside the firm. This section examines the build option in depth: what organic growth entails, when it makes strategic sense, what advantages it offers, and where its limitations become binding constraints.

Organic growth is the process of expanding through the internal development of new resources, capabilities, products, or markets. Rather than acquiring another firm or partnering with an external organization, the firm relies on its own people, knowledge, processes, and investments to close the strategic resource gap. It is also called *internal development* or, when entering entirely new markets, *greenfield development*, a term that evokes the image of building something from the ground up on an empty site, with no preexisting structures or legacies to accommodate.

Organic growth can take many forms: a consumer goods company developing a new product line in its existing R&D labs, a retailer opening new store locations using its own operational expertise, or a technology firm expanding its software platform to serve a new customer segment. What unites these activities is that the firm draws on internal resources to generate expansion rather than looking outside its boundaries for the capabilities it needs.

This distinction matters because the mode of growth shapes the nature of the capabilities that result. Resources developed through organic growth are built incrementally, layer by layer, through the firm's own experience and investment. They become embedded in the firm's routines, culture, and organizational knowledge. As a result, organically developed capabilities tend to be deeply integrated with the firm's existing operations and, critically, tend to be more difficult for competitors to imitate, a point that connects directly to the path dependence concepts developed in Chapter 3 (Barney, 1991).

5.2.2 When Organic Growth Makes Sense

The Build, Borrow, Buy framework identifies resource relevance as the primary criterion for choosing organic growth. But what does "resource relevance" look like in practice? Several conditions signal that internal development is the most appropriate path (Capron & Mitchell, 2012).

Existing resources are highly relevant to the new opportunity. This is the foundational condition. A firm should build when its current resource base — its technology, its talent, its brand, its operational know-how — can be extended, adapted, or recombined to serve the new opportunity. The more overlap between what the firm already does well and what the growth opportunity requires, the stronger the case for organic growth. A pharmaceutical company with deep expertise in oncology drug development pursuing a new cancer therapeutic is operating well within the relevance zone. A pharmaceutical company with the same expertise attempting to enter agricultural biotechnology is not; the knowledge base, regulatory environment, and customer relationships are fundamentally different.

The firm's brand, technology, or customer knowledge transfers to the new area. Organic growth is most effective when existing intangible assets can be leveraged. A strong brand that carries trust into adjacent categories, customer knowledge that transfers when the new opportunity serves similar segments, and technology platforms that extend to new use cases all reduce the cost and risk of entering the new space.

Significant overlap exists between the existing business and the target business. Overlap can be technological (the new product uses similar engineering principles), operational (the new market can be served through existing manufacturing or distribution), or relational (the new customers are reached through existing channels). The greater the overlap, the more the firm can reuse existing infrastructure and knowledge rather than building entirely from scratch. High overlap means the incremental investment required for expansion is low relative to the value created, a favorable economic equation that tips the balance toward internal development.

Specialized knowledge is standardized and skilled workers are available. Organic growth is easier when the labor market has a supply of people with the relevant skills. If a firm wants to expand its data analytics capabilities and qualified data scientists are available, it can hire and develop talent internally without acquiring another organization. When the required expertise is extremely scarce and deeply embedded in a few firms' organizational contexts, internal development becomes much harder.

New technology integrates with existing processes. When a growth opportunity involves technology that complements the firm's current infrastructure, organic development is natural. When the required technology is radically different, requiring entirely different toolchains, methodologies, or scientific foundations, the case for internal development weakens.

Speed is not critical. This condition is often the decisive one. Organic growth is inherently slower than acquisition because the firm must develop capabilities step by step rather than purchasing them fully formed. If the competitive environment allows time for gradual development, if the market opportunity is not being rapidly claimed by competitors, if network effects are not creating winner-take-all dynamics, and if first-mover advantages are not decisive, then the speed disadvantage of organic growth is manageable. If speed is essential, the firm may need to borrow or buy even if its internal resources are relevant, simply because the window of opportunity will not remain open long enough for internal development to bear fruit (Teece et al., 1997).

5.2.3 Advantages of Organic Growth

When the conditions described above are met, organic growth offers several significant strategic advantages over external growth modes.

Maintains strategic control and organizational culture. Internal development allows the firm to retain full control over the direction, pace, and character of its growth. There are no partners to negotiate with and no acquired firm's culture to reconcile with the parent's. The firm can align the new initiative with its existing strategic vision without compromise. This control extends to organizational culture, one of the most difficult elements to manage in acquisitions and alliances. When a firm grows organically, it extends its existing culture into the new activity rather than attempting to merge two different cultures, a process that frequently fails (Larsson & Finkelstein, 1999).

Avoids the integration risks of acquisitions. As Chapter 5.4 will discuss in detail, acquisitions carry substantial integration risks: cultural clashes, employee attrition, operational disruption, and the destruction of the very capabilities that made the target attractive. Organic growth sidesteps these risks entirely. There are no key employees who might leave, no incompatible IT systems to merge, and no two different ways of doing things to reconcile.

Builds path-dependent capabilities that are difficult for competitors to imitate. Capabilities developed through organic growth are the product of the firm's unique history, decisions, and accumulated experience. As discussed in Chapter 3, path dependence creates barriers to imitation because the capability was built through a specific sequence of events, investments, and learning that cannot simply be purchased or replicated by a competitor. An acquired capability, by contrast, was built by someone else, and the fact that it was available for purchase suggests that, under certain conditions, it might be available to other buyers as well. Organically developed capabilities are more firmly embedded in the firm's identity and harder for rivals to observe, understand, or copy. Each internal investment, each iteration of learning, each adjustment to organizational routines adds another layer of path-dependent complexity that raises the barriers to imitation.

Leverages and deepens existing core competencies. Organic growth does not merely use the firm's existing core competencies — it strengthens them (Prahalad & Hamel, 1990). Each new project, each market expansion, and each product extension provides the firm with additional experience that deepens its expertise. A firm that grows organically into related areas accumulates knowledge that reinforces its competitive advantage in its original business as well. The R&D team that develops a product for a new market segment brings lessons back to the core business. The sales force that learns to serve a new customer type develops insights applicable across the entire portfolio. This deepening effect creates a virtuous cycle: organic growth makes the firm's competencies stronger, which makes further organic growth more feasible, which deepens competencies further.

This virtuous cycle also connects to the resource stocks concept from Chapter 3. Organic growth is, in essence, a sustained investment in the firm's resource inflows, adding new knowledge, new relationships, new routines, and new experience faster than the natural outflows of forgetting, attrition, and obsolescence can erode them. A firm that grows organically is actively filling its resource "bucket" from the inside, building the kind of deep, multi-layered capability stocks that are most resistant to competitive erosion (Penrose, 1959).

5.2.4 Limitations of Organic Growth

Despite these advantages, organic growth is not always feasible or desirable. Several limitations constrain its applicability.

Slower than acquisition for entering new markets. Building capabilities internally takes time — often years or decades for complex capabilities in unfamiliar domains. When Facebook acquired Instagram in 2012, it was not because Facebook lacked the technical ability to build a photo-sharing app. But Instagram had already captured 30 million users and was growing explosively. The time required to build a competing platform organically, and the risk that Instagram would become entrenched during that period, made acquisition the superior choice. Speed was the binding constraint that rendered organic growth strategically inferior despite Facebook's highly relevant internal resources.

Requires existing resource relevance; difficult when entering unrelated areas. Organic growth is predicated on the assumption that the firm has a foundation to build on. When a firm seeks to enter a domain where it has little or no existing expertise, internal development means building from scratch against incumbents with years of path-dependent capability development. The learning curve is steep, the investment is high, and the probability of success is low. A consumer packaged goods company attempting to organically develop capabilities in semiconductor manufacturing would face an almost insurmountable gap. When resource relevance is low, the Build, Borrow, Buy framework correctly directs the firm to look externally.

May miss windows of opportunity where speed matters. Some competitive environments reward early movers and penalize latecomers. In markets with strong network effects, the first firm to achieve critical mass can lock in an advantage that later entrants cannot overcome. In industries undergoing rapid technological change, the window for entering profitably may be measured in months rather than years. The deliberate pace of organic growth can mean arriving after the opportunity has passed.

Can lead to incrementalism and strategic myopia. A more subtle limitation is that organic growth, by its nature, tends to push firms toward adjacent opportunities rather than transformative ones. Because the build option works best when existing resources are highly relevant, firms that rely exclusively on organic growth may find themselves expanding only into areas that closely resemble their current business. Over time, this pattern can produce a form of strategic myopia: the firm becomes very good at what it already does but fails to develop capabilities in areas that represent the future of its industry. Kodak is a cautionary example: the company had deep expertise in chemical photography and grew organically within that domain for decades, but its existing resource base was not relevant to the digital photography revolution that ultimately destroyed its core business. Organic growth reinforced Kodak's commitment to its existing competencies at the expense of developing new ones.

5.2.5 Organic Growth and the Build, Borrow, Buy Decision

It is worth emphasizing that organic growth is not inherently superior to alliances or acquisitions; it is superior *in specific circumstances*. The Build, Borrow, Buy framework is a decision tree, not a ranking. The right growth mode depends on the characteristics of the resource gap, not on any a priori preference for one approach over another.

In practice, many firms use organic growth as their default mode and turn to alliances or acquisitions only when internal development is clearly inadequate. This default is understandable, as building internally feels natural, avoids the complexity of external deals, and aligns with managers' desire to maintain control. But defaulting to organic growth when the conditions do not support it can be just as costly as defaulting to acquisition when simpler approaches would suffice. A firm that attempts to build its way into a market that demands speed is making the same category of error as a firm that acquires when a licensing agreement would have been cheaper and less risky. Strategic discipline requires matching the growth mode to the resource gap, not simply choosing the mode that feels most comfortable.

EX: 3M's Organic Growth Through Core Technology Platforms

3M (Minnesota Mining and Manufacturing Company) is one of the most frequently cited examples of successful long-term organic growth. The company operates in dozens of industries, from healthcare to consumer products to industrial manufacturing to electronics, and has generated the vast majority of its diversification through internal development rather than acquisition.

The foundation of 3M's organic growth strategy is its investment in core technology platforms that can be applied across multiple industries and product categories. The company organizes its R&D around approximately 50 core technologies, including adhesives, abrasives, films and coatings, nonwoven materials, and nanotechnology, and encourages researchers to find new applications for these technologies across the company's diverse business units. A single adhesive technology might find applications in healthcare (surgical tapes), consumer products (Post-it Notes and Scotch Tape), automotive (bonding strips), and electronics (thermal management films). Each application extends the technology into a new market without requiring 3M to acquire external capabilities.

Several features of 3M's approach illustrate the principles of effective organic growth. The company's existing resources are highly relevant to each new application; its scientists and engineers already understand the underlying technology and can adapt it to new contexts. The company invests heavily in maintaining conditions that support internal development: 3M famously allows its researchers to spend up to 15 percent of their time on projects of their own choosing, creating space for serendipitous discoveries. And because each new product application builds on existing knowledge, the process deepens 3M's core competencies rather than merely deploying them. 3M's technology base, built over more than a century of continuous R&D investment, cannot be replicated through a single acquisition; the organizational routines, cross-divisional collaboration norms, and institutional memory are deeply path-dependent.

EX: Coca-Cola's Organic Expansion into Adjacent Beverage Categories

The Coca-Cola Company illustrates organic growth driven by brand and distribution leverage rather than technology platforms. For most of its history, Coca-Cola was essentially a single-product company. Its expansion into water (Dasani), sports drinks (Powerade), and tea (Gold Peak) shows how a firm can grow into adjacent categories when existing resources are directly transferable.

Coca-Cola's core resources include one of the world's most recognized brands, the most extensive beverage distribution network on the planet, and deep customer relationships with retailers, restaurants, and vending operators worldwide. When Coca-Cola develops a new product, it can immediately place it in millions of points of sale through existing bottling and distribution partnerships, infrastructure built over more than a century that competitors cannot easily replicate. Expanding from cola into water or sports drinks requires adaptation of formulation, packaging, and marketing competencies, but not their reinvention.

However, Coca-Cola's experience also illustrates the limitations of organic growth. When the company wanted to enter premium coffee, a category with different supply chains, preparation methods, and retail formats, its existing resources were insufficient. This led to the acquisition of Costa Coffee in 2019 for $4.9 billion, reflecting Build, Borrow, Buy logic: when existing resources lack relevance, the firm must look externally. The Coca-Cola example demonstrates both the power and boundaries of organic growth, highly effective within the zone of resource relevance, but insufficient beyond it.

References

Barney, J. B. (1991). Firm resources and sustained competitive advantage. *Journal of Management, 17*(1), 99–120.

Capron, L., & Mitchell, W. (2012). *Build, borrow, or buy: Solving the growth dilemma.* Harvard Business Review Press.

Larsson, R., & Finkelstein, S. (1999). Integrating strategic, organizational, and human resource perspectives on mergers and acquisitions: A case survey of synergy realization. *Organization Science, 10*(1), 1–26.

Penrose, E. T. (1959). *The theory of the growth of the firm.* John Wiley & Sons.

Prahalad, C. K., & Hamel, G. (1990). The core competence of the corporation. *Harvard Business Review, 68*(3), 79–91.
Teece, D. J., Pisano, G., & Shuen, A. (1997). Dynamic capabilities and strategic management. *Strategic Management Journal, 18*(7), 509–533.

5.3 Strategic Alliances & Joint Ventures (Borrow) — *When should firms partner?*

5.3.1 The Increasing Prevalence of Strategic Alliances

The previous section examined organic growth, the build option in the Build, Borrow, Buy framework (Capron & Mitchell, 2012), and established that internal development works best when a firm's existing resources are highly relevant to the growth opportunity. But what happens when a firm needs resources it does not possess and cannot efficiently develop on its own, yet full acquisition is either unnecessary, too expensive, or too risky? This is the domain of the borrow option: strategic alliances, joint ventures, licensing arrangements, and other cooperative strategies that allow firms to access external resources without taking full ownership.

Strategic alliances have undergone a dramatic transformation in their prevalence and strategic importance over the past half-century. In the 1970s, alliances between firms were relatively rare, and most growth occurred either through internal development or outright acquisition. By the 1990s and into the 2000s, strategic alliances had become one of the most common mechanisms for corporate growth. The trend has continued and even accelerated: a 2026 EY-Parthenon survey of 1,200 global CEOs found that 79 percent planned to pursue joint ventures or strategic alliances in the coming year, up from 62 percent the prior year (EY-Parthenon, 2026). Today, major corporations maintain dozens or even hundreds of alliance relationships simultaneously, and the ability to manage alliances effectively has itself become a source of competitive advantage.

Several forces have driven this increase. Globalization has made cross-border partnerships essential for firms entering unfamiliar markets. The accelerating pace of technological change has made it increasingly difficult for any single firm to develop all the capabilities it needs internally. The rise of modular and platform-based business models has created opportunities for firms to specialize and collaborate rather than integrate. And the growing complexity of competitive environments has made flexibility a strategic priority, as alliances allow firms to access resources quickly without the permanent commitment of an acquisition.

Before proceeding, an essential distinction must be drawn. Strategic alliances are cooperative arrangements in which independent firms voluntarily combine resources to create mutual value while remaining separate organizations. They are fundamentally different from *collusive alliances*, in which firms cooperate to restrict competition, raise prices, or divide markets. Collusive alliances are illegal under antitrust law in most jurisdictions and will be addressed briefly at the end of this section.

5.3.2 Types of Strategic Alliances

Strategic alliances vary significantly in their structure, the degree of commitment they require, and the closeness of the relationship they create. Understanding these structural differences is critical because the choice of alliance type should match the characteristics of the resource gap, a principle connecting directly to the tradability and closeness decisions in the Build, Borrow, Buy framework (Ch 5.1).

5.3.3 Nonequity Strategic Alliances

A nonequity strategic alliance is a contractual relationship in which two or more firms agree to share some of their resources and capabilities without creating a separate legal entity and without either firm taking an equity stake in the other. The alliance is governed entirely by the terms of the contract: licensing agreements, supply agreements, co-marketing arrangements, distribution agreements, and similar arm's-length cooperative structures.

Nonequity alliances are the most common form of strategic alliance and the least complex to establish and dissolve. They are particularly well suited to situations where the resources being shared are highly tradable, where they can be clearly specified in a contract and transferred without deep organizational integration. The Build, Borrow, Buy framework identifies these as situations where the needed resources can be "borrowed" through a straightforward contractual arrangement.

EX: NFL and Nike Licensing Agreement

The licensing agreement between the National Football League and Nike illustrates the nonequity alliance in its simplest form. The NFL possesses enormously valuable intellectual property — team logos, names, and the league brand itself — but does not have the manufacturing capabilities or design expertise to produce high-quality athletic apparel. Nike possesses world-class capabilities in apparel design, manufacturing, and distribution but does not own NFL intellectual property. Through a licensing agreement, Nike gains the right to produce officially branded NFL uniforms and merchandise, while the NFL receives licensing fees and benefits from Nike's design and manufacturing excellence. No separate entity is created. No equity changes hands. The relationship is governed by a contract that specifies the terms under which Nike may use NFL intellectual property, the quality standards that must be met, the financial arrangements, and the duration of the agreement.

This type of alliance works because the resources being exchanged are highly tradable. The NFL's intellectual property can be clearly defined and contractually transferred. Nike's capabilities are applied to a specified product category. Neither party needs to fundamentally alter its organizational structure or integrate its operations. The alliance creates value for both parties without requiring the organizational closeness that would justify an equity arrangement.

5.3.4 Equity Strategic Alliances

An equity strategic alliance involves two or more firms sharing resources through equity ownership, structured in one of several ways: the partners may create a legally independent company in which they hold different (that is, unequal) percentages of ownership, one firm may take a partial ownership stake in another, or the partners may take stakes in each other. The defining feature is the equity investment: one or both partners commit capital that creates a shared financial interest in the alliance's success.

Equity alliances represent a deeper commitment than nonequity arrangements. By investing capital, the partners create financial incentives that go beyond what a contract alone can provide, including shared exposure to profits and losses that aligns incentives and reduces the risk of opportunistic behavior or underinvestment.

Equity alliances are appropriate when the resources being accessed are not highly tradable, when they are embedded in organizational routines, tacit knowledge, or cultural practices, and when the degree of closeness required is high but not so extreme as to require full acquisition.

EX: Toyota's Equity Alliances — NUMMI and Tesla

Toyota's alliance history illustrates both the versatility and strategic logic of equity alliances. In 1984, Toyota and General Motors created New United Motor Manufacturing, Inc. (NUMMI), a jointly owned manufacturing facility in Fremont, California. Toyota contributed its legendary Toyota Production System (TPS), while GM contributed its existing facility, workforce, and knowledge of the American regulatory and labor environment. Each partner gained access to resources difficult to develop internally: Toyota learned to manufacture in the United States using American labor, and GM gained direct exposure to Toyota's manufacturing methods. The equity structure provided stronger incentives for genuine knowledge sharing than a licensing arrangement would have offered.

In 2010, after NUMMI's closure following GM's bankruptcy, Toyota entered an equity alliance with Tesla Motors, purchasing a $50 million stake and agreeing to collaborate on electric vehicle development. This gave Toyota access to Tesla's battery technology and electric powertrain expertise, while Tesla gained manufacturing expertise, credibility, and a production facility. The equity investment created financial alignment that incentivized genuine cooperation beyond what a simple licensing arrangement would have produced.

5.3.5 Joint Ventures

A joint venture is a legally independent company created by two or more parent firms with equal (or roughly equal) equity shares. The key distinction from an equity strategic alliance is the equal ownership structure and shared governance. Each parent firm contributes resources, including capital, technology, personnel, market access, or other assets, and shares in the profits, losses, and decision-making authority of the new entity.

Joint ventures represent the deepest form of alliance short of acquisition. They create a separate organization with its own management, its own objectives, and its own operations, governed jointly by the parent firms. This structure is well suited to initiatives that require sustained investment, operational independence, and close coordination between the partners' contributions, situations where the resources being combined are deeply embedded and the degree of closeness required is high.

EX: Hulu — A Joint Venture Among Competitors

The creation of Hulu in 2007 illustrates how a joint venture can enable competitors to collaborate on an initiative that none could pursue as effectively alone. NBC Universal and News Corp (Fox) founded the venture, each holding vast libraries of television content while facing a common threat: the rise of digital streaming led by Netflix. Each network could have launched its own platform independently, but doing so would have fragmented content across services, making none individually compelling enough to attract a critical mass of subscribers.

By pooling their content libraries into a jointly owned entity, the networks created a platform with sufficient breadth to compete in the streaming market. The joint venture structure was appropriate because no single network wanted to cede control of its content to a rival, and the initiative required deep operational integration that a licensing agreement could not support. The venture's value proposition proved compelling enough that a third rival, Disney (ABC), bought in as an equity partner in 2009 — competitors choosing to pool content with competitors rather than go it alone.

Hulu's history also illustrates the inherent tensions in joint ventures between competitors. As each parent developed its own streaming ambitions, with Disney launching Disney+ and NBCUniversal launching Peacock, the alignment that originally justified the venture broke down. Disney eventually acquired full control of Hulu by 2024, underscoring a recurring theme: alliances are often transitional structures, and the conditions that justify them can change as markets and strategies evolve.

5.3.6 Why Firms Enter Strategic Alliances

The structural variety of alliances reflects the variety of strategic motivations that drive firms to partner. While each alliance is unique, the reasons for entering cooperative arrangements cluster around several recurring themes.

Strengthen competitive position. Alliances can enhance a firm's competitive position by combining complementary resources in ways that neither partner could achieve alone. A firm with strong technology but weak distribution can partner with a firm that has the opposite profile, creating a combined offering more competitive than either firm's standalone capabilities.

Access critical complementary assets. Complementary assets are resources that enhance the value of a firm's own assets when combined (Ch 4.5). A pharmaceutical company with a promising drug candidate but no sales force might partner with a firm that has an established physician network and distribution infrastructure. The drug and the sales force are individually valuable but dramatically more valuable together. Alliances allow firms to access these complementary assets without bearing the full cost of developing or acquiring them.

Hedge against uncertainty. In rapidly changing industries, firms face uncertainty about which technologies, markets, or customer preferences will prevail. Alliances provide a way to place multiple strategic bets without committing fully to any single one. A technology firm might form alliances with several potential platform partners, positioning itself to benefit regardless of which platform achieves dominance.

Learn new capabilities. One of the most strategically significant motivations for alliance formation is organizational learning. Alliances provide a structured mechanism for observing and absorbing a partner's capabilities, including management practices, technologies, market knowledge, or operational processes, that the firm can then internalize and apply independently. This learning motive is powerful but also creates risks, as we will discuss in the competitive risks section below.

Enter new markets, especially cross-border. International expansion is one of the most common motivations for alliance formation. Entering a foreign market involves navigating unfamiliar regulations, cultural norms, customer preferences, and competitive dynamics. A local partner can provide knowledge and relationships that would take years to develop independently. Cross-border alliances reduce the risk and cost of international expansion while providing access to local market expertise that is often embedded in the partner's organization and not easily acquired through other means.

Speed up R&D and share costs. In industries where research and development costs are enormous — pharmaceuticals, aerospace, semiconductors, automotive — alliances allow firms to share the financial burden of innovation. Battery technology development in the automotive industry illustrates this dynamic: multiple automakers that compete fiercely in finished vehicle markets collaborate on pre-competitive battery research because the costs of developing next-generation battery technology exceed what any single firm can efficiently bear. By sharing R&D expenses through alliances, firms reduce their individual financial risk while accelerating the pace of innovation.

In every case, the fundamental economic logic is the same: the expected benefits of the alliance must exceed its costs. Alliance costs include not only direct financial commitments but also transaction costs of negotiating and monitoring, opportunity costs of management attention, risks of knowledge leakage, and strategic costs of dependence on a partner whose interests may diverge. Firms that enter alliances without rigorously assessing this equation often find the partnership creates less value than anticipated.

5.3.7 Business-Level vs. Corporate-Level Cooperative Strategies

Strategic alliances can serve different strategic purposes depending on whether they support the firm's business-level or corporate-level strategy. The distinction matters because it affects the type of alliance that is appropriate and the criteria by which its success should be evaluated.

Business-level cooperative strategies are alliances designed to strengthen the firm's competitive position within a single industry. These typically take the form of complementary alliances, partnerships in which firms contribute different but mutually enhancing resources. Complementary alliances can be vertical (partnering with a firm at a different stage of the value chain) or horizontal (partnering with a firm at the same stage, such as two technology firms sharing a platform standard). The goal is to improve the combined competitive offering without changing the scope of the business.

Corporate-level cooperative strategies are alliances designed to help the firm expand its scope, entering new industries, new markets, or new product categories. Three forms are particularly important.

Diversifying alliances allow a firm to enter a new business or market by partnering with a firm already operating there. Rather than building the needed capabilities internally or acquiring a firm in the target industry, the diversifying firm borrows access to the partner's market knowledge, distribution channels, or customer relationships. The North American Coffee Partnership between Starbucks and PepsiCo illustrates this: Starbucks sought to enter the ready-to-drink beverage market, sold through grocery and convenience channels it did not serve, by borrowing PepsiCo's national bottling and distribution network, while PepsiCo gained access to Starbucks's premium coffee brand to compete in the growing packaged-coffee category.

Synergistic alliances combine the resources of two firms to create a new product or service that neither could produce as effectively alone. The partnership between Cargill and Coca-Cola to create Truvia illustrates this well. Cargill possessed expertise in stevia production but lacked the consumer marketing and distribution network to turn it into a mainstream product. Coca-Cola possessed distribution infrastructure and branding power but lacked agricultural processing expertise. By combining these complementary resources, the alliance created the leading natural sweetener brand in the United States, a result neither firm could have achieved as efficiently on its own.

Franchising is a cooperative strategy in which one firm (the franchisor) grants another (the franchisee) the right to use its brand, business model, and operational systems in exchange for fees and adherence to the franchisor's standards. The franchisee borrows the franchisor's brand recognition, proven model, and supply chain relationships, while the franchisor borrows the franchisee's local market knowledge, capital, and entrepreneurial effort. From a corporate-level perspective, franchising allows rapid geographic expansion without the capital investment required to own and operate each location.

5.3.8 Cross-Border Alliances

Cross-border alliances deserve special attention because international expansion is one of the most common and challenging applications of cooperative strategy. When a firm enters a foreign market, it faces resource gaps in local market knowledge, relationships with domestic suppliers and distributors, understanding of regulations and cultural norms, and the credibility that comes from being perceived as a local entity. A domestic partner can bridge these gaps by contributing local expertise that complements the foreign firm's products, technology, or business model.

EX: Walmart and Cifra Group in Mexico

Walmart's entry into Mexico through a partnership with Cifra Group illustrates both the logic and lifecycle of cross-border alliances. In the early 1990s, Walmart sought to expand internationally but lacked knowledge of the Mexican consumer market. Cifra, Mexico's largest retailer, possessed deep local market knowledge but lacked Walmart's supply chain management systems and cost efficiency model.

The alliance combined Walmart's operational systems with Cifra's local expertise, creating co-branded stores that applied Walmart's logistics and pricing disciplines to a product assortment tailored for Mexican consumers. However, as Walmart learned the Mexican market and built its own local capabilities, the original motivation for the partnership diminished. Walmart eventually acquired Cifra outright, converting the alliance into a wholly owned subsidiary (now Walmex).

Cross-border alliances carry distinctive risks. The foreign firm may plan to discard the local partner once it has learned enough to operate independently, as Walmart did with Cifra. Conversely, the domestic partner may absorb the foreign firm's knowledge and then compete directly against it once the alliance dissolves. In both cases, one partner uses the alliance as a learning vehicle, and the other risks being left behind.

5.3.9 Alliance Design and Governance

The success or failure of a strategic alliance depends heavily on how it is structured and governed. Governance refers to the mechanisms through which the partners monitor each other's behavior, resolve disputes, allocate resources, and ensure that both parties fulfill their commitments.

The three alliance types described above also represent a spectrum of governance intensity. Nonequity alliances rely primarily on contracts and are appropriate when resources are clearly definable and the risk of opportunism is low. Equity alliances add financial governance: the ownership stake aligns incentives and provides monitoring rights. Joint ventures add organizational governance: the separate entity has its own management structure and operational processes that serve as a permanent coordinating mechanism between the parents.

Inter-organizational trust is a critical dimension of alliance success that operates alongside, and sometimes substitutes for, formal governance mechanisms. Trust develops over time through repeated interactions, fulfilled commitments, and demonstrated reliability. High-trust alliances spend less on monitoring and enforcement because the partners have confidence in each other's good faith. They also adapt more quickly to changing conditions because decisions can be made informally rather than requiring renegotiation of formal contracts. Research consistently shows that trust between alliance partners is one of the strongest predictors of alliance performance (Dyer & Singh, 1998).

However, trust and formal governance involve a fundamental tradeoff. Investing heavily in contractual monitoring signals distrust and can poison the cooperative relationship. But relying too heavily on trust without adequate protections exposes the firm to exploitation. Effective alliance governance typically combines both: formal contracts that establish baseline expectations, supplemented by trust-building activities that develop the informal cooperative norms needed for the alliance to generate value beyond the contractual minimum.

For an alliance to become a source of sustained competitive advantage, the partnership needs to create resource combinations that satisfy the VRIO criteria from Chapter 3.3. This requires relation-specific investments that commit the partners in ways that create unique value, knowledge-sharing routines that allow the partners to develop joint capabilities, and interfirm trust that reduces monitoring costs and enables deep cooperation (Dyer & Singh, 1998). These elements reinforce each other and build over time through repeated successful interactions. Alliance capability, like any organizational capability, is path-dependent.

5.3.10 Alliance Networks

In the contemporary business environment, most large firms do not maintain a single alliance; they manage portfolios of alliances that collectively form a network. A firm may simultaneously hold licensing agreements, equity stakes in startups, joint ventures in different markets, and contractual relationships with dozens of suppliers and distributors. The firm's position within that network becomes a strategic asset in its own right.

Network position affects a firm's access to information, resources, and bargaining power (Gulati, 1998). A firm that serves as a hub, connected to many partners who are not themselves connected to each other, occupies a structurally advantageous position. It sees information flowing through the network that its partners cannot see, and it can broker connections between otherwise disconnected firms. The major technology firms illustrate this dynamic: Apple, Google, Microsoft, and Amazon each maintain hundreds of alliance relationships, and their positions as central hubs provide informational and bargaining advantages that complement their internal capabilities.

5.3.11 Competitive Risks of Cooperative Strategy

Strategic alliances create value, but they also create risks that are distinctive to cooperative arrangements. Unlike organic growth, where the firm retains full control, and acquisitions, where one firm absorbs the other, alliances involve ongoing relationships between independent organizations whose interests may diverge.

Inadequate contracts. Contracts are inherently incomplete — they cannot anticipate every contingency, every market shift, or every technological development that might affect the alliance. When unforeseen circumstances arise, the gaps in the contract become sources of conflict. Partners may disagree about how to allocate costs, share revenues, or respond to competitive threats that the original agreement did not address. The more complex and longer-lasting the alliance, the more likely that contractual gaps will become significant.

Misrepresentation of competencies. A firm may enter an alliance expecting its partner to contribute specific resources, only to discover that the partner's competencies were overstated. The partner may have presented capabilities in the most favorable light during negotiations, or the firm may have failed to verify claims rigorously. Either way, the alliance produces less value than expected because one partner's contribution falls short.

Failure to utilize complementary resources. Even when both partners possess genuinely valuable and complementary resources, organizational politics, cultural differences, or operational incompatibilities can prevent effective combination. Engineers from different corporate cultures may resist sharing proprietary information. Competing priorities within each parent firm may divert management attention from the alliance. The result is that complementary resources that look powerful on paper fail to produce value in practice.

Partners holding each other hostage. When one partner makes significant relation-specific investments, investments valuable only within the partnership, it becomes vulnerable to holdup by the other partner. The investing partner cannot easily exit without losing its investment, giving the other partner leverage to demand more favorable terms. This is the holdup problem: when asset specificity (Ch 5.1) is high, the investing partner's commitment becomes a source of leverage for the other side (Williamson, 1985).

The "learning race." Perhaps the most strategically significant risk is the learning race, the dynamic in which each partner attempts to learn as much as possible from the other while limiting what the other learns in return. A partner that learns faster can eventually replicate the other's capabilities and compete directly, rendering the alliance and the slower-learning partner obsolete. This dynamic is particularly acute in cross-border alliances, where one partner may be using the alliance primarily as a vehicle for knowledge absorption.

Mitigating alliance risks. Firms can manage these risks through several mechanisms. Detailed contracts that specify obligations, performance metrics, dispute resolution, and exit provisions provide a baseline of protection. Monitoring through joint governance structures and regular performance reviews helps detect problems early. But the most effective mitigation is the development of trusting relationships. Trust does not eliminate risk, but it reduces the probability that partners will exploit contractual gaps or engage in learning races, and it enables the flexible adaptation that allows alliances to respond to unexpected challenges.

Firms that manage alliances repeatedly develop an **alliance management capability**, an organizational competence in forming, governing, and adapting partnerships that improves with experience (Kale & Singh, 2009). Like other organizational capabilities, alliance management capability is path-dependent: firms that have successfully managed many alliances develop routines, knowledge, and institutional norms that make subsequent alliances more likely to succeed. This capability itself can become a source of competitive advantage, enabling the firm to extract more value from cooperative strategies than competitors who lack similar experience.

5.3.12 Collusive Strategies: A Brief Treatment

Although this section focuses on legitimate strategic alliances, a brief discussion of collusive strategies is warranted to clarify the boundary between lawful cooperation and illegal coordination.

Explicit collusion occurs when firms directly coordinate their competitive behavior, agreeing to fix prices, divide markets, limit production, or rig bids. Explicit collusion is illegal under antitrust law in virtually every major jurisdiction and is subject to severe criminal and civil penalties. Globalization and the strengthening of antitrust enforcement have made explicit collusion increasingly rare and risky.

Tacit collusion, also called mutual forbearance, involves firms responding to each other's competitive signals without any formal agreement. One firm takes an action, such as raising a price or adding a fee, and competitors follow suit, recognizing that matching the move is more profitable than competing it away. The airline industry provides a frequently cited example: when one major airline introduces a baggage fee or fuel surcharge, competitors typically adopt the same fee within days.

Tacit collusion occupies a legal gray area. Because there is no agreement between the firms, it is generally not prosecutable under antitrust law. However, firms that facilitate tacit collusion through information-sharing mechanisms or public pricing announcements may attract regulatory scrutiny. The Apple e-book pricing case is instructive: major publishers coordinated with Apple to adopt an "agency model" that raised e-book prices, and the arrangement was ultimately found to constitute illegal price-fixing. What began as seemingly independent decisions was determined to involve sufficient coordination to cross the line into explicit collusion.

References

Capron, L., & Mitchell, W. (2012). *Build, borrow, or buy: Solving the growth dilemma.* Harvard Business Review Press.

Dyer, J. H., & Singh, H. (1998). The relational view: Cooperative strategy and sources of interorganizational competitive advantage. *Academy of Management Review, 23*(4), 660–679.

EY-Parthenon. (2026). *CEO Outlook 2026: AI, transformation and growth.* EY. https://www.ey.com/en_us/ceo/ceo-outlook-global-report

Gulati, R. (1998). Alliances and networks. *Strategic Management Journal, 19*(4), 293–317.

Kale, P., & Singh, H. (2009). Managing strategic alliances: What do we know now, and where do we go from here? *Academy of Management Perspectives, 23*(3), 45–62.

Williamson, O. E. (1985). *The economic institutions of capitalism: Firms, markets, relational contracting.* Free Press.

5.4 Mergers & Acquisitions (Buy) — *When should firms acquire?*

5.4.1 Merger vs. Acquisition: Definitions and Reality

The first two growth modes in the Build, Borrow, Buy framework (Capron & Mitchell, 2012) — organic growth and strategic alliances — allow firms to close resource gaps while maintaining organizational independence. Organic growth preserves the firm's existing boundaries, and alliances create partnerships between firms that remain separate entities. The third growth mode, acquisition, is fundamentally different: it eliminates the boundary between the acquiring firm and the target, absorbing the target's resources, capabilities, and people into the acquiring organization.

A **merger** is the consolidation or combination of two firms of roughly similar size into a single new entity. In a true merger, the firms join forces as relative equals, combining their resources and governance structures into a new organization. An **acquisition** is the outright purchase of one firm by another, in which ownership of the target transfers to the acquiring firm. The target may be absorbed into the acquirer, operated as a subsidiary, or restructured following the purchase, but in all cases, the acquiring firm assumes control.

In practice, the distinction between mergers and acquisitions is far less clear than the definitions suggest. Most transactions described as "mergers" are, in reality, acquisitions in which one firm is the dominant partner. True mergers of equals are rare because it is unusual for two firms of genuinely comparable size and power to agree on governance terms that treat both parties identically. The language of "merger" is often preferred for public relations purposes because it sounds more collaborative than "acquisition."

The 1998 combination of Daimler-Benz and Chrysler Group illustrates this gap between rhetoric and reality. The deal was publicly described as a "merger of equals," but Daimler-Benz was the dominant partner from the beginning. The share exchange terms gave Daimler shareholders approximately 57 percent control of the new company. Key management decisions were soon dominated by Daimler executives. The lesson is straightforward: when evaluating corporate combinations, focus on the economic and governance realities rather than the language used to describe them.

5.4.2 Reasons for Acquisitions

Acquisitions have become an increasingly prominent growth strategy over recent decades, driven by globalization, deregulation across many industries, and legislation that has generally been favorable toward corporate combinations. Despite the well-documented risks of acquisitions, which we will examine in detail, firms continue to acquire for several compelling strategic reasons.

Increase market power. Acquiring a competitor or a firm in a related market can significantly increase the acquiring firm's market share, pricing power, and bargaining leverage with suppliers and customers. When a firm acquires a direct competitor, it reduces the number of rivals in the industry and increases its own scale, both of which can shift competitive dynamics in its favor. This is one of the most straightforward motivations for horizontal acquisitions and connects directly to Porter's Five Forces analysis (Ch 4.3): an acquisition that reduces competitive rivalry or increases the firm's bargaining power relative to suppliers or buyers structurally improves the firm's industry position.

Overcome entry barriers. Some markets are protected by barriers that make organic entry extremely difficult, including regulatory requirements, established distribution networks, entrenched customer relationships, or specialized knowledge that takes years to develop. Acquisition allows a firm to vault over these barriers by purchasing a firm that already operates inside them. This is particularly common in international expansion, where acquiring a local firm gives the entrant immediate access to regulatory approvals, customer relationships, and market knowledge that would take years to build organically.

Avoid product development costs and increase speed to market. Developing a new product or technology internally can be slow and expensive, with uncertain outcomes. Acquisition allows a firm to purchase a fully developed product, a proven technology, or an established customer base, avoiding the time and expense of internal R&D while dramatically accelerating the firm's time to market. In fast-moving industries where product cycles are short and competitive windows are narrow, this speed advantage can be decisive. As discussed in Chapter 5.2, the primary limitation of organic growth is its inherent slowness; acquisition directly addresses this limitation by allowing the firm to buy capabilities that would take years to build.

Reduce risk of entering a new business. Entering an unfamiliar industry through organic growth means starting from a position of competitive disadvantage. Acquisition reduces this risk by purchasing a firm already operating profitably in the target industry, providing an immediate base of operations, a proven revenue stream, and employees with domain expertise. The acquiring firm is buying a going concern rather than building one from scratch.

Increase diversification. As we will explore in Chapter 5.6, firms may seek to diversify their operations across multiple industries or markets to reduce their dependence on a single business line. Acquisition is the fastest path to diversification, as the firm can enter a new industry immediately by purchasing an established participant rather than spending years developing internal capabilities. This speed advantage makes acquisition the default entry mode for unrelated diversification, where the firm's existing resources have low relevance to the target industry and organic growth is therefore impractical.

Avoid excessive competition. In some cases, firms acquire potential competitors not because they want the target's resources but because they want to prevent those resources from being deployed against them. Facebook's acquisitions of Instagram (2012) and WhatsApp (2014) were motivated in significant part by the desire to neutralize potential competitive threats, emerging platforms that could have eroded Facebook's dominance in social networking if they had remained independent or been acquired by a competitor. This defensive use of acquisition is strategically rational from the acquiring firm's perspective, though it raises regulatory concerns about anticompetitive behavior that we will address in Chapter 6.

Learn and develop new capabilities (acqui-hiring). Some acquisitions are motivated primarily by the desire to acquire human capital. This practice, known as "acqui-hiring," is particularly common in technology industries where the scarcity of skilled talent makes individual recruitment insufficient. By acquiring a small startup or specialized firm, the acquirer gains not just products or technology but people and the tacit knowledge they carry.

Increase firm size — and CEO pay. Finally, acquisitions increase the overall size of the firm, which has implications for executive compensation. CEO pay is strongly correlated with firm size, and the larger the firm, the higher the typical compensation package. This creates a personal financial incentive for CEOs to pursue acquisitions even when the strategic rationale is weak (Jensen, 1986). The relationship between firm size, executive compensation, and acquisition incentives is a principal-agent problem that will be examined in detail in Chapter 6's discussion of corporate governance.

5.4.3 The Acquisition Process

Acquisitions unfold through a process that moves from initial strategic idea through due diligence and negotiation, to the transaction itself, and then into the often-difficult work of integration. Understanding this process is important because different types of problems emerge at different stages, and the roots of many acquisition failures can be traced to errors made early in the process that only become visible much later (Haspeslagh & Jemison, 1991).

The process begins with an **idea**, the recognition of a strategic resource gap that might be addressed through acquisition. This idea may emerge from the Build, Borrow, Buy analysis described in Chapter 5.1, from competitive intelligence about a target firm's capabilities, or from an opportunistic awareness that a desirable target has become available.

The idea then moves into **justification, due diligence, and negotiation**. Due diligence is the systematic evaluation of the target firm, encompassing its financial condition, its strategic assets, its liabilities, its cultural characteristics, its key personnel, and its market position. Effective due diligence requires rigorous, dispassionate analysis. The acquiring firm must determine what the target is genuinely worth, what synergies are realistically achievable, and what integration challenges are likely to arise. Negotiation determines the purchase price and the terms of the transaction.

Decision-making process problems can emerge during this pre-acquisition phase. Managers may overestimate the value of the target or the magnitude of expected synergies. They may suffer from hubris — the belief that they can manage the acquired firm better than its current management (Roll, 1986). Competitive bidding dynamics can drive the purchase price above the target's intrinsic value. And the organizational momentum of the acquisition process can create pressure to proceed even when the analysis suggests the deal is marginal.

Following the transaction, the **integration** phase begins, and this is where acquisitions most frequently fail. Integration involves combining the operations, cultures, systems, and personnel of two previously independent organizations. Even when the strategic logic of the acquisition is sound, integration difficulties can prevent the combined firm from capturing the value that justified the deal.

Integration process problems include cultural clashes, the departure of key employees, operational disruptions as systems are consolidated, and the managerial complexity of running two organizations simultaneously while merging them. The acquiring firm's management must devote enormous attention to integration, which can distract from ongoing operations of both businesses. The final stage, **results**, reflects the cumulative effect of how well the acquisition was conceived, evaluated, negotiated, and integrated. A too-high purchase price of an excellent company can undo the effects of a subsequent decade of favorable business developments (Buffett, 1982).

5.4.4 Acquisition Risks

Research consistently shows that the majority of acquisitions fail to create value for the acquiring firm's shareholders (King et al., 2004). The acquisition premium, the amount paid above the target's pre-acquisition market value, must be recovered through synergies, cost savings, or revenue growth, and in many cases it is not. Several recurring risks explain this disappointing track record (Hitt et al., 2001).

Inadequate evaluation of target (poor due diligence). When the acquiring firm fails to thoroughly assess the target's true condition, including its hidden liabilities, its genuine competitive position, and the real quality of its assets, the acquisition is built on a flawed foundation. Overpayment is the most common consequence of inadequate due diligence: the acquirer pays a price that reflects the target's optimistic self-presentation rather than its actual strategic value. Once the transaction is complete and the true condition of the acquired firm becomes apparent, the acquirer discovers that it has purchased less than it believed.

Integration difficulties. Combining two organizations is inherently difficult, and the difficulty increases with the degree of cultural, operational, and strategic difference between the firms. Cultural integration is particularly challenging because organizational culture is deeply embedded, socially complex, and resistant to deliberate change, as explored in Chapter 3's discussion of culture as a source of competitive advantage. When employees from the acquired firm feel that their culture is being overridden or disrespected, morale drops, key personnel leave, and the very capabilities that made the target attractive begin to erode. Operational integration, including merging IT systems, aligning supply chains, and consolidating facilities, creates disruption that can reduce productivity during the transition period. Strategic integration, aligning the two firms' competitive positions, customer relationships, and product portfolios, requires difficult decisions about which activities to keep, which to eliminate, and how to reconcile different strategic priorities.

Large debt taken on in purchase. Many acquisitions are financed with debt, and the resulting leverage can constrain strategic flexibility. Debt service payments consume cash flow that could otherwise be invested in innovation or further development. In extreme cases, the debt burden can push the combined firm toward financial distress, forcing cost-cutting that undermines the strategic rationale for the acquisition.

Inability to achieve synergy. Synergy, the idea that the combined firm will be worth more than the sum of its parts, is the most commonly cited justification for acquisitions. But synergies that look compelling in a presentation often prove elusive in practice (Sirower, 1997). Cost synergies (eliminating redundant operations) are generally more achievable than revenue synergies (cross-selling, leveraging combined market position), but even cost synergies require difficult organizational changes, including layoffs, facility closures, and system migrations, that take time and generate resistance. Revenue synergies frequently depend on customer behavior that the acquiring firm cannot control: the assumption that customers of the acquired firm will readily purchase the acquirer's products, or vice versa, often proves optimistic.

Too much diversification. As Chapter 5.6 will discuss, there is a curvilinear relationship between diversification and performance: moderate levels of related diversification tend to improve performance, but excessive diversification overwhelms managerial capacity and destroys value. Firms that pursue acquisitions aggressively can find themselves managing a portfolio of businesses that is too broad and too diverse for their organizational capabilities. Each additional acquisition adds complexity, and at some point the costs of managing the portfolio exceed the benefits of diversification.

Managers overly focused on acquisitions. The acquisition process is exciting, high-profile, and personally rewarding for executives. A major acquisition generates media attention, demonstrates strategic boldness, and can increase executive compensation through increased firm size. These rewards create incentives for managers to devote disproportionate attention to acquisition activity at the expense of existing operations. While senior management is consumed with evaluating targets and managing integration, the day-to-day business receives less attention, and the core business often suffers precisely when management is pursuing acquisitions intended to improve overall performance.

Resulting firm too large — bureaucracy. Acquisitions increase firm size, and increased size brings organizational complexity. Decision-making slows, management layers multiply, and communication becomes more difficult. The entrepreneurial agility that characterized one or both pre-acquisition firms can be smothered by bureaucratic processes. This risk is particularly acute when the acquired firm was a smaller, more nimble organization whose advantage depended on speed and flexibility.

5.4.5 Characteristics of Effective Acquisitions

Despite the long list of risks, some acquisitions succeed, and they tend to share several common characteristics. Understanding these characteristics helps managers distinguish between acquisitions that are likely to create value and those that are likely to destroy it.

Complementary resources between the acquiring and target firms. The most effective acquisitions involve target firms whose resources and capabilities complement rather than duplicate those of the acquirer. Complementary resources create the foundation for genuine synergies: the acquirer contributes capabilities the target lacks, and the target contributes capabilities the acquirer lacks, producing a combined firm that is stronger than either was alone. This connects directly to the strategic resource gap concept from Chapter 5.1: the acquisition should close a real gap in the acquiring firm's resource base, not merely add more of what the firm already has.

Thorough due diligence. Effective acquisitions are preceded by rigorous, honest evaluation of the target, encompassing not just its financial statements but its strategic position, its organizational culture, its key personnel, and the realistic magnitude of achievable synergies. Thorough due diligence reduces the risk of overpayment and helps the acquiring firm develop realistic integration plans. It also identifies potential deal-breakers early in the process, before the organizational momentum of the acquisition makes it psychologically difficult to walk away.

Friendly acquisition facilitating integration. Acquisitions in which the target firm's management and employees support the transaction are significantly more likely to succeed than hostile takeovers. A friendly acquisition preserves goodwill, facilitates cultural integration, and reduces the risk that key employees will leave. Hostile takeovers create an adversarial dynamic from the outset, making integration far more difficult.

Low to moderate debt levels maintained. Effective acquisitions maintain the combined firm's financial flexibility by avoiding excessive leverage. This can be achieved through the acquirer's existing cash reserves, by selling off non-essential portions of the acquired firm to reduce the net purchase price, or by structuring the transaction to limit the amount of debt incurred. Financial slack, the availability of cash or unused debt capacity, gives the newly combined firm time to work through integration challenges without the pressure of immediate debt service obligations.

Financial slack providing time to integrate. Integration takes time, and synergies often take longer to materialize than projected. A firm with adequate financial reserves can absorb transition costs, invest in integration activities, and weather temporary performance dips without premature cost-cutting that undermines the acquisition's strategic rationale.

Acquiring firm has experience with acquisitions. Like any organizational capability, acquisition expertise improves with practice. Firms that have completed multiple acquisitions develop institutional knowledge about how to evaluate targets, negotiate deals, and manage integration. They build dedicated teams with acquisition experience, establish integration playbooks, and develop pattern recognition for the warning signs of problematic deals. A first-time acquirer is far more likely to make costly mistakes than a firm with a track record of completed transactions and the organizational learning that comes with it.

Emphasis on R&D and innovation in the new firm. Effective acquisitions maintain a focus on innovation and research within the combined firm. This criterion may seem counterintuitive: if the acquisition is itself a substitute for internal development, why emphasize R&D afterward? The answer is that acquisitions are point-in-time transactions that address current resource gaps, but competitive advantage requires ongoing capability development. A firm that stops innovating after an acquisition, treating the acquired capabilities as a permanent solution rather than a starting point, will see those capabilities erode over time as competitors advance and markets evolve. The best acquisitions use the acquired capabilities as a platform for continued innovation rather than as a replacement for it.

EX: DaimlerChrysler — A Cautionary Tale

The 1998 combination of Daimler-Benz and Chrysler Group stands as one of the most frequently cited examples of acquisition failure in the strategic management literature. The deal, valued at $37 billion, created a combined entity with joint revenues of $130 billion, sales of 4.4 million cars, and a market capitalization of approximately $95 billion. The stated vision was to create a global automotive powerhouse that could compete across every market segment, from Chrysler's mass-market vehicles to Mercedes-Benz's luxury offerings, while achieving substantial cost synergies through shared platforms, purchasing power, and global distribution.

The synergies never materialized. The two companies' products served fundamentally different market segments with different customer expectations, and attempts to share platforms risked diluting Mercedes-Benz's luxury brand. Cultural integration proved catastrophic: Daimler's engineering-driven German corporate culture clashed with Chrysler's more entrepreneurial American style, producing friction at every level of the organization. Key Chrysler executives departed. Employee morale plummeted. Operational decisions that should have been routine became battlegrounds for cultural conflict.

The financial trajectory tells the story. By 2001, Chrysler was struggling with high costs and lackluster sales, prompting a restructuring that cut $2 billion in costs and eliminated 20 percent of its workforce. By 2003, the combined market capitalization had fallen to $38 billion, less than Daimler-Benz's standalone value of $47 billion before the merger. In 2000, DaimlerChrysler had purchased a 34 percent stake in Mitsubishi Motors for $2 billion to boost its Asian presence; by 2004, the board refused to approve an additional $7 billion investment needed to keep Mitsubishi afloat. The Daimler CEO stepped down in 2005 after a decade at the helm. In February 2007, Chrysler reported an operating loss of $1.5 billion and announced another 13,000 job cuts. By May 2007, Cerberus Capital Management acquired an 80 percent stake in Chrysler for $7.4 billion, an estimated $36 billion loss from the pre-merger market capitalization.

Dieter Zetsche, CEO of DaimlerChrysler at the time of the Cerberus sale, offered a remarkably understated assessment: "We obviously overestimated the potential of synergies." The DaimlerChrysler case illustrates virtually every acquisition risk described above: inadequate evaluation of cultural compatibility, integration difficulties that proved insurmountable, inability to achieve the promised synergies, excessive diversification (the Mitsubishi investment compounded the problems), management distraction from core operations, and a resulting organization too large and complex to manage effectively. It remains a canonical example of how acquisition failure can destroy billions of dollars of shareholder value.

EX: Cooper Industries — Disciplined Acquisition as a Repeatable Strategy

Cooper Industries made acquisition the centerpiece of its corporate strategy and succeeded through discipline and rigorous adherence to published guidelines. Founded in 1833, Cooper originally produced plows, kettles, and stoves before shifting to steam engines and supplying engine components for U.S. Navy vessels during World War II. After the war, Cooper recognized that its defense-related businesses were cyclical and vulnerable to peacetime contractions, so it pursued diversification through systematic acquisition.

Cooper expanded into electrical products and away from cyclical industries such as automotive and petroleum. Its success stemmed from published acquisition guidelines that specified three criteria: seek acquisitions with stable or countercyclical earnings patterns to smooth revenue volatility; acquire products serving basic, essential needs derived from proven technologies in stable markets with predictable growth; and acquire manufacturing companies with high-quality products that are leaders in their respective markets.

These guidelines embody several characteristics of effective acquisitions identified earlier in this section. Cooper sought complementary resources whose earnings patterns balanced its existing portfolio. It insisted on thorough evaluation, acquiring only proven market leaders rather than speculative ventures. It maintained financial discipline, targeting stable, cash-generating businesses that would not require massive additional investment. And it built acquisition experience over decades, developing institutional knowledge for evaluating, negotiating, and integrating targets consistently.

Cooper's approach also illustrates how acquisition strategy connects to broader corporate-level strategy. By acquiring market leaders in stable industries with countercyclical earnings, Cooper constructed a portfolio designed to reduce risk and generate consistent cash flows across economic cycles, a fundamentally different philosophy than growth for its own sake, and one that explains why Cooper's record stands in stark contrast to DaimlerChrysler's.

5.4.6 Acquisitions in the Build, Borrow, Buy Framework

Returning to the framework that organizes this chapter, acquisitions represent the buy option, the growth mode appropriate when the firm's internal resources are not relevant to the opportunity (ruling out build), the needed external resources are not easily tradable through contracts (ruling out simple borrowing), the required organizational closeness is extreme (ruling out alliances), and the acquiring firm has the capacity to integrate the target successfully.

The Build, Borrow, Buy framework emphasizes that acquisition should not be the default growth strategy. It is the most expensive, most complex, and most risk-laden option in the framework. It requires the acquiring firm to pay a premium over the target's standalone value, to manage a difficult integration process, and to generate enough synergies to justify the premium and the integration costs combined. The framework positions acquisition as a last resort — the option chosen after build and borrow have been carefully considered and found inadequate.

Yet acquisitions remain enormously popular, driven by the strategic reasons enumerated above and by the personal incentives of the executives who pursue them. The challenge for strategic management is not to avoid acquisitions altogether but to distinguish between acquisitions that address genuine strategic resource gaps and those that are driven by managerial hubris, empire-building impulses, or a failure to seriously consider the build and borrow alternatives. The most effective acquirers, firms like Cooper Industries or, in a different era, Berkshire Hathaway, succeed not because they acquire more aggressively than their peers but because they acquire more selectively, evaluate more rigorously, and integrate more carefully.

References

Buffett, W. E. (1982). *Chairman's letter to the shareholders of Berkshire Hathaway Inc.* Berkshire Hathaway. https://www.berkshirehathaway.com/letters/1982.html

Capron, L., & Mitchell, W. (2012). *Build, borrow, or buy: Solving the growth dilemma.* Harvard Business Review Press.

Haspeslagh, P. C., & Jemison, D. B. (1991). *Managing acquisitions: Creating value through corporate renewal.* Free Press.

Hitt, M. A., Harrison, J. S., & Ireland, R. D. (2001). *Mergers and acquisitions: A guide to creating value for stakeholders.* Oxford University Press.

Jensen, M. C. (1986). Agency costs of free cash flow, corporate finance, and takeovers. *American Economic Review, 76*(2), 323–329.

King, D. R., Dalton, D. R., Daily, C. M., & Covin, J. G. (2004). Meta-analyses of post-acquisition performance: Indications of unidentified moderators. *Strategic Management Journal, 25*(2), 187–200.

Roll, R. (1986). The hubris hypothesis of corporate takeovers. *Journal of Business, 59*(2), 197–216.

Sirower, M. L. (1997). *The synergy trap: How companies lose the acquisition game.* Free Press.

5.5 Horizontal/Vertical Integration — *What should firms integrate?*

The preceding sections examined the three primary growth modes available to firms — build, borrow, and buy — and the strategic logic for choosing among them. This section addresses a related but distinct question: in which *direction* should the firm expand? When a firm decides to grow, whether through organic development, alliance, or acquisition, it must also decide whether to expand vertically (into different stages of the value chain), horizontally (at the same stage of the value chain), or into entirely new businesses (diversification, which Ch 5.6 addresses). The direction of expansion shapes the firm's scope, its competitive position, and the risks it faces.

Vertical integration was introduced in Chapter 4 in the context of Porter's Five Forces, where it served as mechanisms for shifting bargaining power within an industry. Here in Chapter 5, we revisit integration as a corporate-level strategy, a deliberate decision about the boundaries and scope of the firm. The analytical question shifts from "how does integration affect bargaining power?" to "should the firm expand its scope in this direction, and if so, how far?"

5.5.1 Vertical Integration

> *"I've always wanted to own and control the primary technology in everything we do." — Steve Jobs*

Vertical integration occurs when a firm expands into different stages of its value chain — the sequence of activities that transforms raw materials into a finished product delivered to the end customer. Rather than purchasing inputs from external suppliers or selling through external distributors, the vertically integrated firm performs these activities itself.

The concept connects directly to Coase's theory of the firm (Ch 1.1): the boundary of the firm is determined by whether the costs of performing an activity internally are lower than the costs of transacting for it through the market. When transaction costs, including searching for suppliers, negotiating contracts, monitoring quality, and enforcing agreements, are high, bringing the activity inside the firm can be more efficient. When transaction costs are low and external specialists can perform the activity more cheaply or effectively, the firm is better off relying on the market. Vertical integration, at its core, is the firm's answer to the question: where along the value chain should my boundaries extend?

5.5.2 Backward Integration

Backward integration means moving upstream in the value chain, as the firm begins producing inputs that it previously purchased from suppliers. The firm, in effect, becomes its own supplier. Backward integration reduces dependence on external suppliers, gives the firm greater control over input quality, cost, and delivery timing, and can eliminate the margins that suppliers capture on the transaction.

EX: Apple Designing Its Own Processors

As discussed in Chapter 4, Apple's decision to design its own processors represents one of the most consequential backward integration moves in recent business history. For years, Apple purchased processors from Intel (for Mac computers) and relied on Samsung and other manufacturers for mobile device chips. These suppliers controlled critical components and held considerable bargaining power, as Apple was dependent on their product roadmaps, pricing decisions, and production schedules.

Beginning in 2010, Apple started designing its own chips for the iPhone and iPad. By 2020, it announced the transition of its entire Mac lineup to Apple Silicon, replacing Intel processors entirely. This backward integration eliminated dependence on Intel's development timeline, allowed Apple to optimize chip performance specifically for its hardware and software ecosystem, reduced costs by cutting out the supplier's margin, and created a proprietary technology advantage that competitors relying on general-purpose processors could not easily match.

From a corporate-level strategy perspective, Apple's chip design program is organic backward integration; Apple built the capability internally. The choice of build over buy was strategic: Apple's existing engineering talent was highly relevant to the new activity, and developing the capability internally preserved the tight integration between hardware and software that is central to its differentiation strategy.

5.5.3 Forward Integration

Forward integration means moving downstream in the value chain, as the firm begins distributing, retailing, or selling directly to end customers rather than relying on intermediary buyers. Forward integration allows the firm to capture value that would otherwise be extracted by downstream intermediaries, build direct customer relationships, and control how its products are presented to the market.

EX: Disney Launching Disney+

Disney's launch of the Disney+ streaming platform in 2019 is a textbook case of forward integration. For decades, Disney's content reached consumers through third-party channels such as theaters, cable networks, and streaming platforms like Netflix. These distributors controlled access to audiences and could negotiate licensing terms that captured a significant share of the value Disney's content created.

Disney+ bypassed these intermediaries entirely. Disney captured subscription revenue directly, controlled how its content was presented, and built a direct relationship with over 100 million subscribers in its first two years. The forward integration also strengthened Disney's bargaining position with remaining distribution partners, who now faced the reality that Disney could pull its content and distribute it exclusively through its own platform.

Disney's forward integration was enabled by its uniquely deep library of intellectual property spanning Disney Animation, Pixar, Marvel, Lucasfilm, and National Geographic. These assets were directly relevant to operating a streaming platform, and the firm had the brand recognition and financial resources to compete in a market that rewards scale. A content company with a thinner library or weaker brand would have faced a much harder calculation.

5.5.4 The Transaction Cost Logic of Vertical Integration

The decision to integrate vertically rests on the same economic logic introduced in Chapter 1.1. Coase (1937) and Williamson (1985) established that the boundary of the firm is determined by the relative costs of internal organization versus market exchange. Vertical integration is the appropriate choice when the total costs of performing an activity internally, including the costs of building new capabilities, managing additional operations, and the potential inefficiencies of internal production, are lower than the total costs of procuring the activity through the market, including transaction costs.

The transaction cost framework identifies several conditions that push toward integration. When the inputs are highly specific to the firm's needs and cannot be easily sourced from other suppliers, the risk of holdup increases — the supplier may exploit the firm's dependence by raising prices or reducing quality. When uncertainty about future conditions makes it difficult to write complete contracts, the firm may prefer the flexibility of internal coordination over the rigidity of contractual terms. When the frequency of transactions is high, the overhead of repeated market contracting may exceed the cost of internal management.

The framework also identifies conditions favoring market procurement. When the input is a commodity available from many suppliers, transaction costs are low and the market provides both price discipline and innovation incentives that internal production may lack. When the activity requires specialized expertise the firm does not possess, external specialists may perform it more efficiently. When the firm's capital and attention are better deployed in core activities, managing a peripheral operation may outweigh the cost savings.

In practice, the decision is rarely absolute. The choice between internal production and market procurement is not binary but falls along a **make-or-buy continuum**, a spectrum of governance structures running from arm's-length market transactions at one extreme to full internal production at the other. Between those poles lie short-term contracts, long-term contracts, licensing arrangements, equity alliances, joint ventures, and parent-subsidiary relationships. Each represents a different balance between the flexibility of the market and the control of the hierarchy, and each carries a different mix of transaction costs.

5.5.5 Horizontal Integration

While vertical integration extends the firm along the value chain, horizontal integration extends the firm at the same stage. Horizontal integration occurs when a firm acquires or merges with another firm operating at the same stage of the production process, often, but not always, a direct competitor.

Horizontal integration can serve several strategic objectives (Porter, 1980). It can increase market share and market power by absorbing a competitor, directly reducing rivalry in the industry (connecting to Porter's Five Forces from Ch 4.3). It can generate economies of scale by combining operations, including shared manufacturing facilities, consolidated distribution networks, and combined purchasing volume that can reduce per-unit costs (connecting to the economies of scale concepts from Ch 2.4). It can provide access to new customer segments, geographic markets, or product lines that the acquired firm serves but the acquirer does not. And it can eliminate a competitor whose continued independence would threaten the acquirer's market position.

Facebook's acquisition of Instagram in 2012 illustrates horizontal integration at its most strategically aggressive. Both companies operated at the same stage of the social media value chain; they were platforms that connected users and generated revenue through advertising. Instagram was not a supplier to Facebook or a distributor for Facebook; it was a potential competitor that served a similar function through a different product format (photo-sharing rather than general social networking). By acquiring Instagram, Facebook expanded the breadth of its social media platform portfolio, absorbed a fast-growing competitive threat, and gained capabilities in mobile-first visual content that complemented its existing text-and-photo platform.

Not all horizontal integrations involve competitors. A firm may horizontally acquire another company that operates at the same value chain stage but serves a different market or product category. A brewery acquiring another brewery that specializes in a different beverage segment (craft versus mass-market, for instance) is pursuing horizontal integration; both firms are manufacturers, but they may not have been direct competitors. The common thread is that the acquisition expands the firm's breadth at its current position in the value chain.

5.5.6 Why Integrate Vertically?

The strategic motivations for vertical integration cluster around three primary benefits.

Improve profits by eliminating the middleman. When a firm integrates backward, it eliminates the margin that suppliers capture. When it integrates forward, it eliminates the margin that distributors or retailers capture. But the qualifying phrase "if run well" is critical. Vertical integration does not automatically improve profits. If the firm manages the integrated activity less efficiently than the external specialist it replaces, because it lacks the expertise, scale, or focused attention, the costs of internal production may exceed the savings. Integration improves profits only when the firm can perform the activity at competitive cost while capturing the intermediary's margin.

Better coordination and quality assurance. Vertical integration gives the firm direct control over the quality, timing, and specifications of the integrated activity. A manufacturer that produces its own critical components does not need to negotiate quality standards with a supplier, wait for supplier deliveries, or worry about the supplier prioritizing another customer's orders. A firm that controls its own distribution channels can ensure that its products are displayed, marketed, and serviced in ways that align with its brand standards. This coordination advantage is particularly valuable when the firm's differentiation strategy depends on tight control over quality, customer experience, or delivery timing, activities where even small deviations by external parties can undermine the brand promise.

Reduce dependence or uncertainty. Vertical integration insulates the firm from risks inherent in market-based relationships: supply disruptions, price volatility, quality inconsistency, and the bargaining power of concentrated suppliers or buyers. A firm that depends on a single supplier for a critical input faces strategic vulnerability. By integrating backward, the firm eliminates this dependency. Similarly, forward integration eliminates dependence on dominant buyers by creating an alternative path to the customer.

5.5.7 Risks of Integration

Despite its potential benefits, vertical integration carries significant risks that must be weighed against the advantages.

High capital investment. Integration requires the firm to invest in new capabilities, facilities, equipment, and personnel, capital that could otherwise be deployed in the firm's core business or returned to shareholders. Building a semiconductor fabrication facility, launching a streaming platform, or developing a retail distribution network requires billions of dollars in investment. This capital is committed and largely irreversible; once the firm has built the facility or launched the platform, it cannot easily redeploy those resources if the integration proves unsuccessful.

Loss of strategic focus. Every activity the firm brings in-house adds to the range of operations it must manage. Each additional activity competes for management attention, organizational resources, and strategic bandwidth. The risk is that the firm spreads itself too thin, managing too many activities adequately rather than managing its core activities superbly. The connection to core competencies (Ch 3) is direct: integration makes strategic sense only for activities central to competitive advantage. Peripheral activities are better outsourced to specialists.

Increased operational and managerial complexity. Integration makes the organization larger, more complex, and harder to coordinate. Decisions that previously involved only existing operations now require coordination with the integrated activity. Organizational structures that worked for a focused firm may not scale effectively, and the added complexity can slow decision-making and reduce agility.

Reduced flexibility and innovation. A firm relying on external suppliers retains the flexibility to switch partners as conditions change. Integration sacrifices this flexibility, as the firm's investment in internal capabilities creates a commitment to a particular way of performing the activity, and switching to an external alternative means writing off sunk investment. Integration can also reduce innovation incentives: an internal division with a guaranteed customer (the parent firm) may face less competitive pressure to innovate than an external supplier that must constantly earn the firm's business.

Supplier or partner alienation. When a firm integrates backward, it becomes a competitor to its former suppliers. When it integrates forward, it competes with former distribution partners. This competitive shift can damage relationships the firm still depends on. A manufacturer that begins producing one component in-house may find remaining suppliers less cooperative. Disney's launch of Disney+ strained its relationships with cable networks who now viewed Disney as both content supplier and direct competitor.

Potential regulatory issues. Vertical and horizontal integration can attract regulatory scrutiny, particularly when the combined entity's market power raises antitrust concerns. Horizontal integration that significantly increases market concentration may be challenged or blocked by competition authorities. Vertical integration that forecloses competitors' access to critical inputs or distribution channels may be scrutinized under theories of anticompetitive harm. Firms pursuing integration strategies must account for regulatory risk as a meaningful constraint on their strategic options.

5.5.8 Vertical Integration Alternatives

Full integration is not the only option. Two alternatives allow firms to capture some of the benefits of integration without bearing its full costs and risks.

Taper integration is partial backward or forward integration in which the firm performs some portion of the activity internally while sourcing the remainder externally (Harrigan, 1984). A manufacturer that produces 30 percent of a critical component in-house while purchasing 70 percent from suppliers is practicing taper integration. This approach offers several strategic advantages. First, it establishes the credibility of the integration threat discussed in Chapter 4: because the firm has demonstrated that it can produce the input, suppliers know that pushing too hard on price or terms could lead the firm to shift more production in-house. Second, internal production provides direct cost benchmarking information, giving the firm detailed knowledge of the supplier's true cost structure and eliminating the information asymmetry that suppliers often exploit in negotiations. Third, it creates a buffer against supply disruptions, ensuring continuity even if external suppliers face capacity constraints or quality issues. Finally, it preserves the benefits of external sourcing, including access to supplier innovation, competitive discipline, and the flexibility to adjust sourcing ratios as conditions change.

Taper integration is particularly valuable when a firm wants to build integration *capability* without committing to full integration. A firm that develops small-scale internal production of a critical input — enough to demonstrate technical feasibility — has established the credibility of the threat. The investment pays for itself through improved bargaining terms, even if the capability is never scaled to full production.

Strategic outsourcing is the reverse of integration: the firm moves existing internal activities to external specialists. Outsourcing makes sense when the activity is not central to competitive advantage and when external specialists can perform it more efficiently or at lower cost. The connection to core competencies is direct: integrate activities central to competitive advantage; outsource the rest.

Outsourcing decisions must account for the bargaining power dynamics analyzed in Chapter 4. Outsourcing is most viable when supplier power is low — when multiple capable suppliers compete for the firm's business, giving the firm leverage over terms. If supplier power is high, outsourcing may expose the firm to unfavorable bargaining dynamics that could have been avoided through internal production. A firm that outsources a critical activity to a concentrated supplier market may find itself dependent on partners with the leverage to extract increasingly unfavorable terms over time.

Together, taper integration and strategic outsourcing represent points along the make-or-buy continuum. Neither is a pure market transaction nor full integration; each occupies a deliberate middle position that preserves some of the market's price discipline while retaining some of the hierarchy's control. The optimal position on the continuum depends on the transaction costs involved, the strategic importance of the activity, the firm's core competencies, and the bargaining power dynamics of the industry.

5.5.9 Connecting Integration to the Broader Strategic Framework

Vertical and horizontal integration connect to virtually every strategic concept covered in this book.

Connection to Porter's Five Forces (Ch 4.3). As discussed in Chapter 4, vertical integration is a mechanism for shifting bargaining power. Backward integration reduces supplier power; forward integration reduces buyer power. The credible threat of integration can be as powerful as actual integration in reshaping bargaining dynamics. Integration can also affect rivalry (horizontal integration reduces the number of competitors), barriers to entry (a vertically integrated firm may control access to critical inputs or distribution channels), and the threat of substitutes (a firm that controls its own distribution can respond more quickly to substitute threats).

Connection to Core Competencies (Ch 3.3). The core competency framework provides the most important guideline for integration decisions: integrate activities central to competitive advantage; outsource the rest. Apple's backward integration into chip design made strategic sense because processor performance is central to its product differentiation. A firm whose advantage rests on marketing and branding would have much less reason to integrate into component manufacturing.

Connection to Transaction Cost Economics (Ch 1.1). The make-or-buy decision that underlies all integration choices is fundamentally a transaction cost calculation. When the costs of market exchange, including search, negotiation, monitoring, and the risk of opportunism, exceed the costs of internal organization, the firm should integrate. When market exchange is efficient and external specialists offer superior capabilities, the firm should remain focused. The Build, Borrow, Buy framework (Ch 5.1) provides the structured decision process for making this calculation in the context of corporate growth strategy.

The integration question, what should the firm bring inside its boundaries and what should it leave to the market, is one of the most consequential decisions in corporate strategy. It determines the firm's scope, capital requirements, organizational complexity, and competitive position. The most effective firms approach integration not as an all-or-nothing proposition but as a calibrated strategic choice, using the full spectrum of the make-or-buy continuum to position themselves where they create the most value.

References

Coase, R. H. (1937). The nature of the firm. *Economica, 4*(16), 386–405.

Harrigan, K. R. (1984). Formulating vertical integration strategies. *Academy of Management Review, 9*(4), 638–652.

Porter, M. E. (1980). *Competitive strategy: Techniques for analyzing industries and competitors.* Free Press.

Williamson, O. E. (1985). *The economic institutions of capitalism: Firms, markets, relational contracting.* Free Press.

5.6 Diversification — *Should firms enter related or unrelated businesses?*

5.6.1 What Is Diversification?

The previous sections examined how firms grow (build, borrow, or buy) and in which direction they extend their boundaries (vertical or horizontal integration). This section addresses a broader question: how widely should the firm spread across different industries? Diversification is the corporate-level strategy of operating in multiple industries or product markets simultaneously, creating a multi-business enterprise whose scope extends beyond a single competitive domain.

Diversification is, in many ways, the quintessential corporate-level strategy question. Business-level strategy asks "how do we compete in this industry?" Diversification asks "which industries should we be in?", a question that only arises when the firm considers expanding beyond its original business. The moment a firm enters a second industry, it has diversified, and it now faces the challenge of creating value not just within each business but across the portfolio as a whole.

Firms diversify to create value through three primary mechanisms. First, **economies of scope** arise when the cost of producing two or more different products together within one firm is lower than the cost of producing them separately in independent firms (Panzar & Willig, 1981). Shared marketing, R&D, logistics, and distribution infrastructure can reduce per-unit costs across the portfolio. Second, **market power** can be enhanced when a diversified firm leverages its size and presence across multiple markets to negotiate more favorable terms with suppliers, customers, and capital providers, or when it uses cross-subsidization to compete more aggressively in one market using profits generated in another. Third, **financial economies** emerge when the diversified firm can allocate capital more efficiently across its business units than external capital markets would, channeling cash from mature, cash-generating businesses into high-growth opportunities that might otherwise struggle to attract external funding.

Diversification also serves as a form of **risk reduction**, analogous to diversifying a stock portfolio. A firm operating in a single industry is entirely exposed to that industry's risks. A firm operating across multiple industries spreads its exposure so that a downturn in one business can be offset by stability in others. This logic is intuitive, though it carries an important caveat: shareholders can diversify their own portfolios far more cheaply than corporate managers can diversify a firm's operations.

5.6.2 Levels of Diversification

> *"Put all your eggs in one basket, and watch that basket."* — *Andrew Carnegie*

Diversification is not a binary condition; firms are not simply "diversified" or "undiversified." Rather, diversification exists on a spectrum, and the strategic implications differ significantly depending on where a firm falls on that spectrum. Five levels of diversification capture the range of possibilities (Rumelt, 1974).

Single business. A single-business firm earns more than 95 percent of its revenue from one line of business. The firm may sell multiple products or serve multiple customer segments, but they all fall within a single industry or closely related product category. The strategic focus is entirely on competing effectively in that one domain.

WD-40 is a classic example. The product was developed in 1953 after 40 attempts to perfect a rust-prevention solvent for the aerospace industry, hence WD-40 (Water Displacing formula, 40th attempt). The product was so successful that the company never developed its planned broader product line, eventually renaming itself after its only product. WD-40 represents the extreme of strategic focus: one product, one market, one set of core competencies deployed with remarkable consistency.

Dominant business. A dominant-business firm earns between 70 and 95 percent of its revenue from its main line of business, with a smaller secondary business contributing the remainder. The firm has begun to diversify but remains primarily defined by its core business. Donatos Pizza illustrates this level: the company earns the majority of its revenue from its roughly 200 company-owned and franchised restaurants across several states, but it also operates a secondary business selling take-and-bake pizzas through grocery stores. The restaurant business dominates, but the grocery channel represents a meaningful, if subordinate, second revenue stream.

Related-constrained diversification. A related-constrained firm earns less than 70 percent of its revenue from its main line of business, and its other business lines share product, technological, or distribution linkages with the main business. The key word is "constrained": the firm's diversification is constrained by the requirement that all businesses be closely related. Every business unit shares significant resources, capabilities, or market relationships with the others.

PepsiCo exemplifies related-constrained diversification. Originally a carbonated beverage company, Pepsi expanded into snacks through a merger with Frito-Lay in 1965, subsequently acquiring Tropicana Products (1998) and Quaker Oats (2001). By 2017, food accounted for 53 percent of PepsiCo's $63.5 billion in revenue. But the businesses remain tightly linked: they share distribution networks, marketing expertise in consumer packaged goods, and customer relationships with convenience stores and grocery chains. The linkages are extensive and deliberate, and each business unit benefits from its connection to the others.

Related-linked diversification. A related-linked firm operates in related markets, but fewer linkages exist between the business lines than in a related-constrained firm. Some business units share resources and capabilities with each other, but not all of them do; there are clusters of related businesses that may have limited connections to other clusters.

The Walt Disney Company illustrates related-linked diversification. Disney operates in film and television production, theme parks and resorts, consumer products, streaming media (Disney+), broadcast television (ABC), sports media (ESPN), and cruise lines. Some businesses are tightly linked: a Disney animated film generates characters that drive theme park attractions, consumer merchandise, and streaming content. But others, such as ESPN's sports broadcasting, have fewer direct linkages to the core character-driven entertainment model. There is some overlap and cross-promotional opportunity, but the businesses are not all constrained to a single set of shared resources.

Unrelated diversification. An unrelated diversifier operates in multiple product categories and markets with few or no linkages between them. The businesses do not share technology, customers, distribution channels, or core competencies in any meaningful way. The firm creates value not through operational synergies but through financial management, including efficient capital allocation, disciplined acquisition and restructuring, and corporate-level bargaining power.

United Technologies Corporation (UTC) exemplified unrelated diversification, manufacturing products ranging from aircraft engines and helicopters to HVAC systems, elevators, fire and security systems, and missile systems. The connections between manufacturing elevators and producing military helicopters are tenuous at best. UTC's value creation came not from sharing resources across these businesses but from allocating capital efficiently, applying rigorous financial controls, and leveraging corporate size for favorable terms with lenders and suppliers.

5.6.3 Related Diversification

Related diversification creates value primarily through operational synergies, the sharing and transferring of resources and capabilities across business units. Two mechanisms are particularly important.

Economies of scope are the cost savings that arise when producing two or more different products together is cheaper than producing them separately. The concept is related to but distinct from economies of scale (Ch 2.4), which involve spreading fixed costs over a larger volume of the same product. Economies of scope involve spreading shared resources across different products (Teece, 1982). When PepsiCo uses the same distribution trucks to deliver both chips and cola to the same convenience store, it achieves an economy of scope. When Procter & Gamble uses centralized R&D laboratories to develop innovations applied across Tide, Gillette, and Pampers, it achieves economies of scope in research and development.

Economies of scope are most available in related diversification because the shared resources must be applicable across business units. When businesses are unrelated, these opportunities are minimal or nonexistent.

Leveraging core competencies across business lines is the second major mechanism for value creation in related diversification (Prahalad & Hamel, 1990). As discussed in Chapter 3, core competencies are the superior capabilities that differentiate the firm and drive competitive advantage. Related diversification allows a firm to deploy these competencies across multiple businesses, generating returns from the same capability in multiple markets. 3M's ability to apply its adhesive and materials science technologies across dozens of industries — from healthcare to electronics to consumer products — is a textbook example of leveraging core competencies through related diversification. The competency was developed once but generates value repeatedly across the portfolio.

Firms can also create value by **transferring corporate-level competencies** from one business to another. A firm with exceptional supply chain management practices can transfer that expertise to a newly acquired business unit, improving performance beyond what it could achieve independently, provided the businesses are related enough for the transferred competency to be applicable.

5.6.4 Unrelated Diversification

Unrelated diversification creates value through fundamentally different mechanisms than related diversification. Because unrelated business units share few or no operational resources, the synergies must come from corporate-level financial management rather than business-level operational sharing.

Efficient resource allocation between business units. A diversified corporation operates as an internal capital market. Corporate headquarters collects cash flows from all business units and reallocates capital to opportunities with the highest expected returns. In theory, this internal capital market can be more efficient than external markets because corporate managers have better information about their own businesses; they can observe operations directly and evaluate opportunities with proprietary knowledge. By shifting capital from mature, cash-generating businesses to high-growth opportunities, the diversified firm can fund investments that might not attract external financing on favorable terms.

Acquiring, restructuring, and placing firms under rigorous financial controls. Some unrelated diversifiers create value by acquiring underperforming firms, restructuring operations to eliminate inefficiencies, and imposing disciplined financial management. The corporate parent adds value not through operational expertise in the acquired firm's industry but through superior financial discipline, governance, and performance management.

Creating financial economies through corporate size. A large, diversified corporation can negotiate better terms with lenders, insurers, and financial institutions than individual business units could alone. The corporation's size, cash flow stability, and asset base provide creditworthiness that individual units lack.

5.6.5 Benefits of Diversification

Diversification, whether related or unrelated, can deliver several strategic benefits.

Economies of scope. As discussed above, sharing marketing, R&D, logistics, distribution, and other resources across multiple business units reduces costs and improves efficiency. These economies are strongest in related diversification but can exist in limited forms (shared corporate services, for example) even in unrelated portfolios.

Leveraging core competencies into new products and markets. A firm with a distinctive capability can generate additional returns by applying it to new competitive contexts. This benefit is strongest when the core competency is genuinely transferable, when it addresses similar customer needs or technological requirements across the firm's business units.

Risk reduction. Operating in multiple industries reduces exposure to any single industry's risks. This portfolio effect is genuine, though shareholders can achieve the same risk reduction by diversifying their own investment portfolios. The risk-reduction benefit is therefore most valuable when shareholders cannot easily replicate the diversification themselves, or when the firm's internal capital allocation genuinely outperforms external markets.

Growth opportunities. When a firm's core market is mature or saturated, diversification provides avenues for continued growth. A company that has captured the maximum feasible share of its original market must look elsewhere to expand, reinvesting cash flows in new markets rather than in increasingly low-return expansions of the core business.

Market power and synergy. A diversified firm may enjoy enhanced bargaining power due to its overall size and cross-selling opportunities. A firm serving the same customer from multiple business units can bundle products, negotiate volume discounts, and create switching costs that single-business competitors cannot match.

Financial synergies. The internal capital market allows the diversified firm to allocate capital more efficiently than external markets in some circumstances, and the corporation's overall financial strength provides favorable terms from external capital providers.

Strategic renewal. Perhaps the most underappreciated benefit is diversification's role in strategic renewal. A single-business firm whose industry is disrupted faces an existential threat. A diversified firm can absorb the disruption of one business unit while using others as platforms for adaptation, providing the time and resources to develop new capabilities without the pressure of an immediate survival crisis.

5.6.6 Risks of Diversification

> *"Diversification is protection against ignorance. It makes little sense if you know what you are doing."* — *Warren Buffett*

For every benefit of diversification, there is a corresponding risk. These risks help explain why the empirical relationship between diversification and performance is curvilinear rather than linear, and why more diversification does not automatically produce more value.

Loss of strategic focus. The most fundamental risk of diversification is that it dilutes strategic clarity. Every business unit added demands managerial attention, capital, and resources. As the portfolio expands, leadership must divide its focus across an increasing number of competitive contexts. Core competencies that once drove advantage may atrophy as resources spread more thinly. A company that was once the best in its industry becomes merely adequate in several, sacrificing depth for breadth.

Managerial overconfidence. Diversification decisions are particularly susceptible to managerial hubris — the belief that skills producing success in one industry will transfer seamlessly to another. This overconfidence is compounded by the self-reinforcing nature of corporate success: executives repeatedly rewarded for bold decisions may underestimate how much of their previous success was context-dependent rather than transferable.

Capital misallocation. In practice, internal capital markets frequently fail to allocate resources optimally. Profitable business units may subsidize underperformers, not because those units represent genuine growth opportunities but because division heads have political influence, the corporate center is reluctant to admit a prior acquisition was a mistake, or exit barriers make divestiture difficult. Cash that could have been returned to shareholders or invested in the firm's strongest businesses is instead funneled into mediocre units that external markets would never have funded on the same terms. As we will examine in Chapter 6, this is a manifestation of the principal-agent problem: managers may prefer a larger, more diversified portfolio because it increases their compensation and prestige, even when shareholders would be better served by a more focused firm.

Increased bureaucracy and coordination costs. Diversification inevitably increases organizational complexity. Each additional business unit requires coordination mechanisms, including reporting structures, planning processes, performance metrics, and transfer pricing, that consume managerial time and resources. Decision-making slows, and information flowing across more organizational boundaries creates opportunities for distortion and delay. These coordination costs are real economic costs that offset the synergies diversification is supposed to produce.

Integration challenges. When diversification is achieved through acquisition, the firm must integrate the acquired business into its existing organization. Cultural clashes can undermine morale and productivity. Key employees may leave, taking the knowledge that made the acquisition attractive. Systems must be harmonized at significant cost and disruption. The more different the acquired business, the more severe these challenges, because fewer routines and practices transfer between dissimilar businesses.

Regulatory and brand risks. Entering new industries exposes the firm to unfamiliar regulatory environments and legal liabilities. Beyond regulatory risk, diversification can create brand risk: a failure or scandal in one business unit can damage the reputation of the entire portfolio, particularly when businesses share a corporate brand.

Shareholder redundancy. Perhaps the most incisive critique of diversification as a risk-reduction strategy comes from financial theory. Shareholders can diversify their own investment portfolios far more cheaply than corporate managers can diversify a firm's operations. An investor wanting exposure to both technology and healthcare can simply buy shares in companies in each industry. There is no need for a single corporation to operate in both industries on the investor's behalf, and doing so imposes all the costs described above that portfolio-level diversification avoids. This is why the risk-reduction argument for corporate diversification is weaker than it appears: the benefit is real, but shareholders can replicate it at near-zero cost. The conglomerate discount, the empirical finding that diversified firms are often valued at less than the sum of their parts, reflects the market's recognition that the costs of corporate diversification frequently outweigh the benefits shareholders cannot achieve on their own (Berger & Ofek, 1995).

EX: General Electric's Diversification and Value Destruction

General Electric under CEO Jack Welch became the iconic American conglomerate, operating in industries ranging from jet engines and power generation to financial services, media (NBC), healthcare equipment, and home appliances. Welch's philosophy — be number one or number two in every industry, or exit — imposed discipline, and GE's stock price rose dramatically during his tenure. But GE Capital, the financial services arm, eventually accounted for more than half of profits and introduced enormous financial risk. When the 2008 financial crisis struck, GE Capital's exposure to subprime mortgages nearly brought the entire conglomerate down, requiring a $139 billion government-backed debt guarantee.

Under successor Jeff Immelt, the costs of extreme diversification became increasingly apparent. The corporate center struggled to allocate capital across such disparate businesses, and the stock price stagnated even as the broader market soared. GE's response was prolonged de-diversification: selling NBC Universal, divesting GE Capital, spinning off healthcare, and ultimately announcing in 2021 a breakup into three separate companies focused on aviation, healthcare, and energy. Investors greeted the breakup with enthusiasm, signaling that the individual businesses were worth more apart than together. GE's journey from conglomerate icon to breakup candidate is a cautionary tale about every diversification risk described above.

5.6.7 Typical Diversification Performance: The Curvilinear Effect

Given these potential benefits, one might expect that more diversification is always better. The empirical evidence tells a different story. Research across multiple industries and geographies consistently finds a **curvilinear relationship** between diversification and firm performance, an inverted U-shape that reveals the limits of diversification's benefits (Palich, Cardinal, & Miller, 2000).

Performance typically improves as a firm moves from a single business toward moderate levels of related diversification. The firm captures economies of scope, leverages core competencies across multiple businesses, and reduces its exposure to single-industry risks. The incremental value from each additional related business unit is positive, because the shared resources and capabilities generate synergies that exceed the costs of managing a more complex organization.

Performance tends to peak around the related-constrained or related-linked level of diversification. At this point, the firm has captured the major available synergies, including shared distribution, cross-leveraged R&D, and transferred management competencies, while maintaining enough focus that managerial attention and organizational systems can effectively coordinate the portfolio.

Performance declines as the firm moves toward unrelated diversification. The operational synergies that drive value in related diversification are unavailable when business units share few linkages. Managerial complexity increases faster than the benefits, decision-making slows, and the corporate center's ability to add value diminishes. The internal capital market, which in theory should allocate resources more efficiently, often fails in practice as corporate managers may engage in political allocation rather than economically optimal allocation. At the extreme, the diversified conglomerate may actually destroy value: the sum of the parts may be worth more as independent businesses, the "conglomerate discount."

The curvilinear effect does not mean unrelated diversification always fails. The resource-based view (Ch 3) reminds us that some firms develop distinctive capabilities in corporate management or capital allocation that allow them to succeed where most cannot. Berkshire Hathaway under Warren Buffett and Cooper Industries (Ch 5.4) are examples. But these are exceptions: the typical firm achieves its best performance at moderate levels of related diversification, and performance deteriorates as the portfolio becomes broader and less related.

5.6.8 Entry Mode: Greenfield vs. Acquisition

Once a firm has decided to diversify, to enter a new industry or market, it must choose how to enter. This choice is the Build, Borrow, Buy decision from Chapter 5.1 applied to diversification. **Greenfield entry corresponds to *build*** — the firm develops the new business internally using its own resources. **Acquisition entry corresponds to *buy*** — the firm purchases an existing participant and brings it inside the firm's boundaries. The third option, ***borrow***, takes the form of a strategic alliance or joint venture that provides access to the new market without full ownership, the cooperative structures examined in Chapter 5.3. Because the borrow option was treated there, this section focuses on the two ownership-based modes that sit at the build and buy ends of the continuum: greenfield development and acquisition.

Greenfield entry means the firm organically expands into the new industry using its own resources, brand, technology, and customer knowledge. The speed and feasibility depend heavily on the overlap between existing businesses and the new one. When overlap is high, greenfield entry can be efficient. When overlap is low, it becomes slow and expensive, because the firm must build from scratch capabilities that incumbents have developed over years.

Acquisition entry means the firm buys its way in by purchasing an existing participant. Acquisition is generally faster because the acquired firm is already operating in the target industry, but it carries the integration risks discussed in Chapter 5.4.

The choice between greenfield and acquisition depends on several assessable factors. **Brand strength** matters: if the firm's brand is well-known in the new market, greenfield can leverage it; if not, acquiring an established brand may be faster. **Customer similarity** matters: if new customers resemble existing ones, customer knowledge transfers and greenfield is feasible. **Channel access** matters: if distribution channels are scarce or controlled by incumbents, acquiring a firm with established relationships may be the only practical option. **Human capital** requirements matter: if relevant skills are standardized and available, the firm can hire for greenfield entry; if expertise is tacit or concentrated, acqui-hiring may be necessary. **Technology overlap** matters: compatible technology favors greenfield; fundamentally different technology favors acquisition. And **speed requirements** matter: if rapid entry is needed, acquisition's speed advantage may be decisive; if gradual entry is acceptable, greenfield preserves more strategic control.

In practice, many diversification moves combine modes. A firm may acquire a small platform company and then grow it organically, capturing acquisition's speed while leveraging organic-growth strengths. Alternatively, a firm may borrow first, entering through an alliance or joint venture to learn the market at lower risk, and then deepen its commitment in one of two ways. It may convert the partnership into full ownership through acquisition. Or it may move beyond the partnership to build out its own operations organically, as Walmart did in Mexico: it entered in 1991 through a joint venture with the retailer Cifra, and once it had absorbed enough local market knowledge, it expanded across the country largely by opening its own stores.

5.6.9 Diversification and the Corporate Strategy Framework

Diversification is not an end in itself; it is a means to an end. The relevant question is never "should we diversify?" but "will diversification create more value than the alternatives?" The Build, Borrow, Buy framework provides the decision logic, the levels of diversification provide the vocabulary, the curvilinear performance relationship provides the empirical warning, and the Build, Borrow, Buy entry-mode choice provides the implementation pathway.

The sections that follow examine how diversified firms manage their portfolios, through internal capital markets (Ch 5.7) and portfolio management frameworks (Ch 5.8), and how corporate governance (Chapter 6) ensures that diversification decisions serve shareholder interests rather than managerial ones.

References

Berger, P. G., & Ofek, E. (1995). Diversification's effect on firm value. *Journal of Financial Economics*, *37*(1), 39–65.

Palich, L. E., Cardinal, L. B., & Miller, C. C. (2000). Curvilinearity in the diversification–performance linkage: An examination of over three decades of research. *Strategic Management Journal*, *21*(2), 155–174.

Panzar, J. C., & Willig, R. D. (1981). Economies of scope. *American Economic Review*, *71*(2), 268–272.

Prahalad, C. K., & Hamel, G. (1990). The core competence of the corporation. *Harvard Business Review*, *68*(3), 79–91.

Rumelt, R. P. (1974). *Strategy, structure, and economic performance.* Harvard University Press.

Teece, D. J. (1982). Towards an economic theory of the multiproduct firm. *Journal of Economic Behavior & Organization*, *3*(1), 39–63.

5.7 Internal Capital Markets — *How do diversified firms allocate resources?*

> *"The heads of many companies are not skilled in capital allocation." — Warren Buffett*

When a firm operates a single business, capital allocation is straightforward: reinvest profits, return cash to shareholders, or hold reserves. When a firm operates multiple business units across different industries, however, a fundamentally different mechanism comes into play. The diversified firm can allocate capital internally, directing cash from one business unit to fund investments in another, without accessing external capital markets at all. This internal capital market is one of the central mechanisms through which diversified firms attempt to create value, and understanding when it works and when it fails is essential to evaluating any corporate-level diversification strategy.

5.7.1 What Are Internal Capital Markets?

An internal capital market exists whenever a diversified firm's corporate headquarters collects cash flows from its business units and redistributes that capital based on strategic priorities. Rather than each unit independently raising funds through banks or equity offerings, the parent corporation acts as an intermediary, pooling resources and directing investment where it sees the greatest returns.

This is fundamentally an extension of the transaction cost logic from Chapter 1. Just as firms exist because internal coordination can sometimes be more efficient than market exchange (Coase, 1937), internal capital markets exist because internal allocation of financial resources can sometimes be more efficient than external markets. The diversified corporation is, in effect, acting as its own bank (Williamson, 1975).

The theoretical case rests on an informational argument. Corporate headquarters possesses information about its business units that external investors do not have: detailed operating data, internal forecasts, knowledge of competitive dynamics, and assessments of management talent. This allows headquarters to identify the best investment opportunities more accurately than outsiders relying on quarterly earnings reports and analyst coverage. Beyond informational advantages, internal allocation avoids the transaction costs of external financing, including underwriting fees of 3 to 7 percent of capital raised, plus legal, accounting, and regulatory compliance expenses (Eckbo et al., 2007). Internal allocation also offers speed and flexibility: corporate headquarters can redirect capital almost immediately to seize time-sensitive opportunities without waiting weeks or months for external financing.

5.7.2 When Internal Capital Markets Create Value

Internal capital markets are most likely to create value when three conditions are met simultaneously. First, corporate managers must genuinely possess better information than external investors. This is most likely when business units operate in industries that are difficult for outsiders to evaluate, perhaps because the technology is complex, the competitive dynamics are opaque, or the key value drivers are not well captured by standard financial metrics. In industries where information is readily available and easily interpreted by analysts, the informational advantage of headquarters diminishes considerably.

Second, the firm's business units must have meaningfully different capital needs and growth profiles. If every unit has similar investment needs and return profiles, there is little benefit to reallocating capital among them. The value of internal allocation comes from redirecting cash from units that generate more than they need toward units with better growth opportunities. A portfolio combining mature, cash-generating businesses with younger, capital-hungry growth businesses is well-positioned to benefit.

Third — and most critically — allocation decisions must be made on strategic and economic merit rather than internal politics or organizational inertia. This condition is far harder to satisfy than the first two, and its frequent violation is the primary reason internal capital markets often destroy rather than create value.

EX: Berkshire Hathaway's Capital Allocation Model

Berkshire Hathaway under Warren Buffett provides perhaps the most celebrated example of an internal capital market functioning effectively. Berkshire's portfolio includes insurance operations (GEICO, General Re), railroads (BNSF), utilities (Berkshire Hathaway Energy), manufacturing firms, and retail operations, among many others. The insurance businesses generate enormous cash flows through their "float" — premiums collected before claims are paid — and Buffett's role as capital allocator involves directing this capital toward the highest-return opportunities across the entire portfolio. When BNSF needed billions in capital expenditure to upgrade rail infrastructure, Berkshire could fund it internally without accessing debt markets. When attractive acquisition targets appeared, Berkshire could move quickly with cash on hand. The model works because Buffett and his team maintain rigorous, economically rational allocation discipline and because Berkshire's decentralized management structure gives corporate headquarters genuine informational advantages, as subsidiary managers report directly and candidly in ways they might not to external analysts. Crucially, Buffett has been transparent that when he cannot find internal investment opportunities that meet his return thresholds, he returns capital to shareholders rather than deploying it into subpar investments, demonstrating the discipline that separates value-creating internal capital markets from value-destroying ones (Cunningham, 2014).

5.7.3 When Internal Capital Markets Destroy Value

If the theoretical case is compelling, the empirical record is more sobering. Research consistently finds that diversified firms trade at a discount relative to the combined value of their individual units as standalone companies, a phenomenon known as the "diversification discount" or "conglomerate discount" (Berger & Ofek, 1995; Lang & Stulz, 1994). Misallocation through internal capital markets is one of the most widely cited explanations.

The fundamental problem is that internal allocation decisions are made by people with their own interests and biases (Scharfstein & Stein, 2000). Three specific pathologies recur. **Cross-subsidization** occurs when headquarters uses cash from profitable units to prop up underperforming ones. A struggling unit described as having "turnaround potential" or facing "temporary headwinds" continues receiving capital that external markets would refuse to provide. This is particularly insidious because consolidated financial statements may show adequate overall returns even as enormous value is destroyed through internal transfers from strong units to weak ones. Only when the firm is eventually broken up does the full extent of cross-subsidization become apparent.

Empire building arises because division managers have strong personal incentives to grow their units regardless of whether growth creates shareholder value. Larger divisions typically mean higher compensation, more prestige, greater organizational power, and more career opportunities for the division's management team. These incentives create persistent pressure on headquarters to allocate capital to divisions that want to grow rather than to divisions where growth would generate the highest returns. This connects directly to the principal-agent problems we will examine in Chapter 6.

Political allocation occurs when capital flows to units with the most influential managers rather than the best opportunities: who has the CEO's ear, which division head is the most persuasive presenter, which unit has the most organizational allies. This problem worsens as firms grow more complex and headquarters must rely increasingly on the representations of the very managers who have incentives to overstate their needs and understate their risks.

These pathologies point to a fundamental tension: for internal allocation to create value, corporate headquarters must exercise the same discipline that external markets impose. External markets force firms to justify investments to investors who have alternatives. A struggling standalone company would be forced to restructure or shut down. An internal capital market has no such automatic discipline — a struggling division can continue receiving capital as long as headquarters provides it. This is why the quality of corporate management is the single most important determinant of whether an internal capital market creates or destroys value. Headquarters must be willing to starve underperforming units, reallocate resources even when it creates conflict, and divest businesses that cannot justify the capital they consume. One tool for imposing this discipline is the BCG Growth–Share Matrix, which we examine in the next section.

EX: General Electric's Capital Allocation Failures

General Electric under CEO Jeff Immelt illustrates how internal capital markets can destroy value at enormous scale. GE Capital, the company's financial services arm, generated massive cash flows that were redirected across GE's sprawling portfolio of industrial businesses. Rather than returning excess capital to shareholders or investing only where returns clearly exceeded the cost of capital, GE used its internal capital market to fund acquisitions and investments in units that consistently underperformed, including a poorly timed \$10.6 billion acquisition of Alstom's power business in 2015, just as the global power market was entering a structural decline. The informational advantages that theoretically justified GE's diversified structure were overwhelmed by the political dynamics of a complex conglomerate: division heads competed for capital, corporate headquarters lacked the specialized expertise to evaluate opportunities across dozens of industries, and the sheer complexity of the organization made disciplined allocation nearly impossible. GE's market capitalization fell from nearly \$600 billion at its 2000 peak to under \$100 billion by 2018, and the company was eventually broken into three separate companies — an implicit admission that its internal capital market was destroying rather than creating value (Gryta & Mann, 2020).

5.7.4 Implications for Diversification Strategy

The analysis of internal capital markets raises a fundamental question from the investor's perspective: why should a diversified corporation allocate capital on behalf of shareholders when those shareholders could make the same decisions themselves? If PepsiCo's snack business generates excess cash, investors might prefer that PepsiCo return it as dividends and let them decide whether to invest in beverages, snacks, or something entirely different. The internal capital market is only justified if corporate headquarters can allocate capital more effectively than the external market, meaning that informational and transaction cost advantages must outweigh the agency costs and political distortions that internal allocation introduces.

This investor perspective helps explain why diversified firms that fail to demonstrate disciplined allocation face pressure from activist investors to break up. When activist funds push conglomerates to separate their business units, the underlying argument is that shareholders would be better served by standalone companies that each raise capital in the external market. The threat of such activism serves as an external check on internal capital markets, a reminder that the privilege of allocating capital internally must be justified by superior results.

This analysis also reinforces the curvilinear relationship between diversification and performance discussed in the previous section. Moderate, related diversification is most likely to support effective internal capital allocation because headquarters can realistically maintain informational advantages and allocation discipline. As diversification becomes broader and more unrelated, informational advantages erode and corporate managers cannot be experts in dozens of industries, while political and agency problems intensify. For managers evaluating diversification strategy, the key question is not whether internal capital allocation is theoretically possible but whether the firm's headquarters has the information, analytical capability, and organizational discipline to allocate capital better than external markets would. Firms that can honestly answer yes have a legitimate basis for diversification. Firms that cannot should think carefully about whether their strategy is creating or destroying shareholder value.

References

Berger, P. G., & Ofek, E. (1995). Diversification's effect on firm value. *Journal of Financial Economics, 37*(1), 39–65.

Coase, R. H. (1937). The nature of the firm. *Economica, 4*(16), 386–405.

Cunningham, L. A. (2014). *Berkshire beyond Buffett: The enduring value of values.* Columbia University Press.

Eckbo, B. E., Masulis, R. W., & Norli, Ø. (2007). Security offerings. In B. E. Eckbo (Ed.), *Handbook of empirical corporate finance* (Vol. 1, pp. 233–373). Elsevier.

Gryta, T., & Mann, T. (2020). *Lights out: Pride, delusion, and the fall of General Electric.* Houghton Mifflin Harcourt.

Lang, L. H. P., & Stulz, R. M. (1994). Tobin's q, corporate diversification, and firm performance. *Journal of Political Economy, 102*(6), 1248–1280.

Scharfstein, D. S., & Stein, J. C. (2000). The dark side of internal capital markets: Divisional rent-seeking and inefficient investment. *Journal of Finance, 55*(6), 2537–2564.

Williamson, O. E. (1975). *Markets and hierarchies: Analysis and antitrust implications.* Free Press.

5.8 The BCG Growth–Share Matrix — *How do we manage business portfolios?*

> *"To be successful, a company should have a portfolio of products with different growth rates and different market shares." — Bruce Henderson*

The previous section established that internal capital markets are only as effective as the discipline corporate headquarters brings to allocation decisions. But discipline requires a framework, some structured way to evaluate which business units deserve investment, which should be maintained, and which should be divested. Without such a framework, allocation decisions default to internal politics and organizational inertia, producing exactly the value-destroying outcomes we examined in Chapter 5.7. The BCG Growth–Share Matrix, developed by the Boston Consulting Group in 1970, is the most widely known tool for imposing that structure (Henderson, 1970). Despite its age and significant limitations, the matrix remains a useful starting point for thinking about portfolio management in diversified firms.

5.8.1 What Is the BCG Growth–Share Matrix?

The BCG matrix is a portfolio planning tool that classifies a diversified firm's business units along two dimensions: the growth rate of the market in which the unit competes, and the unit's relative market share within that market. Market growth rate is plotted on the vertical axis (from low to high) and relative market share on the horizontal axis (from low to high). Together, these two dimensions create a two-by-two matrix with four quadrants, each of which implies a different strategic posture and a different role in the firm's internal capital allocation.

The logic behind these two dimensions draws on concepts introduced earlier in this textbook. Market growth rate matters because high-growth markets present greater opportunities for revenue expansion and because competitive positions are more fluid in growing markets, where it is easier to gain share when the overall pie is expanding than when competitors must fight over a fixed pool of customers. Relative market share matters because of the connection between market share and cost advantage. As we discussed in Chapter 2, firms with larger market share tend to benefit from economies of scale and learning curve effects, giving them lower per-unit costs than smaller competitors. A firm with high relative market share is therefore likely to be more profitable and to generate more cash than its smaller rivals.

The term "relative" in relative market share is important. The BCG matrix does not simply measure a firm's absolute market share but rather its share relative to its largest competitor. A business unit with 20 percent market share in an industry where the next largest competitor holds 10 percent has a relative market share of 2.0, meaning it is twice the size of its nearest rival. The same 20 percent share in an industry where the leader holds 40 percent yields a relative market share of only 0.5. This relative measure captures the competitive position of the unit more accurately than absolute share alone, because it reflects whether the unit is likely to enjoy scale and experience advantages or to suffer from them.

5.8.2 The Four Quadrants

Stars (high growth, high relative share) are a firm's most promising business units. They hold strong competitive positions in fast-growing markets, generating substantial revenue while being well-positioned to capture expanding demand. However, stars also require significant investment to maintain their positions because high-growth markets attract competitors, and sustaining a leading position requires continuous spending on capacity expansion, marketing, and product development. As a result, stars tend to be roughly cash-neutral: they generate a great deal of cash but also consume a great deal. The strategic recommendation is to invest heavily to maintain or strengthen competitive position. A star that receives inadequate investment risks losing share and sliding into the question mark quadrant.

Cash cows (low growth, high relative share) hold dominant positions in mature markets where growth has slowed. Because the market is no longer expanding rapidly, there is less need for heavy investment in capacity or market development. At the same time, high relative market share means the unit benefits from scale economies and experience advantages that produce strong margins. The combination of high profitability and low investment requirements makes cash cows the primary generators of free cash flow within a diversified portfolio. The recommendation is to maintain the unit's position with only the investment necessary to sustain operations, while harvesting excess cash to fund stars and promising question marks. Cash cows are the engine of the internal capital market: without them, the diversified firm has no surplus cash to allocate.

Question marks (high growth, low relative share) compete in attractive, fast-growing markets but lack dominant positions. They present a conundrum: the high growth rate suggests significant potential, but low relative share means the unit is at a cost disadvantage. Turning a question mark into a star requires substantial investment with no guarantee of success. The recommendation is to evaluate each carefully, investing aggressively in those with realistic potential to become stars and divesting those unlikely to achieve leadership.

Dogs (low growth, low relative share) hold weak positions in stagnant markets. They generate little profit and may operate at a loss. With limited growth opportunity and insufficient scale advantages, the standard recommendation is to divest. However, some dogs serve complementary strategic purposes, such as providing critical components to a star, and may warrant continued support, though such rationales should be carefully scrutinized to avoid cross-subsidization (Ch 5.7).

5.8.3 Portfolio Life Cycle and Restructuring

One useful feature of the BCG matrix is its illustration of how units move through the portfolio over time. The ideal trajectory begins as a question mark, moves rightward to become a star as market share grows, then downward to cash cow as the market matures, generating the surplus cash that funds the next generation. This connects directly to the industry life cycle concepts in Chapter 4. A healthy portfolio should contain units at multiple stages: cash cows to generate funding, stars for future growth, and carefully selected question marks to ensure a pipeline. The goal is balance across quadrants, using the internal capital market to transfer resources from units that generate cash to those that need it most.

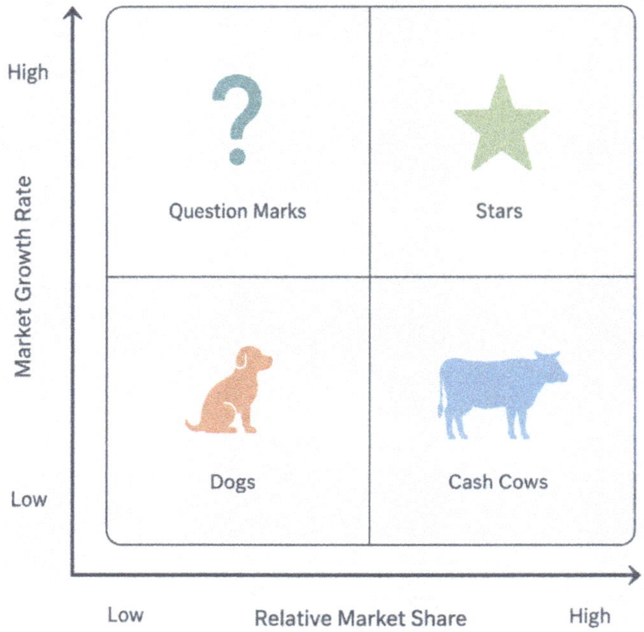

BCG Growth–Share Matrix

When a diversified firm finds itself over-diversified or burdened with too many dogs and underperforming question marks, restructuring becomes necessary. The BCG matrix helps identify which units to keep, invest in, or divest. Three primary restructuring strategies exist. **Downsizing** focuses on reducing labor costs and overhead by eliminating duplications and shutting down underperforming units. While it delivers immediate savings, research consistently finds that downsizing in isolation tends to harm long-term performance because short-term savings rarely compensate for erosion of organizational capability (Cascio, 1993). **Downscoping** reduces the firm's level of diversification by divesting units outside its core strategic focus. Of the three strategies, downscoping is most closely associated with performance improvements because it reduces managerial complexity and allows headquarters to focus attention on fewer businesses (Hoskisson et al., 1994). **Leveraged buyouts (LBOs)** involve taking a firm or division private through debt-financed purchases. The high debt load imposes financial discipline — every dollar must earn its return or the firm risks default — eliminating the slack that enables empire building and cross-subsidization (Jensen, 1989). The goal is to improve efficiency sufficiently to return the firm to public markets or sell it within five to eight years.

EX: Dell's Leveraged Buyout

Dell's $24.4 billion leveraged buyout in 2013 illustrates how an LBO can facilitate strategic restructuring. By the early 2010s, Dell was a publicly traded company facing intense pressure from Wall Street to deliver quarterly earnings growth, even as the PC market — the foundation of its business — was declining. The quarterly earnings pressure made it difficult for Dell's management to invest in the long-term strategic pivot the company needed: a transition from consumer PCs toward enterprise hardware, software, and services. Michael Dell, the company's founder, partnered with Silver Lake Partners to take the company private. Freed from the short-term pressures of public markets, Dell was able to make large, risky bets on its enterprise business, including the $67 billion acquisition of EMC Corporation in 2016, a deal that would have been nearly impossible to execute as a publicly traded company facing quarterly earnings scrutiny. By

2018, Dell had grown its enterprise business and returned to public trading through a $23.9 billion buyout of its DVMT tracking stock, completing the cycle that the LBO was designed to facilitate (de la Merced, 2013, 2018).

5.8.4 Limitations of the BCG Matrix

Despite its intuitive appeal, the BCG matrix has significant limitations. First, the matrix relies on only two dimensions to characterize a business unit's strategic position. In reality, profitability depends on the firm's business-level strategy (Ch 2), core competencies (Ch 3.3), rivalry intensity (Ch 4.2), and bargaining dynamics (Ch 4.3). A "dog" occupying a well-defended niche with strong differentiation might be quite profitable, while a "star" might be unprofitable if competitive dynamics are unfavorable.

Second, the matrix assumes a direct relationship between relative market share and profitability, grounded in scale and experience effects. While this holds in many industries, it is not universal. In industries where differentiation matters more than cost, such as luxury goods, creative industries, and professional services, smaller firms with distinctive capabilities can be highly profitable despite modest share.

Third, as discussed in Chapter 4, defining market boundaries is not straightforward, yet the matrix's recommendations depend entirely on how the market is defined. A unit might appear to be a cash cow in "beverages" but a star in "premium energy drinks."

Fourth, the matrix is static: it captures a snapshot at one point in time without accounting for disruption, regulatory changes, or competitive dynamics that can rapidly shift a unit's position.

Finally, the matrix can encourage mechanistic thinking that ignores interdependencies between units. Divesting a dog that provides critical components to a star, or harvesting a cash cow too aggressively, can damage the broader portfolio. Portfolio management requires holistic thinking that a two-by-two matrix cannot fully capture (Seeger, 1984).

Despite these limitations, the BCG matrix endures because the alternative, allocating capital based on intuition or politics, is worse. The most effective strategists use it not as a decision-making algorithm but as a diagnostic that raises the right questions: Which units generate cash and which consume it? Are we investing in genuine growth potential or subsidizing units that should be divested? Do we have a balanced portfolio that sustains long-term performance? These are the questions disciplined internal capital markets must answer, and the BCG matrix — for all its imperfections — provides a useful framework for asking them.

References

Cascio, W. F. (1993). Downsizing: What do we know? What have we learned? *Academy of Management Perspectives, 7*(1), 95–104.

de la Merced, M. J. (2013, February 5). Dell to be taken private in $24 billion deal. *The New York Times.* https://archive.nytimes.com/dealbook.nytimes.com/2013/02/05/dell-to-be-taken-private-in-24-billion-deal/

de la Merced, M. J. (2018, July 2). Dell to return to public trading, but still in its founder's hands. *The New York Times.* https://www.nytimes.com/2018/07/02/business/dealbook/dell-public-vmware.html

Henderson, B. D. (1970). The product portfolio. *BCG Perspectives.* Boston Consulting Group.

Hoskisson, R. E., Johnson, R. A., & Moesel, D. D. (1994). Corporate divestiture intensity in restructuring firms: Effects of governance, strategy, and performance. *Academy of Management Journal, 37*(5), 1207–1251.

Jensen, M. C. (1989). Eclipse of the public corporation. *Harvard Business Review, 67*(5), 61–74.

Seeger, J. A. (1984). Reversing the images of BCG's growth/share matrix. *Strategic Management Journal*, *5*(1), 93–97.

Chapter 6

Corporate Governance & Business in Society

6.1 Principal-Agent Problems — *Why do shareholders and managers have conflicting interests?*

6.1.1 Why Corporate Governance Matters

Throughout Chapters 1 through 5, we examined how firms create value, develop competitive advantages, analyze their environments, and pursue growth through corporate-level strategies. All of these strategic decisions, however, share a common assumption: that the people making them are acting in the best interests of the firm and its owners.

This chapter challenges that assumption. Corporate governance is the set of mechanisms used to manage the relationships among stakeholders, determine the strategic direction of organizations, and control their performance (Daily et al., 2003). It asks a deceptively simple question: who controls the firm, and are they exercising that control in the interests of the people who own it? As we discussed in our treatment of stakeholders (Chapter 1.6), different groups have competing claims on the firm. The principal-agent tension between shareholders and managers is among the most consequential of these conflicts, and addressing it is the central task of corporate governance.

Governance is not merely a compliance exercise. The governance structures a firm adopts directly shape the strategic decisions it makes. A CEO whose compensation is tied entirely to short-term stock price will make different strategic choices than one whose incentives reward long-term value creation. A board that functions as a rubber stamp for management will oversee a very different firm than one that exercises genuine oversight. Understanding corporate governance is therefore essential for understanding why firms pursue the strategies they do, and why those strategies sometimes serve management's interests rather than the firm's.

6.1.2 The Separation of Ownership and Control

> *"The directors of such companies, however, being the managers rather of other people's money than of their own, it cannot well be expected, that they should watch over it with the same anxious vigilance." — Adam Smith*

The governance problem does not exist in all firms. When the owner of a small business also serves as its manager, there is no separation between the person who bears the financial risk of ownership and the person who makes the operating decisions. The owner-manager's interests are perfectly aligned with those of the firm because they are the same person. If the business succeeds, the owner profits. If it fails, the owner bears the loss. This direct alignment of risk and reward eliminates the need for governance mechanisms.

The governance problem emerges as firms grow and ownership becomes dispersed. When a firm goes public and sells shares to thousands of investors, the people who own the firm are no longer the people who run it. Shareholders provide capital and bear financial risk, but they delegate decision-making authority to professional managers who may have little or no ownership stake. This separation of ownership and control is a defining characteristic of the modern corporation (Berle & Means, 1932).

Adam Smith recognized this problem more than two centuries ago, observing that managers of other people's money cannot be expected to watch over it with the same anxious vigilance with which they would watch over their own (Smith, 1776). When you are spending someone else's money, the personal cost of a bad decision is lower, the temptation to pursue personal comfort is higher, and the incentive to take bold action on behalf of owners is weaker.

Most modern shareholders are not owners in the traditional sense. An individual who holds one hundred shares of a Fortune 500 company has no meaningful control over corporate decisions, limited access to operational information, and virtually no ability to influence management behavior. Their primary governance tool is the ability to sell their shares, to exit rather than exercise voice (Hirschman, 1970). This dispersed ownership structure means that no single shareholder has sufficient incentive to bear the costs of monitoring management, creating a collective action problem that governance mechanisms must address (Fama & Jensen, 1983).

6.1.3 Agency Theory

Agency theory provides the foundational framework for understanding the governance problem. An agency relationship is created when one party — the principal — delegates decision-making authority to another party — the agent — who is expected to act on the principal's behalf. In the corporate context, shareholders are the principals who hire and compensate managers (agents) to run the firm and make decisions that maximize shareholder value (Jensen & Meckling, 1976).

The agency problem arises because the interests of principals and agents are not naturally aligned. Agency theory poses three core questions that illuminate why this misalignment occurs. First, what happens when the goals of the principal and the agent conflict? Shareholders want to maximize the long-term value of their investment. Managers may want to maximize their own compensation, job security, prestige, or comfort. These goals frequently diverge, and when they do, managers, as the ones actually making decisions, may pursue their own interests at shareholders' expense.

Second, what happens when it is difficult or expensive for the principal to verify what the agent is actually doing? Shareholders cannot observe every decision a CEO makes. They see quarterly earnings reports and annual filings, but they cannot assess whether the CEO is making optimal strategic decisions or pursuing value-destroying pet projects. This information gap gives agents significant latitude to act in ways that benefit themselves rather than their principals.

Third, what happens when the principal and the agent have different attitudes toward risk? Shareholders, who can diversify their investment portfolios across dozens of companies, are generally willing to accept higher risk in exchange for higher expected returns. Managers, whose human capital is concentrated in a single firm, tend to be more risk-averse. A CEO whose career, reputation, and compensation are all tied to one company has a very different risk appetite than a shareholder who holds that company's stock as a small fraction of a diversified portfolio.

Jensen and Meckling's (1976) seminal work formalized these insights and demonstrated that the separation of ownership and control imposes real costs on the firm. These agency costs include monitoring expenditures principals incur to oversee agents (such as auditing and board oversight), bonding expenditures agents incur to signal alignment with principals' interests (such as accepting stock-based compensation), and the residual loss that occurs because no monitoring or bonding arrangement can perfectly align interests.

6.1.4 How Agency Problems Manifest

Agency problems are not merely theoretical concerns — they manifest in concrete, observable patterns of managerial behavior that can significantly harm shareholder value.

Managerial empire building is perhaps the most common manifestation. Managers may pursue growth through acquisitions and diversification not because these strategies maximize shareholder value, but because managing a larger firm increases their compensation, prestige, and power. CEO compensation is strongly correlated with firm size, creating a direct financial incentive to grow the firm even when growth destroys value (Tosi et al., 2000). As we discussed in Chapter 5.4, the majority of acquisitions fail to create value for the acquiring firm's shareholders, yet acquisitions remain enormously popular. Agency theory helps explain this paradox: acquisitions that destroy shareholder value may still serve managerial interests by increasing firm size and expanding the CEO's scope of authority.

Excessive diversification represents a closely related agency problem. As we examined in Chapter 5.6, firm performance tends to follow a curvilinear pattern across levels of diversification: performance improves as firms move toward related-constrained diversification but declines as firms continue diversifying into unrelated businesses (Palich et al., 2000). The optimal level of diversification for profitability, what shareholders want, is related-constrained. Managers, however, may prefer higher levels of diversification because it reduces their personal employment risk. Just as an investor diversifies a stock portfolio to reduce exposure to any single company's failure, a manager can diversify the firm's business portfolio to reduce the probability that a downturn in any one industry will produce a catastrophic quarter. The key difference is that shareholders can easily diversify their own portfolios; managers cannot easily diversify their employment across multiple firms. By over-diversifying the firm, managers effectively create a diversified portfolio at their one job, reducing personal risk at the expense of firm profitability.

Managerial employment risk, the risk of losing one's job, bonus, or reputation due to firm performance, drives much of this behavior. Managers are not primarily trying to maximize returns; they are trying to minimize variance. A steady stream of acceptable results is safer for a manager's career than a volatile pattern of spectacular wins and painful losses, even if the volatile pattern produces higher average returns.

Resistance to takeover bids provides another clear illustration. When an acquiring firm makes a bid that would deliver a substantial premium to shareholders, the target firm's managers may resist not because the bid undervalues the company, but because the acquisition would cost them their jobs. Managers may deploy defensive tactics such as poison pills, staggered boards, or golden parachutes that entrench existing management at the expense of shareholder interests (Gompers et al., 2003).

Finally, shirking and perquisite consumption represent a more subtle form of agency costs. Managers may consume private benefits at shareholder expense: lavish offices, corporate jets, excessive staffing, and unnecessary travel that improve the manager's quality of life without contributing to firm value (Jensen & Meckling, 1976). While individually these expenditures may seem trivial, they signal a broader pattern of managerial self-interest and can be symptomatic of deeper governance failures.

6.1.5 Information Asymmetry

Information asymmetry compounds every agency problem described above. Managers possess far more detailed information about the firm's operations, strategic prospects, and internal challenges than shareholders or even board members (Eisenhardt, 1989). A CEO knows which projects are underperforming, which divisions are being mismanaged, and which strategic initiatives are driven by genuine opportunity versus personal ambition. Shareholders, reviewing summary financial statements and listening to carefully scripted earnings calls, see only what management chooses to reveal.

This information advantage gives managers considerable latitude. Even well-intentioned governance mechanisms can be undermined when the people being monitored control the flow of information to those doing the monitoring.

Diversification exacerbates the information asymmetry problem. As we discussed in Chapter 5.6, highly diversified firms operate across multiple industries, each with its own competitive dynamics and performance drivers. The more business units a firm operates, the harder it becomes for outside shareholders, and even board members, to evaluate whether each unit is being managed effectively. A conglomerate operating in fifteen industries is inherently more opaque than a focused firm operating in one, and that opacity gives managers more room to pursue their own interests.

6.1.6 Principal-Principal Conflicts

The classic principal-agent framework assumes dispersed ownership, where many small shareholders face a collective action problem in monitoring professional managers. This model describes the governance challenge in the United States and the United Kingdom reasonably well. However, in many other countries, the primary governance issue is not a conflict between shareholders and managers but between controlling shareholders and minority shareholders. These are known as principal-principal conflicts (Young et al., 2008).

In countries where concentrated or family ownership is common, including much of continental Europe, East Asia, and Latin America, one shareholder or family group may hold enough shares to exercise effective control. Unlike dispersed shareholders, controlling shareholders can directly shape corporate strategy, appoint executives, and determine resource allocation. The governance problem in this context is that controlling owners may act against minority owners' interests. A controlling family might use the firm's resources to fund family members' pet projects, engage in related-party transactions that transfer wealth to family-controlled entities, or pursue strategies that preserve family control even when those strategies reduce firm value.

Business groups, such as the Japanese keiretsu and the Korean chaebol, represent a particularly important form of concentrated ownership internationally. These groups consist of networks of companies with interlocking ownership, shared management, and coordinated strategies. While business groups can create value through resource sharing, they can also facilitate the exploitation of minority shareholders when the controlling group prioritizes its own interests (Khanna & Yafeh, 2007). At the same time, cultural factors in some countries often restrict businesses within the same group from taking any action that would disadvantage one another, reinforcing mutual obligation and reciprocity across affiliated firms. Furthermore, many countries with concentrated ownership systems have fewer external regulatory constraints than the United States or the United Kingdom, making minority shareholders more vulnerable to expropriation.

Understanding principal-principal conflicts is increasingly important for strategic managers operating in a global economy. Firms pursuing international expansion must navigate governance systems that differ dramatically from the Anglo-American model. The assumption that shareholders share a common interest in maximizing firm value does not hold when one group of shareholders has the power and the incentive to redirect value toward themselves.

EX: Enron and the Failure of Governance

The collapse of Enron Corporation in 2001 remains one of the most powerful illustrations of how agency problems, information asymmetry, and governance failures can combine to produce catastrophic outcomes. At its peak, Enron was the seventh-largest company in the United States by revenue, widely praised for its innovation and aggressive growth strategy (McLean & Elkind, 2003).

Behind that reputation, Enron's senior executives were engaged in a systematic campaign to conceal the firm's true financial condition. CEO Jeffrey Skilling and CFO Andrew Fastow created a complex network of off-balance-sheet special purpose entities (SPEs) used to hide billions of dollars in debt and inflate reported earnings. These SPEs allowed Enron to move liabilities off its books while recording associated revenues, creating the appearance of profitable growth when the underlying businesses were often losing money (Healy & Palepu, 2003).

The agency problems at Enron were severe. Executives were compensated primarily through stock options, creating powerful incentives to drive up the short-term stock price regardless of underlying economic reality. Fastow personally profited from the SPEs he managed, earning tens of millions of dollars from entities that were supposed to be independent of Enron — a direct conflict of interest that exemplifies the principal-agent problem at its worst.

The board of directors failed in its monitoring role. Despite having access to information about the SPE structures, the board waived Enron's own code of ethics to allow Fastow's conflicted role, and the audit committee did not adequately scrutinize the complex financial arrangements (Bratton, 2002). Enron's financial structures were deliberately designed to be difficult for outsiders to understand, and the few insiders who raised concerns were marginalized or ignored. Arthur Andersen, Enron's external auditor, faced its own conflicts of interest: the firm earned more from consulting fees with Enron than from its audit work, undermining its independence as a monitor.

When the truth emerged in late 2001, Enron's stock price collapsed from over $90 per share to less than $1. The firm filed for what was, at the time, the largest bankruptcy in American history. Thousands of employees lost their jobs and their retirement savings, which had been heavily invested in Enron stock. Shareholders lost approximately $74 billion in value. The scandal directly led to the passage of the Sarbanes-Oxley Act of 2002, which imposed sweeping new governance requirements on publicly traded companies, requirements we will examine in the following sections of this chapter.

Enron illustrates that agency problems are not abstract theoretical constructs. When governance mechanisms fail to monitor and align managerial behavior, the consequences can be devastating for shareholders, employees, and the broader economy.

References

Berle, A. A., & Means, G. C. (1932). *The modern corporation and private property.* Macmillan.

Bratton, W. W. (2002). Enron and the dark side of shareholder value. *Tulane Law Review, 76*(5–6), 1275–1361.

Daily, C. M., Dalton, D. R., & Cannella, A. A. (2003). Corporate governance: Decades of dialogue and data. *Academy of Management Review, 28*(3), 371–382.

Eisenhardt, K. M. (1989). Agency theory: An assessment and review. *Academy of Management Review, 14*(1), 57–74.

Fama, E. F., & Jensen, M. C. (1983). Separation of ownership and control. *Journal of Law and Economics, 26*(2), 301–325.

Gompers, P., Ishii, J., & Metrick, A. (2003). Corporate governance and equity prices. *Quarterly Journal of Economics, 118*(1), 107–156.

Healy, P. M., & Palepu, K. G. (2003). The fall of Enron. *Journal of Economic Perspectives, 17*(2), 3–26.

Hirschman, A. O. (1970). *Exit, voice, and loyalty: Responses to decline in firms, organizations, and states.* Harvard University Press.

Jensen, M. C., & Meckling, W. H. (1976). Theory of the firm: Managerial behavior, agency costs and ownership structure. *Journal of Financial Economics, 3*(4), 305–360.

Khanna, T., & Yafeh, Y. (2007). Business groups in emerging markets: Paragons or parasites? *Journal of Economic Literature, 45*(2), 331–372.

McLean, B., & Elkind, P. (2003). *The smartest guys in the room: The amazing rise and scandalous fall of Enron.* Portfolio.

Palich, L. E., Cardinal, L. B., & Miller, C. C. (2000). Curvilinearity in the diversification–performance linkage: An examination of over three decades of research. *Strategic Management Journal, 21*(2), 155–174.

Smith, A. (1776). *An inquiry into the nature and causes of the wealth of nations.* W. Strahan and T. Cadell.

Tosi, H. L., Werner, S., Katz, J. P., & Gomez-Mejia, L. R. (2000). How much does performance matter? A meta-analysis of CEO pay studies. *Journal of Management, 26*(2), 301–339.

Young, M. N., Peng, M. W., Ahlstrom, D., Bruton, G. D., & Jiang, Y. (2008). Corporate governance in emerging economies: A review of the principal–principal perspective. *Journal of Management Studies, 45*(1), 196–220.

6.2 Board Roles and Governance — *How do boards oversee management?*

6.2.1 What Is a Board of Directors?

Chapter 6.1 established that the separation of ownership and control creates agency problems: managers may pursue their own interests rather than those of shareholders. If the problem is that principals cannot directly monitor their agents, the solution is to create an intermediary body with the authority, information, and incentive to do so. That intermediary is the board of directors.

A board of directors is a group of individuals elected by shareholders to represent their collective interests. The board is the primary internal governance mechanism responsible for overseeing management and ensuring that the firm is led in a manner consistent with shareholders' objectives (Fama & Jensen, 1983). Corporate governance thus involves three key relationships: the owners (shareholders) who provide capital, the managers (led by the CEO) who make strategic and operational decisions, and the board of directors who serve as the elected representatives of owners and the overseers of management. The board occupies a critical intermediary position — it is neither ownership nor management, but stands between the two to ensure that one is accountable to the other.

In theory, this structure provides an elegant solution to the agency problem. Shareholders, who are too dispersed to monitor management directly, delegate that monitoring function to a smaller, more informed body. In practice, however, the effectiveness of boards varies enormously, and the history of corporate governance is in many ways a history of efforts to make boards work as they are supposed to.

6.2.2 Board Composition

The composition of a board, who sits on it and what relationships those individuals have with the firm, is a primary determinant of its effectiveness as a governance mechanism.

Boards in the United States and the United Kingdom are typically composed of three categories of directors. Inside directors are current employees of the firm, most commonly the CEO and other senior executives. They bring deep operational knowledge but their employment relationship with the firm, and particularly their reporting relationship to the CEO, compromises their independence. An inside director is unlikely to challenge the CEO who controls their career advancement and compensation.

Outside directors, also called independent directors, are individuals with no material relationship to the firm. They are not current or recent employees, do not provide consulting or legal services to the company, and have no family ties to management. Their independence from management is what makes them valuable as monitors, since they have no personal stake in protecting the CEO and no career consequences for asking difficult questions.

Related outsiders occupy a gray area between these two categories. These are individuals who have some prior connection to the firm: former employees, consultants, family members of executives, or professionals whose firms do business with the company. While they are technically not insiders, their relationships with management may compromise their willingness to exercise truly independent oversight (Dalton et al., 1998).

The trend in corporate governance over the past several decades has been decisively toward majority-independent boards. This shift accelerated dramatically with the passage of the Sarbanes-Oxley Act (SOX) of 2002, enacted in the wake of the Enron, WorldCom, and other corporate scandals discussed in Chapter 6.1. SOX imposed new requirements on board composition, mandating that audit committees be composed entirely of independent directors and requiring at least one member with financial expertise. The legislation reflected a straightforward governance logic: if boards had failed to prevent massive fraud, the solution was to ensure that boards had the independence and expertise necessary to fulfill their monitoring function (Romano, 2005).

The benefits of outsider dominance on boards include broader access to knowledge and independent oversight of strategy. However, outside directors also face disadvantages: they have less direct access to operational information than insiders, fewer opportunities to build relationships with non-board executives, and may lack the deep industry-specific knowledge necessary to evaluate complex strategic decisions (Adams & Ferreira, 2007). Effective boards typically include a mix of insiders and outsiders, leveraging insiders' operational knowledge while relying on outsiders' independence for oversight. The case for insiders is not only operational: the type of career experience shaping a manager's human capital affects how accurately they can judge their firm's strategic prospects, as revealed by the foresight in managers' open-market stock purchases ahead of new product launches (Asghar et al., 2026).

6.2.3 Key Roles of the Board

The board of directors performs several critical functions that collectively address the agency problems identified in the previous section.

The most fundamental role is monitoring the executive. The board ensures that the CEO and senior management are making decisions that serve shareholders' interests. This includes reviewing strategic plans, evaluating financial performance, questioning major capital allocation decisions, and holding management accountable for results. Effective monitoring requires that board members be willing to ask difficult questions and challenge management's assumptions.

Executive compensation design is another essential board function. As we will explore in detail in Chapter 6.3, the structure of CEO compensation is one of the most powerful tools available for aligning managerial and shareholder interests. The board, typically through a dedicated compensation committee, determines how much the CEO is paid, how that pay is divided between salary, bonuses, and equity-based incentives, and what performance metrics trigger variable compensation. Getting compensation design right is one of the most impactful governance decisions a board makes.

Succession planning is a board responsibility that often receives insufficient attention until a crisis forces the issue. The board must identify and prepare potential successors for the CEO role, ensuring that the firm has qualified leadership available in the event of an unexpected departure. Companies that lack succession plans face significant strategic risk, and the best boards maintain active plans that are updated regularly (Berns & Klarner, 2017).

Auditing and financial oversight ensure the accuracy and integrity of financial reporting. The board's audit committee is responsible for overseeing the relationship with external auditors, reviewing financial statements, and monitoring internal controls. This function is directly tied to the information asymmetry problem discussed in Chapter 6.1: if managers control the flow of financial information, the audit committee serves as an independent check on the reliability of that information.

Many board members also serve as strategic advisors. Because directors are often current or former CEOs and senior executives at other firms, they bring substantial strategic expertise that can benefit the company. However, this advisory role creates a tension with the monitoring function. If the board recommends a strategic course of action and the CEO follows that advice and it fails, the board is then in a difficult position to hold the CEO accountable for poor performance, since the CEO was, after all, following the board's own guidance. This tension means boards must carefully balance their advisory and oversight roles.

Finally, board members can serve an advocacy function. Directors who hold positions at major financial institutions, other corporations, or industry associations can leverage those relationships to benefit the firm, for instance by helping secure more favorable financing terms or facilitating strategic partnerships.

6.2.4 Board Effectiveness and Evolving Expectations

For much of the twentieth century, boards of directors at many large American corporations were, to put it bluntly, rubber stamps. Boards were frequently populated with the CEO's friends, business associates, and social connections. Board meetings were brief, perfunctory affairs in which directors approved management's proposals with minimal discussion and even less dissent. Directors faced no personal liability for governance failures, and the compensation they received, while not trivial, was treated more as a social perk than as payment for serious oversight work (Lorsch & MacIver, 1989).

This culture changed dramatically in the early 2000s. The wave of corporate scandals that produced the

Sarbanes-Oxley Act also transformed the expectations placed on boards and their individual members. Post-SOX and post-financial-crisis reforms introduced the possibility of personal liability for directors who fail to exercise adequate oversight. This single change — making directors personally accountable for governance failures — had a profound effect on board behavior. When a directorship carried the risk of a lawsuit rather than merely the reward of a quarterly stipend, directors became far more engaged.

The results of this shift are measurable. Board committees met more frequently in the post-SOX period, directors and officers (D&O) insurance premiums roughly doubled, and median director pay at large firms rose more than fifty percent between 2001 and 2004 — outpacing the increase in CEO pay over the same period. Boards also became larger and more independent, with a greater representation of financial experts, lawyers, and retired executives rather than current operating executives (Linck et al., 2009).

Board compensation has risen in tandem with these expanded responsibilities. Directors of S&P 500 companies now average roughly $300,000 or more in annual compensation, reflecting the expectation that they will devote significant time and effort to governance. This compensation increasingly includes equity components, such as stock grants and options, that tie directors' financial interests to firm performance, further aligning their incentives with those of shareholders.

6.2.5 CEO Duality

One of the most debated questions in corporate governance is whether the same individual should serve as both the CEO and the chairperson of the board of directors. This practice, known as CEO duality, is common in the United States but less so internationally.

Proponents of duality argue from a unity-of-command perspective. Having one person serve as both CEO and chair provides clear strategic focus, eliminates potential confusion about who speaks for the company, and enables faster decision-making based on firsthand operational knowledge. When the CEO also chairs the board, there is no ambiguity about strategic direction and no risk of conflicting signals from the two most powerful positions in the firm (Finkelstein & D'Aveni, 1994).

Opponents of duality argue from the agency theory perspective that has grounded this entire chapter. If the board's primary function is to monitor the CEO, then allowing the CEO to also lead the board creates an inherent conflict of interest. The CEO-chair effectively oversees their own performance, a structure that undermines board independence. When the same person sets the board's agenda, controls information flow to directors, and leads the meetings at which their own performance is evaluated, meaningful oversight is difficult to achieve.

International practice varies considerably on this question. In the United Kingdom, separation of the CEO and chair roles is effectively required under corporate governance codes. Many other countries, including Singapore and Russia, recommend or require separation. The United States, by contrast, has historically been more permissive of duality, though the trend has moved toward separation in recent years as governance reforms have emphasized board independence (Krause et al., 2014).

6.2.6 Shareholder Activism and Ownership Concentration

While the board of directors is the primary internal governance mechanism, shareholders themselves also play an important role in disciplining management, particularly when ownership is concentrated enough to overcome the collective action problems described in Chapter 6.1.

Ownership concentration refers to the extent to which a firm's shares are held by large-block shareholders, typically defined as investors holding at least one percent of the company's outstanding shares. Large-block shareholders have both the incentive and the ability to monitor management that dispersed individual shareholders lack. Because they have a substantial financial stake in the firm, the returns from effective monitoring exceed the costs of exercising that oversight.

Institutional investors — pension funds, mutual funds, and index funds that pool the resources of individual investors into large investment portfolios — have become the dominant force in American equity markets. Institutional investors now own roughly 70–80 percent of the shares in U.S. publicly listed companies, a dramatic increase from approximately 7–8 percent in 1950 (Blume & Keim, 2012). This concentration of ownership has fundamentally altered the governance landscape. Where individual shareholders once faced an insurmountable collective action problem, institutional investors now have the scale and the organizational capacity to engage directly with management on issues of strategy, compensation, and governance.

Institutional investors are increasingly active in exercising their voting power. Rather than simply selling shares when dissatisfied with management (the "Wall Street Walk"), large institutional investors now routinely engage with boards, propose shareholder resolutions, and vote against management on contentious issues. The rise of passive index funds has paradoxically intensified this activism: because index funds cannot sell shares of underperforming companies without abandoning the index, they have a strong incentive to improve governance at companies they are effectively required to hold (Appel et al., 2016).

Activist investors represent a more aggressive form of shareholder engagement. These are typically hedge funds that acquire significant positions in companies they believe are undervalued due to poor management. Activists then publicly or privately pressure management to make specific changes: divesting underperforming divisions, returning capital to shareholders, replacing board members, or pursuing a sale. The market for corporate control, in which poorly managed firms become targets for hostile takeovers, serves as the ultimate external governance mechanism: if internal mechanisms fail to discipline management, the threat of an outside acquirer removing management provides a final check on agency problems (Jensen, 1986).

EX: The Board Transformation at General Electric

General Electric provides a compelling illustration of how board composition, effectiveness, and shareholder activism interact in practice. For decades under CEO Jack Welch (1981–2001), GE's board was widely regarded as a model of corporate governance. The company was consistently profitable, its stock price rose dramatically, and the board was populated with high-profile business leaders. Yet in retrospect, the board's relationship with Welch exhibited many characteristics of the rubber-stamp era, marked by deep deference to a powerful, charismatic CEO who dominated strategic decision-making (Gryta & Mann, 2020).

The governance weaknesses became apparent under Welch's successor, Jeff Immelt, who led GE from 2001 to 2017. During Immelt's tenure, GE's stock price declined significantly, the company's aggressive diversification strategy produced disappointing returns, and its financial services division, GE Capital, exposed the firm to enormous risk during the 2008 financial crisis. Despite these mounting problems, the board was slow to act. Immelt remained in the CEO role for sixteen years, and the board continued to approve substantial executive compensation packages even as shareholder value eroded. Critics argued that the board lacked the independence and willingness to challenge a CEO who had inherited the authority and prestige of the Welch era (Gryta & Mann, 2020).

The turning point came through shareholder activism. In 2015, activist investor Trian Fund Management, led by Nelson Peltz, acquired a roughly $2.5 billion stake in GE and began publicly pushing for strategic changes. Trian argued that GE was over-diversified, that its conglomerate structure destroyed value, and that the company needed to divest non-core businesses and return capital to shareholders. The pressure contributed to Immelt's departure in 2017 and the appointment of John Flannery as CEO, followed by Larry Culp in 2018 — the first outside CEO in GE's history. Under Culp, GE undertook a radical restructuring, ultimately splitting into three separate publicly traded companies focused on aviation, healthcare, and energy, a dramatic reversal of the diversification strategy that the board had supported for years (Gryta & Mann, 2020).

The GE case illustrates several themes from this section. The board's deference to a powerful CEO undermined its monitoring function for years. The shift toward independent, engaged boards, accelerated by post-SOX reforms, eventually changed board expectations, but cultural inertia delayed reform at GE. Ultimately, it was external pressure from activist shareholders, not internal board initiative, that forced the strategic changes necessary to address GE's decline. The case demonstrates that governance mechanisms work best not in isolation but as a system: when one mechanism fails, others, particularly shareholder activism and the market for corporate control, can step in to correct course.

References

Adams, R. B., & Ferreira, D. (2007). A theory of friendly boards. *Journal of Finance, 62*(1), 217–250.

Appel, I. R., Gormley, T. A., & Keim, D. B. (2016). Passive investors, not passive owners. *Journal of Financial Economics, 121*(1), 111–141.

Asghar, N., Coff, R., Mawdsley, J. K., & Meyer-Doyle, P. (2026). Human capital and strategic foresight: Evidence from managers' stock purchases. *Strategy Science*. Advance online publication. https://doi.org/10.1287/stsc.2024.0328

Berns, K. V. D., & Klarner, P. (2017). A review of the CEO succession literature and a future research program. *Academy of Management Perspectives, 31*(2), 83–108.

Blume, M. E., & Keim, D. B. (2012). *Institutional investors and stock market liquidity: Trends and relationships* (Working paper). Wharton School, University of Pennsylvania.

Dalton, D. R., Daily, C. M., Ellstrand, A. E., & Johnson, J. L. (1998). Meta-analytic reviews of board composition, leadership structure, and financial performance. *Strategic Management Journal, 19*(3), 269–290.

Fama, E. F., & Jensen, M. C. (1983). Separation of ownership and control. *Journal of Law and Economics, 26*(2), 301–325.

Finkelstein, S., & D'Aveni, R. A. (1994). CEO duality as a double-edged sword: How boards of directors balance entrenchment avoidance and unity of command. *Academy of Management Journal, 37*(5), 1079–1108.

Gryta, T., & Mann, T. (2020). *Lights out: Pride, delusion, and the fall of General Electric.* Houghton Mifflin Harcourt.

Jensen, M. C. (1986). Agency costs of free cash flow, corporate finance, and takeovers. *American Economic Review, 76*(2), 323–329.

Krause, R., Semadeni, M., & Cannella, A. A. (2014). CEO duality: A review and research agenda. *Journal of Management, 40*(1), 256–286.

Linck, J. S., Netter, J. M., & Yang, T. (2009). The effects and unintended consequences of the Sarbanes-Oxley Act on the supply and demand for directors. *Review of Financial Studies, 22*(8), 3287–3328.

Lorsch, J. W., & MacIver, E. (1989). *Pawns or potentates: The reality of America's corporate boards.* Harvard Business School Press.

Romano, R. (2005). The Sarbanes-Oxley Act and the making of quack corporate governance. *Yale Law Journal, 114*(7), 1521–1611.

6.3 CEO Incentives and Compensation — *How do we align manager and shareholder interests?*

6.3.1 The Logic of Incentive Alignment

> *"Show me the incentive and I will show you the outcome." — Charlie Munger*

The previous two sections established that the separation of ownership and control creates agency problems (Ch 6.1) and that the board of directors serves as the primary internal mechanism for monitoring management (Ch 6.2). But monitoring alone is insufficient. Even the most engaged, independent board cannot observe every decision a CEO makes. If governance relied entirely on monitoring, the costs would be prohibitive and the gaps would be exploitable. The complementary approach is to design compensation structures that make the agent's interests converge with the principal's, so that self-interested behavior by the CEO also serves shareholders.

This insight is not new. Adam Smith observed that we do not expect our dinner from the benevolence of the butcher, the brewer, or the baker, but from their regard to their own interest (Smith, 1776). The logic of executive compensation follows exactly this principle: rather than relying on managerial goodwill or the hope that executives will voluntarily prioritize shareholders, governance systems use financial incentives to ensure that what is good for the CEO is also good for the owners. Compensation design is therefore not merely a reward for services rendered — it is a strategic governance tool, one of the most powerful mechanisms available for aligning the interests of principals and agents (Jensen & Murphy, 1990).

The challenge, as we will see, is that compensation design is far more difficult to get right than this clean theoretical logic suggests. Poorly designed incentives can create perverse outcomes that make agency problems worse rather than better.

6.3.2 Components of Executive Compensation

Modern executive compensation packages typically consist of several components, each serving a distinct function in the overall incentive structure.

Base salary is the fixed component of compensation, providing the CEO with a predictable income regardless of firm performance. Base salary serves an important role in attracting and retaining qualified executives, since few top-tier candidates would accept a position where one hundred percent of their compensation was at risk. However, because base salary does not vary with performance, it does nothing to align the CEO's interests with those of shareholders. A CEO earning a $1.5 million base salary receives that amount whether the stock price doubles or drops by half.

Annual bonuses are tied to short-term performance metrics such as revenue growth, net income, operating margins, or specific operational targets. Bonuses introduce a variable component that rewards executives for achieving specific goals within a given fiscal year. The strength of bonus structures is their ability to focus managerial attention on measurable outcomes. Their weakness is that they emphasize short-term results, potentially at the expense of long-term value creation. A CEO who can earn a substantial bonus by hitting this year's earnings target may be tempted to cut R&D spending, defer maintenance, or engage in earnings management to reach the threshold, actions that boost short-term numbers while undermining the firm's competitive position over time.

Long-term incentives are designed to address this short-term bias. Stock options give the CEO the right to purchase company shares at a predetermined price (the strike price) at some future date. If the stock price rises above the strike price, the CEO profits; if it falls below, the options are worthless. Restricted stock units (RSUs) grant the CEO actual shares of stock that vest over a multi-year period, requiring the executive to remain with the firm to receive the full benefit. Performance shares tie equity grants to the achievement of specific long-term performance metrics; for example, the CEO might receive shares only if the firm's total shareholder return exceeds an industry benchmark over a three-year period. Each of these instruments is designed to tie the CEO's personal wealth to the long-term value of the firm, creating a financial incentive to make decisions that benefit shareholders over an extended horizon (Frydman & Jenter, 2010).

Stock ownership requirements take this logic one step further by requiring CEOs to become substantial owners of company stock, not just recipients of options or RSUs, but genuine shareholders with a significant personal financial stake. Many boards now require that CEOs hold stock worth several multiples of their base salary. The goal is straightforward: when the CEO owns a meaningful amount of the company's stock, their financial interests are directly aligned with those of other shareholders. Gains and losses are shared proportionally, and the CEO has a personal stake in the long-term health of the firm that goes beyond any single year's bonus or option grant.

6.3.3 The CEO Pay Problem

While the theoretical logic of incentive alignment is sound, the practical application has produced outcomes that generate significant controversy. CEO compensation at major corporations has grown dramatically over the past several decades, both in absolute terms and relative to the pay of average workers. The CEO-to-worker pay ratio at large American firms significantly increased from 21-to-1 in 1965 and peaked at 366-to-1 in 2000 at the height of the dot-com bubble, when CEOs earned in a day what their typical employee earned in a year (Mishel & Wolfe, 2019). While this ratio has moderated somewhat, it remains extraordinarily high by historical and international standards.

Part of the explanation for rising CEO pay is straightforward market dynamics: the demand for executive talent, particularly at the largest and most complex firms, has increased while the supply of individuals with the requisite skills and experience remains limited. But agency theory offers a more troubling explanation that is rooted in the very incentive structures designed to solve the principal-agent problem.

For compensation to function as an effective incentive, it must represent a meaningful percentage of the CEO's existing wealth. A \$5 million bonus is a powerful motivator for an executive whose net worth is \$10 million; it is far less motivating for an executive whose net worth is \$500 million. As CEOs accumulate wealth through successive years of generous pay packages, ever-larger packages become necessary to maintain the same incentive effect. This creates a self-reinforcing cycle: high pay leads to greater wealth, which requires even higher pay to produce the same proportional incentive, which leads to still greater wealth, and so on. The result is a compensation escalator that boards find difficult to reverse, particularly when compensation committees benchmark CEO pay against peer groups, a practice that tends to ratchet pay upward across the entire market as each firm tries to pay its CEO at or above the median (Bizjak et al., 2008).

Board compensation committees face the unenviable task of navigating these dynamics. They must set pay levels high enough to attract and retain top talent, structure incentives that genuinely align managerial and shareholder interests, and do so under intense public scrutiny. The Dodd-Frank Act of 2010 introduced "say-on-pay" provisions requiring publicly traded firms to hold non-binding shareholder votes on executive compensation packages, adding another layer of accountability, though the non-binding nature of these votes limits their practical impact (Thomas et al., 2012).

6.3.4 Unintended Consequences of Incentive Design

Perhaps the most important lesson of executive compensation is that incentive structures often produce outcomes their designers did not intend. The history of CEO pay is littered with examples of compensation mechanisms that, while theoretically sound, created perverse incentives in practice.

Stock options, long regarded as the gold standard of incentive alignment, illustrate this problem clearly. Options have an asymmetric payoff structure: if the stock price rises above the strike price, the CEO's gain is theoretically unlimited, but if the stock price falls, the CEO simply does not exercise the options and loses nothing beyond the opportunity cost. This asymmetry can incentivize excessive risk-taking. A CEO with a large options package has a strong incentive to pursue high-risk strategies that could produce dramatic stock price increases, because the upside is captured in full while the downside is limited. From the CEO's perspective, a strategy with a fifty percent chance of doubling the stock price and a fifty percent chance of cutting it in half is enormously attractive — the expected value of their options is strongly positive. From shareholders' perspective, this same gamble may be far less appealing, particularly if the downside scenario threatens the firm's survival (Sanders & Hambrick, 2007).

Stock options can also incentivize short-term stock price manipulation rather than genuine long-term value creation. Because options become more valuable as the stock price rises, CEOs have an incentive to boost the stock price in the short term through aggressive earnings guidance, accounting manipulation, share buybacks timed to option vesting periods, or other tactics that inflate the price without creating real economic value. The wave of accounting scandals in the early 2000s, including Enron and WorldCom (discussed in Ch 6.1), was driven in part by option-heavy compensation packages that rewarded executives for reported earnings rather than actual performance.

Annual bonuses tied to specific financial thresholds create their own perverse incentives. When a CEO's bonus is triggered by reaching a particular earnings target, behavior tends to cluster around that threshold. If the firm is clearly going to miss the target, the CEO may have an incentive to take a "big bath," writing off as many losses as possible in the current period to set up an easier target for the following year. If the firm has already exceeded the target, the CEO may defer revenue or accelerate expenses into the current period to bank performance for future bonuses. These behaviors, known collectively as earnings management, can distort financial reporting and mislead shareholders about the firm's true performance (Healy, 1985).

Recognizing these problems, governance experts have increasingly advocated for multi-dimensional performance metrics that reduce the ability to game any single measure. Balanced scorecards that incorporate financial performance, customer satisfaction, internal process quality, and innovation metrics provide a more complete picture of managerial performance and make it harder for executives to optimize one measure at the expense of others (Kaplan & Norton, 1992). Similarly, the shift from stock options toward RSUs and performance shares, instruments with less extreme payoff asymmetry, reflects an effort to reduce the risk-taking incentives embedded in traditional option-based compensation.

6.3.5 Golden Parachutes and Change-of-Control Provisions

Golden parachutes are large severance packages that are triggered when a change in corporate control occurs, typically an acquisition or merger. These packages can be worth tens or even hundreds of millions of dollars, and they are among the most controversial elements of executive compensation.

The governance rationale for golden parachutes is grounded directly in the agency problems discussed in Chapter 6.1. As we noted, managers may resist takeover bids that would benefit shareholders because the acquisition threatens their jobs. This resistance represents a clear case of managerial self-interest overriding shareholder welfare. Golden parachutes are designed to solve this problem by eliminating the financial penalty associated with job loss. If the CEO knows they will receive a substantial severance package regardless of whether the acquisition proceeds, they have less reason to resist a deal that serves shareholders' interests. The golden parachute reduces managerial employment risk, freeing managers to evaluate acquisition offers on their merits for shareholders rather than on the personal consequences for their own careers (Lambert & Larcker, 1985).

The connection to the market for corporate control is direct. As discussed in Chapter 6.2, the threat of hostile takeover serves as an external governance mechanism: poorly managed firms become acquisition targets, and the acquiring firm replaces incumbent management. For this mechanism to function effectively, incumbent managers cannot be allowed to block value-creating acquisitions solely to protect their own positions. Golden parachutes, in this view, facilitate the market for corporate control by reducing managerial resistance to takeovers (as discussed in Ch 5.4 on mergers and acquisitions).

Critics, however, see golden parachutes very differently. From this perspective, golden parachutes reward executives for failure — managers receive enormous payouts precisely when they have performed so poorly that the firm becomes an attractive takeover target. The packages can also make acquisitions more expensive for the acquiring firm, since the cost of triggering multiple golden parachutes is factored into the deal price. And because golden parachutes are negotiated by the very executives who benefit from them, albeit with board approval, they raise concerns about managerial self-dealing that echo the broader agency problems governance is supposed to address.

EX: Wells Fargo and the Limits of Incentive Design

The Wells Fargo fake accounts scandal, which came to public attention in 2016, provides a powerful illustration of how compensation incentives can cascade through an organization with devastating consequences. Wells Fargo had long been admired on Wall Street for its consistent cross-selling performance, the number of products (checking accounts, credit cards, mortgages, insurance) held by each customer. CEO John Stumpf regularly highlighted the firm's cross-sell ratio as a key performance metric, and the bank's compensation system at all levels was designed to reward employees for increasing that ratio (Independent Directors of the Board of Wells Fargo & Company, 2017).

The incentive structure was straightforward: branch employees received bonuses and could avoid termination by meeting aggressive sales targets tied to the number of new accounts opened. Managers were evaluated on their branches' sales numbers. Regional leaders were assessed on aggregate cross-selling performance. And the CEO's compensation and public reputation were tied to the firm-wide metrics that all of these individual targets fed into. In theory, this cascading incentive structure should have aligned employee behavior with shareholder value, since more products per customer meant more revenue and deeper customer relationships.

In practice, the pressure to meet unrealistic sales targets led thousands of employees to open millions of unauthorized accounts in customers' names. Employees created fake email addresses, forged signatures, and transferred customer funds without consent to inflate their sales numbers. The behavior was not the work of a few rogue employees — investigations revealed that approximately 3.5 million accounts may have been opened without customer authorization over a period of years, involving thousands of employees across the organization (Independent Directors of the Board of Wells Fargo & Company, 2017).

The case illustrates several lessons about incentive design. First, compensation metrics that are too narrowly focused invite gaming. Wells Fargo's obsessive focus on cross-sell ratios created an environment in which employees optimized the measurable metric, new accounts opened, without regard for whether those accounts represented genuine customer value. Second, incentive problems are not limited to the CEO suite. Compensation structures cascade through organizations, and poorly designed incentives at any level can produce destructive behavior at scale. Third, the board's monitoring function failed. Despite internal reports and employee complaints about the aggressive sales culture, the board did not intervene effectively until the scandal became public.

The consequences were severe. Wells Fargo paid over \$3 billion in fines and settlements. CEO Stumpf resigned under pressure and was forced to forfeit approximately \$41 million in unvested equity compensation, a rare example of clawback provisions being enforced. The bank's reputation suffered lasting damage, and regulators imposed an unprecedented asset cap that limited Wells Fargo's growth for years. The scandal demonstrates that compensation design is not merely a governance technicality — it shapes organizational behavior at every level, and when the incentives are wrong, the consequences can extend far beyond the executive suite (Tayan, 2019).

References

Bizjak, J. M., Lemmon, M. L., & Naveen, L. (2008). Does the use of peer groups contribute to higher pay and less efficient compensation? *Journal of Financial Economics, 90*(2), 152–168.

Frydman, C., & Jenter, D. (2010). CEO compensation. *Annual Review of Financial Economics, 2*(1), 75–102.

Healy, P. M. (1985). The effect of bonus schemes on accounting decisions. *Journal of Accounting and Economics, 7*(1–3), 85–107.

Independent Directors of the Board of Wells Fargo & Company. (2017). *Sales practices investigation report.* Wells Fargo & Company.

Jensen, M. C., & Murphy, K. J. (1990). Performance pay and top-management incentives. *Journal of Political Economy, 98*(2), 225–264.

Kaplan, R. S., & Norton, D. P. (1992). The balanced scorecard — Measures that drive performance. *Harvard Business Review, 70*(1), 71–79.

Lambert, R. A., & Larcker, D. F. (1985). Golden parachutes, executive decision-making, and shareholder wealth. *Journal of Accounting and Economics, 7*(1–3), 179–203.

Mishel, L., & Wolfe, J. (2019). *CEO compensation has grown 940% since 1978: Typical worker compensation has risen only 12% during that time.* Economic Policy Institute.

Sanders, W. G., & Hambrick, D. C. (2007). Swinging for the fences: The effects of CEO stock options on company risk taking and performance. *Academy of Management Journal, 50*(5), 1055–1078.

Smith, A. (1776). *An inquiry into the nature and causes of the wealth of nations.* W. Strahan and T. Cadell.

Tayan, B. (2019). The Wells Fargo cross-selling scandal. *Stanford Closer Look Series*, Corporate Governance Research Initiative.

Thomas, R. S., Palmiter, A. R., & Cotter, J. F. (2012). Dodd-Frank's say on pay: Will it lead to a greater role for shareholders in corporate governance? *Cornell Law Review, 97*(5), 1213–1266.

6.4 Ethical Decision-Making — *How should leaders navigate ethical dilemmas?*

6.4.1 Why Ethics Belongs in a Strategy Textbook

> *"In looking for people to hire, you look for three qualities: integrity, intelligence, and energy. And if they don't have the first, the other two will kill you." — Warren Buffett*

Strategy is ultimately about choices — which markets to enter, which capabilities to develop, how to compete, how to grow. Many of these choices have ethical dimensions that are inseparable from their strategic consequences. A pharmaceutical company deciding how to price a life-saving drug is making both a strategic and an ethical decision. A manufacturer choosing whether to source from a low-cost supplier with questionable labor practices is weighing competitive advantage against moral responsibility. A technology firm deciding what user data to collect confronts tradeoffs between profitability and privacy that no purely strategic framework can resolve.

This chapter has argued that effective governance produces better strategic outcomes by aligning the interests of managers and shareholders (Ch 6.1–6.3). But governance serves a broader purpose as well: effective governance produces ethical behavior in formulating and implementing strategies (Paine, 1994). A firm with a brilliant strategy executed unethically faces legal penalties, reputational damage, and the erosion of stakeholder trust that can undermine its competitive position far more decisively than any rival's actions. As we discussed in Chapter 1.6, ethical behavior is often what determines whether the firm maintains the trust of its stakeholders, and without stakeholder trust, even the most well-crafted strategy will eventually fail.

Ethics is not a constraint on strategy; it is a component of it. The firms that endure are not merely those that create the most value in the short term, but those that create value in ways that their stakeholders, their employees, and the broader society regard as legitimate.

6.4.2 Common Ethical Dilemmas in Business

Strategic managers routinely face ethical dilemmas, situations in which there is no course of action that satisfies all moral obligations simultaneously. Understanding the most common categories of ethical dilemmas helps managers recognize them when they arise and reason through them more effectively.

Conflicts of interest occur when the personal interests of managers or board members diverge from their fiduciary duties. As Chapter 6.1 established, the entire principal-agent problem is fundamentally a conflict of interest. But conflicts extend beyond the executive suite. A board member who sits on the boards of two companies negotiating a contract faces a conflict that cannot be resolved simply by serving both firms well. Recognizing and disclosing conflicts is the first step; managing them requires governance structures, including recusal policies, independent oversight, and transparent decision-making, that minimize the opportunity for self-dealing.

Information asymmetry and disclosure present another category of ethical dilemma. Managers possess information that shareholders, regulators, and customers do not have. Securities law establishes minimum disclosure requirements, but legal minimums do not necessarily coincide with ethical obligations. A company that discovers a potential safety defect faces a choice: disclose immediately and accept recall costs, or wait until the problem is confirmed and risk consumer harm. In each case, the ethical obligation to transparency may conflict with short-term financial interest.

Competitive practices raise questions about where aggressive competition ends and unethical behavior begins. Industrial espionage, predatory pricing designed to destroy smaller competitors, and misappropriation of trade secrets clearly cross ethical lines. But many practices fall into gray areas. Is it ethical to hire a competitor's key engineer primarily to gain access to their knowledge? Is it acceptable to lobby for regulations that disadvantage rivals without serving the public interest? Strategic managers must navigate these questions with an awareness that competitive advantage pursued without ethical boundaries can produce short-term gains at the cost of long-term reputational damage.

Supply chain ethics have become increasingly prominent as firms globalize their operations. When a company sources materials or components from suppliers in developing countries, it assumes some degree of responsibility for the labor practices, environmental standards, and human rights conditions in those supply chains. A firm that profits from low-cost manufacturing while its suppliers employ child labor or subject workers to unsafe conditions faces both moral criticism and practical risk, as consumers, regulators, and advocacy groups increasingly hold firms accountable for conditions throughout their supply chains, not just within their own facilities (Locke, 2013).

Product safety dilemmas arise when cost optimization pressures conflict with consumer welfare. Every product design involves tradeoffs between cost, performance, and safety, and the ethical question is how those tradeoffs should be resolved. As we will see in the extended example below, the consequences of prioritizing cost reduction over safety can be catastrophic, not only for the consumers who are harmed but for the firm itself.

Going Deeper: Five Lenses for Ethical Analysis

When confronting an ethical dilemma, strategic managers benefit from structured frameworks that clarify the competing considerations at stake. Most business ethics texts draw on secular philosophical traditions, but religious foundations shape how many leaders actually reason about moral questions and deserve a place alongside them. Five lenses are particularly useful for evaluating business decisions.

The utilitarian approach evaluates actions based on their consequences, seeking the greatest good for the greatest number of people (Mill, 1863). Under this framework, a manager would assess the total benefits and costs of a decision across all affected parties and choose the option that produces the best net outcome. Utilitarianism is intuitive and widely applied in business, as cost-benefit analysis is essentially a utilitarian exercise. However, it can justify decisions that harm a minority if the benefits to the majority are sufficiently large, and it requires predicting consequences that may be uncertain or difficult to measure.

The rights-based approach holds that certain fundamental rights, including the rights to life, safety, privacy, and honest dealing, must be respected regardless of consequences (Kant, 1785/1993). Under this framework, an action that violates someone's fundamental rights is wrong even if it produces a net positive outcome for society. A company cannot ethically expose consumers to a known safety risk simply because the cost of a recall exceeds the expected cost of injuries. Rights-based reasoning provides strong protections for individuals but can be difficult to apply when rights conflict with one another; for instance, a firm's right to competitive information may conflict with an individual's right to privacy.

The justice approach focuses on the fair distribution of benefits and burdens across stakeholders (Rawls, 1971). Are the costs of a strategic decision distributed equitably, or do they fall disproportionately on those with the least power? A plant closure that generates savings for shareholders while devastating a local community raises justice concerns even if it is strategically sound. The justice framework is particularly relevant to stakeholder management, as it forces managers to consider whether the most vulnerable stakeholders are bearing an unfair share of the consequences.

Virtue ethics takes a different approach entirely, asking not what consequences an action produces or what rules it follows, but what a person of good character would do in this situation (Aristotle, trans. 2009). This framework emphasizes the moral qualities of the decision-maker, such as honesty, courage, fairness, and compassion, rather than the mechanics of the decision itself. Virtue ethics is valuable because it acknowledges that ethical behavior is not simply a matter of following rules but of cultivating judgment, integrity, and moral awareness over time.

Faith-based ethics anchors moral obligations in religious foundations rather than in secular reasoning alone. The Judeo-Christian tradition, for example, draws on natural law (the idea that there is a moral order discoverable through reason and revelation), stewardship (the principle that managers hold resources in trust rather than owning them outright, with corresponding duties to use those resources wisely), and covenant (a relational commitment that extends obligations to employees, communities, and partners beyond what any contract specifies). Islamic business ethics provides a parallel structure, shaping global finance through prohibitions on interest (*riba*) and excessive uncertainty (*gharar*). For many leaders and employees, faith is not supplementary to ethical reasoning but its primary foundation, and it often arrives at conclusions consistent with the secular frameworks while grounding those conclusions in a different source of authority.

No single framework provides complete answers to every ethical dilemma. In practice, ethical reasoning requires weighing multiple perspectives and accepting that reasonable people may reach different conclusions. The value of these frameworks is not that they produce definitive answers but that they ensure managers consider the full range of moral dimensions before making strategic choices.

6.4.3 The Role of Organizational Culture in Ethical Behavior

Individual ethical reasoning matters, but organizational behavior is shaped far more powerfully by culture. As we discussed in Chapter 3.5, organizational culture refers to the shared values, beliefs, and norms that govern how people within a firm think, behave, and make decisions. Culture determines whether employees feel empowered to raise ethical concerns or pressured to cut corners, whether whistleblowers are protected or punished, and whether ethical behavior is genuinely valued or merely professed.

The concept of "tone at the top" captures the outsized influence that senior leadership has on organizational ethics. Employees at every level observe what leaders actually do — not what they say in speeches or write in codes of conduct — and calibrate their own behavior accordingly. A CEO who tolerates minor ethical lapses when they produce good financial results sends a clear signal that the firm's stated values are negotiable. A manager who pressures subordinates to meet unrealistic targets without asking how those targets are being met creates conditions in which ethical shortcuts become rational responses to institutional incentives. Research consistently shows that leadership behavior is the single strongest predictor of ethical culture within organizations (Treviño et al., 2006).

Formal ethics programs, including codes of conduct, ethics hotlines, compliance training, and dedicated compliance officers, play an important supporting role, but they are insufficient without a cultural foundation that takes ethics seriously. A code of conduct that prohibits fraud is meaningless if the firm's culture rewards the kind of aggressive behavior that leads to fraud. An ethics hotline that employees are afraid to use because they fear retaliation provides no real protection. The most effective organizations pair formal compliance structures with informal cultural norms that reinforce ethical behavior through everyday expectations, peer accountability, and leadership example. The Wells Fargo scandal, discussed in Chapter 6.3, demonstrated how a culture of intense sales pressure overrode formal compliance mechanisms and led to systemic misconduct across the organization.

6.4.4 Legal Compliance vs. Ethical Responsibility

> *"It takes 20 years to build a reputation and five minutes to ruin it. If you think about that, you'll do things differently."* — *Warren Buffett*

A common misconception in business is that legal compliance and ethical behavior are the same thing. They are not. Legal compliance means adhering to the laws and regulations that govern business activity. Ethical responsibility means doing what is right, which may go well beyond what the law requires — and may, in rare cases, mean questioning whether the law itself is just.

Actions can be legal but ethically questionable. A firm may legally pay its workers the minimum wage while generating enormous profits, but whether this is ethical depends on one's view of the firm's obligations to its employees. A company may legally exploit tax loopholes to minimize its obligations, but doing so may undermine public trust and invite regulatory backlash.

Conversely, actions can be illegal but ethically defensible. A manager who violates a confidentiality agreement to blow the whistle on corporate fraud is breaking a legal obligation in service of a larger ethical duty.

The regulatory environment sets minimum standards of acceptable behavior. The Sarbanes-Oxley Act of 2002 and the Dodd-Frank Act of 2010 were both legislative responses to ethical failures in corporate America: SOX addressed the accounting scandals of the early 2000s (discussed in Ch 6.1), while Dodd-Frank responded to the governance failures that contributed to the 2008 financial crisis. These laws raised the floor of required behavior, but ethical leadership means going beyond minimum compliance. The firms that build the strongest reputations and the deepest stakeholder trust are those that treat legal compliance as a starting point rather than a destination (Paine, 1994).

EX: Boeing and the 737 MAX

The Boeing 737 MAX crisis illustrates how ethical failures at multiple levels, including product safety decisions, disclosure practices, organizational culture, and regulatory relationships, can compound to produce catastrophic outcomes. In October 2018 and March 2019, two 737 MAX aircraft crashed within five months of each other, killing 346 people. Investigations revealed that a flawed flight control system known as MCAS (Maneuvering Characteristics Augmentation System) played a central role in both crashes (House Committee on Transportation and Infrastructure, 2020).

The ethical dimensions of the crisis were layered. Boeing designed the 737 MAX as an update to the existing 737 platform rather than developing an entirely new aircraft. This decision was driven by competitive pressure: rival Airbus had launched the A320neo, and Boeing needed to respond quickly to prevent airlines from switching. The choice to modify an existing airframe rather than build a new one saved time and money, but it created engineering challenges that led to the MCAS system. MCAS was designed to compensate for handling characteristics introduced by the MAX's larger engines, but a single faulty sensor could trigger the system and push the aircraft's nose down repeatedly, overriding pilots' attempts to correct the descent (Gates, 2019).

From a utilitarian perspective, Boeing's cost-benefit analysis was deeply flawed. The company prioritized speed to market and cost containment, underweighting the catastrophic downside risk of a safety failure. From a rights-based perspective, airline passengers had a fundamental right to safe air travel, and Boeing's failure to adequately disclose the MCAS system and its risks violated that right. Boeing did not include detailed information about MCAS in pilot training materials, and many pilots were unaware of the system's existence until after the first crash. From a justice perspective, the burden of Boeing's cost-cutting decisions fell entirely on the most vulnerable stakeholders, the passengers and crew who had no knowledge of the risks they were assuming.

The cultural dimensions were equally significant. Internal communications revealed that Boeing employees had expressed concerns about the 737 MAX's design and the pressure to meet production schedules during development, yet these concerns did not alter the company's course. One employee wrote that the aircraft was designed by clowns supervised by monkeys — a remark that reflected deep internal unease about the prioritization of schedule and cost over engineering rigor (House Committee on Transportation and Infrastructure, 2020). The tone at the top emphasized financial performance and competitive urgency, and the organizational culture did not provide effective channels for safety concerns to override commercial pressures.

The regulatory dimension added another layer. Boeing had cultivated a close relationship with the Federal Aviation Administration (FAA), and the FAA had delegated significant portions of the 737 MAX's safety certification process to Boeing itself. This arrangement, while common in the aviation industry, created a conflict of interest in which the entity responsible for safety certification was also the entity with the strongest financial interest in rapid certification. The regulatory relationship reflected a broader pattern in which legal compliance structures proved inadequate without genuine ethical commitment from the firm.

The consequences were devastating. Beyond the 346 lives lost, Boeing faced over $20 billion in costs from the 737 MAX grounding, lost orders, and legal settlements (Josephs, 2021). The firm's reputation, built over a century as a premier aerospace company, suffered lasting damage. The case demonstrates that ethical failures in product safety are not abstract moral concerns but strategic catastrophes that can threaten the survival of even the largest firms.

References

Aristotle. (2009). *The Nicomachean ethics* (D. Ross, Trans.; L. Brown, Rev.). Oxford University Press. (Original work ca. 340 BCE)

Gates, D. (2019, June 22). Flawed analysis, failed oversight: How Boeing and FAA certified the suspect 737 MAX flight control system. *The Seattle Times*.

House Committee on Transportation and Infrastructure. (2020). *Final committee report: The design, development, and certification of the Boeing 737 MAX*. U.S. House of Representatives.

Josephs, L. (2021, January 7). Boeing to pay more than $2.5 billion to settle criminal conspiracy charge over 737 Max. *CNBC*.

Kant, I. (1993). *Grounding for the metaphysics of morals* (J. W. Ellington, Trans.). Hackett Publishing. (Original work published 1785)

Locke, R. M. (2013). *The promise and limits of private power: Promoting labor standards in a global economy.* Cambridge University Press.

Mill, J. S. (1863). *Utilitarianism.* Parker, Son, and Bourn.

Paine, L. S. (1994). Managing for organizational integrity. *Harvard Business Review, 72*(2), 106–117.

Rawls, J. (1971). *A theory of justice.* Harvard University Press.

Treviño, L. K., Weaver, G. R., & Reynolds, S. J. (2006). Behavioral ethics in organizations: A review. *Journal of Management, 32*(6), 951–990.

6.5 Non-Market Strategy — *How do firms shape their political and social environment?*

6.5.1 What Is Non-Market Strategy?

Throughout Chapters 2 through 5, we examined how firms compete in the marketplace through differentiation and cost leadership (Chapter 2), by leveraging internal resources and capabilities (Chapter 3), by navigating industry structure and external forces (Chapter 4), and by pursuing growth through alliances, acquisitions, and diversification (Chapter 5). These are all elements of market strategy: competing through products, pricing, innovation, and operational excellence. Market strategy assumes that the rules of the competitive game, including the regulatory environment, the legal framework, the tax structure, and the trade policies, are given. Firms take these rules as they find them and compete within them.

Non-market strategy challenges that assumption. It recognizes that the political, legal, regulatory, and social environment in which firms operate is not simply a given — it is a variable that firms can actively shape (Baron, 2013). When a company lobbies Congress for favorable tax treatment, files a lawsuit to block a competitor's merger, or launches a public relations campaign to influence consumer opinion on regulation, it is pursuing non-market strategy. The external environment we analyzed through PESTEL in Chapter 4.9, the political, economic, social, technological, environmental, and legal forces that shape industry conditions, is not merely something firms must adapt to. It is something firms can influence, and the most successful firms are effective at both market and non-market competition.

Non-market strategy complements market strategy; it does not replace it. A firm with a superior product and efficient operations still benefits from a favorable regulatory environment. A firm with a weak competitive position cannot compensate through political influence alone, at least not sustainably. But for many firms, particularly those in heavily regulated industries, non-market strategy is as important to profitability as any product innovation or cost reduction initiative. Understanding how firms shape their external environment is therefore essential to a complete picture of strategic management.

6.5.2 The Political Environment as a Competitive Arena

> ***Business has to be involved in the political process because the political process is involved in business.* — *David Baron***

Government policy directly affects industry profitability. Regulations determine what firms can sell and how they can sell it. Tax policy affects the after-tax returns on investment. Subsidies channel resources toward favored industries and away from others. Trade policy, including tariffs, quotas, and trade agreements, determines which foreign competitors can access domestic markets and on what terms. Antitrust enforcement shapes the boundaries of permissible competitive behavior, merger activity, and industry consolidation. Every one of these policies creates winners and losers, and firms have strong incentives to influence policy in their favor.

The connection to Porter's Five Forces (Ch 4.3) is direct. Government regulation affects all five forces that determine industry profitability. Regulations can raise or lower barriers to entry; licensing requirements protect incumbents while deregulation invites new competitors. Environmental or safety regulations can increase supplier power by limiting the number of qualified suppliers. Consumer protection laws and price regulations affect buyer power. Government subsidies for alternative technologies can strengthen the threat of substitutes. And regulations that constrain competitive behavior, such as price floors, service requirements, and operating restrictions, directly affect the intensity of rivalry among existing firms.

Because government policy is so consequential for profitability, the political environment functions as a competitive arena in its own right. Firms do not merely accept the regulatory framework passively; they actively compete to shape it. This competition takes place in legislatures, regulatory agencies, courts, and the court of public opinion — venues where the skills that determine success are quite different from those that win in the marketplace. Understanding this parallel competitive arena is what non-market strategy is about.

6.5.3 Tools of Non-Market Strategy

Firms employ a range of tools to influence the political, legal, and social environment. Each tool operates through a different mechanism and carries different costs, risks, and strategic implications.

Lobbying is the most direct form of political engagement. Firms hire lobbyists, often former legislators, regulators, or government officials, to meet with policymakers, present information and arguments, and advocate for specific legislative or regulatory outcomes. Lobbying is pervasive: in the United States, total federal lobbying expenditures reached a record $4.4 billion in 2024, with the largest spenders concentrated in industries most directly affected by government regulation, including pharmaceuticals, technology, energy, and financial services (Drutman, 2015; OpenSecrets, 2025). Effective lobbying requires not just financial resources but deep knowledge of the policymaking process, established relationships with key decision-makers, and the ability to frame the firm's interests in terms that resonate with broader public policy goals.

Campaign contributions and political action committees (PACs) provide another avenue for political influence. Firms and industry groups contribute to the campaigns of sympathetic legislators, building relationships that provide access, the opportunity to present their case directly to policymakers. While campaign contributions cannot legally purchase specific votes, they create a dynamic in which legislators who receive significant industry funding are more likely to hear and be sympathetic to that industry's concerns. The rise of Super PACs and independent expenditure groups has expanded the scale of corporate political spending, though it has also increased public scrutiny of the relationship between money and political influence.

Trade association membership allows firms to pursue collective action on shared political interests. Industry trade associations, such as the National Association of Manufacturers, the American Petroleum Institute, or PhRMA (the pharmaceutical industry's lobbying group), pool resources from member firms to lobby on issues that affect the industry as a whole. Trade associations are particularly effective when an industry faces a common regulatory threat, because they can speak with a unified voice and spread the costs of political engagement across many firms (Olson, 1965).

Grassroots mobilization involves organizing employees, customers, suppliers, or community members to express support for the firm's political positions. When a company encourages its workforce to contact their congressional representatives about a pending regulation, or when it mobilizes local communities to oppose zoning restrictions that would affect its operations, it is using grassroots tactics to amplify its political voice. Grassroots mobilization is particularly effective because legislators are more responsive to constituent pressure than to corporate lobbying alone.

Public relations and media strategy shape the broader public discourse in ways that create favorable conditions for policy outcomes. A firm that successfully frames a regulatory debate in terms of consumer benefit rather than corporate interest is more likely to achieve its political objectives. Media campaigns, op-eds, sponsored research, and social media engagement all serve to influence how the public and policymakers understand the issues at stake.

Litigation uses the legal system as a strategic tool. Firms may file lawsuits to block competitor actions, challenge unfavorable regulations, or establish legal precedents that benefit their competitive position. Litigation can be expensive and time-consuming, but it offers the advantage of binding legal outcomes that lobbying and public relations cannot guarantee. In some cases, the mere threat of litigation is sufficient to deter competitors or regulators from pursuing actions that would harm the firm.

Regulatory capture represents the most extreme form of non-market influence. It occurs when the regulated industry exerts disproportionate influence over the regulatory body that is supposed to oversee it, effectively co-opting the regulator to serve industry interests rather than the public interest (Stigler, 1971). Regulatory capture can result from the revolving door between industry and government — regulators who expect future employment in the industry they oversee may be reluctant to impose strict standards — or from the informational advantage that industry participants have over regulators who lack comparable technical expertise. While regulatory capture benefits the firms involved, it undermines the legitimacy of the regulatory system and can produce outcomes that harm consumers and the broader economy.

6.5.4 Strategic Implications of Non-Market Activities

Non-market strategy is not merely about defensive responses to regulatory threats. It can be used proactively as a competitive weapon, a means of shaping the competitive environment to the firm's advantage.

One of the most strategically significant applications is raising rivals' costs. A firm can lobby for regulations that impose compliance costs on all industry participants, knowing that it is better positioned to absorb those costs than smaller or less well-capitalized competitors. Environmental regulations, for example, may require expensive pollution control equipment that large firms can afford but that smaller firms cannot, effectively creating a barrier to entry that protects incumbents. Similarly, complex licensing and certification requirements increase the costs of entering an industry, reducing the threat of new entrants and benefiting established firms (Salop & Scheffman, 1983).

Non-market strategy can also create barriers to entry directly. Zoning restrictions, professional licensing requirements, and regulatory approval processes all limit the number of firms that can operate in a given market. Incumbent firms that lobby to maintain or strengthen these requirements are using non-market strategy to protect their competitive positions. In the telecommunications industry, for instance, incumbent providers have historically lobbied against municipal broadband initiatives that would create publicly owned competitors. In agriculture, subsidy programs that favor large-scale producers make it more difficult for smaller farms to compete on cost.

Trade policy represents another arena where non-market strategy has direct competitive implications. Tariffs that protect domestic producers from foreign competition, trade agreements that open export markets for specific industries, and sanctions that restrict competitors' access to key inputs are all examples of government policy shaping competitive outcomes. Firms that effectively influence trade policy can gain significant advantages over rivals who cannot access the same markets, resources, or cost structures.

6.5.5 Risks and Ethical Considerations

Non-market strategy carries significant risks that must be weighed against its potential benefits.

Public backlash is an ever-present danger. Citizens and consumers are increasingly skeptical of corporate influence on government, and firms that are perceived as using political power to advance narrow interests at the public's expense can suffer reputational damage that offsets any regulatory gains. The growth of social media has amplified this risk by making corporate political activity more visible and more easily criticized. A lobbying campaign that succeeds in blocking a popular regulation may win the legislative battle but lose the reputational war.

Legal risks are substantial, particularly for firms operating internationally. The Foreign Corrupt Practices Act (FCPA) prohibits U.S. firms from bribing foreign government officials to obtain business advantages, and violations carry severe criminal and civil penalties. The line between legitimate political engagement and illegal corruption is not always clear, and firms that operate in countries where bribery is culturally normalized face heightened compliance challenges. Similar anti-bribery statutes, including the U.K. Bribery Act, impose additional legal constraints on global firms (Klaw, 2012).

Reputational risk extends beyond specific legal violations to the broader perception of how the firm competes. A company that is seen as relying on political manipulation rather than genuine value creation may lose the trust of customers, employees, and investors. This reputational concern is particularly acute in an era when corporate purpose and social responsibility have become important dimensions of brand identity, as we will discuss in Chapter 6.6.

The deepest tension in non-market strategy is the distinction between legitimate advocacy and rent-seeking. Legitimate advocacy involves firms providing information, expertise, and perspective to policymakers who benefit from industry knowledge when making regulatory decisions. Policymakers cannot be experts in every industry, and industry input is a valuable — even essential — component of sound policymaking. Rent-seeking, by contrast, involves firms using political influence to obtain economic benefits, such as favorable regulations, subsidies, and protection from competition, that they could not earn through market competition alone (Tullock, 1967). Rent-seeking transfers value from consumers and taxpayers to politically connected firms without creating any new economic value, and it represents a fundamental misallocation of resources. The ethical challenge for strategic managers is to ensure that their non-market activities fall on the legitimate advocacy side of this line, that they are seeking to inform policy rather than to capture it.

EX: Big Tech and the Politics of Antitrust

The technology industry's engagement with antitrust policy in the United States illustrates the full range of non-market strategy tools and the tensions they create. For much of the 2000s and 2010s, major technology companies, including Google, Amazon, Apple, and Meta (formerly Facebook), operated in a relatively permissive regulatory environment. U.S. antitrust enforcement had been influenced by the Chicago School of economics, which held that antitrust intervention should focus narrowly on consumer harm as measured by price effects, and that large firms achieving dominance through superior products and efficiency should generally be left alone (Bork, 1978). This framework benefited technology firms, whose services were often provided free to consumers, making traditional price-based antitrust analysis difficult to apply.

As these companies grew to dominate their respective markets, however, political sentiment shifted. Critics argued that the platforms had accumulated excessive market power, engaged in anticompetitive practices (such as self-preferencing their own products in search results or app stores), acquired potential competitors before they could become threats, and amassed enormous quantities of user data that created insurmountable barriers to entry (Khan, 2017). Bipartisan support for tighter regulation of technology companies began to emerge in Congress, culminating in multiple antitrust lawsuits filed by the Department of Justice and the Federal Trade Commission against Google and Meta, among others.

The technology industry responded with a comprehensive non-market strategy. Lobbying expenditures by major tech firms increased dramatically, and the industry collectively became one of the largest lobbying spenders in Washington. Companies hired former government officials and regulatory experts to represent their interests. Trade associations such as the Computer & Communications Industry Association (CCIA) and the Information Technology Industry Council (ITI) coordinated industry-wide advocacy against specific legislative proposals. Individual firms launched public relations campaigns framing proposed regulations as threats to innovation, consumer choice, and American competitiveness.

The strategic implications were significant. Technology companies argued that proposed antitrust legislation, which would have restricted platforms from favoring their own products, required data interoperability, and made certain acquisitions presumptively illegal, would undermine the product integration and ecosystem strategies that created value for consumers. Critics responded that this framing was precisely the kind of self-serving argument that non-market strategy is designed to produce, and that the real purpose of the lobbying campaign was to protect monopoly profits from competitive discipline.

The case illustrates the tension between legitimate advocacy and rent-seeking that defines the ethical boundary of non-market strategy. Technology firms have genuine expertise about how proposed regulations would affect their products and their users, and policymakers benefit from that expertise. But these same firms also have billions of dollars at stake in the outcome, creating powerful incentives to frame their arguments in whatever terms are most likely to produce favorable policy outcomes regardless of the broader public interest. For strategic managers, the technology antitrust debate is a reminder that non-market strategy is a powerful tool — but one that must be wielded with awareness of its ethical dimensions and reputational risks.

References

Baron, D. P. (2013). *Business and its environment* (7th ed.). Pearson.

Bork, R. H. (1978). *The antitrust paradox: A policy at war with itself.* Basic Books.

Drutman, L. (2015). *The business of America is lobbying: How corporations became politicized and politics became more corporate.* Oxford University Press.

Khan, L. M. (2017). Amazon's antitrust paradox. *Yale Law Journal, 126*(3), 710–805.

Klaw, B. W. (2012). A new strategy for preventing bribery and extortion in international business transactions. *Harvard Journal on Legislation, 49*(2), 303–372.

Olson, M. (1965). *The logic of collective action: Public goods and the theory of groups.* Harvard University Press.

OpenSecrets. (2025). *Federal lobbying set new record in 2024.* https://www.opensecrets.org/news/2025/02/federal-lobbying-set-new-record-in-2024

Salop, S. C., & Scheffman, D. T. (1983). Raising rivals' costs. *American Economic Review, 73*(2), 267–271.

Stigler, G. J. (1971). The theory of economic regulation. *Bell Journal of Economics and Management Science, 2*(1), 3–21.

Tullock, G. (1967). The welfare costs of tariffs, monopolies, and theft. *Western Economic Journal, 5*(3), 224–232.

6.6 Beyond Profits: CSR / ESG — *What are firms' broader responsibilities?*

6.6.1 The Shareholder vs. Stakeholder Debate Revisited

In Chapter 1.6, we introduced the fundamental question of who the firm serves. The shareholder primacy perspective, most forcefully articulated by Milton Friedman, holds that a business already contributes to society by selling goods and services that customers value above many competing alternatives while operating within the rules of the game (Friedman, 1970). A firm that fails to create sufficient value for its customers will not survive, so the discipline of the market ensures that pursuing profit and serving society are, for the most part, the same activity. Managers, in this view, are agents of shareholders and owe no operational duty beyond that relationship; diverting firm resources toward social goals that do not increase shareholder value amounts to spending other people's money for social ends they did not choose. It also casts managers as unelected arbiters of the public good, substituting their own judgment about worthy causes for that of the shareholders, customers, and employees whose money it is.

The stakeholder perspective, advanced by R. Edward Freeman, rejects this narrowing of duty. Freeman argues that firms and their managers bear a direct operational responsibility to benefit society by creating value for all parties who affect or are affected by the firm's activities, including employees, customers, suppliers, communities, and society at large (Freeman, 1984). This responsibility is practical as well as ethical: a firm depends on the cooperation of these groups to survive, and one that consistently neglects its workforce, its suppliers, or its community will eventually find that neglect reflected in its performance.

This debate has evolved considerably. In 2019, the Business Roundtable, an association of CEOs from nearly two hundred of America's largest corporations, issued a revised statement on the purpose of a corporation, explicitly committing to delivering value to all stakeholders rather than prioritizing shareholders alone (Business Roundtable, 2019). Whether this represents a genuine philosophical shift or a public relations gesture remains contested, but it reflects a growing recognition that the shareholder-versus-stakeholder dichotomy may be a false choice.

This section examines corporate social responsibility (CSR) and environmental, social, and governance (ESG) criteria, frameworks through which firms and investors have attempted to operationalize the stakeholder perspective, along with their strategic implications, criticisms, and international variation.

6.6.2 Corporate Social Responsibility (CSR)

Corporate social responsibility refers to a firm's voluntary actions to address social, environmental, and ethical concerns beyond what the law requires. The key word is voluntary — CSR goes beyond legal compliance (Ch 6.4) to encompass actions that firms undertake because they believe them to be right, strategically beneficial, or both.

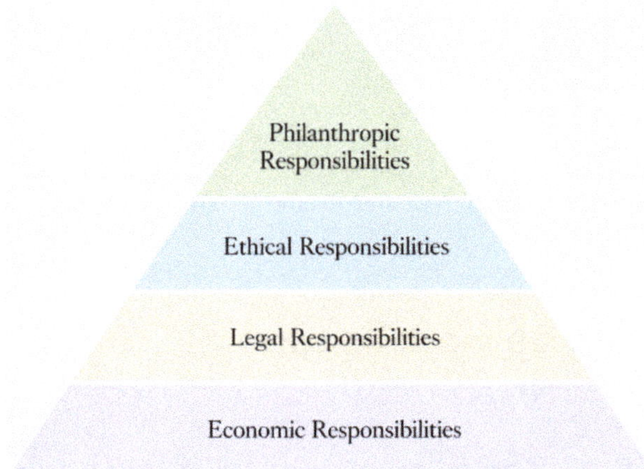

Archie Carroll's CSR Pyramid

Archie Carroll's CSR Pyramid provides a widely used framework for understanding the different layers of corporate responsibility (Carroll, 1991). At the base of the pyramid are economic responsibilities: the firm must be profitable, because without economic viability none of its other responsibilities can be fulfilled. The second layer consists of legal responsibilities: the firm must obey the laws and regulations that govern its activities. The third layer encompasses ethical responsibilities: the firm should do what is right and fair, even when not required by law. At the top of the pyramid are philanthropic responsibilities: the firm should be a good corporate citizen, contributing resources to improve quality of life in the communities where it operates. Carroll's framework is useful because it makes clear that CSR is not a substitute for profitability or legal compliance; it is an additional set of obligations that builds on top of those foundational requirements.

A critical strategic question is whether CSR activities can also serve the firm's competitive interests. Purely altruistic CSR, philanthropy motivated solely by moral obligation, is conceptually clean but strategically limited. Strategic CSR seeks opportunities where social benefit and competitive advantage overlap. Michael Porter and Mark Kramer advanced this idea through the concept of shared value: creating economic value in ways that simultaneously create value for society (Porter & Kramer, 2011). A food company that invests in sustainable agriculture may improve supply chain reliability while addressing environmental concerns. A technology firm that provides digital literacy programs in underserved communities may cultivate a future customer base while fulfilling a social mission. The shared value concept argues that the most powerful CSR strategies are those where doing good and doing well are mutually reinforcing.

6.6.3 Environmental, Social, and Governance (ESG) Criteria

While CSR describes what firms do, ESG describes how investors evaluate what firms do. Environmental, social, and governance criteria have emerged as a framework through which institutional investors assess firms on dimensions beyond traditional financial performance.

The environmental dimension evaluates a firm's impact on the natural environment: carbon emissions, energy and resource usage, waste management, pollution, and exposure to climate-related risk. The social dimension assesses how a firm manages relationships with its workforce, customers, and communities: labor practices, workplace safety, diversity and inclusion, community relations, product safety, and data privacy. The governance dimension, the most directly connected to the topics we have covered in Chapters 6.1–6.3, examines the quality of a firm's internal oversight mechanisms: board independence, executive compensation structures, transparency, anti-corruption policies, and shareholder rights (Eccles et al., 2014).

The rise of ESG has been driven primarily by institutional investors, the pension funds, mutual funds, and index funds that, as discussed in Chapter 6.2, now own roughly 70–80 percent of U.S. equities. These investors increasingly recognize that environmental and social risks translate directly into financial risks. A company with poor environmental practices may face regulatory penalties or stranded assets. A firm with weak labor practices may suffer reputational damage and operational disruptions. Poor governance, as Chapters 6.1–6.3 have demonstrated, can lead to fraud and corporate collapse. ESG analysis attempts to capture these risks systematically, providing investors with a more complete picture of long-term prospects than financial statements alone.

The growth of ESG ratings agencies, firms such as MSCI, Sustainalytics, and S&P Global that evaluate companies on ESG criteria, has given the framework institutional weight. These ratings influence capital allocation by signaling which firms are better or worse positioned on environmental, social, and governance dimensions. A strong ESG rating can attract investment from ESG-focused funds, while a poor rating can restrict access to capital.

Because what gets measured gets managed, the concentration of grading power in a small number of large ratings agencies and institutional investors gives those firms substantial influence over corporate behavior. When a handful of well-capitalized players define the criteria and assign the scores, companies have strong incentive to manage toward whatever those scorecards reward, whether or not the underlying activity creates real social value.

6.6.4 The Strategic Case for CSR/ESG

Beyond the moral arguments, there is a pragmatic strategic case for why firms should invest in CSR and attend to ESG performance.

Reputation and brand value are directly affected by perceived social responsibility. Consumers increasingly consider a firm's social and environmental record when making purchasing decisions, particularly in markets where products are otherwise difficult to differentiate. A reputation for responsible behavior creates a form of differentiation (Ch 2.2) that competitors cannot easily replicate, because reputation is path dependent (Ch 3.4) and socially complex (Ch 3.5).

Talent attraction and retention have become significant strategic considerations, particularly as younger generations of workers express strong preferences for employers whose values align with their own. Firms with strong CSR and ESG profiles have a competitive advantage in labor markets where talented candidates can choose among multiple offers. The cost of employee turnover makes retention a meaningful financial consideration, and a firm's social reputation directly affects its ability to retain high-performing employees (Turban & Greening, 1997).

Risk management is perhaps the most concrete strategic benefit. Proactive environmental and social practices reduce the likelihood of costly incidents, such as environmental disasters, product safety failures, labor disputes, and regulatory penalties, that can destroy shareholder value overnight. The cases of Enron (Ch 6.1), Wells Fargo (Ch 6.3), and Boeing (Ch 6.4) all illustrate how governance and ethical failures can produce financial losses that dwarf the cost of preventive measures.

Access to capital is increasingly tied to ESG performance. As ESG-focused investment capital grows, firms with strong profiles gain access to a larger and potentially cheaper pool of financing, while firms with poor ESG performance may find themselves excluded from certain investment mandates.

Finally, sustainability constraints can drive innovation. When firms are forced to reduce waste, improve energy efficiency, or redesign products to meet environmental standards, the constraints can stimulate creative problem-solving. Circular economy business models, in which firms design products for reuse, repair, and recycling rather than disposal, represent an emerging form of sustainability-driven innovation that can also reduce costs and create new revenue streams.

6.6.5 Criticisms and Challenges

CSR and ESG are not without significant criticisms, and strategic managers must understand these challenges to navigate them effectively.

Greenwashing — the practice of presenting a positive public image on social and environmental issues without making substantive changes to actual practices — is perhaps the most damaging criticism. When firms invest more in marketing their sustainability credentials than in actual sustainability improvements, they undermine the credibility of CSR and ESG more broadly. Greenwashing erodes stakeholder trust and can produce severe reputational backlash when the gap between rhetoric and reality is exposed (Lyon & Maxwell, 2011).

Measurement challenges remain a fundamental obstacle. Unlike financial performance, which is reported according to standardized accounting rules, ESG performance lacks universally accepted metrics. Different ratings agencies use different methodologies, weight different factors, and frequently produce conflicting assessments of the same firm. This lack of standardization makes meaningful comparison difficult and creates opportunities for selective reporting. Ongoing efforts to standardize ESG disclosure aim to address this problem, but standardization remains incomplete.

Cost concerns are legitimate. CSR and ESG initiatives may increase short-term costs, through higher-quality materials, better wages, and cleaner production processes, without clearly measurable short-term returns. For firms in intensely competitive markets with thin margins, these costs can be difficult to justify when competitors who do not invest in CSR may undercut them on price.

Political backlash has emerged as a significant challenge, particularly in the United States. That a small number of unelected ratings agencies and large investors effectively set the standards against which firms are judged has helped shift ESG from a technical investment consideration into a politically contested topic in recent years. The anti-ESG movement, driven by critics who argue that ESG investing imposes a political agenda on capital markets, has produced state-level legislation restricting the use of ESG criteria in public pension fund investment decisions. Several states have divested from or blacklisted financial firms that incorporate ESG factors, arguing that fiduciary duty requires maximizing financial returns without regard to social or environmental considerations.

The fundamental tension underlying these criticisms is whether firms can genuinely serve shareholders and society simultaneously. Proponents argue that the interests converge in the long run, that responsible firms outperform irresponsible ones over time. Critics argue that this convergence is empirically unproven and that managers' primary obligation remains maximizing shareholder returns.

6.6.6 International Variation in Corporate Governance and CSR

The shareholder-versus-stakeholder debate does not play out uniformly across countries. Different national governance systems reflect different assumptions about whose interests the corporation should serve, and these differences have direct implications for how CSR and ESG are understood and practiced.

The United States has historically been the strongest proponent of shareholder value maximization.

American corporate law, financial markets, and governance norms have traditionally prioritized shareholders above other stakeholders, though the Business Roundtable statement and the growth of ESG investing suggest a gradual shift toward a broader stakeholder orientation.

Germany offers the most striking institutional counterpoint through its system of codetermination. Under German law, companies with more than 500 employees must reserve one-third of their supervisory board seats for employee representatives. Companies with more than 2,000 employees must allocate nearly half of board seats to employees (Fulton, 2020). This system institutionalizes the stakeholder perspective by giving employees formal governance authority, a structural commitment to balancing shareholder and employee interests that has no equivalent in Anglo-American governance. Notably, some German firms near the 2,000-employee threshold use outsourcing and other strategies to remain below it, illustrating the tension between governance ideals and managerial self-interest that pervades this chapter.

Japan has historically featured minimal shareholder activism and a governance culture characterized by long-term relationships among firms, banks, and employees. In recent years, however, Japan has seen emerging activist investors and governance reforms aimed at increasing board independence, reflecting gradual convergence toward international norms.

The United Kingdom combines strong shareholder rights with governance requirements that exceed American standards in several respects, including the effective requirement that CEO and board chair roles be separated and higher expectations for board independence. The U.K. Corporate Governance Code operates on a "comply or explain" basis, requiring firms to either follow best practices or publicly justify their departures.

The broader trend is convergence. As firms globalize, they increasingly adopt governance practices that satisfy multiple national systems. A multinational corporation listed on exchanges in both the United States and Europe must navigate different governance codes, disclosure requirements, and stakeholder expectations simultaneously. The practical result is a gradual standardization around international best practices, a process that is far from complete but that is steadily narrowing the differences among national systems.

EX: Patagonia and the Limits of Shareholder Primacy

Patagonia, the outdoor clothing and gear company, has become one of the most frequently cited examples of a firm that has embedded stakeholder and environmental values into its core business strategy — and in 2022, it took the most radical step any major company has taken to resolve the shareholder-versus-stakeholder tension permanently.

Founded by Yvon Chouinard in 1973, Patagonia built its brand around environmental activism and responsible business practices. The company donated one percent of annual sales to environmental organizations, pioneered the use of recycled materials in outdoor apparel, and famously ran a Black Friday advertisement in 2011 telling customers not to buy its jacket, an anti-consumerism message that paradoxically reinforced the brand's authenticity and drove long-term customer loyalty (Chouinard, 2016). Patagonia's environmental commitment was not a marketing overlay; it was embedded in the firm's culture, supply chain decisions, and product design, making it an example of strategic CSR that created both social value and competitive differentiation.

The strategic tension, however, was real. As a profitable private company, Patagonia's ownership structure meant that any eventual sale or IPO would transfer control to new owners who might not share the founding family's environmental commitments. Chouinard described the conventional options, selling the company or taking it public, as paths that would inevitably compromise the firm's mission, because new owners or public market shareholders would prioritize financial returns over environmental goals.

In September 2022, Chouinard announced that he and his family were transferring ownership of Patagonia to two new entities: the Patagonia Purpose Trust, which holds all voting stock and is designed to ensure the company's values are maintained, and the Holdfast Collective, a nonprofit organization that receives all of Patagonia's profits, approximately $100 million annually, to fund environmental causes. The Chouinard family retained no ownership stake and receives no ongoing financial benefit from the company (Gelles, 2022).

The Patagonia case illustrates both the power and the limits of the CSR/ESG framework. On one hand, Patagonia demonstrates that a firm can build a highly successful business while genuinely prioritizing environmental and social values. On the other hand, Chouinard's decision to give the company away reflected his conclusion that traditional corporate structures could not permanently guarantee stakeholder interests would take precedence over shareholder returns. The very governance mechanisms examined throughout this chapter, boards, compensation structures, shareholder activism, and the market for corporate control, are designed to protect shareholder interests, and Chouinard judged that these mechanisms would eventually override the firm's mission under conventional ownership. His solution was to remove shareholders from the equation entirely — a resolution available to very few firms and one that highlights the enduring difficulty of reconciling shareholder and stakeholder interests within the standard corporate governance framework.

References

Business Roundtable. (2019). *Statement on the purpose of a corporation.* https://www.businessroundtable.org

Carroll, A. B. (1991). The pyramid of corporate social responsibility: Toward the moral management of organizational stakeholders. *Business Horizons, 34*(4), 39–48.

Chouinard, Y. (2016). *Let my people go surfing: The education of a reluctant businessman* (2nd ed.). Penguin Books.

Eccles, R. G., Ioannou, I., & Serafeim, G. (2014). The impact of corporate sustainability on organizational processes and performance. *Management Science, 60*(11), 2835–2857.

Freeman, R. E. (1984). *Strategic management: A stakeholder approach.* Pitman.

Friedman, M. (1970, September 13). The social responsibility of business is to increase its profits. *The New York Times Magazine.*

Fulton, L. (2020). *Codetermination in Germany: A beginner's guide* (Mitbestimmungspraxis No. 32). Hans-Böckler-Stiftung.

Gelles, D. (2022, September 14). Billionaire no more: Patagonia founder gives away the company. *The New York Times.*

Lyon, T. P., & Maxwell, J. W. (2011). Greenwash: Corporate environmental disclosure under threat of audit. *Journal of Economics & Management Strategy, 20*(1), 3–41.

Porter, M. E., & Kramer, M. R. (2011). Creating shared value. *Harvard Business Review, 89*(1/2), 62–77.

Turban, D. B., & Greening, D. W. (1997). Corporate social performance and organizational attractiveness to prospective employees. *Academy of Management Journal, 40*(3), 658–672.

www.ingramcontent.com/pod-product-compliance
Lightning Source LLC
LaVergne TN
LVHW070853210926
848482LV00016B/921
* 9 7 9 8 9 9 7 2 3 2 7 0 2 *